THIRTEEN WAYS OF LOOKING FOR A POEM

A Guide to Writing Poetry

WENDY BISHOP

Florida State University

An imprint of Addison Wesley Longman, Inc.

New York • Reading, Massachusetts • Menlo Park, California • Harlow, England
Don Mills, Ontario • Sydney • Mexico City • Madrid • Amsterdam

Editorial Director: Richard Wohl
Acquisitions Editor: Laura McKenna
Associate Editor: Liza Rudneva
Marketing Manager: Melanie Goulet
Full Service Production Manager: Valerie Zaborski
Project Coordination, Text Design, and Electronic Page Makeup: Elm Street Publishing
 Services, Inc.
Cover Designer/Manager: Nancy Danahy
Cover Illustration: *Western Raven* by Timothy Janda
Senior Print Buyer: Hugh Crawford
Printer and Binder: The Maple-Vail Book Manufacturing Group
Cover Printer: The Lehigh Press, Inc.

Library of Congress Cataloging-in-Publication Data

Bishop, Wendy.
 Thirteen ways of looking for a poem: a guide to writing poetry / Wendy Bishop.
  p.   cm.
 Includes bibliographical references and index.
 ISBN 0-321-01130-9 (pbk.)
 1. Poetry—Authorship. I. Title
PN1059.A9 B58 2000
808.1 21—dc21   99-045079
                                                               CIP

Please visit our website at http://www.awlonline.com

ISBN 0-321-01130-9

  4 5 6 7 8 9 10-MA-05 04

ACKNOWLEDGMENTS

Boundless thanks to poetry students, poetry group members, and poetry friends—I have been blessed. I have
three main muses: my daughter, Morgan; my son, Tait; and Dean, who listens.
    Former and current editors and editorial assistants at Longman's have worked long and hard on this pro-
ject. Thank you: Lisa Moore, Laura McKenna, Janice Wiggens Clark and Liza Rudneva; Natalie Hart and
Ruth Halikman. Pavel Zemliansky helped greatly with permissions. Reviewers challenged me and taught me
how to better teach myself about poetic craft. Thanks to Alan Ainsworth, Houston Community College;
Laura Arnold, Reed College; Barry Bauska, University of Puget Sound; Greg Bernard, Illinois Valley
Community College; Patrick Bizzaro, East Carolina University; David Citino, Ohio State University; Bill
Clemente, Peru State College; Susan Cole, Albertus Magnus College; Elizabeth Davis, University of California,
Davis; Nancy Edwards, Bakersfield College; Edward J. Gleason, Saint Anselm College; Matthew Graham,
University of Southern Indiana; Jeffrey Gray, Seton Hall University; Eloise Klein Healy, Antioch University;
Jack Hicks, University of California, Davis; Marianna Hofer, University of Findlay; Margaret Holley; Colleen
McElroy, University of Washington; Scott McKelvie, University of Missouri; Joy Passanante, University of
Idaho; Katherine Riegel, Southern Illinois University; Richard Robbins, Mankato State University; Barry
Spacks, University of California, Santa Barbara; Sue Standing, Wheaton College; David Starkey, North
Central College, Aurora, IL; Terry Stokes, University of Cincinnati; Lee Upton, Lafayette College; and
Kathleen West, New Mexico State University.

CONTENTS

Note: The symbol ❖ indicates published poems about writing or reading poetry. The symbol * indicates draft poems created using "Invention Exercises."

APPENDIX

THREE CASE STUDIES IN FORM AND REVISION 374

INTRODUCTION

Ars Poetica ❖
RITA DOVE

Thirty miles to the only decent restaurant
was nothing, a blink
in the long dull stare of Wyoming.
Halfway there the unknown but terribly
important essayist yelled Stop!
I wanna be *in* this; and walked
fifteen yards onto the land
before sky bore down and he came running,
crying Jesus—there's nothing out there!

I once met an Australian novelist
who told me he never learned to cook
because it robbed creative energy.
What he wanted most was
to be mute; he stacked up pages;
he entered each day with an ax.

What I want is this poem to be small,
a ghost town
on the larger map of wills.
Then you can pencil me in as a hawk:
a traveling x-marks-the-spot.

Poets care deeply about the processes and products of poem-making. Their poems are shaped by their beliefs. Consider these claims:

> And of course, the constant, underlying purpose of poetry toward which I always aim first is pleasure—joy in the language and its motions, pleasure in the surprise and turning of thought and perception, happiness in the sound and music of the words, ebullience in the praise that any act of creation assumes. —Pattiann Rogers (Buckley and Merrill 123)

> [W]riting poetry is not a way of saying only what one already has the words for, but a way of saying what one didn't know one knew. This is true of everything about poetry, including meter and rhyme. While meter and rhyme create specific effects of expression, they are there in the poem because the poet wanted to be led, somewhat, by the language into saying things previously unexpressed, at least by him or her. —Marvin Bell (Duke and Jacobsen 22)

You'll often find poets' beliefs embodied in an **ars poetica**—an attempt to define the art of poetry writing, like Rita Dove's, as well as in a textbook like *Thirteen Ways of Looking for a Poem*. Examining the beliefs and advice of other poets, like the insights of Pattiann Rogers and Marvin Bell, can help you better understand the worlds of poetry that are available to you, as reader and writer, as you pencil yourself in—a hawk on the complicated map of thought we call a poem.

As you use this book to help you write into and out of poetic forms, I encourage you to play, to have fun with writing poetry as well as to work at it, to come back again and again to different aspects of the craft through the use of varied invention exercises. There is rewarding work in writing because it is through practice that you internalize skills. Marge Piercy claims that "Good work habits are nothing more than habits that let you work, that encourage you to pay attention" (Duke and Jacobsen 16). Writing a solid sonnet approxima-tion—what I call in chapter 12 a 10 × 14 sonnet—allows you eventually to write a better traditional sonnet, if you choose to do so. "I started imitating Shakespeare's sonnets when I was in high school," says Diane Wakowski, "It's still the best way to learn many, many things" (Packard 213).

Exploring traditional fixed forms can prove essential for enlarging and informing your repertoire of **free verse** composing strategies. Equally, if you come to poetry primarily as a prose writer, experience with poetry will help you use poetic effects—metaphor, image, condensed language, rhyme, and rhythm—to better advantage in your prose.

You may find several features of this book worth considering before you begin. First, I share my observations here out of my belief that everyone can learn about poetry by writing poetry and, by doing so, improve his or her writ-ing in general. Second, writing poetry is an essential act of the human heart and mind and serves many needs for us all, but different needs for each writer and reader. You may use poetry to explore your life and share it with others, to create a pleasing artistic object that meets your developing aesthetic taste, or for the pleasure of experimenting with and shaping ideas in words. At different times in your life, you may do only one or all of these things.

Third, this book is eclectic and democratic. In it, you'll discover in-progress and polished drafts—the work of emerging poets and the work of well-known, regularly published poets—because all of these examples and options offer you lessons, provide strategies to borrow, and offer insight into the usually hidden inner mechanics of poem-building, as well as into my instructional tastes and abilities. Since a teaching textbook to some degree replicates the teaching meth-ods of its author, I would be unable to "teach" here without reproducing my classroom methods. Such a policy also leads me to share the insights that can be gained from reading poems in draft state as well as from reading previously published works.

Some readers will wonder at the choice of a published poem by Poet R and not by Poet T. Overall, I chose poems that worked, in the classroom and in my own and my friends' writing lives, to provoke more poems and to help us investigate the art of poetry-writing. Regularly I use my own poems as drafting examples because with these texts, I can freely turn lines inside out and show and analyze poetic processes as I know them, for the writer herself is often most aware of what is not yet clear, what is being fudged or covered up, as well as what works and why. In doing this, I also can show you one poetic voice struggling, sometimes more successfully than at other times, with a variety of forms. Not all forms fit a person, place, or poetic intention, though each form can usefully inform your developing poetic sensibility. I hope and trust that your writing teacher and writing peers will do the same: share their work with you as you begin to share yours.

In *The New Book of Forms,* Lewis Turco chooses a double strategy, presenting some poems under his own name and some under the pseudonym Wesli Court, an anagram of his own name. John Hollander in *Rhyme's Reason* writes poems about forms, utilizing each form. That is, directions for writing sonnets are written as a sonnet. There is a tradition supporting Hollander: many poets improve their understanding of the practice of poetry by writing poems about their processes. This can be seen in the collection *What Will Suffice,* whose editors Christopher Buckley and Christopher Merrill explain: "Each decision the writer makes concerning subject matter, form, diction, and tone reveals something about his or her vision of the world. Nowhere is that vision more on display than in an ars poetica, which is where a poet takes stock, writing down his or her articles of faith. An ars poetica is also a barometer for the cultural climate of one's times . . ." (xvi).

You'll notice in that spirit that I've included poems about writing or reading poetry in nearly every chapter of *Thirteen Ways* (indicated by the ❖ after the title). This one, by Archibald MacLeish, is a well-known example:

Ars Poetica ❖
ARCHIBALD MACLEISH

A poem should be palpable and mute
As a globed fruit,

Dumb
As old medallions to the thumb,

Silent as the sleeve-worn stone
Of casement ledges where the moss has grown—

A poem should be wordless
As the flight of birds.

A poem should be motionless in time
As the moon climbs.

Leaving, as the moon releases
Twig by twig the night-entangled trees.

Leaving, as the moon behind the winter leaves,
Memory by memory the mind—

A poem should be motionless in time
As the moon climbs.

A poem should be equal to:
Not true.

For all the history of grief
An empty doorway and a maple leaf.

For love
The leaning grasses and two lights above the sea—

A poem should not mean
But be.

In each chapter of *Thirteen Ways,* I define form(s) and often some variations on each form. I share professional examples chosen for their general worth. That is, each is a poem I value and have learned from. These examples function as exemplars of—or as alternatives to—the tradition. Most chapters include process notes from writers who are drafting and examining their drafts because I believe there is worth in such self-examination. At times, I share quotations like this one, from published poets and prosodists who help me make my points more ably or who provide useful meditative insights on issues of craft:

Whatever remains most constant is the poem's prosody.
—Lewis Turco, 19

Most important, throughout *Thirteen Ways* you'll encounter invention exercises aimed at easing you into a form, although just as often I say: jump in, try it, wander around in the form. At the same time, some exercises are aimed at encouraging you to ease *out* of the form at certain crucial revision points.

The poem "Thirteen Ways of Looking at a Blackbird" by Wallace Stevens influenced the direction of this book. This poem is sometimes referred to as a haiku sequence and it certainly reminds us of the haiku form's brevity and associational qualities.

Thirteen Ways of Looking at a Blackbird
WALLACE STEVENS

I

Among twenty snowy mountains,
The only moving thing
Was the eye of the blackbird.

II

I was of three minds,
Like a tree
In which there are three blackbirds.

III

The blackbird whirled in the autumn winds.
It was a small part of the pantomime.

IV

A man and a woman
Are one.
A man and a woman and a blackbird
Are one.

V

I do not know which to prefer,
The beauty of inflections
Or the beauty of innuendoes,
The blackbird whistling
Or just after.

VI

Icicles filled the long window
With barbaric glass.
The shadow of the blackbird
Crossed it, to and fro.
The mood
Traced in the shadow
An indecipherable cause.

VII

O thin men of Haddam,
Why do you imagine golden birds?
Do you not see how the blackbird
Walks around the feet
Of the women about you?

VIII

I know noble accents
And lucid, inescapable rhythms;
But I know, too,
That the blackbird is involved
In what I know.

IX

When the blackbird flew out of sight,
It marked the edge
Of one of many circles.

X

At the sight of blackbirds
Flying in a green light,
Even the bawds of euphony
Would cry out sharply.

XI

He rode over Connecticut
In a glass coach.
Once, a fear pierced him,
In that he mistook
The shadow of his equipage
For blackbirds.

XII

The river is moving.
The blackbird must be flying.

XIII

It was evening all afternoon.
It was snowing.
And it was going to snow.
The blackbird sat
In the cedar-limbs.

When my first college poetry teacher read this poem with my class and asked us all to come up with our own imitations, I went home and wrote "Six Ways of Looking for Ghosts," a poem I never knew I had in me. This was my first poem in many ways, though I had written some verse in high school. This assignment proved to be inventive and exciting enough to keep me writing up to today. Wallace Stevens' poem points to the significance of the seemingly insignificant as blackbirds become greater than themselves—flying, resting, watching, and shadowing the speaker's thoughts. The variations and possibilities of this poem, evoked through a reader's attention, remind me of the variations and possibilities of form evoked through the poet's attention. It is the infinite possibilities of form that Kelly Cherry celebrates when she says:

> Poetic forms, established or nonce, are like maps of places no one's ever been. They lead the writer into uncharted territory; they show the writer where to go, even though they cannot know the way. This paradox is what keeps poetic form eternally interesting. . . . she knows only that the form is there like a flashlight or map and that she will see what the form reveals and go where the form takes her. She knows, too, that the form *will* take her somewhere, *will* show her a place never before seen or seen so clearly. (Finch 39)

While reading a collection of African American poets, *Every Shut Eye Ain't Asleep*, I found another poet who thought Stevens' poem crucial, a paradoxical map and a flashlight illuminating his thoughts. Raymond Patterson's "Twenty-Six Ways of Looking at a Blackman" is the title poem of his similarly titled collection. What for me was a class exercise became, for Patterson, a prompt that helped him move more deeply into his subject. By substituting the image of the blackman for the blackbird of the Stevens poem, Patterson momentarily aligns with his precursor and then immediately breaks free, exploring his own political and poetic contexts. The poem, in twenty-six sections, opens like this (the complete poem appears in chapter 6):

> I
> On the road we met a blackman,
> But no one else.

> II
> Dreams are reunions. Who has not
> On occasion entertained the presence
> Of a blackman?

> III
> From brown paper bags
> A blackman fills the vacancies of morning
> With orange speculations.

In *Thirteen Ways* you'll encounter poems about blackbirds, ghosts, a blackman, serious and resonant poems, and humor, word play, imitation, and parody. And you'll hear students trying carefully to read and understand the poetic traditions they are beginning to align with. For example, Ed Flagg muses on a poem by Hans Ostrom that you'll read below:

xxxvi   THIRTEEN WAYS OF LOOKING FOR A POEM

Response to "Ways of Looking at Wallace Stevens"

I love this poem for the deflation of this wizard with words [Stevens]. . . . his observations about people of color were probably off or "colored" by his prejudice. I like this poem for what it teaches me about Stevens. At first, I was disappointed that Ostrom was harassing the poet—then right in the middle of the parody, we learn about Stevens' [possible] racism, and I began to not mind so much the terms "enormous white belly" and "Bird shit: on the head of a bald poet." I like this poem for its playfulness. "Ecallaw Snevets" is just plain fun and it reminds me of "shallow" and "snivel," both of which seem to apply here to Stevens. . . . I can imagine the secretaries talking about Stevens while Stevens is eating that meal. —Ed Flagg

A line in Hans' poem has Ed wondering about the poet's beliefs and biographical background. To determine the accuracy of his reading, Ed will need to research the life and times of Wallace Stevens. Just as, to better enjoy the parodic response to Stevens by Hans Ostrom that follows, it helps to know that Stevens wrote poems called "Anecdote of the Jar," "The Palm at the End of the Mind," and "The Idea of Order at Key West" and that he is often mentioned as an example of a poet who held a regular, paying job in insurance.

*Ways of Looking at Wallace Stevens**
  Hans Ostrom

1. I placed a miniature insurance salesman inside a jar in Tennessee.
2. Consider Wallace Stevens' enormous white belly in the sunlight—there, next to the swimming pool beside the motel at the end of the mind.
3. The blackbird looked back at the poet, who was only more refracted light in blackbird optics.
4. Bird shit: on the bald head of a bald poet who removed his gray flannel hat in the park.
5. Please note: Wallace Stevens is a major American poet.
6. Please note: The phrase "niggers in Ethiopia" appears in one of Wallace Stevens' letters.
7. It is 1938, and two secretaries joke about the pomposity of their boss, Mr. Stevens. Their lipstick is red. They are paid by the week.
8. After a steak dinner, there is only the plate, and Mr. Stevens, and the check.
9. Ecallaw Snevets.
10. The plural of Steven is Stevens.
11. Black. Bird. Black. Bird. Black. Black. Black. Ethiopia.
12. The Idea of An Insurance Policy In Key West.
13. In heaven, Zora Neale Hurston holds down Wallace Stevens. Emily Dickinson tickles him. Gertrude Stein, taking notes, takes notes, and takes note, please.

Depending on your experience with poetry and your investment in the poetic tradition, you may be entertained or irritated by this send-up of a poetic icon. I think poetry should do both—entertain and sometimes irritate—and much more. Poems can/must/do imitate, echo, and outrun other poems. I resist the urge to view poems as sacred objects as often as I resist the urge to view poetry-writing as trivial or unconnected to the way I lead my life. We can make poetry central to our lives by making use of it, by playing with and by it. When we do this, we praise previous poems and poets. We can improvise on the forms others adore and experiment with. In fact, that's what practicing poets do: they enter the conversation of poetry, reading each other, writing back and forth in praise and in imitation of and in response to each other. For example, looking through James Tate's work, I realized his poem "A Guide to the Stone Age" was a response to Charles Simic's poem "Stone."

Stone
CHARLES SIMIC

Go inside a stone
That would be my way.
Let somebody else become a dove
Or gnash with a tiger's tooth.
I am happy to be a stone.

From the outside the stone is a riddle:
No one knows how to answer it.
Yet within, it must be cool and quiet
Even though a cow steps on it full weight,
Even though a child throws it in a river;
The stone sinks, slow, unperturbed
To the river bottom
Where the fishes come to knock on it
And listen.

I have seen sparks fly out
When two stones are rubbed,
So perhaps it is not dark inside after all;
Perhaps there is a moon shining
From somewhere, as though behind a hill—
Just enough light to make out
The strange writings, the star-charts
On the inner walls.

A Guide to the Stone Age
JAMES TATE

For Charles Simic

A heart that resembles a cave,
a throat of shavings,
an arm with no end and no beginning:

How about that telephone?
—Not yet.

The cave in your skull,
a throat with a crack in it,
a heart that still resembles a cave:

How about the knife?
—Later.

The fire in the cave of your skull,
a beast who died shaving,
a cave with no end and no beginning:

A big ship!
—Shut up.

Instructions which ask you to burn other instructions,
a circle with a crack in it,
a stone with an arm:

A hat?
—Not the hat.

A ship with a knife in it,
a telephone with a hat over it,
a cave with a heart:

The Stone Age?
—There is no end to it.

Poets write poems. They write poems to each other's poems. Poems squared. Thirteen becomes 169. Couplets become quatrains. List poems loosen into free verse jazz. A sonnet doubles and becomes a twenty-eight line meditation. Odes turn humorous, and ghazals and pantoums invite us into odd conjoinings of language and thought. To help you understand how poems form and are formed, I include the process narratives of "apprentice" poets who are apprenticing to the genre, to the traditions. Their free-write or journal comments will appear in the typeface of Ed Flagg's response above.

All poem *drafts* will be indicated in the following manner:

Your face turns toward the Pacific, away

These drafts range from first tries to nearly polished (written and rewritten) drafts. Some of the poems marked typographically as "published" in this book were once classroom drafts, just as some of the drafts you are currently reading will see journal publication before this book reaches your hands.

Poems published by the time this book goes to press will be presented as in a collection of poetry: with author's name and poem title (as in the poems by Charles Simic and James Tate above).

Invitations to write will be listed as:

➤ INVENTION EXERCISES ➤

And poems generated from these (or from any exercise) will be marked by an asterisk after the title, like this:

*Gardenia**

Because this book looks at modern approaches to form-making, it's no surprise that many of the poets included share observations about poetic processes. Poems in this genre—poetry about writing poetry—are indicated with a symbol, as in:

Ars Poetica ❖

As Mara High observes: "Poets tend to return again and again to a few familiar subjects—'poetry' is currently popular, as are women's lives, and the relations adults have with their children or parents" (*Spreading the Word* 5). Certainly you'll find poems about poetry, women's lives, and parents and children gathered here. But those impulses are not just familiar and current: they are also historical, as you'll see when you read Ben Jonson's sixteenth century elegies for his children who died young.

Invitations to discuss aspects of poetry through journal entries, class discussion, or with writing group members will be indicated this way:

ᴄᴏ READING INTO WRITING ᴏᴄ

To read more actively and accurately, you may need reading resources. Suggestions for using the Internet and World Wide Web to gather information—

for finding online rhyming dictionaries or sites where poets can be "heard"
reading their own works or practicing their radical textual experiments—will be
indicated with the symbol shown in the margin. Used judiciously, the Web offers
wonderful possibilities for joining a nationwide and worldwide poetry community.

Although my choice of poems and poets to include in *Thirteen Ways* reflects
my training and preferences, I hope you'll search out more poems by the poets
I've shared here, and that you'll do the same with those poets I've had to leave
out—due to space, time, taste, or teaching constraints. Find poets and poems.
Listen to them live or on the Web. Read poems aloud. Read poets' biographies
and study the contexts of their lives. Type their poems into your computer files
and paste poems into your notebooks as I did while compiling this text. I
promise you: it is invigorating to inhabit the lines and lives of others, even for
a little while.

While I don't explicate poems or provide detailed readings or interpretations,
I don't want you to forget that I've fallen in love with many of these poems and
return to them often for understanding, consolation, and encouragement about
life. I hope at least some of the poems I've included will speak this way to you.
And though these exercises have been life- and field-tested, they are good for
you only if they help you produce your own best writing. Try them, work
through them, around them, beyond them.

This book's chapters are arranged alphabetically because there is no preor-
dained order for learning forms or apprenticing yourself to a life in poetry. You
or your teacher will enter where you will, as you need to. However, like most
endeavors, it seems like we/you/I need to learn and know everything all at once
and to create a common language (for instance, understanding and defining *ars
poetica*) and a common reading history.

For this reason, chapter 1 orients the reader to general writing issues, and
chapters 2 and 3 offer more introductions to technical terms and definitions
than do subsequent chapters in order to provide a *lingua franca* for discussions
that follow. Terms that appear in **bold** during chapter discussions appear in the
Pocket Definitions section at the end of that chapter, and those definitions
appear again at the end of *Thirteen Ways*. Also, I have informally cross-refer-
enced the chapters throughout, suggesting you look at discussions in other sections of the text, since any attempt to divide techniques into parts is bound to
fail. Those interested in writing and revision processes will find windows into
the inner workings of poem construction in the three revision case studies in the
appendix. Devan Cook, William Snyder, and Rex West were generous in sharing their work-in-progress with us.

Finally, indexes: An *author* and *title* index may help you find other poems by
poets you enjoy in one section, and indexes of *forms*, *themes*, and *terms* let you
see how a single poem can fit into and illuminate discussions on several technical points. This happens because the prose poem may use rhyme; the list poem
may also be an elegy; aubades are a thematic form that can utilize free verse

forms or stanza forms; and so on. I'll try to remind you of those overlaps and interconnections even as we freeze-frame some of these forms for intense study.

Over many years of professional writing, and particularly in the course of writing this textbook, I consulted and re-consulted and now quote from a number of reference books. These guides are all written with skill and generosity. I hope this text will join their ongoing conversations and might rest with these on your bookshelf. Thanks to the following editors and authors for their fine work:

Adams, Stephen. *Poetic Designs.* Orchard Park, NY: Broadview Press, 1997.

Ahmad, Aijaz, ed. *Ghazals of Ghalib.* New York: Columbia University Press, 1971.

Ammons, A. R., ed. *The Best American Poetry.* New York: Scribner's, 1994.

Behn, Robin and Chase Twichell. *The Practice of Poetry.* New York: HarperCollins, 1992.

Buckley, Christopher and Christopher Merrill. *What Will Suffice.* Salt Lake City, UT: Gibbs-Smith, 1995.

Corn, Alfred. *The Poem's Heartbeat.* Brownsville, OR: Story Line Press, 1997.

Dacey, Philip and David Jauss, eds. *Strong Measures.* New York: Harper and Row, 1986.

Drury, John. *Creating Poetry.* Cincinnati, OH: Writer's Digest Books, 1991.

Duke, Charles R. and Sally A. Jacobsen. *Poets' Perspectives.* Portsmouth, NH: Boynton/Cook, 1992.

Finch, Annie, ed. *A Formal Feeling Comes.* Brownsville, OR: Storyline, 1994.

Fry, Paul H. *The Poet's Calling in the English Ode.* New Haven, CT: Yale University Press, 1980.

Furness, Tom and Michael Bath. *Reading Poetry.* New York: Prentice-Hall, 1996.

Fussell, Paul. *Poetic Meter and Poetic Form.* New York: Random House, 1979.

Hartman, Charles O. *Free Verse: An Essay on Prosody.* Princeton, NJ: Princeton University Press, 1980.

Hass, Robert, ed. *The Essential Haiku.* New York: Ecco Press, 1994.

Heninger, Jr., S. K. *The Subtext of Form in the English Renaissance.* University Park, PA: Pennsylvania State University Press, 1994.

Higginson, William with Penny Harter. *The Haiku Handbook.* New York: McGraw Hill, 1985.

Hollander, John. *Rhyme's Reason.* Cambridge, MA: Yale University Press, 1989.

Kirby-Smith, H. T. *The Origins of Free Verse.* Ann Arbor, MI: University of Michigan Press, 1996.

Lowitz, Leza, Miyuki Aoyama, and Akemi Tomika, eds. and trans. *A Long Rainy Season.* Berkeley: Stone Bridge Press, 1994.

Myers, Jack and Michael Simms. *The Longman Dictionary of Poetic Terms.* New York: Longman, 1989.

Owen, Stephen. *Traditional Chinese Poetry and Poetics.* Madison, WI: University of Wisconsin Press, 1985.

Packard, William, ed. *The Poet's Craft.* New York: Paragon, 1987.

Padgett, Ron, ed. *The Teachers and Writers Handbook of Poetic Forms.* New York: Teachers & Writers Collaborative, 1987.

Preminger, Alex and T. V. F. Brogan, eds. *The New Princeton Encyclopedia of Poetry and Poetics.* Princeton, NJ: Princeton University Press, 1993.

Sacks, Peter M. *The English Elegy.* Baltimore, MD: Johns Hopkins University Press, 1985.

Spreading the Word: Editors on Poetry. Columbia, SC: Bench Press, 1990.

Turco, Lewis. *The New Book of Forms.* Hanover, NH: University Press of New England, 1986.

1

ABOUT WRITING AND READING POETRY

Western Wind
ANONYMOUS
(13th century)

Western wind, when wilt thou blow,
The small rain down can rain?
Christ, if my love were in my arms,
And I in my bed again!

The Bed
THOM GUNN
(20th century)

The pulsing stops where time has been,
    The garden is snowbound,
The branches weighed down and the paths filled in,
    Drifts quilt the ground.

We lie soft-caught, still now it's done,
    Loose-twined across the bed
Like wrestling statues; but it still goes on
    Inside my head.

Two love poems. The poets who wrote them lived approximately seven hundred years apart. One poet is unknown, one writes during the second half of the twentieth century. Because both poems are short and intense reading experiences, both poems call attention to form. In "Western Wind," much is said and implied in four lines (a rhymed **quatrain**, with the **rhyme scheme** of *abcb—blow, rain, arms, again*) about the speaker's desire to be reunited with a loved one. In "The Bed," much is said and implied in eight lines (two rhymed quatrains—*abab, abab*—*been, snowbound, in, ground; done, bed, on, head*) about the way lovemaking takes place in memory/imagination as well as with a partner in bed. In addition, the lines of "The Bed" are typographically arranged to echo the drifts of snow. Both poets utilize the particulars of the world—beds and weather—to help us feel what they feel. Their poems make us consider constancy of **prosody** (of line length, rhythm, stanza, rhyme pattern, and theme) even as their poems' story, message, image, and meaning calls on us for emotional and intellectual responses.

"Western Wind" and "The Bed" are microcosms of the worlds of poetry writing that this book addresses. Each poem reminds us of the pleasures of reading and writing poetry: so much can happen within a few lines, a few stanzas in the rhyme (full and slant), meter (regular and irregular), alliteration, assonance, imagery, hyperbole, and understatement. Each poem plays the reader as the reader plays with it. We read to determine how the poet achieved the poem's technical effects as well as how the poet wrote about love. We also read to discover the ways the contemporary poet, Thom Gunn, stakes out new territory in the world of love and of poetry in the late twentieth century. One poet discusses, we assume, heterosexual love. One discusses, we assume (from biographical knowledge of the poet), homosexual love, or, more inclusively, lovers of either gender. We can speculate this way because the speakers of these poems are distinct—not interchangeable—yet connected. We may assume Thom Gunn is aware of his anonymous precursor, for "Western Wind" is a much quoted, highly regarded lyric. We're lucky to have these poems. We can learn from their interconnected variety and collect writing ideas from both poets.

When I first discussed these poems in this manner, some reviewers of this book took exception to my claims. At least two readers wanted to know why gender was an issue when looking at these poems. And one reader asked why I thought Thom Gunn was aware of the poem "Western Wind." Their questions can encourage you to ask—and answer—similar questions. I raised the issue of gender, as I'll continue to raise issues of gender, race, and class as we read poems in *Thirteen Ways,* because biographical and historical information can, does, and will change and challenge our readings of poems. Amiri Baraka says: "The first thing I tell them [writing students] is, it's all political. I begin by letting them see how in art and writing, the first thing you look for is the stance" (Packard 315).

It is true that for years, some readers of poetry—often termed the New Critics—insisted we address only the words on the page, and although we'll often do that in this book because we're trying to learn how to create the best pattern for our words on the page, recent literary critics emphasize other ways of reading. They assume that reading a poem one way (just the text, for example) and then in other ways (informed by biographical information or a feminist perspective, for example) deepens our understanding of a poem. The more readings we complete, the more likely we are to have evoked the many possibilities of a text, created a reliable interpretation, and learned how better to construct our own poems. Rachel Hadas claims that "All writing is rewriting. . . .

writing, far from being easier than reading (as beginning poets often think), is instead a difficult *form* of reading" (Finch 98).

 To support my reading of these poems, I did what any contemporary reader with access to the World Wide Web might do, as I encourage you to do: I researched current resources. The results were quick and informative. An Internet search for "Thom Gunn" produced a number of Web sites, including a site that provides a sample poem, read by Gunn, as well as useful biographic data: "Thom Gunn (b. 1929) is a British poet who has lived in the United States since 1954. He has published over thirty books of poetry, a collection of essays, and four edited collections. His work is extensively represented in literary anthologies. Gunn combines an interest in traditional poetics with less traditional subjects, such as Hell's Angels, LSD, and homosexuality" (http://www.lib.umd.edu/UMCP/ARCV/gunn.html). As a visit to this site and to another that listed further bibliographical resources made clear, understanding the poet's sexual identity *may* be of use in understanding this poem. Another site provided library reference books for studying Thom Gunn's poems: *Contemporary Authors, Dictionary of Literary Biography, Critical Survey of Poetry, Contemporary Poets, Concise Encyclopedia of English and American Poets and Poetry,* and *The Gay and Lesbian Literary Heritage.* The last reference clearly suggests that Thom Gunn is claimed by others for inclusion in literary discussions based on sexual identity. For "Western Wind" less information was available, but what I found reminded me again that this poem has received wide circulation in Great Britain, Thom Gunn's birthplace. Besides being listed in most anthologies of English poetry, this poem "was a secular tune often used as a basis for settings of the Mass" in Tudor England (Amazon.com review of the CD recording *Taverner, Tye, Sheppard: Western Wind Masses*).

Within minutes, a student of poetry with Web access can hear Thom Gunn reading his work, learn about the poet's life, and find a CD of the several Tudor masses composed from "Western Wind." Does every student of poetry need to do that with every poem in this book? No, but the active writer will want to do some of this some of the time, particularly when interpretive or compositional questions arise that use of this technology can illuminate.

FREE AND FORMAL VERSE

The poem is the language of an act of attention.
—Charles O. Hartman, 12

As we move from the World Wide Web back to the world, consider the degree to which most humans are collectors. We all try to impose order on our world(s). When I rake the oak leaves on Sunday, I don't say, "That's a 'good' oak leaf and that's a 'bad' oak leaf," leaving one kind and collecting only another. I gather them all up against the fence for mulch. However, as a collector who presses colored leaves in books, I might try to find what I think is the best of its kind—an elegant red-gold oak leaf—that models what I think a classic fall leaf should look like. And that's the one I'll take some extra care with.

The same happens at the ocean. You may pick up first one and then another shell, finding what you think for a moment is the perfect shell and then another and then another, each new discovery modifying your definition of what you call a classic shell. So too, some of us collect owl figurines, CDs, antique cars, clothes, Scottie-dog statues, beer cans—or poems. In each collection, we revel at the similarity and dissimilarity, the ideal and its variations. This love poem and that love poem. Traditional poems are best understood in conjunction with the freer verse that followed; and free verse would not exist without the traditions they break away from, play with, against, into. By learning both the conventions and where those conventions might most profitably be challenged, we learn the most. As H. T. Kirby-Smith explains, "The best free-verse poems take advantage of the tension between tradition and revolt, working contrapuntally. . . . dressing down rather than up, and sometimes cross-dressing" (x), and he warns us that the poet who doesn't pay attention to those tensions, the one who thinks anything goes, will be creating poems "devoid of rhythmic interest" (x).

Good and bad are useful or unavoidable terms at times. Certainly those writing poetry in classes are trying to get good grades, and those writing poetry professionally are trying to write well enough to garner publication. For now, deploy the terms good and bad in your own best interests. Lewis Turco points out the poet's need for constancy. As a practicing poet, I find that formal constancy is worth seeking through craft and worth setting aside at times in order to follow a line of thought or an intuition, in order to create a more effective poem.

In this spirit, you need to take chances, try new forms, examine your drafts, and develop your work critically and enthusiastically, because you learn to write poetry from your own attempts and variations. To do this, you'll need to write. A lot. Alone and in the company of other writers.

In the remainder of this chapter, I review a number of issues that allow you to embark on a course of study in poetry, looking at forms, trying them out, and sharing them in a workshop setting. Like anyone entering into new territory, you need to have the right gear and the knowledge of how to use that gear, but you also have to use the gear immediately, often before you feel ready to do so. For the most part, learning is like that: you just have to dive in. The same is true about learning to write poetry. Some guides tell you quite a lot about what to do and not to do—such as, avoid **clichéd** language and aim for precise, concrete images. While I agree with those exhortations and will emphasize some of these issues myself, overall I see my job differently. I want to encourage you *to begin* and *to write often*. Over time, as we explore and mature together as poets entering the world of contemporary poem-making, we'll learn about what doesn't work by working toward what does work.

Still, it's pretty easy to become overwhelmed in this territory and grow annoyed at poets and prosodists when they talk of formal verse, free verse, metrical verse, unrhymed verse, fixed forms (sonnet, villanelle), formal techniques (stanza, alliteration), genre and form (prose poem is to poem? Poem is to story? To nonfiction? To drama?).

I remember early in my schooling, as part of a poetry class project, taking a tape deck from office to office in the English department and asking each professor to define poetry. Most demurred, others rephrased the question, and still others offered me cut-and-dried definitions that **poetry** was a certain thing (often connected to their understandings developed through a literary affiliation). Not surprisingly, I found that no one could or would adequately define poetry. Everyone seemed to offer partial or tentative definitions, and no one seemed to arrive at the same definition. Poetry, I found then, and know even more surely now, is alive and changing—an act, a process—which is why I encourage you to begin, to participate, and then (almost immediately) to examine and reflect and define and refine. Prosody can be experienced but not nailed down. I found this to be the case when I consulted other textbooks and specialized prosody manuals. Contemporary poets need to be attuned to dialects, regional speech patterns, and the current musical but complicated linguistic rhythms of our multicultural society; they also need to learn to find the strengths, the regularities, and the idiosyncrasies of those languages and to understand how our current presentations of rhythmic speech approach and stray from older, more traditionally measured metrical patterns and literary dialects.

Remember, however, that while poetry resists definition, it does seem to yield to practice.

> The purity of the Aristotelian distinction between form and what is often called structures has rarely been kept. . . . At its least encompassing level, form is used to refer to metrical patterns as well as lexical, syntactic, and linear arrangements: for example, the form of the heroic couplet or the Spenserian stanza. At this level the term has to do with matters of technique and style. . . . A more encompassing view considers form as structure, put most simply as the overall "mode of arrangement" . . . of the text; that is, the way textual materials are organized so as to create shape. —Alex Preminger and T. V. F. Brogan, 451

In response to this quotation I'm tempted to say, exactly, or (im)precisely. *Forms are what we pour some poems into and form(ing) is what we do to words to make them convey meaning in a poetic way.* With this in mind, you'll find me emphasizing the tools of the poet's craft and simultaneously examining how we use those tools to craft certain poetic structures.

Here's another way to categorize—adapted from a chart provided in John Drury's book *Creating Poetry:*

	POETRY		PROSE

VERSE

UNMETRICAL VERSE	METRICAL VERSE
• Long-lined Free Verse	• Rhymed Verse
• Free Verse	• Blank Verse
	• Syllabics
	• Accentual Verse

For purposes of discussion, Drury contrasts poetry and prose and then distinguishes among types of formally measured and counted (metrical) verse and types of unmeasured (unmetrical) verse. Notice that he doesn't include the genre categories of humorous, light, or nonacademic verse, or song although he might have.

In *The New Book of Forms,* Lewis Turco organizes his handbook according to this taxonomy:

- typographical level (how poetry looks on the page is certainly different than how prose looks)
- sonic level (what poetry sounds like—how sounds and rhythms are organized in lines)
- sensory level (how figures of speech such as similes and images are used within poems)
- ideational level (grammar and syntax)
- forms (a matter of counting and naming shapes, such as two-line or four-line stanzas and more complicated forms with repeating lines and/or words)

Paul Fussell divides his discussion in *Poetic Meter and Poetic Form* into those two guiding categories—**meter** and form. In my textbook *Working Words* I focus on genre boundaries. Because I talk about creating in both prose and poetry, in this book I examine genre borderlands: where/if/how prose becomes poetry, for instance, or how narrative verse partakes of dramatic, fictional, and poetic conventions, and so on.

It's time for me to say again that you're going to have to experiment with forms and with forming. Later in this chapter, I'll illustrate this by talking you through the class invention exercise that resulted in a published poem for me, in order to show you how the three elements of this text—reading other poets, creating an invention exercise or self-assignment that triggers poetic exploration, forming a poem from those prompts—might work for you.

If you do these explorations yourself, you'll discover what breaking out of form teaches you, since fixed forms—sonnet, pantoum, villanelle, haiku—are time-, culture-, and context-bound. The English sonnet, for instance, came into popularity for particular reasons. Sonnets from the past are often elegant and moving. Yet sonnets from the past can also sound overly stylized and archaic to a modern ear. A great part of the joy of exploration through form, then, results from matching formal demands to current contexts. If full rhymes (moon/June) seem ponderous to our modern ear, let's discover the work that slant rhymes (splice/place) can perform within our poems. And maybe, out of joy and mischievousness, let's try to slip a full rhyme in anyway—maybe not in end words, but internally, within a line where the full rhyme makes music but doesn't sound out a fire alarm.

> To see how free verse actually works, we will have to ask what conventions remain after metrical rules are abandoned.
> —Charles O. Hartman, 24

Conversely, ways of forming (deciding to write in metrical or nonmetrical verse, choosing to honor lyric over narrative, and so on) are also choices of custom and may mark your decision to participate in a particular poetic culture.

> I can't imagine how Romantic poets like Blake, Burns, Wordsworth, the Brownings, Tennyson, Christina Rossetti, Elizabeth Hands, Ann Yearsly, Joanna Baillie (just to name a few) worked in tight form all their lives. I can only imagine the freedom Whitman must have felt in abandoning all the rigidity of form. And yet there is a pride I felt after working on this villanelle. It was damn hard work. And, somehow, maybe a poet has to be even more creative to write a successful formal poem. It's a different kind of creativity: when writing a villanelle, I feel more conscious of the process than I do writing in free verse. Yet my impulses are still driven by a curiosity to see what happens. —Rex West

For now, discover what happens when you explore the music of words, the constraints and excesses of boundary-making and boundary-breaking, the architectures and skeletons upon which we hang our ideas and feelings. If on the journey, you write a good villanelle or a nearly perfect, classic sestina, take that much more satisfaction in what you have accomplished within these fixed forms.

> Poetry is methodology—more process than genre. It's important to me to try to understand the architecture of an idea, the context for the architecture, and the dynamics of how the idea spins out. I spend a great deal of time thinking about a poem before it ever emerges as words. Once the poem has shown itself, I take the poem through any number of revisions and permutations to try to see what it is I'm saying in those words. —Monifa Love

But back to free verse. Free verse began as a movement against formal constraints, first in France in the seventeenth century when **syllabic verse** forms were liberated. By the nineteenth century, there was a rebellion against meter—the carefully counted iambic pentameter of the English sonnet or blank verse—

and by the time Walt Whitman composed *Leaves of Grass* in 1855, he helped poets see how to respond to regularity with planned irregularity by using syntax or typography to measure lines.

from *Song of Myself*
WALT WHITMAN

1

I celebrate myself, and sing myself,
And what I assume you shall assume,
For every atom belonging to me as good belongs to you.

I loafe and invite my soul,
I lean and loafe at my ease observing a spear of summer grass.

My tongue, every atom of my blood, form'd from this soil, this air,
Born here of parents born here from parents the same, and their parents
    the same,
I, now thirty-seven years old in perfect health begin,
Hoping to cease not till death.

Creeds and schools in abeyance,
Retiring back a while sufficed at what they are, but never forgotten,
I harbor for good or bad, I permit to speak at every hazard,
Nature without check with original energy.

Whitman's first stanza reads like an ars poetica. And reading him in that manner, poets began to give themselves permission to write past the constraints of full-stopped rhymes and common prosody meters.

Whitman brought back into poetry strong stress at unpredictable places, grammatical emphasis and parallelism, anaphora, and long lines. His oral-derived form is expansive, asymmetrical, mixing dialects and modes, and above all, personal." —Alex Preminger and T. V. F. Brogan, 425

In the twentieth century, another strand of free verse developed in the avant-garde sense of explicit experimentation. Poets developed prosodic theories based on breath length, or played with readers' expectations by giving syntactic units like articles (*a, an, the*) or conjunctions (*and, but, for, nor, yet*) unexpected accent and importance, or composed concrete poetry where typography took on an important, poster-like dimension.

Because free verse finds form through alternate methods—relying on repetition, parallelism, explorations of the relationship of auditory and visual voicing—in one sense, much of the formal work presented in this book is free verse inspired since I don't spend much time teaching (or following) metrical patterns, nor do I usually advocate full rhyme. (The reference books listed in the preface, however, provide fine resources for those interested in further study of formal prosody.) Instead, I urge you to use formal patterns (often of stanza and repetition) initially, and then to free your poems as you draft and redraft. It's most important to understand that writers can be neither free nor formal in isolation. We learn conventions both by accepting and by rebelling. We see what can be learned from conforming and from breaking with expectation, but there is no breaking and no unexpected excitement unless we know and cultivate and play with reason and constraint.

> Free verse, to succeed as poetry, *must depart in a distinctive and recognizable way from one or more conventions that have in the past governed the organization of the poetic line, or the stanza taken as a whole.* It is analogous, on an enlarged scale, to the familiar idea of metrical substitution, or expressive variation, which takes place within the accentual-syllabic line. —H. T. Kirby-Smith, 10–11

If you have wondered in the past just what is so free about free verse, I hope you can now begin to see that you learn to write free verse by learning both fixed verse forms and then the ways poets—you included—choose to depart from those forms. A number of poets believe that improving your free verse results from improving your control over your technical repertoire. Jane Greer claims, "[T]he only point of poetry [is] delight: To refuse rhyme or meter is to limit the delight. And no one has poetic license to do that" (Finch 79).

CONTEMPORARY POETRY

Many students of poetry haven't yet read a lot of contemporary poetry. Their (your?) influences may primarily be popular song and historical poems, most of which rely on strong rhyme and regular stanza patterns and easily memorizable, repeatable phrases. It's easy to assume contemporary poetry will require the same techniques. Well, yes and no. Sometimes, but often not. For instance, contemporary poets prefer rhyme that doesn't call attention to itself; concrete, particular images; and conversational (though carefully chosen and arranged) language. Poets look for unexpected phrases and strong sensory details. These poems often have, as I've come to term it, their feet on the ground, describing or memorializing particular, exact spots and using the five senses of sight, taste, touch, smell, and sound. Although there are historical distinctions between narrative and lyrical poems, the first telling a long story, the second capturing a moment or emotion, most contemporary poets speak from the point of view of people much like themselves—poet to contemporary reader: poem's **speaker** or **persona** (a created/assumed character) to reader. In a great deal of contemporary poetry, someone is at home. Someone (the speaker, who is distinct from but often very similar to the poet) is telling about his/her life and feelings. Someone lives somewhere and says something particularly appropriate to that time and place.

Popular songs, on the other hand, are intentionally more portable, intended to trigger your memories more than let you into the insights of the poet as he or she shares a special, vivid vision of the world. Neither poem nor song is preferable; each has different uses and strengths. Contemporary poetry is not more or less valuable than historical poetry or popular songs. It is simply different, addressed to different concerns, representative of its particular time and place.

Poetry is about making words fit well together. —Karl Hofmeister

I have learned to strive to write with clear, fresh, unique ideas. That is to not just write "dead tired"—an overused clichéd description. But to think [about how] to describe tired in a way that has not been described before. —Sharel Mitchell

I think my poems are contemporary poems for a number of reasons. I used concrete descriptions of specific settings and events and tried to include precise detail in my writing. . . . I also worked to avoid overly flowery imagery and focused on avoiding clichés. —Natasha Clews

⮂ READING INTO WRITING ⮀

To test out these writers' theories, use the following songs and poems to explore definitions for yourself. After reading the four texts below, describe the techniques each writer uses. Then, alone or with group members, compose a definition of Poem and Song, based on your observations. (Note: I know my taste in song and poetry is not your taste: I've picked samples that illustrate differences. I'm aware that I could have picked songs that are more like contemporary poems, say lyrics by Natalie Merchant or Alanis Morissette, because songs often do perform like poems and vice versa: Counting Crows references Bob Dylan the way poets reference other poets; David Byrne parodies everyone and everything; Bruce Cockburn and Van Morrison have sections of their CDs that feel like spoken word poetry performances; you might swear by REM, etc. But that's not the point here. Right now I need to show differences that allow you to develop an ear for the nuances of an effective contemporary poem. If you find yourself arguing with my choices, fine. This shows how you could profitably continue this discussion in the pages of your own journal to examine more songs and more contemporary poems, and to work on these distinctions to your own satisfaction.)

Tears in Heaven
ERIC CLAPTON AND WILL JENNINGS

Would you know my name
if I saw you in heaven?
Would you feel the same
if I saw you in heaven?
I must be strong and carry on
'Cause I know I don't belong here in heaven . . .

Would you hold my hand
if I saw you in heaven?
Would you help me stand
if I saw you in heaven?
I'll find my way through night and day
'Cause I know I just can't stay here in heaven.

Time can bring you down,
time can bend your knees
Time can break your heart,
Have you begging please . . .

Beyond the door there's peace I'm sure
And I know there'll be no more tears in heaven.
(Repeat stanzas 1 and 2.)

Traveling Through the Dark
WILLIAM STAFFORD

Traveling through the dark I found a deer
dead on the edge of the Wilson River road.
It is usually best to roll them into the canyon:
that road is narrow; to swerve might make more dead.

By glow of the tail-light I stumbled back of the car
and stood by the heap, a doe, a recent killing;
she had stiffened already, almost cold.
I dragged her off; she was large in the belly.

My fingers touching her side brought me the reason—
her side was warm; her fawn lay there waiting,
alive, still, never to be born.
Beside that mountain road I hesitated.

The car aimed ahead its lowered parking lights;
under the hood purred the steady engine.
I stood in the glare of the warm exhaust turning red;
around our group I could hear the wilderness listen.

I thought hard for us all—my only swerving—
then pushed her over the edge into the river.

A Blessing
JAMES WRIGHT

Just off the highway to Rochester, Minnesota,
Twilight bounds softly forth on the grass.
And the eyes of those two Indian ponies
Darken with kindness.
They have come gladly out of the willows
To welcome my friend and me.
We step over the barbed wire into the pasture
Where they have been grazing all day, alone.
They ripple tensely, they can hardly contain their happiness
That we have come.
They bow shyly as wet swans. They love each other.
There is no loneliness like theirs.
At home once more,
They begin munching the young tufts of spring in the darkness.
I would like to hold the slenderer one in my arms,
For she has walked over to me
And nuzzled my left hand.
She is black and white,
Her mane falls wild on her forehead,
And the light breeze moves me to caress her long ear
That is delicate as the skin over a girl's wrist.
Suddenly I realize
That if I stepped out of my body I would break
Into blossom.

Across the Great Divide
KATE WOLF

I've been walkin' in my sleep
Countin' troubles 'stead of countin' sheep
Where the years went I can't say
I just turned around and they've gone away

I've been siftin' through the layers
Of dusty books and faded papers
They tell a story I used to know
And it was one that happened so long ago

Chorus

It's gone away in yesterday
Now I find myself on the mountainside
Where the rivers change direction
Across the Great Divide

Now, I heard the owl a-callin'
Softly as the night was fallin'
With a question and I replied
But he's gone across the borderline

Chorus, one further stanza
And Chorus Twice

There are many free verse poems in this book. You can locate them in the Forms Index and you'll note their prevalence in the chapters on Elegies and Aubades, Listing and Repetition, Odes and Praise songs. We'll begin to examine free verse techniques by reading the six, themed, free verse poems below by professional and emerging poets. All deal with interpersonal relationships and all are "expansive, asymmetrical, mixing dialects and modes, and above all, personal" (Preminger and Brogan 425).

The One Girl at the Boys Party
SHARON OLDS

When I take my girl to the swimming party
I set her down among the boys. They tower and
bristle, she stands there smooth and sleek,
her math scores unfolding in the air around her.
They will strip to their suits, her body hard and
indivisible as a prime number,
they'll plunge in the deep end, she'll subtract
her height from ten feet, divide it into
hundreds of gallons of water, the numbers
bouncing in her mind like molecules of chlorine
in the bright blue pool. When they climb out,
her ponytail will hang its pencil lead
down her back, her narrow silk suit
with hamburgers and french fries printed on it
will glisten in the brilliant air, and they will

see her sweet face, solemn and
sealed, a factor of one, and she will
see their eyes, two each,
their legs, two each, and the curves of their sexes,
one each, and in her head she'll be doing her
wild multiplying, as the drops
sparkle and fall to the power of a thousand from her body.

Grating Parmesan
BARBARA CROOKER

A winter evening,
sky, the color of cobalt,
the night coming down like the lid on a pot.
On the stove, the ghosts of summer simmer:
tomatoes, garlic, basil, oregano.
Steam from the kettle rises,
wreathes the windows.
You come running when I reach for the grater,
"Help me?" you ask, reversing the pronouns,
part of your mind's disordered scramble.
Together, we hold the rind of the cheese,
scrape our knuckles on the metal teeth.
A fresh pungency enters the room.
You put your fingers in the fallen crumbs:
"Snow," you proudly exclaim, and look at me.
Three years old, nearly mute,
but master of metaphor.
Most of the time, we speak without words.

Outside, the icy stones in the sky
glitter in their random order.
It's a night so cold, the very air freezes flesh,
a knife in the lungs, wind rushing
over the coil of the planet
straight from Siberia,
a high howl from the wolves of the steppes.
As we grate and grate, the drift rises higher.
When the family gathers together,
puts pasta in their bowls,
ladles on the simmered sauce,
you will bless each one
with a wave of your spoon:
"Snowflakes falling
all around."

You're the weatherman
of the kitchen table.
And, light as feathers,
the parmesan sprinkles down,
its newly fallen snow
gracing each plate.

Appetite
MAXINE KUMIN

I eat these
wild red raspberries
still warm from the sun
and smelling faintly of jewelweed
in memory of my father

tucking the napkin
under his chin and bending
over an ironstone bowl
of the bright drupelets
awash in cream

my father
with the sigh of a man
who has seen all and been redeemed
said time after time
as he lifted his spoon

men kill for this.

Eating Together
LI-YOUNG LEE

In the steamer is the trout
seasoned with slivers of ginger,
two sprigs of green onion, and sesame oil.
We shall eat it with rice for lunch,
brothers, sister, my mother who will
taste the sweetest meat of the head,
holding it between her fingers
deftly, the way my father did
weeks ago. Then he lay down
to sleep like a snow-covered road
winding through pines older than him,
without any travelers, and lonely for no one.

The Window
C. J. HANNAH

Roy, Mother spoke softly,
her back to us as she washed
the supper's dishes. Dad
sat at the round oak table, reading.
Roy, I would so like a window here,
above the sink. It's so dark and no
amount of lighting seems to help.

Ummm, He mused, looking up
as if studying the problem.
Bad time of the year for that.
The first frost'll be here this week.

I looked at the wall wondering what
mother wanted to see out her window . . .
the peach orchard, now autumn barren,
and a mile away above the orchards,
the bookcliffs looming
like monstrous battleships.
In spring she'd see pink blossoms,
fragrant clouds caught in the branches,
in summer, dark green leaves curling
finger-like 'round the swelling fruit,
and in fall, along the canal,
cottonwoods exploding into a yellow
so bright it hurts the eyes.

Spring eased into summer,
the peaches ripened
from almond size
to that of baseballs.
Dad came in for lunch one day
and stopped, stunned,
just inside the door. A faint cloud of
white dust drifted in the air, and a
smell of wood long hidden from the sun.
A ten pound sledge hammer lay on the floor.
Mother stood near the sink, staring sharp eyed
at him, as he stared at
the hole smashed in the wall
above the sink, dripping white chunks
of plaster and laths.
A gentle, warm breeze blew down the canyon

and through the hole
filling the kitchen with
the smell of ripening peaches.
Mother pointed to the ragged hole.
That is where I want the window.

Under Stars
TESS GALLAGHER

The sleep of this night deepens
because I have walked coatless from the house
carrying the white envelope.
All night it will say one name
in its little tin house by the roadside.

I have raised the metal flag
so its shadow under the roadlamp
leaves an imprint on the rain-heavy bushes.
Now I will walk back
thinking of the few lights still on
in the town a mile away.

In the yellowed light of a kitchen
the millworker has finished his coffee,
his wife has laid out the white slices of bread
on the counter. Now while the bed they have left
is still warm, I will think of you, you
who are so far away
you have caused me to look up at the stars.

Tonight they have not moved
from childhood, those games played after dark.
Again I walk into the wet grass
toward the starry voices. Again, I
am the found one, intimate, returned
by all I touch on the way.

☙ READING INTO WRITING ❧

1. Consider the way Sharon Olds breaks her lines. Read the poem aloud,
   several times. Or have several members of a writing group each read
   the poem aloud. What do you make of (and how do you read) the several lines ending on "and"—a coordinating conjunction that some
   poets feel does not belong at the focal point of a line break?

2. Again, using Sharon Olds' poem, look at her use of **metaphor** and particular detail. Discuss who is speaking and to whom. What is the reader's role in this poem? How would you feel if your mother wrote a poem like this about you?

3. Read "Grating Parmesan" and then write an initial response to/ explication of/exploration of this poem. Barbara Cooker breaks lines differently than does Sharon Olds. The speaker in her poem also seems to have a less explicit relationship to the "you" in the poem. Is this her daughter or son (does it matter)? After writing your response, compare it to the response written by Ellen Schendel, below, or to responses written by members of a peer group.

4. Maxine Kumin writes her poem in three five-line stanzas and closes with a single dramatic line. Decide if this poem is free or formal verse. Why or why not?

5. The speakers in the Maxine Kumin and Li-Young Lee poems are both discussing their fathers. Write about each speaker's relation-ships with a father as we learn about them in the poem. (Quote lines for support of your interpretation.) Then, write for five minutes nonstop about your relationship to your own father. What metaphor would best represent that relationship? Investigate this metaphor in a poem draft.

6. The C. J. Hannah poem "The Window" was chosen most often when I asked class writers to pick a poem that interested them from the class anthology. Write an explanation of why you think it was chosen by your peers as an interesting or moving poem. What would you like to steal from it and why? Try to do so.

7. I often use the Tess Gallagher poem "Under Stars" to build a com-munity consensus by sharing it in parts—the first stanza only, then the next, then the next—while we discuss and try to agree on the gist of the poem. Try this in a small group with any poem in the book. Take a poem new to you all and cover all but the first few lines or first stanza, discussing a few lines at a time until you agree on mean-ing and interpretation, then uncovering a few more lines until your reading is complete. With "Under Stars" we can usually achieve fair agreement until the last stanza. Focus on this stanza in your reading. What is going on? Why/how has the tone changed? Does/how does the last stanza change your reading of the poem?

8. Reread these six poems to discover how each poet achieves a sense of **closure** without heavy rhyme, without repetition of line, and without the expected techniques of formal verse patterns. How does each say to you, the reader, "This poem is finished"?

READING POEMS FOR WRITING POEMS

Poems need to be read, both aloud and internally, and usually more than once. To appreciate a poem, you need to hear it and rehear it in your own voice or the voices of others. (That's why poets like to go to live readings by other poets, just as musicians and music lovers go to concerts.) You also have to read it with both your emotional and analytic minds, which again means reading a poem several times. Reading theorist Louise Rosenblatt posits that we come to any text from one of two main stances—the aesthetic or the efferent. We look for the artistic (aesthetic) qualities and for the informational (efferent) qualities of a text. While I agree those are useful reading stances, I think a poet comes to poems for even more reasons and from many different angles. I encourage you to read and reread the poems of others (and your own drafts) in multiple ways—artificially trying several at first to broaden your options for ways of reading and then creating more utilitarian mixes of reading strategies. Journal editors like David St. John, find that their business of reading is a complicated but rewarding one: "I felt that each time I returned to these two poems I learned something new about them, and about myself as well. These were poems that one could not 'get' on a first reading. Like all the best poems, they yielded slowly, like blossoms unfolding. It was their mystery, offered with impeccable style, that dazzled me" (*Spreading the Word* 4). This is the place to remind you again that reading histories—our politics, our affiliations, and our beliefs—will affect our readings of the poem just as those issues affected the poet's composing.

There is no best order for employing reading strategies, but these are some that have proven useful overall:

1. Read a poem and retell the poem's *story* or *feeling* by trying to capture the *gist* of the text in your own words. This may read like a summary or an investigation.

2. Read the poem line by line, with a dictionary, a poetry encyclopedia, and books of myths, etc. Mark all the vocabulary and sayings you don't understand and try to find out what they mean, first with your books, then by asking other readers. Then recopy the poem in slightly longer form—but in much the same shape—inserting plainer words to clarify meaning, untangling and regularizing syntax if that helps.

3. A variant on the previous method: turn the poem into a prose version. Add missing words, untangle syntax, and simplify/clarify/explore **allusions**.

4. Read the poem associationally. (This is a reader-response technique.) Underline the passages that trigger resonate memories or experiences in your own life and freewrite about those experiences. Let the poem

open you up to yourself before you return to it for a second reading where you connect your experiences to the poet's presentation of life.

5. Read the poem and narrate the play of your mind as it untangles meanings. (Peter Elbow calls this providing a "movie of the reader's mind.") You can do this into a tape recorder or on a computer with the screen turned off. Quote the text, respond, then analyze how your mind responds to and explicates the poem.

6. Read the poem for technical information. Take all your craft knowledge and say what the poet did structurally and/or rhetorically. Is the poem in fixed form? How well does it adhere to or break away from the form?

7. Read the poem to divine meaning and intention. Look at the poet's play of metaphor, symbols, and allusions, and guess at his/her intentions. Share your interpretation of what the poet is getting at with another reader and negotiate a middle ground that you can both agree on. If two readers can't agree, add a third and a fourth reader until some type of consensus is reached. Or start with four readers and read the poem aloud together, negotiating meaning as you go.

8. Read the poem historically and with a consideration of how the poet's race, class, or gender (and the race, class, and gender politics of the time of composition) may influence your reading. As demonstrated above, you can use the Internet as a resource for this type of reading.

9. Read the poem using a theoretical lens, many of which are available. You can read the poem from a feminist perspective, or from a psychological perspective, from a deconstructive perspective (look for what isn't being said in the poem and what is being avoided). Patrick Bizzaro's book *Responding to Student Poems: Applications of Critical Theory* (National Council of Teachers of English, 1994) can offer you samples of several types of these useful ways of reading poetry.

Do you have to read a poem nine times and in nine different ways? (With theoretical variants we could call this thirteen ways.) No. But it would never hurt. And when you do so, poems you formerly hadn't appreciated may begin to blossom and unfold for you if you give them your repeated attention. Each reading is different because you're a different person each time you read, with different attitudes toward the poem you (re)encounter.

We should celebrate the play of poetry. Careful reading helps us do this. Right next to a love of form, poets have in common a dedication to experimentation, to weaving and unweaving, and to structuring and releasing their words in draft after draft. Words are crucial, as are phrases and sentences, lines and stanzas. With words, we come to understand our world; we make use of language, arranging it into beauty and into knowledge. Our subjects are our lives, as Raymond Carver points out in his poem "Sunday Night."

Sunday Night ❖
RAYMOND CARVER

Make use of the things around you.
This light rain
Outside the window, for one.
This cigarette between my fingers,
These feet on the couch.
The faint sound of rock-and-roll,
The red Ferrari in my head.
The woman bumping
Drunkenly around in the kitchen . . .
Put it all in,
Make use.

Particularly, if you want to imitate a poet and/or learn from his or her poetic moves, you'll benefit from doing the following:

a. Copy the poem by hand or by typing it into your computer. There is something important about making the exact technical and typographical moves a poet made. Also, you might choose to memorize a poem or portion of a poem.

b. Read more than one poem by the poet to see how this poem confirms or experiments with his/her style.

c. Then write a journal entry using one or usually more than one of the reading techniques shared here.

d. Finally, begin to imitate, spring off of, or let yourself be lightly influenced by that poet.

Reading is the first way in. Equally, all these reading techniques increase your skill at reading peers' poems in workshops and your own poems as you look toward revision. You'll see the poets doing this type of close reading of their own drafts in the revision case studies in the appendix. There is no single way to read for writing poems, but I encourage you to work hard at reading because this work will repay you in increased confidence and comfort as you approach each new text.

Ellen Schendel completed the following reading response to decide which of two poems—both of which she admired—she would choose to imitate.

Reading Journal Response to "Grating Parmesan," by Barbara Crooker
Prose Translation:

It's a winter evening, dark growing darker. On the stove, the last remnants of summer vegetables simmer: tomatoes, garlic, basil, oregano. Steam from the kettle rises, steams up the windows. You, my child, come running when I reach for the grater. You say "help me?" in that too child-like way of yours, where you reverse the pronouns; your mind is a busy (and confused?) place these days, and you often mix up your words. Together, we hold the block of cheese, sometimes accidentally scraping our knuckles on the metal teeth of the grater as we grate the parmesan. The smell of parmesan fills the room. You put your hands in the shreds of cheese: "Snow," you say looking at me. You are proud of your analogy. You are three years old, can barely speak (after all, you mix up your words, sometimes), but still an astute observer. Besides, most of the time, you and I communicate without speaking because we know each other so well.

  Outside, the stars and snow glitter in the sky. It's such a cold night that we'd get chill-bumps if we went outside; it's the kind of cold that burns your lungs when you breathe. It's windy, so windy that it seems as if the gusts come from all over the world. As we grate and grate, the snowdrift of cheese gets larger. When the rest of the family joins us for a meal of pasta and meat sauce, you will spoon parmesan onto each bowl, saying "Snowflakes falling all around." You are our little weatherman. You sprinkle parmesan, light as feathers, and like newly-fallen snow it gracefully lands on each plate.

Structural Analysis/Reader Response/Chasing Down
Allusions, Gaps, Absences, Symbols:

I love that this poem is so tight: snow, cooking, family. Each stanza ties those ideas together. Cold, windy outside, but intimate inside—and yet, the chilliness of the outside and the steaminess of the kitchen are tied together by the image of snow/cheese, the role of the little boy as weatherman (I think the child is a boy—"master" and "weatherman" are masculine; but the kid could be a girl, too).

  More about the child: although when I first read the poem I was not sure why he confuses his words and is almost mute. It didn't dawn on me to assume that the child is mentally handicapped in some way. Upon re-reading this poem—and my response to it—I think that there is more to the child than I first thought. If he is handicapped (and I think there's a great chance that he is), it makes the whole "little weatherman" and "most of the time we speak without words" parts stronger. If he's mentally handicapped and doesn't have advanced language skills, these times together in the kitchen doing things (not talking) are more intimate than I at first thought. That he is a weatherman, the center of attention at the end of the poem, and very much in control (the weatherman being the one who produces "snow") makes the ending more powerful: it is still about intimacy with his mother, but it is also about his words "'Snowflakes falling all around'" having power.

The title, "Grating Parmesan," places the emphasis/focus of the poem squarely on the act of grating cheese, the thing that the mother and child do together inside, where it's warm and steamy. I think this is significant: it would be a different kind of poem if it were something about snowing or cold. Cooking = warmth and coziness and happiness to me, and I think that the tone of this poem is one of intimacy, a time cherished by a mother (I guess we don't know for sure that this poem is about a mother, either—but since the poet is a woman and I think women write about food/kitchens as comfort zones, I can't help but assume that the poem is about a mother).

Why bring up the cold, windy outside anyway? I'm not exactly sure. It is a good contrast to the warmth (literally and metaphorically) in the kitchen. It seems to be a realistic and natural comparison—grated parmesan to snow— that the child makes, since it is snowing (and gathering in drifts) outside. I like the ambiguity of the start of stanza two: I like how the "icy stones" make me think of both stars and snow; I like that "As we grate and grate, the drift rises higher" seems to refer both to the snow outside and the cheese inside. The ambiguity here implies that the mother-son bonding matches the strength of the cold outside; a weather metaphor, perhaps, for the natural strength of the parent-child (and mother-son) bond?

Because I think meta-texts are neat, I can't help but notice the discussion of language going on throughout the poem. The little boy, not very language-adept, is the one who makes the connection between grated parmesan and snow. It's the metaphor that is important, the underlying meaning, the unspoken words between parent and child, that matter most in this poem; it's the underlying meaning of the poem, the metaphor of cheese and snow for parent-child bonding that is the real point of this poem.

⌒ READING INTO WRITING ⌒

1. Monifa Love uses the analogy of form as architecture, Rex West makes obeying or disobeying form sound like putting on and taking off tight clothes, and I compare form to instances of natural symmetry and repetition although I might also call form the skeleton for the poem's body. Do some freewriting to explore those comparisons and/or come up with your own analogy for poetic form. Molly Peacock claims: "If you think of form as the outside of an Inside, that is only half the truth. Verse form is also inside the Inside. It acts as a skeleton as well as a skin. It is a body" (Finch 178).

2. It's sometimes easier to see the form of a song, because songs depend (often) on regular stanzas, rhymes, and refrains; these techniques are most familiar to many of us from church hymns. Look at the poems in the preface and try to sketch out their "music" or "skeleton" or "architecture." What repeats and what calls attention to itself?

3. Take your favorite poem and do the same sketching or mapping. Since even free verse relies on certain types of regularity, how do you know you're looking at a poem? How does the poem declare itself? What techniques does the poet use to let you know you should read this as a "poem"? Consider, for instance, Raymond Carver's poem.

4. There are multitudes of shapes and sizes and attitudes and occasions for poems: formal poems, free verse poems, poems you encounter in everyday use (the Hallmark card, the advertising jingle, the poem your daughter or parent or significant other writes and includes in a present or letter), and poems that are archived in books that we most often find in libraries or academic classrooms. What are the attributes of public and private, academic and popular verse? How do you know one from the other? Why does such a distinction matter? Would you be as happy to have the next poem you write appear on the back of a cereal box as in the student literary magazine? Why or why not?

5. Read any of the poems in this book actively using the World Wide Web as I did with Thom Gunn's "The Bed" at the beginning of this chapter and/or with off-line resources (including a dictionary—the essential reference tool for a poet). Phillip Levine claims any seventeen-year-old should, with the information provided by such research, be able to read his work. For this activity, choose a poem that is slow to yield its meaning to you and work on it for a few days, preparing an introduction to that poem for a seventeen-year-old friend or for an English class at your local high school.

> It would seem to me that all of my poems would be accessible to a bright person of sixteen or seventeen, given that the opportunity is presented for that person to know the essentials. If the poem is about a particular event, they have to know the event; if the poem is about certain kinds of conditions in the thirties that I happen to be writing about, they have to know what those conditions are; or if the poem makes a reference to people living in Spain in the thirties, they have to know about the Civil War. Anybody could present that to them. I hope my poems are available to bright seventeen-year-olds. —Phillip Levine (Duke and Jacobsen 48)

➤ INVENTION EXERCISES ➤

Here's an example of one journey into and out of form. As you'll see below, Tom Heise has written what he calls a nonce **sonnet**. Nonce means the poet has decided upon the terms of formal regularity for his text. In this case, Tom's nonce sonnet has fourteen lines altogether, but the lines don't occur in traditional sonnet meter (iambic pentameter) or rhyme scheme (*abab, cdcd, efef, gg*), nor does his sonnet follow the expected rhetorical structure, making a statement in the first eight lines and resolving them in the last six lines. Instead, Tom uses all he is learning about sonnets to allow him to put his ideas into dialogue with the tradition.

*One Winter Morning**

> There's not much life here this time
> of year, even the low moans of the factory seem
> forced. The snow that comes up past my knees
> as I wade to my car, reminds
> me of a sick child's face, pale, but slightly gray.
> The tree branches cast such thin shadows, they might be taken for
>   spider webs.
>
> The car door snaps shut, cleanly breaking
> a fresh sheet of ice, and when I look through
> the frosted windows, it's like trying to see through
> stained glass; everything's enchanting, yet fractured, cold and silent.
> My brother's lips, heavy with the scent
> of coffee, are strangely captivating, as he stands
> in the doorway to his apartment mouthing words
> I can't comprehend, like please write, good-bye, I love you.

"One Winter Morning" was recently written as the final assignment for my summer Poetic Technique course. Though the course was my initiation to formal verse . . . even within those forms I experimented with liberties that allowed me to remain true to the poem's basic pattern, but still introduced a freshness to the words. "One Winter Morning" is an example of such an experiment. It is a nonce sonnet with a deep structure that abandons tradition-al rhetoric and resolution; ending instead with the beginning of questioning.
—Thomas Heise

Essentially, without the sonnet to spark his experimentation, Tom's poem wouldn't have developed as it did. To break form, he needed to explore and honor form. To judge the effects of experimentation, he had to understand the fixed forms as well as how to deviate from them.

In Tom's sonnet, we've seen a considered variation on a theme. He's written his sonnet in a reversed rhetorical pattern: instead of an eight-line thought asking for a six-line resolution, he's given us a six-line description, followed by an eight-line elaboration that, if we read his composing notes shared above, we learn was done intentionally to resist expected resolution. "We all," Tom explains, "have an emotional chasm between ourselves and those we love (or hope to love), that cannot be bridged, but vainly we try anyway to cross. The poem conveys this sentiment without becoming sentimental. On these levels the poem is successful."

I want to make much here of Tom's qualification—"on these levels the poem is successful"—because I am encouraging you to undertake the process of finding poems through the invitations offered to writers by traditional forms. My goal is not to teach you to write the perfect Shakespearean sonnet (though you're sometimes encouraged to try to imitate perfectly, for there is much learning involved in that act). I do hope you'll work *through* forms to understand their uses, to discover the ways theme and variation, imitation and parody, and accent and repetition create music with words. Writing poetry is about both freedom and control.

> Can I take a rigid vessel (usually a form originated centuries ago) and fill it with living, fluid poetry? Like the ongoing relationship between water and its retainers, the experience can be peaceful or exhilarating, powerful, sometimes fearful. —Jane Austin Geir (Finch 79)

Tom used reading as a source of poetic invention and self-assignment, and I've come to rely on similar "exercises." When I was first introduced to poetry writing, I was handed an immensely thick anthology of poetry and told to go home and read and write—to bring a poem back to the next class. Unsure of how to go about this act-of-faith type of drafting, I spent a long weekend analyzing the anthology. I looked at the index of titles and first lines and found poets often chose similar themes (lost love, rare moments of insight into everyday life, historical themes) and that titles fell into patterns—"For My Mother" and "For a Lady I Know" (for this or that person); "On Seeing the Elgin Marbles" and "On Being Asked for a War Poem" (on doing this or that, reading this or that); or that one-word titles like "Outlaw" or "Ozmandias" led poets into philosophical explorations which those titles only partially pointed toward.

Next I started reading the poems, noting historical movements from fixed stanza forms to more loosely lined poems; from third-person work or dramatic apostrophes to informal, everyday, first-person accounts; from meditative and mournful to darker and more ironic poems. I learned to read for clues that I could then embody in assignments I call invention exercises: asking, if these poets did this, what happens—and what are the steps—that might prompt the same excursion for other writers? In fact, I'd like to encourage you and your fellow writers never to leave one of my sets of invention exercises in this book without adding a few of your own, based on your own similar explorations.

In sum, where do invention exercises come from? From my own practice and from my own years as a student of poetry and working with students of poetry. From my reading of poets and working backwards—saying, as you might say, "This poet achieved this effect: I bet if I did this and this and this, I could achieve the same or a similar effect in my work." From imitation and analysis. And they do work.

Here is an example from an exercise, completed with my writing class, and then revised and submitted to a literary magazine—*The Georgia Review*—that I had been sending poems to for nearly fifteen years, hoping they would find one just right for one of their issues. To my pleasure, it was the poem "Gardenia" below, written from the following class prompts that finally caught the editor's attention.

Early each summer in Florida, where I now live, the gardenia bushes outside my bedroom windows bloom, their strong scent wafting into the house. About that time of the year, I'm teaching summer school, and we're working on concrete detail in our poems, on learning to observe and re-observe—to do primary observational research on the natural world. So I fill a brown paper bag full of rain-wet gardenias and take them into the classroom, placing one on each desk. The dusty institutional room fills with gardenia perfume, and we each write about our gardenia. The prompts I use have developed from my desire to push writers to look and look again at the actual plant, to make metaphoric comparisons, and from my memory of flower poems I've read in the past that I've loved, particularly in the work of D. H. Lawrence and Mary Oliver, some of whose poems appear in this book. I accompany the gardenia exercise with a picture from an illustrated dictionary that a poetry student gave me one year at the end of class, which gives the scientific name for all the parts of a flowering plant. I encourage students to do similar secondary research as they revise— looking in flower catalogs, botanical textbooks, and at Internet resources. The poet, I believe, does not simply try to paint a word picture (though that can be effective and pleasurable) but also explores, learns, studies, refracts, and reflects a new vision of a common human experience. Here are the prompts we followed that day in class:

1. Place your gardenia on your desk.
2. Describe it literally.
3. Explore its smell: what color is the smell, what taste, what texture, what secret does the smell hold?
4. Relate the gardenia to other things.
5. Tell what the gardenia is or is not like.
6. Give someone directions for "inventing" the first gardenia and/or create a modern myth about the gardenia.
7. Let the gardenia speak. What would it say, and to whom?

   - In class, use these freewrites to write a letter/prose poem to someone who doesn't live in North Florida (preferably to a friend or family member who has never lived here). Let describing the gardenia and this location be the occasion for writing the letter, include the feel of a North Florida summer, and try to capture some essence of being outdoors here this time of year.

- At home, do more research, revise this into a poem on the summer season or on gardenias or a combination of both.

As you'll see, the poem that resulted for me sticks very closely to the prompts and even to the prompt sequence even though the prompts, or stanzas, could easily be re-ordered and a new poem direction would undoubtedly result.

*Gardenia**

WENDY BISHOP

Eleven white petals the shape of flattened baseball bats, white-turning-brown
   edges curled back.
Sexual parts looking like an upside-down spider—five tawny stamen legs
   waving toward this lonely, light-yellow banana-shaped pistil.
Meaty green leaves in lilypad layerings but not in lilypad sizes.
Formed like citrus leaves but a deeper, glossy green.

A white, yeast-infection-thick-scent, like heaven gone bad.
A bottle of fume blanc.
A musty secret, something kept moist for ages, edges blurring back toward
   raw earth.
A sky on the Fourth of July: heavy humidity expected, in fact, invited.
The secret of all indulgence, overkill, and destruction and the draw of the
   same.

Like a funeral *and* a birth: this is an occasion. A moment waited-for that
   arrives, too large, too big, too fast.
Like fantasies.
Like expensive and undercooked meats.
Like guilt, glut, sin, but squat—
   not roses on their imperious high-heeled stalks
   not snapdragons, frivolous and blown in the winds.

When a girl first feels her hips touch her palms at night without asking.
When a girl first pushes cotton sheets out of the bottom of the tightly tucked
   bed.
When a girl first eats her own tears and likes them: too sweet, too light to
   lunch on for long yet irresistible.
When a girl first passes her message from hand to hand.

The gardenia is re-invented.

As mentioned earlier, you should view the invention sequences, such as this one and those that follow, as opportunities to draft new poems and to learn how to make your own best future self-assignments.

━ INVENTION EXERCISES ━

1. One poem does not equal a poet. Go to the Web, the library, or a bookstore and find a collection by one of the poets shared in this chapter. Read a section of the collection or the whole book and then make some notes about the degree to which the poem I've shared here is typical or atypical of this poet, and why you think this. Quote lines. Then, imitate one of the poet's poems. Before you draft, make a wish list of what you are aiming for. After you draft and revise, write a drafting coda. How did you achieve or deviate from that wish list?

2. Like the three poets—Devan Cook, Bill Snyder, and Rex West—in the appendix, keep notes for your own revision case study in which you look particularly at your decisions in regard to form and free verse.

3. Move from one chapter of this book to the next, completing exercises using the same theme. First, freewrite, say, on family and turn it into a **prose poem** (chapter 9).

   a. Find a **haiku** (chapter 6) in the freewrite or carve one out of the prose poem.
   b. Find a line in the freewrite (or take the haiku and straighten three lines into one longer line) and turn it into the repeating line in a pantoum (chapter 5) or a villanelle (chapter 11).
   c. Choose six end words from the freewrite and write a sestina, using the six words as repeat words (chapter 11).
   d. Recast the freewrite into a sonnet-like draft—a 10 × 14 (chapter 12).

   To better understand this transformation process (taking a freewrite into and out of several forms), read the sections of my drafts below. Move backward from the last version (couplets) through earlier versions, marking what was carried from an earlier version into a later version. Which draft/form do you like best and why? Explain this to and share conclusions with group members. Try the same exercise taking a prose poem to narrower free verse to syllabic verse (any syllable length you choose) to **couplets** (or any stanza form you choose).

Suburban Lightning Strike*
   Prose Poem (Section)

My children wail like sirens, one a hacking drawn out "uhuuu, uhuuu," the
other ends on a keening "Mom-meeeeeeeee?" I've just seen them running to
the center of the house, long limbs caught in the strobe that still feels
imprinted on my brain. And we're all turning in circles like the ceiling fan.
Ears ringing, I reassemble the backyard, bring it from the dark of gathering
storm clouds and echoing thunder in the distance, to center stage, the kliegs
have just snapped on, and the weather-bent live oaks fling their hair back,
shaking leaves like green tambourines, leaves that never sounded so loud as
in the silence after the hit. Why this ghostly headache? What would placate
such a spirit in its suddenly tangible ionic steam of atmosphere, the charge
grounding in the back fence where it snapped three 4 inch fence posts into
splinters, shrapnel of raw wood littering the mulch pile of grass clippings, an
eight inch round metal thermometer thrown down from another post, a
marker where we've sometimes stood.

Suburban Lightning Strike*
   Free Verse (section)

My children wail like sirens,
one a hacking drawn out "uhuuu, uhuuu,"
the other ends on a keening "Mom-meeeeeeeee?"
I've just seen them running to the center of the house,
long limbs caught in strobe light
that still feels imprinted on my brain.
And we're all turning in circles
like the ceiling fan. Ears ringing,
I reassemble the backyard, bring it
from the dark of gathering storm clouds
to center stage. The kliegs have just snapped on,
and weather-bent live oaks fling their leaves
that never sounded so loud as in the silence after the hit.

Suburban Lightning Strike*
   Twelve-Syllable Lines (first five lines)

And we're all turning in circles like the ceiling
fan. Ears ringing, I reassemble the backyard,
bring it from the dark of gathering storm clouds to
center stage, the kliegs have snapped on, and the weather-
bent live oaks shake leaves like green tambourines, leaves that

Suburban Lightning Strike*
   Couplets (first five of twelve)

   And we're all turning in circles
   like the ceiling fan. Ears ringing,

   I reassemble the backyard, bring it from the dark
   of gathering storm clouds to center stage,

   the kliegs have snapped on,
   and the weather-bent live oaks shake leaves

   like green tambourines, leaves
   that never sounded so loud as in the silence

   after the hit. Why this ghostly headache?
   The charge grounding in the back fence

MAKING RULES AND BREAKING RULES

As you read the poems in *Thirteen Ways*, consider how they play with and against conventions and formal constraints. Note which techniques the poets rely on and which school of contemporary poetry a poet seems to affiliate with. The subtypes in the field are varied. There are confessional poets who draw on autobiographical detail; surrealist poets who leap, associate, or dive deep; modernist poets who rely on image; poets who resist poetic closure; L-A-N-G-U-A-G-E poets who focus on the sound of the language and even the etymology of the words; new formalist poets who are interested in fixed stanza and verse patterns; and so on. The writing conventions for poets affiliated with one of these schools, or poetic movements, are not necessarily the conventions followed by poets in a different group, school, or movement. You should real-ize that journal editors, who will eventually read and review your poems if you choose to submit them for publication, have their internalized "rules" for what makes a good poem. Insights into how these editors read can be found in *Spreading the Word*. Here is one example from Hale Chatfield:

> I searched my mind and came up with the check-list I used to select
> poems [for the journal *The Hiram Review*] all these years, and now I use
> it to measure my *own* poems: (1) I want a poem to be *unique*. (I want to
> know right away I've never seen another poem quite like it); (2) I want it
> to be *competent*. (Wallace Stevens says we read poetry with our nerves;
> that's a real investment of ourselves—something like submitting to a
> lover. Incompetence in prosody, or even in diction, spelling, or punctua-
> tion, is painful to a poetry reader.); (3) I want it to be *concise*. (I want to
> have the feeling that every word in the poem is necessary, that no word or

phrase is there just for padding. When I encounter an adjective, I don't want to feel that it might have been omitted if its noun had been more carefully selected.); perhaps above all (4) I want the poem to be *filled with adventure*. (At every point in the poem I want a sense of excitement about what must be coming next. If I try to guess what is coming next, I want to be proven wrong.) (30–31)

Any practicing poet and any book on poetry will offer you other—sometimes contradictory—writing rules and suggestions. Over time, you'll learn to glean from these imperatives and warnings, choosing to pay primary attention to those that are most useful to you or that seem to be repeated most consistently. For instance, my first rule is:

- always break a rule to make a poem *work* or to keep up your interest in writing.

Having said that, I also believe it is essential to learn by undertaking exercises, by setting up and then sticking (at least temporarily) to rules. Equally, it's useful to develop a set of rules that support your artistic aesthetic or taste and help you understand what you've accomplished and what you want to accomplish. Here is a set of advice offered to one group of poets to guide them toward revisions that would accentuate the contemporary aspects of their poems. I composed these after reading the first set of poems they wrote:

- Use a first-person, everyday voice.
- Focus on the particulars you know rather than the universal that you may only guess at.
- Include images and metaphors in a rhyming poem (or you're left with empty sounding words).
- I often don't know what you're saying, to whom, and why; use your language to be precise and in control of the picture or story that you present to a reader.
- Take advantage of a title to set up your reader's expectations.
- Evoke a mood and/or tell a story. Know your point so the reader can too.
- Avoid archaic and sci-fi personas—damsels in distress and personified concepts—time, eternity, and so on.

This list once was numbered, but there's really no order of importance to writing advice—there's only what works. These days I'd add a few more suggestions, which shows that do/don't lists are meant to be tinkered with. In fact, I hope you'll construct your own best advice for you as writer as you read this book.

- As soon as you move from private journal sharing to the public forum of a workshop, you have some obligation to a reader.
- When writers aren't writing, they're reading.

- Poets revel in sheer word play. As often as they're trying to share their thoughts and feelings, they're word musicians, trying to figure out how words and sentences, sound and sense, work together
- Honor your own life and vision as a writer by keeping your poem's feet on the ground; that is, locate and celebrate your physical and emotional location(s) in life
- Cultivate your knowledge of the particular: collect dictionaries, field guides to plants and animals, local myths, stories and tales, books on arcane subjects (meteorology, alchemy, astrology, modern physics, Hopi rituals, "how-to" books on plumbing).

(An example: On e-mail, a friend described to me her trip to Wakulla Springs, a local state park, using her poet's eye, and I enjoyed the message because of the wonderful words she taught me, and the particulars she shared—

> at Wakulla Springs there are fuzzy-headed yellow herons in the nests, and ospreys are nesting, and eagles, and also common moorhen biddies— they're bald, and then their mothers, who are as mean as all common moorhens supposedly are, peck on their heads too!

From her detailed description, I learn much more than that there are birds at Wakulla Springs this time of year.)

Finally (for now):

- As Raymond Carver reminds us in "Sunday Night"—"make use of the things around you."

POCKET DEFINITIONS

Allusions—When a poet intentionally refers to something else—a person, place, time, pop cultural event—she is said to be alluding to something outside, behind, or beyond the work at hand in the hope of enriching your reading of the work (if you understand, or work to understand, that connection or reference).

Cliché—Clichéd language is language that offers the easy, the overly familiar, and the predictable and represents, for the poet, a missed opportunity to relate her particular vision of the world through words. Clichés are certainly generational. What is clichéd (old, expected, predictable, like "have a nice day") to one reader, is not necessarily clichéd to a younger person who might hear that phrase for the first time and be enchanted by it. *Trite, stereotyped, platitudinous, predictable, too easy, imprecise* are words you might substitute for cliché. Clichés are useful placeholders when you're drafting, but you need to reread and replace the easy with the exact, the first choice with the best choice. If you've read it on a bumper sticker or poster or hear your friends using it regularly or often read the comparison or term in poetry from an earlier time—it's clichéd. Your job is to think of new ways to discuss the timeless ideas and images humans care about saying, observing, and describing. And language is generative enough to allow you to do so—if you listen, read widely, and increase your vocabulary so you know you're picking the exact best way to say what you want and need to say. A thesaurus and dictionary can sometimes help, but paying attention—trying out words as you listen to the words (written and spoken) of others—is the better long-term tool.

Closure—Readers of poems develop an expectation of how the work will end, what might provide a satisfying resolution or sense of ending and textual stability. This sense of closure can be thematic and/or technical. For instance, an initial line or image may be repeated, or the regularity of a stanza form can be varied to signal that the end of a poem has arrived. Some poets prefer to work against such an expectation of regularity or finish, favoring instead an intentionally open-ended effect that rejects closure.

Couplets—Two-line stanzas (or a complete poem in a single, two-line couplet). Often these lines are of the same length. Historically couplets were metered in a similar manner, often achieving closure through full rhyme or parallel syntax.

Haiku—Growing out of Zen Buddhist philosophy (a version of Buddhism that began in India and then spread widely, in which believers seek enlightenment through introspection and intuition rather than through interpretation of a text or scripture), the haiku is obviously well suited for such introspection and intuitive explorations. The Japanese form has been cast by Western poets into a three-line, syllabic poem of 5, 7, 5 syllables per line. Japanese haiku were often presented as single-line poems, and contemporary poets sometimes revert to the single-line presentation and no longer focus on exact syllable counts since the original Japanese form cannot be directly translated into English. Haiku turns on strong natural images and intense emotions, often leading to spiritual insights.

Metaphor—A figure of speech, a comparison of one thing to another. In Sharon Olds' poem "The One Girl at the Boys Party," the speaker compares wet hair to the lead of a child's pencil:

> When they climb out,
> her ponytail will hang its pencil lead
> down her back . . .

In describing the ponytail this way, ponytail = a pencil lead, Olds lets us see it in a new light. The girl's wet hair is as straight and thick and black as a carbon lead. If the poem kept comparing parts of the daughter's body to writing instruments (it doesn't), the poet would be extending a metaphor into a *conceit*, a metaphor that goes beyond the equation of $X = Y$.

If the words *like* or *as* are used to complete the comparison, the writer has produced a different figure of speech, the *simile*. (For an example of simile, see the comparison of the father to a snow-covered road in Li-Young Lee's poem, "Eating Together.")

Special terms used with metaphor—*tenor* and *vehicle* and *ground*—come from the work of critic I. A. Richards. The tenor is considered the literal thing being referred to, the vehicle is the metaphorical (comparative term), and the ground is the relationship/similarities between the two. What sounds simple in definition can be complicated in analytic application. In the Sharon Olds' example above, the terms can be applied and explained fairly directly: ponytail = tenor; pencil lead = vehicle; and ground = the way the wet ponytail momentarily and visually looks like a pencil lead, emphasizing the young swimmer's schoolgirl connection to the math she is doing in her head. Such an analysis is less clear when explored using Robert Burns' line "O my luve's like a red, red rose," where "my luve" = tenor and "a red, red rose" = vehicle, but here the ground is more open to interpretation—the similarity being the freshness of a love and a rose? Like the rich fragility of love and a rose? Use these terms where they aid your understanding and discussion, but where they prove problematic, remember that complexity points to the complexity of metaphoric language itself, an area ripe for lifelong poetic study.

Meter—Metered verse in English relies on accent and syllable counts. All words in English receive particular syllabic stress, like par-TIC-u-lar. Poets can arrange stresses in patterns (poetic feet) and feet can be counted off, with so many feet per line. The most common pattern in English verse has been iambic pentameter (da-Da da-Da da-Da da-Da da-Da) of five iambic (da-DA) feet. Readers interested in meter will want to consult the reference books listed in the preface.

Persona—The persona offers one way of discussing the speaker of the poem (as distinct from the living poet/author of the poem). While most poets prefer readers to assume that the speaker of any poem is always an authorial construction, some poets are clearly choosing a highly autobiographical voice. When the poet signals the construction of a poetic persona, this speaker may provide a mask or alternate identity for the poet. Personas can be a fictional or historical character or a regular person, but one who clearly leads a life different from that of the poet. This everyday persona allows the poet to explore and investigate different perspectives and lifestyles. The persona may be that of a classical, historical, or popular character: someone who once lived or is living now whom the poet inhabits and speaks for. A persona can be and often is a fictional character (such as Robert Browning's speaker in "My Last Duchess" or even a character who embodies (readers suspect or poets admit) a side of that poet—a part of his or her personality, now amplified and given voice (as in John Berryman's dream song sequence).

Poetry—A genre (as opposed to novels, drama, technical reports, and so on); like prose it can be unmetered. Historically, poetry has relied on meter since even free verse is based on creating artful exceptions to our expectations of regularity based in metered lines. Poetry relies on attention to line over paragraph and utilizes condensed and shaped language, including recognizable figures of speech (images, metaphors, and similes), sound patterns (assonance, alliteration, rhyme, and repetition), and countable or analyzable rhythm (meter).

Prose Poem—A block-shaped, usually paragraphed text that relies on the poetic techniques of imagery and condensed, rhythmic, repetitive, often rhymed language and often makes its point via metaphor, analogy, or association, yet still may partake of fictional techniques like character building, plot, dialogue, and so on.

Prosody—The study of verse forms, sounds, and patterns in poetry.

Quatrain—A poetic stanza of four lines, the most common stanza form in English poetry.

Rhyme Scheme—The pattern of repeating sound that occurs in a poem, most often in the words that end lines in a stanza; represented by letters of the alphabet, assigned as each new rhyme appears. The rhyme pattern of "Western Wind" is *blow* (*a*), *rain* (*b*), *arms* (*c*), *again* (*b*) (*rain* and *again* rhyme and are therefore given the same letter designation).

Sonnet—A historical fixed form. The eight-line octave followed by the six-line sestet held numerical significance: it could be reduced to 4 and 3 and the total, 7. All three numbers were important in music composition as well as in religious thinking, four signifying the world and three the trinity, and so on. The Italian sonnet consists of an octave rhyming *abbaabba* and a sestet rhyming *cdcdcd*. The English sonnet, which developed out of the Italian, consists of fourteen lines of iambic pentameter verse: three quatrains and a closing couplet, with the rhyme scheme of *abab, cdcd, efef, gg*. Poets have always adapted this structure, observing most consistently only its fourteen-line length.

Speaker—See *Persona*.

Syllabic Verse—Line length in syllabic poems is fixed by syllable count—say, ten per line—or in a shaped pattern like the 5, 7, 5 syllable pattern that signals a Western haiku.

2

ACCENTUAL AND SYLLABIC VERSE

The Musics of Meters

Question
MAY SWENSON

Body my house
my horse my hound
what will I do
when you are fallen

Where will I sleep
How will I ride
What will I hunt

Where can I go
without my mount
all eager and quick
How will I know
in thicket ahead
is danger or treasure
when Body my good
bright dog is dead

How will it be
to lie in the sky
without roof or door
and wind for an eye

With cloud for shift
how will I hide?

Here's the plainest explanation for what is happening in May Swenson's poem, and what will happen in your poem: Poetry is made of words, and words in English have accented (´) and unaccented (˘) syllables (WHÉRE wĭll Ĭ SLÉEP). Your words can be arranged so that accented syllables fall in regular, repeated, rhythmic order (mȳ HORŚE, mȳ HOÚND), and consonant and vowel sounds can be placed so as to add additional music: chiming (discussed here as **allitera-tion**—house, horse, hound and **assonance**—house, hound) and rhyming (dis-cussed in chapter 3—hunt/mount, sky/eye). This gets more complicated, of course, since multisyllabic words can have primary and secondary accents and since regional pronunciations shift these accents by local customs, which is why we reach for a dictionary to find standard pronunciations, accents, and syl-labic segmentation. Or for a prosody handbook like those listed in the preface.

ACCENT AND ALLITERATION

Any accentual pattern that becomes too regular becomes singsong, monoto-nous, and overly predictable. That doesn't happen in May Swenson's poem because she varies accents, alliteration and assonance, stanza lengths (4-, 3-, 8-, 4-, 2-line stanzas), and so on. While poetry works hard at creating subtle vari-ations that point out, quietly underline, and support the poem's unfolding meaning, humorous verse often derives its strength from a heavier helping of the same elements. Remember discovering "Peter piper picked a peck of pickled peppers" and then chanting it so long your parents or friends asked you to please stop?

As you read Jody Eastman's draft you'll hear the strong accents and repeat-ing consonants —Wait/web, Poised/dan, Peace/pat, Dan/death.

*Waiting**

Waiting in the web,
Poised and dangerous,
A peaceful pattern,
Dandling death,

Motionless movement,
Gently swaying,
A breeze blows,
Wriggling wave,
Across the web,
Poised to prey,
In peaceful stillness.

Attempting an accentual poem—two strong stresses to each line—Jody has arranged the words in her poem to emphasize these downbeats—two strongly accented syllables—per line. It doesn't matter for this form how many quieter, unaccented syllables come between the accented ones: a PEACEful PATtern has five syllables, two with heavy accents. DANdling DEATH, however, is a three-syllable line. Jody has emphasized her pattern by using alliteration, the repeti-tion of consonants (usually the initial consonant). She uses W, P, D in the first stanza and M, G, W, P in the second stanza. She could have made her sound patterns more formally regular (in three places she misses an alliterative second accent). Yet, on two of these three occasions, she alliterates by echoing a sound from an earlier line or looks toward a sound that will come up in the next line. (Only once is our expectation completely broken, in the line "gently swaying," where the *g* sound is not echoed before or after.)

> Poetry's equivalent of musical beat is based on the variable energy required to articulate syllables of each word, and the regular recurrence of verbal accent (or stress) that falls on some of these syllables. Just as music is divided into a series of bars, poems are divided into a series of lines, each line (in traditional practice) containing an assigned number of stresses. Poetry does not, however, specify that the strongest accent in a line is the first. The relative strength of stresses in a line varies according to a number of factors, some having to do with the sound of individual words, others with the line's conceptual and emotional content.—Alfred Corn, 3

Poetry is created out of pattern and variation—expectation and surprise. By counting and manipulating where accented syllables fall in a line of verse, we make poetry memorable in the basic sense: something we can easily retain in memory. Since poetry has long been an important part of oral traditions, helping people encode their histories, myths, and stories, the formal arrangement of sounds became crucially important for the way it allowed poets to create long chains of verse.

The Lay of the Last Survivor
ANONYMOUS

His wit acknowledged
that the treasures gathered and guarded over the years
were his for the briefest while.
Barrow stood ready
on flat ground where breakers beat at the headland,
new, near at hand, made narrow of access.
The keeper of rings carried into it
the earls' holdings, the hoard-worthy part
fraught with gold, few words spoke:

'Hold, ground, the gold of the earls!
Men could not. Cowards they were not
who took it from thee once, but war-death took them,
that stops life, struck them, spared not one
man of my people, passed on now.
They have had their hall-joys. I have not with me
a man able to unsheathe this. . . .
Who shall polish this plated vessel?
This cup was dear. The company is elsewhere.

This hardened helmet healed with gold
shall lose its shell. They sleep now
whose work was to burnish the battle-mask;
so the cuirass that in the crash took
bite of iron amid breaking shields:
it moulders with the man. This mailshirt travelled far,
hung from a shoulder shouldered warriors;
it shall not jingle again.
                           There's no joy from harp-play,
gleewood's gladness, no good hawk
swings through hall now, no swift horse
tramps at threshold. The threat came:
falling has felled a flowering kingdom.'
                           —trans. by Michael Alexander

Some languages rely on syllabic patterns as much or more than accentual patterns, but poetry written in English takes advantage of both and draws from the strong Anglo-Saxon heritage you can hear in Michael Alexander's translation of the Old English (A.D. 650–1066) poem *Beowulf.* You can—as will be suggested later in this chapter—write a poem whose sound scheme relies primarily on accents (the same number of accents per line but varying the unaccented syllables) or syllables (lines with a regular pattern of syllables—say, ten per line—or in a shaped pattern like the 2,- 4-, 6-, 8-, 2-syllable pattern that forms a cinquain). For instance, the stanza of Dylan Thomas' "Fern Hill" follows the general pattern of 14, 14, 9, 6, 9, 14, 14, 7, 9 syllables per line in a nine-line stanza.

METER (JUST THE PRELIMINARIES)

Meter is what results when the natural rhythmical movements of colloquial speech are heightened, organized, and regulated so that pattern—which means repetition—emerges from the relative phonetic haphazard of ordinary utterance. Because it inhabits the physical form of the words themselves, meter is the most fundamental technique of order available to the poet. —Paul Fussell, 4–5

When syllables and accents are arranged together in regular patterns, we find the traditional metrical schemes of English prosody. Poets arrange stresses in patterns (poetic feet). Generally, we use four basic patterns for this:

iamb	dă-DÁ
trochee	DÁ-dă
anapest	dă-dă-DÁ
dactyl	DÁ-dă-dă

And feet can be measured, so many per line:

> dimeter = two feet to the line
> trimeter = three feet to the line
> tetrameter = four feet to the line
> pentameter = five feet to the line
> and so on

> Trochee trips from long to short; ❖
> From long to long in solemn sort
> Slow Spondee stalks; strong foot yet ill able
> Ever to come up with Dactylic trisyllable.
> Iambics march from short to long—
> With a leap and a bound the swift Anapests throng.
> —Samuel Taylor Coleridge

dă-DÁ, dă-DÁ, dă-DÁ, dă-DÁ, dă-DÁ = iambic pentameter

Iambic pentameter, five iambs to each line, is the most frequently occurring pattern in traditional English verse. When shaped into a block of fourteen lines with a set rhyme scheme (*abab, bcbc, cdcd, efef, gg* or *sun, red, dun, head; white, cheeks, delight, reeks; know, sound, go, ground; rare, compare*), iambic pentameter builds the English sonnet. Unrhymed iambic pentameter verse, called **blank verse**, is counted off in five iambic feet to the line but doesn't need to rhyme in predictable patterns.

> A poetic foot is a measurable, patterned, conventional unit of poetic rhythm. Because the idea of the foot has been imported into modern accentual-syllabic scansion from classical quantitative practice, quarrels about its nature and even its existence have been loud and long since the Renaissance. Most authorities would agree that if we are going to use the concept of the foot to describe the rhythmic norm of poetic lines, then the foot consists of one stressed syllable and one or two unstressed syllables. . . . By convention, the feet are conceived of as roughly of the same kind, although variations, produced by the "substitution" of different feet, are not only permissible but desirable so long as these substitutions do not efface for long the repeated pattern of the prevailing or dominant kind of foot. . . . —Paul Fussell, 19

Most readers think of poetry primarily as condensed thought, holding intricate meanings; but for poets, writing poetry is as much about word play and word pleasure—the explorations of and elaboration upon fundamental techniques. Poets tie music to thoughts, and, like musicians, they learn to count their beats and rhythm patterns as they do this.

For instance, try scanning your name as I've done here with two poets whose work you'll read in this book:

ĕ-LIŹ-ă-BÉTH BISH́-ŏp = iambic dimeter + a trochee

WAĹ-lăce STÉ-vĕns = two trochees (trochaic dimeter)

Not only do names scan (have a repeated, pleasing accentual pattern), but parents also appear to have an inclination to alliterate—with repeating, echoing, chiming consonant sounds—their childrens' names. For instance, in my city phone book, I find "Barry Barnett" and "Brian Barnette," "Bob Bass" and "Barbara Bass," "Fred Flowers" and "Sheri Stephens." There's a "John Johnson" in town and a "Robin Robinson" (on Whetherbine Way). This list illustrates the downside of alliteration: too much makes a sentence, poem, or name sound silly. Just the right amount, though, creates word music. In general, as you'll see in the exercises below, it's better to jump in at first and alliterate a lot, exploring the excess of this technique, and then learn to ease some of the sounds out. Eventually, you'll learn to lay on sound with a lighter hand. Kaila Boykin began with an informal freewrite:

> The rigid smell of cigarette smoke in the beauty salon. How in the world can my freshly shampooed hair smell like strawberries if there was a cloud of smoke over my head? The ladies with the cigarettes didn't seem to mind the smell of their hair. Me, I wanted strawberry scented shampoo or apple. Something fruity; my mom paid extra. As the lady finished my hair, she sprayed an aerosol oil around the style. Wow, it looked like smoke, but it smelled like ... I don't know, something sweet and subtle, yet bold and overpowering. Overpowering the cigarettes that is. I walked out with a scented hairdo that shined.

Kaila used class discussions about alliteration and accent to shape her draft for a free verse poem so that alliteration works with typographical line breaks:

*Beauty Salon**
Ripe
rigid smell of cigarette
residue in the midst of
resplendence.

Can my
carefully shampooed hair
   smell of
   strawberries with a
cloud of smoke
   surrounding my
crown?

Ladies with the
Luckys didn't seem to care if smoke
lingered in their hair.

Me, I wanted
   wildberries or
   watermelon, not
Winstons and
   weeds.

Fruity tutti shampoo, I didn't have a care, my
fee had already been paid in
full.

Amazingly she
aerosoled my hair
around and
around.

Imitating smoke yet
   smelling
intimately
inviting.

Sweet but
subtle. Overpowering and
   outspoken.

Departing with a
different
do.
Deodorized and
dancing with luster.

ACCENTUAL-ALLITERATIVE VERSE

In poems, when alliteration combines with an accentual pattern, we hear the antecedents of English poetry, for eleventh-century, Anglo-Saxon scops (minstrel poets who sang with a harp) composed in **accentual-alliterative verse**. This verse was easier to memorize than prose and had set rules for its construction that allowed for easier composition. These poems were generally written down hundreds of years later after being passed from poet to poet as part of their apprenticeship. While we can learn to read Middle English (the English of Geoffrey Chaucer) fairly quickly, Old English requires translation, as in the two poems below (as did "The Lay of the Last Survivor").

These are the opening lines from a much longer poem, "The Seafarer."

from ***The Seafarer***
From the Anglo-Saxon

May I for my own self song's truth reckon,
Journey's jargon, how I in harsh days
Hardship endured oft.
Bitter breast-cares have I abided,
Known on my keel many a care's hold,
And dire sea-surge, and there I oft spent
Narrow nightwatch nigh the ship's head
While she tossed close to cliffs. Coldly afflicted,
My feet were by frost benumbed.
Chill its chains are; chafing sighs
Hew my heart round and hunger begot
Mere-weary mood. Lest man know not
That he on dry land loveliest liveth,
List how I, care-wretched, on ice-cold sea,
Weathered the winter, wretched outcast
Deprived of my kinsmen;
Hung with hard ice-flakes, where hail-scur flew,
There I heard naught save the harsh sea
And ice-cold wave, at whiles the swan cries,
Did for my games gannet's clamour,
Sea-fowls' loudness was for me laughter,
The mews' singing all my mead-drink.
Storms, on the stone-cliffs beaten, fell on the stern
In icy feathers; full oft the eagle screamed
With spray on his pinion.
                                        —trans. by Ezra Pound

Pound's translation offers us the sense of Anglo-Saxon verse, but his translation varies quite a bit from the fairly rigorous scansion pattern of the original, which requires four strongly stressed accents per line with each line broken between accent two and accent three in a pause, called a **caesura**. There can be any number of unaccented syllables, and the accented syllables usually alliterate three times, the first two accents falling in the first half of the line and one of the accents falling in the second half of the line. You'll hear the same accentual-alliterative sounds in Michael Alexander's translation from *Beowulf* of "The Lay of the Last Survivor."

What creates a striking accentual pattern in Old English can feel heavy-handed in present-day English. For that reason, an effective translation often stays close to the original but also makes meaning as important as sound, as in the next poem. Shown first is the initial stanza with the most regular parts of the accentual-alliterative patterns marked. Then these lines are repeated with the whole poem so you can read and hear them with uncluttered pleasure:

THE WIFE'S LAMENT

> Ic þis giedd wrece   bi me ful geomorre,
> minre sylfre sið.   Ic þæt secgan mæg,
> hwæt ic yrmþa gebad,   siþþan ic up weox,
> niwes oþþe ealdes,   no ma þonne nu.
> 5 A ic wite wonn   minra wræcsiþa.
>   Ærest min hlaford gewat   heonan of leodum
> ofer yþa gelac;   hæfde ic uhtceare
> hwær min leodfruma   londes wære.
> Ða ic me feran gewat   folgað secan,
> 10 wineleas wræcca,   for minre weaþearfe.

I have wrought these words together || out of a wryed existence,
the heart's tally, || telling off
the griefs I have undergone || from girlhood upwards,
old and new, || and now more than ever;
for I have never not had || some new sorrow,
some fresh affliction || to fight against.

The Wife's Complaint
ANONYMOUS

I have wrought these words together out of a wryed existence,
the heart's tally, telling off
the griefs I have undergone from girlhood upwards,
old and new, and now more than ever;
for I have never not had some new sorrow,
some fresh affliction to fight against.

The first was my lord's leaving his people here:
crossed crests. To what country I knew not,
wondered where, awoke unhappy.
I left, fared any road, friendless, an outcast,
sought any service to staunch the lack of him.

Then his kinsmen ganged, began to think
thoughts they did not speak, of splitting the wedlock;
so—estranged, alienated—we lived each
alone, a long way apart; how I longed for him!

In his harshness he had me brought here;
and in these parts there were few friendly-minded,
worth trusting.
             Trouble in the heart now:
I saw the bitterness, the bound mind
of my matched man, mourning-browed,
mirk in his mood, murder in his thoughts.

Our lips had smiled to swear hourly
that nothing should split us—save dying—
nothing else. All that has changed:
it is now as if it never had been,
our friendship. I feel in the wind
that the man dearest to me detests me.
I was banished to this knoll knotted by woods
to live in a den dug beneath an oak.
Old is this earthen room; it eats at my heart.

I see the thorns thrive up there in thick coverts
on the banks that baulk these black hollows:
not a gay dwelling. Here the grief bred
by lordlack preys on me. Some lovers in this world
live dear to each other, lie warm together
at day's beginning; I go by myself
about these earth caves under the oak tree.
Here I must sit the summer day through,
here weep out the woes of exile,
the hardships heaped upon me. My heart shall never
suddenly sail into slack water,
all the longings of a lifetime answered.

May the grief and bitterness blast the mind
of that young man! May his mind ache
behind his smiling face! May a flock of sorrows
choke his chest! He would change his tune
if he lived alone in a land of exile
far from his folk.

> Where my friend is stranded
> frost crusts the cracked cliff-face
> grey waves grind the shingle.
> The mind cannot bear in such a bleak place
> very much grief.
> He remembers too often
> less grim surroundings. Sorrow follows
> this too long wait for one who is estranged.
> —trans. by Michael Alexander

I first read this poem in 1974 (in the same class where I learned to imitate Wallace Steven's blackbird poem), and each time I reread it, I marvel at the power of its strong rhythms and complex emotions. "Some lovers in this world/live dear to each other, lie warm together/at day's beginning" and "My heart shall never/suddenly sail into slack water,/all the longings of a lifetime answered" and "The mind cannot bear in such a bleak place/very much grief" are some of my favorite lines of poetry. Other parts of the poem may remain more distant, but certainly these lines of love and sadness continue to reverberate down centuries.

∞ READING INTO WRITING ∞

As you read the following poems, determine what emphasis each poet places on alliteration, assonance (repetition of vowel sounds), and accent. Consider what liberties the poets took with the accentual-alliterative form. Try your own intentional imitations by stating your pattern before drafting. Like some of the poets in this book, Gerard Manley Hopkins wrote during an earlier time period (he lived from 1844–1889), so his culture and vocabulary are sometimes prob-lematic for contemporary readers (*farrier, fatal four disorders, fettle*). The best solution is to read such a poem first with a dictionary in hand. Then the Internet for further resources and discussions. Finally, share readings and definitions in class with other readers to help you decide what is being said, to the best of your knowledge. This is normal work for any reader of poetry: to consider definitions and possibilities, just as with Donald Fikel's poem you might want to look up *jacaranda* to prompt your visual memory—or to educate it for the first time about this plant.

Felix Randal
GERARD MANLEY HOPKINS

Felix Randal the farrier, O he is dead then? my duty all ended,
Who have watched his mould of man, big-boned and hardy-handsome
Pining, pining, till time when reason rambled in it and some
Fatal four disorders, fleshed there, all contended?
Sickness broke him. Impatient he cursed at first, but mended

Being anointed and all; though a heavenlier heart began some
Months earlier, since I had our sweet reprieve and ransom
Tendered to him. Ah well, God rest him all road ever he offended!
This seeing the sick endears them to us, us too it endears.
My tongue had taught thee comfort, touch had quenched thy tears,
Thy tears that touched my heart, child, Felix, poor Felix Randal;
How far from then forethought of, all thy more boisterous years,
When thou at the random grim forge, powerful amidst peers,
Didst fettle for the great grey drayhorse his bright and battering sandal!

Were It Not
ROBERT PACK

For rumors of war and wars
                  men against men
I think I could grow
            gracefully back to earth
This morning warm
          for April in Vermont
Graceful I sit in the sun
             nuzzling a pear
Warming my teeth my tongue
                  to my body's roots
Wet it is warm and wet
             it flows it is good
For the grip of my roots
             here on this morning
In this sun in this sprouting
              April returning now
Here I am sower of children
             there they are
My wife has invented
            coffee again butter bread
They are good and she is good
                and my children
Have redeemed all sorrow now
                one bad blood night ago
Now all is grace
           sun surges in each dew
Nothing can spoil this now
             you are all
Every one of you
          all all are invited
This warm morning
            to my house

Waiting for the Wind
DONALD FINKEL

Wind wafts his fitful
   dispensations—incense,
      wren-song, distant bells.
We reach to catch them.
    As soon catch a cloud
      in a fish-net,
rain in a teaspoon.
    Now he's playing
      with the jacaranda,
rumpling her leaves
    with his clumsy fingers,
      parting her limbs
like slim brown thighs.
    Now he's dragging
      that disreputable nimbus
across the morning's lips
    like a dirty handkerchief.
      Now it's back in his pocket.
Not a breath of rain.

━ INVENTION EXERCISES ━

1. After rereading "The Lay of the Last Survivor" or "The Seafarer,"
   choose a word, image, or line for the landscape you have lived in
   and love best but miss—such as the desert, tropics, arctic, mountains, etc. Place that phrase in the center of a piece of paper. Circle it
   and then free-associate similar words and more descriptions of the
   place and weather, creating a cluster of words and images. If you're
   not familiar with the technique, you can find an example of clustering in Bill Snyder's revision case study in the appendix.

   Since a great deal of Anglo-Saxon poetry is about being a wanderer or outcast from the community, try writing a short passage using
   your cluster images that talks about how you miss this
   landscape/weather. Then fashion some of that description into
   accentual-alliterative lines. As you modernize, you might consider
   the politics of being an outcast or feeling marginalized in contemporary society.

2. Write a letter of complaint to someone you care about but whose
   actions you object to. Indulge yourself—tell that person what both-
   ers you. Remind that person of times you spent together, describing
   each one. Talk a little about what you think happened—did some
   person or event intervene? End with a sense of the emotion you feel
   these days, but try to embody it in an image. After writing this, high-

light phrases. Play with them and see if you can form this longer
letter into a short (say, ten or fifteen lines) complaint or lament, or
write a letter about something lost, using the Old English form. For
more on letter poems, see Pound's "The River-Merchant's Wife: A
Letter" in chapter 9.

3. Take the most effective of your two poems and try a revision where
   you pull back on the alliteration—take out at least fifty percent of
   the intentional chimes.

4. Equally, take this poem and keep the alliteration but cast it as a
   prose paragraph so the accents don't fall as regularly—change the
   accentual pattern to have a more prose-like rhythm. Gerard Manley
   Hopkins is known for both alliteration and accentual experiments—
   what he called sprung rhythm—and both are highlighted here within
   the sonnet form we'll take up in chapter 12.

Note: Inventions 2 to 4 above ask you to remember the basic
premise of this book. Work into a form, but during revision, don't
let the formal demands that you may not yet be able to control keep
a poem from growing. Always release it from constraints where and
when you need to.

"The Lilacs" offers a rare example of a contemporary poem developed in
accentual-alliterative verse:

The Lilacs
RICHARD WILBUR

Those laden lilacs
                at the lawn's end
Came stark, spindly,
                and in staggered file,
Like walking wounded
                from the dead of winter.
We watched them waken
                in the brusque weather
To rot and rootbreak,
                to ripped branches,
And saw them shiver
                as the memory swept them
Of night and numbness
                and the taste of nothing.
Out of present pain
                and from past terror
Their bullet-shaped buds
                came quick and bursting,

As if they aimed
                    to be open with us!
But the sun suddenly
                    settled about them,
And green and grateful
                    the lilacs grew,
Healed in that hush,
                    that hospital quiet.
These lacquered leaves
                    where the light paddles
And the big blooms
                    buzzing among them
Have kept their counsel,
                    conveying nothing
Of their mortal message,
                    unless one should measure
The depth and dumbness
                    of death's kingdom
By the pure power
                    of this perfume.

Richard Wilbur chose this form for another poem titled "Junk" where he finds something noble in an unexpected location: the neighbor's junkheap. That poem opens:

An axe angles
                    from my neighbor's ashcan;
It is hell's handiwork,
                    the wood not hickory,
The flow of the grain
                    not faithfully followed.
The shivered shaft
                    rises from a shellheap
Of plastic playthings,
                    paper plates,
And the sheer shards
                    of shattered tumblers

In both poems, Wilbur has emphasized the caesura—a breath break in the center of the line—by dropping the second half of the line down. This visual indication can prepare you as a reader for the form, helping you read it more rhythmically. I also found such spacing could help me maintain formal consistency while drafting.

*Canyon**

WENDY BISHOP

The long stretches of rock face
             remind us that rivers,
tides and strong weather
             will win our envy.
Here crows caw from pinnacles
             across the canyon
and perch on the rock croppings
             in pure abstract patterns
as below, far below,
             sheep baa uncertainly
while walls fall statically
             from cliff to floor
in red rifts of sandstone,
             spiked and spined and rilled.
We admire such emptiness
             and mismeasure, arms wide,
calculations useless. Cottonwoods trace
             for scale the tight curves
of river. Waters widening in storm
             wrote this record.
In perspective, animals and humans
             make small marks in geology
while wind, earth, and water
             form a true sand painting.

While revising, I loosened the traditional accentual-alliterative pattern by relying on internal assonance (the repetition of vowel sounds) as well as alliteration for my chimes and I didn't worry about accents, or I should say I measured and cut my lines by ear, trying to let the accents fall strongly, but more naturally. All these choices were made, of course, to complete a draft at all.

━━ INVENTION EXERCISES ━━

1. Look for a common event, occupation, or scene in which you can see a heroic side of someone or something—the way a preschool teacher copes with her students, the remains of a battleground or cemetery, a child becoming a teenager, a friend's rehabilitation after an accident, the hopefulness of a wedding you've just attended. Freewrite all the details of that event, occupation, or scene. Get particulars down: what the graves look like, the way your friend smiles

when he/she succeeds at an endeavor, the look each generation—
parents, young children, and so on—had at the wedding. Then, put
your freewrite aside and begin telling the story, working loosely in a
drop-line verse pattern like Wilbur. Decide later if you want to
increase the poem's regularity or leave this as a free verse imitation.

2. Write your own poem that personifies and observes part of the natural landscape as "The Lilacs" and "Canyon" both do. It helps if
you're in the place you're describing. If that's not possible, close
your eyes and recreate the scene—the sounds, scents, and colors. Jot
down lists of particulars, using all your senses as Chanda Langford
does in her draft. Then shape this work into a poem draft, ignoring,
if you like, the tight accentual pattern and craft your poem by ear.

Backyard Backdrop*

Splintered dogwood limb
        straddles crumpled bushes
Day lilies dance
        among the scraggly, unkempt shrubs
Nubby crowns of amaryllis
        remember bygone blossoms
Once respected lawn
        now blotched with callous weeds
Chartreuse-breasted birds
        mark the migratory season
Heroic hickory totems
        lean into sunset's crimson wake
Magnolia's white pinwheels
        swirl in emerald eddies
As twilight-tempered nighttime
        nudges daylight into sleep.

3. Follow the idea set up in "Junk." Write your own imitation using a
yard sale, trash heap, used clothing store, etc. Look as Wilbur did
for the gold that's in the dross. Humans leave their personalities and
their impact on the things they own. Try to capture some sense of
this whether you find it appalling, exciting, ironic, sad, or simply
humorous.

SYLLABIC VERSE

> Linguists divide all languages into two general types: the syllable-timed
> and the accent-timed. Some languages, like French or Greek, are sylla-
> ble-timed: speakers of these languages—quite unconsciously—try to
> equalize the span of time allotted to each syllable, ignoring accent.
> Languages like English and German, however, are accent-timed: speak-
> ers quite unconsciously try to equalize the time span between primary
> accents, regardless of the number of syllables. —Stephen Adams, 4

Although it is difficult to do in English, some poets' variations of accentual
verse lead them into counting syllables as their major organizing principle, creating syllabic verse. They do this because poetry is about language challenges.
It is a pleasure to attempt the difficult and to translate prosodies as well as can
be done from one language to another. But poets also know they need to make
their games seriously productive. That's why a poet like Dylan Thomas in
"Fern Hill" also retains strong connections to Anglo-Saxon verse patterns, a
more natural meter for English than the plain counting of syllables. To achieve
his effects, he uses intense alliteration while manipulating his line length by syllable more than by stress.

Fern Hill
DYLAN THOMAS

Now as I was young and easy under the apple boughs
About the lilting house and happy as the grass was green,
        The night above the dingle starry,
            Time let me hail and climb
        Golden in the heydays of his eyes,
And honored among wagons I was prince of the apple towns
And once below a time I lordly had the trees and leaves
          Trail with daisies and barley
        Down the rivers of the windfall light.

And as I was green and carefree, famous among the barns
About the happy yard and singing as the farm was home,
        In the sun that is young once only,
           Time let me play and be
        Golden in the mercy of his means,
And green and golden I was huntsman and herdsman, the calves
Sang to my horn, the foxes on the hills barked clear and cold,
          And the sabbath rang slowly
        In the pebbles of the holy streams.

All the sun long it was running, it was lovely, the hay
Fields high as the house, the tunes from the chimneys, it was air
        And playing, lovely and watery
             And fire green as grass.
      And nightly under the simple stars
As I rode to sleep the owls were bearing the farm away,
All the moon long I heard, blessed among stables, the nightjars
        Flying with the ricks, and the horses
            Flashing into the dark.

And then to awake, and the farm, like a wanderer white
With the dew, come back, the cock on his shoulder: it was all
        Shining, it was Adam and maiden,
           The sky gathered again
      And the sun grew round that very day.
So it must have been after the birth of the simple light
In the first, spinning place, the spellbound horses walking warm
        Out of the whinnying green stable
           On to the fields of praise.

And honoured among foxes and pheasants by the gay house
Under the new made clouds and happy as the heart was long,
        In the sun born over and over,
           I ran my heedless ways,
        My wishes raced through the house high hay
And nothing I cared, at my sky blue trades, that time allows
In all his tuneful turning so few and such morning songs
        Before the children green and golden
           Follow him out of grace,

Nothing I cared, in the lamb white days, that time would take me
Up to the swallow thronged loft by the shadow of my hand,
        In the moon that is always rising,
           Nor that riding to sleep
      I should hear him fly with the high fields
And wake to the farm forever fled from the childless land.
Oh I was young and easy in the mercy of his means,
        Time held me green and dying
      Though I sang in my chains like the sea.

This poem is also pleasurable for its astonishing linguistic and emotional exuberance as Thomas mixes extravagant metaphors into the rounds of everyday life, as in "the owls were bearing the farm away" standing for something like "the owls were hooting as I fell asleep."

Poet Marianne Moore is equally well known for her explorations with syl-labic verse. And while many poets are influenced by Dylan Thomas, the syllabic form most often undertaken by authors in English is the haiku, derived from the Japanese form and discussed in chapter 6.

➤ INVENTION EXERCISES ➤

1. Take one or two stanzas of Thomas' poem and rewrite them with less alliteration.
2. For a first syllabic poem, try a less-complicated pattern than Thomas'. A **cinquain** (pronounced "sing-cane") is a single stanza poem with the syllabic pattern of 2, 4, 6, 8, 2 syllables per line. The most well-known practitioner of the form is an American poet named Adelaide Crapsey, who wrote the following cinquain:

Triad
ADELAIDE CRAPSEY

These be
Three silent things:
The falling snow . . the hour
Before the dawn . . the mouth of one
Just dead.

    a. Cinquains can be explored through a **found poem** exercise: find anoth-er writer's work (prose or poetry) and take a memorable line and shape it into a cinquain. Titles do a lot of work in this form since they offer extra syllables for extending, underlining, or pointing to your poem's content.
    b. Take your own freewriting or an old poem of your own and find a cinquain within it:

from *Farm Wife*
WENDY BISHOP

Watch the combine paring harvest fields to stubble.
    Remember the hand sheared haircuts of farm boys. **Remember wheat, sheaved and gleaned the old way by women in dark aprons, foreign consonants climbing the autumn air.** And stern Protestants who could not control their dreams at night, who prayed: let not the locusts come, send water, keep our sons from temptation and war.

As I did here:

Harvest*

> Wheat, sheaved
> and gleaned the old
> way, by women in dark
> aprons; foreign consonants cut
> fall air.

> c. Using the form as a guide, pour your description into it, letting the form alter your poem's development as Oliver Ruiz did in class as we played with the form.

Deep

> He yells.
> I'm going to
> Be buried in the sea
> Like a pirate and treasure.
> Down deep.

3. For this draft, choose your own poetic subject, but use Dylan Thomas' syllabic pattern, or your own, or one of the patterns found in the poems by Whitney Balliett, Ted Kooser, James Tate, and Donald Hall that follow. First, of course, you need to analyze their use of syllabic form.

> **Back**
> WHITNEY BALLIETT
>
> We stand inside the door,
> Our feet tangled in bags,
> And listen for the wind
> Vowelling in the chimney
> And the rosebush worrying
> The kitchen screen. We feel
> The old smells of damp and
> Ashes on our cheeks, and dig
> The light creaking down the
> Stairs to count the sheeted
> Chairs in the hall.

> Then
Barney and Max, loosed from
Their box, shoot under the
Hall table, and wait behind
Their yellow lamps. A breeze
Sucks at the front door and,
Stiff as winter, it sighs
And bangs shut. The sound
Startles us, and sends
The cats up the stairs so
Fast they make two straight
Lines—one gray, one black.

Beer Bottle
TED KOOSER

In the burned-
out highway
ditch the throw-

away beer
bottle lands
standing up

unbroken,
like a cat
thrown off

of a roof
to kill it,
landing hard

and dazzled
in the sun,
right side up;

sort of a
miracle.

Miss Cho Composes in the Cafeteria ❖
JAMES TATE

You are so small, I
am not even sure
that you are at all.

To you, I know I
am not here: you are
rapt in writing a

syllabic poem
about gigantic,
gaudy Christmas trees.

You will send it home
to China, and they
will worry about

you alone amid
such strange customs. You
count on your tiny

bamboo fingers; one,
two, three—up to five,
and, oh, you have one

syllable too much.
You shake your head in
dismay, look back up

to the tree to see
if, perhaps, there might
exist another

word that would describe
the horror of this
towering, tinselled

symbol. And . . . now
you've got it! You jot
it down, jump up, look

at me and giggle.

Valley of Morning
DONALD HALL

Jack Baker
rises when
the steeple
clock strikes three
to shape dough
into pans
and wed pale
rising bread
to the fire,
trays shoved in
clay ovens
over wood
coals. After
the summer
sun touches
the church's
steeple, he
pulls from his
bakestove two
hundred loaves,
crusted brown
with damp fire
inside. Now
the valley
of morning
wakes breathing
bread's air, fresh
loaves for the
day's mouth, for
meadow, lane,
and row house.

Reading a *New Yorker* magazine, I came upon the following poem; it moved me deeply and interested me technically. As I read I felt my way through and around the line breaks and shape of the stanzas. I asked myself about its form— as I ask myself about most poems I read. I wondered, Is it a syllabic poem? And started counting off syllables per line. Why, I wondered, would the poet choose syllabics? How does the form emphasize the sense of the poem, add to it, or augment whatever the poet is attempting here? I spent a few minutes thinking about how this would read if it were recast as a longer-lined poem. What would be gained and what would be lost by each decision the poet makes?

Paper Dolls
HENRI COLE

To some it might
have seemed vulgar
or degrading that
he was naked,
but for a wrinkled sheet.
Straight as candles,
his legs exposed
the eroding candelabrum
that was his body.
As directed,
no priest was present.
So when his mouth,
chapped and bleeding,
locked on a breath
we believed was the last,
the other of us
ran wailing down
the long blue corridor
for a nurse
who came to us
as Demeter had
to the frozen earth.
On the windowsill,
red tulips
stopped their grieving
as we kissed
what remained
good-bye
in a scene
at first holy,
then lurid,
as something stirred
beneath the sheet.
On the night table,
paper dolls cut
like shackled lions
roared at his entrance.

As you end this chapter, I encourage you to develop your own form-based reader's questions and investigate your own preferences. How much regularity do you like in a poem? Do you prefer accentual, syllabic, or both as your counting system? Has counting accents gotten in the way of your meaning as you drafted or helped you to find a shape for what you want to say? Is the cinquain a poet's game or a real and viable and challenging poetic form? There are no right answers to these questions, nor are these all the questions you might ask. But keep them in mind as you take some more time to play with these forms, working into and out of them, to see what you find out about your own sound sense.

POCKET DEFINITIONS

Accentual-Alliterative Verse—Poetry that relies on lines of four accented syllables, two on each side of a caesura—a mid-line pause. The lines don't rhyme, but the first three and often the fourth accented syllables alliterate.

Alliteration—Repeated initial consonant sounds, particularly when these are stressed syllables and are close to each other in a line of poetry. For example, in Mary Oliver's poem "Question," in the line "my horse, my hound," *horse* and *hound* alliterate (have initial stressed syllables), and *my* and *my* repeat and could be said to alliterate (although they are unstressed syllables in this line of poetry) because alliteration is partly a visual device.

Assonance—Repeated vowel sounds, as in "with**ou**t my m**ou**nt".

Blank Verse—Unrhymed iambic pentameter verse. Lines are counted off in five iambic feet (ten syllables, five accents—da-DA), but end rhymes do not occur in predictable patterns.

Caesura—"Caesura" is often used freely to mean a pause within a line of poetry—usually at a syntactical clause or phrase boundary. More technically, the term indicates the place a metrical break occurs as happens in the intentional separation of strong accents within a line of Old English verse.

Cinquain—A single stanza poem with the syllabic pattern of 2, 4, 6, 8, 2 syllables per line.

Found Poem—A poem shaped from naturally occurring language elements— magazine or newspaper articles, ad language, professional jargon, bulletin board notices, printed directions—that already have some notable poetic effects. This language is then shaped into poetic form(s) by the poet (by dividing into lines of regular length, and so on).

3

COUPLETS AND THE SOUNDS OF FULL, SLANT, AND NO RHYME

Evening Chess
CHARLES SIMIC

The Black Queen raised high
In my father's angry hand.

Couplets, which are two-line stanzas, can be complete poems, as in "Evening Chess." More often, along with tercets and quatrains discussed in later chapters, couplets can be thought of as basic building blocks of poetry. In studying couplets, writers can learn about line-length choices (**end-stopped**—stopping a phrase, clause, or sentence at the line ending, or **enjambed**—continuing a phrase, clause, or sentence on the next line) and the options in sound that are available at the ends of lines (**full, slant,** and no **rhyme**) and the way alliteration, assonance, or rhyme can be placed internally within a two-line stanza. Couplets can be linked together to develop narratives or can stand alone, producing a striking **image.** When couplet lines are equal lengths, the couplets are called *equal couplets* (as in Charles Simic's couplet), and when the lines are of different lengths, they are called *unequal couplets* (as in William Carlos Williams' poem). When each line is stopped or slowed by punctuation, the couplet is closed (as seen in the Dryden and Pope couplets below); when the couplet enjambs and runs over to the next line, it's called an open couplet. (Such enjambment is highlighted in both William Carlos Williams' and Gwendolyn Brooks' poems below.)

BUILDING WITH COUPLETS

In the past, poets created long chains of couplets to develop complicated narratives like *The General Prologue to the Canterbury Tales* and *The Rape of the Lock.* While there is a long historical pedigree for this form, it's easy to overlook how some of the simplest seeming and most familiar poems in the modern literary canon are built out of two-line stanzas, like this much anthologized piece:

The Red Wheelbarrow
WILLIAM CARLOS WILLIAMS

so much depends
upon

a red wheel
barrow

glazed with rain
water

beside the white
chickens.

In Williams' poem the second line is a word of two syllables and isn't rhymed. In addition, there is no punctuation throughout the poem. Still, the long-line-followed-by-shorter-line progression of these couplets lends a rhythmic punctuation to the image of the wheelbarrow, vivid in the rain beside the chickens, and is famous as a statement about the force of visual detail and the importance of everyday observation to the modern artist. By slowing our reading, segmenting sentences, and developing images around pauses and line breaks, the poet manipulates how we perceive his words and develop our understanding of his poem.

> The sense in prose flows continuously, while in verse it is segmented so
> as to increase information density and perceived structure.
> —Alex Preminger and T. V. F. Brogan, 695

The following, also a well-known couplet poem, displays Gwendolyn Brooks' powerful use of a single, repeated end word, while enjambment creates a strong, jazzy rhythm:

We Real Cool
GWENDOLYN BROOKS

The Pool Players
Seven at the Golden Shovel.

We real cool. We
Left school. We

Lurk late. We
Strike straight. We

Sing sin. We
Thin gin. We

Jazz June. We
Die soon.

∽ READING INTO WRITING ∽

1. Based on your reading of Simic and Williams, compose your own
   unrhymed couplet **image** poem. Do this by walking outside and finding an engaging sight. Make one line shorter than the other (first or
   second is fine) and try to write the poem as a single sentence. You
   might use the title or an opening statement like Williams' "so much
   depends upon . . ." to focus your observations. Try something like:
   "It is always a surprise . . ." or "Every morning . . ." and similar
   ideas. Some readers in one of my classes felt Williams wrote an
   "easy" poem and challenged each other to compose a poem about
   another yard implement, a blue shovel. A draft by Ben Floyd follows. After attempting Williams' form, these writers were quickly
   convinced that the wedding of form and statement found in "The
   Red Wheelbarrow" is far from easy to accomplish. Sometimes less *is*
   more. Sometimes what is easy to read is not so easy to write.

*The Blue Shovel**

So much depends
on

the blue
shovel

caked with orange
clay

lying near the
grave.

2. Try your own version of Gwendolyn Brooks' poem. Write a heavily
   rhymed series of couplets. Perhaps speak for your own high school
   peer group (this might be an ironic poem).

*Father Is Mad at Me**
        Oliver Ruiz

Father is mad. Father
feels bad. Father

yells loud. Father
is proud. Father

was mean. Father
makes scene. Father

throws dart. Father
cold heart.

MOVING INTO AND OUT OF RHYME

[B]y now we are in the territory of approximate rhyme, where a number
of terms are used, such as "off rhyme," "near rhyme," "slant rhyme,"
etc. In this latitudinarian zone, similarities of sound produce rhyming
pairs such as *dark/card, drama/armor, aspirin/inspiring, locate/collate,*
and what have you. This kind of rhyme has been particularly in favor
during the recent revival of interest in metered and rhymed poetry.
—Alfred Corn, 73

Morning Swim
MAXINE KUMIN

Into my empty head there come
a cotton beach, a dock wherefrom

I set out, oily and nude
through mist, in chilly solitude.

There was no line, no roof or floor
to tell the water from the air.

Night fog thick as terry cloth
closed me in its fuzzy growth.

I hung my bathrobe on two pegs.
I took the lake between my legs.

Invaded and invader, I
went overhand on that flat sky.

Fish twitched beneath me, quick and tame.
In their green zone they sang my name

and in the rhythm of the swim
I hummed a two-four-time slow hymn.

I hummed *Abide with Me.* The beat
rose in the fine thrash of my feet,

rose in the bubbles I put out
slantwise, trailing through my mouth.

My bones drank water; water fell
through all my doors. I was the well

that fed the lake that met my sea
in which I sang *Abide with Me.*

In this poem, the poet takes advantage of both full (or true) rhyme and slant (or half) rhyme—*fell/well* is an example of full rhyme, words that have similar sounding vowels and the same number of syllables, but different consonants following the vowel. In other places, the poet chooses slant rhyme—*cloth/growth* and *floor/air.* Here the vowels echo but don't repeat. Slant rhyme is the preferred rhyme of many modern poets since it produces more subtle, less noticeable variations and helps set off contemporary poetry from contemporary song, which still relies heavily on the uses of full rhyme (see the samples in chapter 1). Kumin also uses rhymes that end on stressed syllables—COME/whereFRÓM and NÚDE/SÓL-ĭ-TÚDE. These are called *masculine rhymes.* To make what we call *feminine rhymes,* we'd turn the rhyme TÁME/NÁME into TÁMing/NÁMing. (Stress in a feminine rhyme occurs on the first syllable, followed by an unstressed syllable.)

 To practice rhyme at your computer, you can find a rhyming dictionary on the Web. But just as the best musicians learn to keep much of their music in their heads, you'll want to practice rhyming by playing out the combinations of your own musical vocabulary, trying out word combinations for effect.

There are specific names for the types of sound effects we incorporate into poems. Others are informative, ones you can collect and experiment with. If Maxine Kumin had structured her couplets differently (and less well), beginning each line this way:

I hung my bathrobe on two

pegs. I took the lake between my
legs. Invaded and invader,

I went overhand on that flat
sky

her poem would then turn on *head rhymes*—the rhymes coming at the beginning of each line. We also see poets placing rhymes within the lines, creating what are called *internal rhyme* patterns.

> I hung my bathrobe
> on two *pegs*. I took
>
> the lake between
> my *legs*. Invaded
>
> and invader, *I* went overhand
> on that flat *sky*.

We use *syllabics* to help us understand rhymes, too, as in counting *masculine* and *feminine rhyme* patterns and deciding which syllables of multisyllabic poems actually hold the sound. When choosing *nude/solitude*, Kumin is producing a masculine rhyme (NUDE/sol-i-TUDE) but also joining a single to a *triple syllable rhyme*.

The rhymes in the next couplet poem are unusual for the way the end word of the previous couplet gets echoed in the end word of the first line of the next couplet—this becomes more obvious from the twelfth and thirteenth lines onward: *froth/troughs* and *thrall/seagulls*, and so on.

The Seals in Penobscot Bay
DANIEL HOFFMAN

> hadn't heard of the atom bomb,
> so I shouted a warning to them.
>
> Our destroyer (on trial run) slid by
> the rocks where they gamboled and played;
>
> they must have misunderstood,
> or perhaps not one of them heard
>
> me over the engines and tides.
> As I watched them over our wake
>
> I saw their sleek skins in the sun
> ripple, light-flecked, on the rock,
>
> plunge, bubbling, into the brine,
> and couple & laugh in the troughs
>
> between the waves' whitecaps and froth.
> Then the males clambered clumsily up

and lustily crowed like seacocks,
sure that their prowess held thrall

all the sharks, other seals, and seagulls.
And daintily flipped the females,

seawenches with musical tails;
each looked at the Atlantic as

though it were her looking-glass.
If my warning had ever been heard

it was sound none would now ever heed.
And I, while I watched those far seals

tasted honey that buzzed in my ears
and saw, out to windward, the sails

of an obsolete ship with banked oars
that swept like two combs through the spray

and I wished for a vacuum of wax
to ward away all those strange sounds,

yet I envied the sweet agony
of him who was tied to the mast,

when the boom, when the boom, when the boom
of guns punched dark holes in the sky.

I hardly noticed the pattern until I was typing the poem, but then I began to see how these quiet vertical rhymes support the development of this poem's narrative.

> Where there is no similarity, there is no rhyme. Where the similarity is too great, boredom sets in. Skillful rhyming involves finding a balance between identity and difference." —Alfred Corn, 77

In this poem—as in other poems in this book—you'll notice, perhaps, allusions to other literature. In this case, Hoffman is talking about a famous wanderer and sailor—Odysseus—who poured wax into his sailors ears to keep them from hearing the singing of the sirens.

Readers of Western poetry have long found a reference work like Edith Hamilton's *Mythology* essential for untangling such references. In fact, contemporary readers will probably find it useful to collect books of myths and legends and tales from cultures around the world, as well as to search the Internet for discussions of the same. You'll find sites on Greek and Roman mythology as well as folktales and myths and sites that direct you out of the European traditions into world mythologies. You can also search for myths by subject—finding out worldwide beliefs about, for instance, the moon, seasons, monsters, heroes, rebirth.

THE ECHOES OF COUPLETS PAST

Neither Hoffman nor Kumin relies on the full end rhyme of the **heroic couplet**—two rhyming lines of iambic pentameter in a closed couplet:

dă-DÁ dă-DÁ dă-DÁ dă-DÁ dă-DÁ (end rhyme *a*)
dă-DÁ dă-DÁ dă-DÁ dă-DÁ dă-DÁ (end rhyme *a*)
dă-DÁ dă-DÁ dă-DÁ dă-DÁ dă-DÁ (end rhyme *b*)
dă-DÁ dă-DÁ dă-DÁ dă-DÁ dă-DÁ (end rhyme *b*, and
continuing *cc, dd*, etc.)

In English verse, this form has a lineage that moves through time from Geoffrey Chaucer (1340?–1400) to John Dryden (1631–1700) to Alexander Pope (1688–1744).

from ***The General Prologue to the Canterbury Tales***
GEOFFREY CHAUCER

Whan that Aprill with his shoures soote
The droghte of March hath perced to the roote,
And bathed every veyne in swich licour
Of which vertu engendred is the flour;
Whan Zephirus eek with his sweete breeth
Inspired hath in every holt and heeth
The tendre croppes, and the yonge sonne
Hath in the Ram his halve cours yronne,
And smale foweles maken melodye,
That slepen al the nyght with open ye
(So priketh hem nature in hir courages)
Thanne longen folk to goon on pilgrimages ...

from ***Absalom and Achitophel***
JOHN DRYDEN

With secret Joy, indulgent David view'd
His Youthful Image in his Son renew'd:
To all his wishes Nothing he deni'd,
And made the Charming Annabel his Bride.

from ***The Rape of the Lock***
ALEXANDER POPE

What dire Offence from am'rous Causes springs,
What mighty Contests rise from trivial Things,
I sing—This Verse to Caryll, Muse! is due;
This, ev'n Belinda may vouchsafe to view:
Slight is the Subject, but not so the Praise,
If She inspire, and He approve my Lays.

In all three of these historic poems, "The General Prologue to the Canterbury Tales," "Absalom and Achitophel," and "The Rape of the Lock," narratives dexterously unfold within the constraints of the heroic couplets. Each line ends strongly after a full grammatical phrase or at the punctuated end of a sentence. Using regular meter and the emphasis of full rhyme, the poet measures his meaning within pentameter requirements. The poet turns three-syllable words to two-syllable words (*am'rous*) or counts normally silent syllables (particularly words ending in *ed*) as sounded syllables when needed.

> Regardless of its length, the closed couplet seems both by its nature and its historical associations to imply something special about the materials enclosed in it. It seems to imply a distinct isolation of those materials from related things, a vigorous enclosure of them into a compact and momentarily self-sufficient little world of circumscribed sense and meaning. To construct a closed couplet is to draw a boundary line, to set something off as special and perhaps a trifle fragile.
> —Paul Fussell, 131

Many of us are familiar with the heroic couplet because it appears as the last two lines (thirteen and fourteen) of the Shakespearean sonnet. Certainly the regularity and strength of the rhymed couplet echoes through years of our school reading of poetry and helps define "poems" for us, consciously or unconsciously:

> This thou perceiv'st, which makes thy love more strong,
> To love that well which thou must leave ere long. (Sonnet LXXIII)

and

> For sweetest things turn sourest by their deeds;
> Lilies that fester smell far worse than weeds. (Sonnet XCIV)

This is why new writers of contemporary poetry sometimes feel they are unlearning poetic technique, for, as I mentioned earlier, most contemporary writers avoid the strong closure of the full-rhyme couplet (iambic or not) and opt for slant, alliterative, or random rhyme.

Returning to rhyme and meter in the 1990s is not returning to the attitudes and values associated with the formal poems of the 1950s. Many of the poets who are now returning to formal poetry are bringing with them the spirit of the 1960s and 1970s. —Debra Bruce (Finch 33)

Alan Shapiro's poem "The Letter" is an exception to that observation about contemporary preferences, however. He composes a twenty-five stanza narrative that takes the form of a letter in heroic couplets and includes a recasting of the Orpheus and Eurydice myth, all while weaving full and slant rhyme together with great skill. In his author's notes to this poem, Shapiro explains his intentions this way:

"The Letter" is partly a retelling, in reverse of the Orpheus/Eurydice myth. In the original story, the male lover leads his beloved up out of the underworld, and the beloved vanishes when he turns around; in my version, the beloved leads the speaker down into the underworld and makes him vanish when she turns away. Beyond this, I think the poem expresses both the dangers and attractions implicit in a certain kind of longing. —A. R. Ammons, 244

The Letter
ALAN SHAPIRO

The letter said you had to speak to me.
Please, if you love me, Alan, hurry. Please.

I read it and reread it, running down
the big stone steps into the underground,

and every time, as in an anagram,
the letters rearranged themselves again

as new words cancelling the ones before:
Come or don't come I really couldn't care,

I never meant to hurt you like I did.
I never hurt you. There's nothing to forgive . . .

The letter virulent with changing moods,
now cross, now pleading, accusing and accused,

seemed to infect each place I hurried through:
the slippery concrete of the vestibule,

the long low tunnel, and the turnstiles where
nobody waited to collect my fare,

nobody on the platform either, far
and near no sound within that mineral air,

nothing around me but a fever of clues
of what it was you wanted me to do.

O mother, my Eurydice in reverse,
was it the white line I was meant to cross?

To hear within its Thou Shalt Not a "Shall"
and follow you into a lower hell?

The page went blank. Below me now I saw
barbed wire running where the third rail was,

and in the sharp script of its angry weaving,
suspended in the loops and snares, the playthings

of forgotten life, dismembered dolls,
the frayed tip of a rubber knife, a wheel,

the tiny shatterings of cups and saucers,
and other things worn back into mere matter,

their glitter indecipherable except
as the star burst of some brief interest,

the barbed discarded relics of a wanting
they all intensified by disappointing.

As if they could be words, and those words yours,
obscuring what they substituted for,

each leading to a darker one beyond
the bleak lights of the platform, I jumped down

and there at last among them crawled and read,
burning with comprehension as I bled.

The pain was good, the pain exhilarated,
the pain was understanding, now perfected.

Cauled in my own blood, mute and lame and free
of everything obstructing you from me,

I saw your face above me leaning down.
There's nothing here for you, you said, go home.

It's for your own good, child, believe me, and
I vanished, waking, as you turned around.

The couplet appears, of course, in other literatures. For instance, the couplet has been a building block of Chinese poetry for centuries and was used by poets to explore the ancient Taoist cosmological principles—Yang/fire/sun and Yin/water/moon. The poets composed in parallel couplets and explored pairs—high/low, fire/water, sun/moon, mountain/water, and so on—as in this translation by Stephen Owen of the poet Tu Fu (in *Traditional Chinese Poetry and Poetics* 90):

Plains flow with sunlight, moving over the earth;
The river enters clouds as they cross the mountains.

Reread "The Red Wheelbarrow" with this tradition in mind. While you can see the way line lengths are balanced and rhythmic patterns develop in western poems I share in this chapter, it would be worth complicating those understandings by exploring natural and conceptual pairings in one of your couplet poems. You can also find many Internet sites devoted to exploring eastern philosophies and writing.

> In literary Chinese most conceptual categories occur in compounds of two characters. . . . In a parallel couplet we often find these very compounds, or variations of them, aligned in parallel positions. Furthermore, each line of a parallel couplet can often be seen as the expansion of one term of a common compound. A frequent example occurs in couplets describing landscapes—in Chinese, *shan-shui* . . . "mountain-and-water." The general category through which a poet conceives of his topic is not a unitary idea, a "landscape"; rather, the category is a *pair* of terms, and those terms dispose themselves each into one line of the couplet. The resulting couplet consists of one line on a "mountain" scene set in parallel to a line on a "water" scene. The world was conceptualized in paired terms, and those same terms serve as the basis of parallel relations in a couplet. —Stephen Owen, 88

✒ INVENTION EXERCISES ✒

1. Recast a few stanzas of Daniel Hoffman's poem as heroic couplets by turning his slant rhymes into full rhymes with no stanza breaks. What does this do to the sound of the poem? Equally, what does taking out the stanza pauses do to an unrhymed set of couplets like those in Enid Shomer's poem, on the next page? Does her poem retain its sense of couplet-ness with paired, coupled lines? Or does it change into a less definable free verse poem?

2. Try your hand at casting one of your own poems in both full and slant rhyme; it doesn't matter in which direction you compose. Which do you like better, and why?

3. Try an alternate rhyme pattern for couplets like Hoffman seems to do:

———————————————————*a*
———————————————————*b*

———————————————————*b*
———————————————————*c*

———————————————————*c*
———————————————————*d*

This pattern throws off a reader's visual expectation of where rhymes will occur. In my poem "Your Apple Tree," I chose audible and visual rhyme—alliterative and assonant end words for my couplets instead of either full or slant rhymes *(jelly/jars, apples/appetite)*—and I regularly enjamb many of the couplet stanzas. What does that do your reading of the poem?

4. Try your own poem (couplets or not) that plays with alternative placements of the rhymes.

   Try initial (full or slant) rhyme and/or alliteration:

a———————————————
a———————————————
b———————————————
b———————————————

Try internal (full or slant) rhyme/alliteration:

```
————————a————    ——
————————a————
————b————————
————————b————
```

5. Like Alan Shapiro, retell a classical myth, fairy tale, or folk parable
   in your own couplet poem. Choose iambic pentameter (notice how
   often Shapiro repeats phrases and clauses to achieve his pentameter)
   or, more simply, use ten-syllable lines.

6. Think of your own natural landscape, and consider how you make
   sense out of symmetry and pairings: night/day, sun/moon, cat/dog,
   armadillo/hummingbird, to name a few. Explore why you see these
   as both complementary and opposite sides of your sense of creation
   and natural unity. Then cast your own modern version of single-par-
   allel or linked-parallel couplets, adding to those poems elements of
   the western tradition (such as rhyme patterns) for a pairing of East
   and West.

   In the poems that follow, you'll encounter a variety of couplet patterns.
You'll get a better sense of just how flexible couplets and sound schemes are if
you analyze the way these poets form their couplets to create sound patterns,
and the way these variations support the narrative and imagistic content. Enid
Shomer deploys a variety of half rhymes in expected and unexpected patterns.
As I've pointed out, the end rhymes in my poem "Your Apple Tree" are intentionally obscured—I decided to alliterate the last word of each couplet:
made/may, linked/lay—aiming for a ghost of rhyme instead of a thunderclap at
the line ends.

   Romantic, at Horseshoe Key ❖
   ENID SHOMER

   All day the light breaks up the waves,
   turning them over in dark spadefuls

   while I fish from the pier raised
   like a spyglass into the Gulf.

   There is such eloquence in the factual
   that has no name, in all the ways water

   is patterned in a boat's wake: Laces
   coming undone? A chain slipping its gears?

What should I call the time we ate cherries
by the pound for moisture, the water jug

forgotten on the dock? You said *years*
from now our trees will crown this plot

of water. A surf of blossoms,
our hands branded red as hearts . . . .

I can't subtract you from this place,
from the boat basin's curved

embrace, the red channel markers
that ripen all night in my sleep.

My pale purple line enters the water
and deflects like a censored

thought. Now I see you in your boat
moving quickly through the ink

of my poem. Gulls keep turning
the pages of the sky. I write

the way a shore bird prints her words
in sand to be read by water.

I name it romantic, this belief
that pain is only the bad year of an orchard.

Your Apple Tree
WENDY BISHOP

Unexpectedly, our days were linked
by apples. Some mornings I lay

unwilling to wake on a quilt made
of yellows and greens. Light melted

across the torn window screen after
coming by way of the blossoming apple

that crowded your garden
in a good year or gently

marked the empty rows and drooping
vines during droughts.

One apple tree can fuel a whole
farm. Visiting, I'd find them heaped

in piles on the ground, in buckets
gathered carelessly abundant

on your porch, golden in jars as jelly
for toast, wrinkled in jars,

weathered, dried into slices
like kindling for the stomach.

In winter, the wait for summer apples.
In summer, the dream of winter appetite

for pies before stove fires.
I learned about apples that way, filching

from the overburdened tree before
our walks, discussions punctuated by

the brandished fruit, arguments ended by
that sharp familiar crack of first bite,

chittering birds chased by the cores,
the return, empty handed, to a chore.

The harvest gifts that I took home
were never as good and hardy

apples withered in a bowl
because, less rural, life was too busy

for making pies, so I sliced
one batch to hang before my sink

to dry on a string. Their sweetness
drove flies mad. The string

sagged. That year we changed. I took
a trip and stayed away. In summer heat they

had no choice, the apples spoiled
before they dried. The link between such

days and these is a picture of your apple
tree fragrant in the wind and

the memory of that flight,
the string of rotting apples filling

with scent my abandoned house.

You'll find line-length experiments more along the line of William Carlos Williams' and Gwendolyn Brooks' poems dominating in Melanie A. Rawls' couplets.

*Tallahassee Summer**

It's hot.
The sun burns up the

early morning mist, burns up
the blue of sky, leaves a

blaze of white. It's hot.
The sidewalks blind. The curbs

waver. Dogs struggle a distance of two
feet then flop. Joggers appear under water—

slowed to a fast walk and a determined
pumping of arms. Hot.

Grass keels over. Skin tingles, hair
rises, pulls away from the body. Sweat

is sucked away. So is sound.
Hot.

Sandra McPherson's and Catherine Bowman's poems provide special couplet effects. McPherson's poem is both a direct address to the poet Sappho, but her couplets also loosely rhyme and alliterate in a manner that underlies but does not overwhelm the poem's multilayered textual commentary on texts—a meditation on reading the female body and female poets, mentors and mentees, mothers and daughters, old and young. Catherine Bowman, on the other hand, began to write an **abecedarian poem,** one which uses a letter of the alphabet in order to begin each line. In so doing, she uses the couplets to separate out the twenty-six letters into twelve spaced couplet stanzas. She also lets each line drive the next, with each letter of the alphabet determining the line's development into a playful and surreal poem. To begin to write a poem this seemingly unconnected, try writing a poem that makes no sense, and you'll quickly see how the conventions of syntax and sentence phrasing and image chains start to forge connections you didn't see at first between your lines. Notice, also, how Bowman allows her line lengths to ebb and flow; in general, unequal couplets echo the looser rhythms of free verse, despite the couplet form. In his poem, Darrell Fike echoes McPherson's laundry theme and the play of Bowman's poem, but he also uses couplets to suit a shorter, more unified lyric impulse.

Note to Sappho ❖
SANDRA MCPHERSON

In an age when T-shirts are our libraries,
doing laundry is a literate job.

My daughter puts a clean one on
and her seventeen-year body is an open book.

But when she takes it off, on just another
virgin night, she says Mom it's hard

to sleep against my breasts. Agreed,
but I don't curse them. Sometimes I curse

the mattress springs, get up and read
you under the lamp. Or clear-imaged lines

of my former teacher, lesbian,
you would like. Otherwise, no birds

will sing for two more hours yet.
I hand-do the indecipherable lingerie—

cups that would strain wine!
Then lie down and dream your life

linked in bumpy sleep with mine.

Twins of a Gazelle Which Feed Among the Lilies
CATHERINE BOWMAN

Antlers butting against the full moon.
Bellies lolling on my belly.

Creamy chestnut crania in convex cones.
Dogs they follow me around in circles.

Everything I do they mimic. When I laugh they laugh, when I cry they howl.
Fins breakwater, slice the waves that make up my body.

Galactopoietic forms that feed the Milky Way.
Hunchbacks girdled to the chest for life.

Interwoven compartments of lobules containing a network of tubes.
Joined to the tubes of each lobe are ducts and all ducts lead to the nipple.

Knots for tongues to untie.
Lazy-boy recliners for lips to sit on.

Mushroom explosions taped to the chest.
Naked reminders of the death cup cloud.

O mammilla O
Papilla.

Quivering wolf snouts nose through my dreams.
Rats on a whiskered basso-relievo.

Sleep on our back they point to the stars.
Two points earned at birth. Nightpoints to stick to a crying baby.

U × 2.
Vaulted cupola. Baldheaded misers hoarding the mammon.

Women lie topless, side by side on the beach, from A-flat to C-sharp to 3-D.
Xylophones for the sun to play on.

Yes, to say, Yes
Zeugma. Zucchetto. Zoo.

Laundromat Love
DARRELL FIKE

These freshly laundered sheets
are a meadow in the bedroom

lazy clover scent of honey bee
sweet new grass and wildflower sun

your big blue flea-market pillow
a sudden little lake

the comforter bunched at the bottom of the bed
a bank of springy clouds

and you and me in a giggling heap
wrinkling these newly tucked sheets

two lovers in a meadowed heaven
that will last about a week.

The next two poems, one by Sean Thomas Dougherty and a poem in imitation
of Dougherty by Ellen Schendel, present family stories in a more serious, political vein. You can see in this section how the couplet form has flexibly allowed
poets to develop love poems, family poems, imagistic observations, and social
statements. To the first poem you will bring the primary research of your family
but will benefit from some secondary research—refreshing your understanding
of the 1960s—on the Civil Rights Movement and the Vietnam War. To complete
even more primary research, interview individuals who remember and partici-
pated in those events.

After the Last Great Anti-War Demonstration
SEAN THOMAS DOUGHERTY

The brass buckles
On blue coveralls,

Bright as medals,
Shining on the shoulder straps

Of that young man
With his hair cropped,

Chewing spit
As he pumped our gas.

I was six, maybe seven
When my step-father opened the door

Of our rusty Chevy, his afro
Round as the moon, & that man

Glanced at my mother & said,
"That's a fine white woman

you got in the car, boy."
And the acrid smell—

Like a match being struck,
As my step-father stepped

Up an inch from his eyes,
And whispered, "*That's*

My wife . . ."
And then took out

His wallet, & paid him;
Then he started the car

And drove us north to
Ohio, far away

From that EXXON sign
Just outside D.C.

War Story*
    Ellen Schendel

Shining brass medals
on olive uniform,

bright as new pennies,
sewn to the breast pocket

of my uncle the soldier:
hair cropped, boots shined,

bleeding bone, grinding teeth,
skin melting bones. He plays dead

until the shooting stops
and he crawls to a cottage

two football fields away
in the German countryside—

still in enemy territory
but allowed to bleed

across the farm
to an empty barn.

Straw sticks like needles
into blood and bone,

the farmer, careful
carpenter, saws the leg.

The soldier bites
leather, sweating up

at the ceiling, seeing
skies and stars of Illinois,

dreaming away from
Germany, tanks, farms.

(After Sean Thomas Dougherty's "After the Last Great
Anti-War Demonstration")

⟳ INVENTION EXERCISES ⟳

1. Choose an old family photograph that includes you. Do some
   freewriting to tell the following:

   a. Describe literally everything you see.
   b. Tell a story about this photo.
   c. What/who is just outside the edge of the photo?
   d. Who would you like to have included in this photo (or what person
      who is not there wishes he/she is in the photo)?
   e. Look carefully at the reproduction of you—describe what you see.

   Reread your freewriting, turn the freewriting over, and start to write
   a poem you title "Self-Portrait." Form this poem into couplets with
   any rhyme pattern you prefer.

Self-Portrait*
        Natasha Clews

my hair neatly
tied

lips stenciled
red

smile cheek to
cheek

family arm in
arm

sun lighting the
sky

focus seeming
clear

funny how pictures
lie

*From Self-Portrait**
    Jenny Harvey

Average, full lips, no expression—hidden humor.
I have darker shorter hair.
Freckles paint me younger than I really am.
My face lies without talking.
If I were a fruit, I'd be a mango, crazy fruit
Only appealing to a certain group.
If I were a car, I'd be my old Ford Mustang.
I love to rattle and to complain
Not just about me but complain in general like
My old car that even when you turn it off
It tries to stay on and chug along.
The scar on my nose still shows slightly.

2. Write down four or five words you like within the following cate-
    gories:

   a. flowers or plants:
   b. metals:
   c. animals:
   d. types of landscape or weather:
   e. parts of the body:
   f. words you simply like the sound of:
   g. colors:
   h. scents:

Then, read your favorite poem in this chapter and circle five drive words—words you think are resonant and powerful for the poet who used them. Now choose five of your own drive words. Write a five-stanza couplet poem using one of your words and one of the poet's drive words in each couplet. In this revised draft of such a poem, only four (underlined) drive words remain.

*Treasure Hunting**
     Natasha Clews

Collecting pine cones
in the hands of friends

<u>Tromping</u> through fallen, fall leaves
brushing over the earth

Tasting the <u>sweet</u> and bitterness
of kid-dom and sap on frozen fingers

Shining from the September morning sun
like treasures to ten year old eyes.

Sometimes I'm still called
by the shadow of the pine

Feeling the emptiness of my palm
catching a breath of <u>evergreen</u>

Bending to reach for a <u>bronze cone</u>
even now, feels like capturing a star.

3. Like Ellen Schendel, write an imitation or a poem based on any of the couplet poems in this chapter. In general, imitations seem to work this way:

   a. Imitate the subject matter or comment on it but not in the poet's own form. (In the Preface, Hans Ostrom's parody of Wallace Stevens does this directly, and James Tate comments more indirectly on Charles Simic's poem.) To do this well, you may need to conduct some historical, context-setting research.

   b. Imitate the form, but use your own subject matter. (Devan Cook's imitation of John Ashbery's "31 haiku" and my imitation of her imitation in chapter 6 work this way.) You might want to write your own abecedarian poem like Catherine Bowman did in "Twins of a Gazelle Which Feed Among the Lilies" using the alphabet to prompt lines (in couplets or not in couplets), using—as she says she did in her author's notes to the poem—the letter to prompt the line.

   c. Do a little of both (sometimes I call this writing across a poem). Michele Liles does this to a certain degree with "Why I Love the

Midwest," an imitation of Gary Snyder's "Why I Take Good Care of My Macintosh" in chapter 7. You could do this with Sandra McPherson's "Note to Sappho" by choosing your own mythic, heroic, and/or pop cultural character and using that individual as a sounding board for your thinking about something in your life. Look up your character on the Internet and be prepared for an avalanche of usable trivia as well as some serious investigations and provocative speculations about his or her life and times.

After experimenting with couplets—with rhythm, meter, and rhyme—you'll understand how this stanza form encourages a poet to develop flexibility with the *line*—repeating it, rhyming it, and placing spaces between lines at intervals. A reader can climb down couplet stanzas like a ladder or balance across the stepping stones of line breaks. Although you may not agree completely, you'll see why poet Janet Lewis urges you toward such work: "Rhythm and meter go together, supporting one another, yet rhythmical units of verse run counter to the metrical as much as they run with it. And that's what makes it interesting. The rhythm and meter comment on each other. We need meter. Otherwise, we fall into prose" (Finch 152).

The couplet allows a great deal of space and breathing room for readers and writers to meet in, and it has proven flexible when rhymed and end-stopped strongly in the heroic couplet or as an enjambed, more open exploration as in this closing poem where Mary Oliver uses a memory to speak on the passage of time, maturity, and mortality.

An Old Whorehouse
MARY OLIVER

We climbed through a broken window,
walked through every room.

Out of business for years,
the mattresses held only

rainwater, and one
woman's black shoe. Downstairs

spiders had wrapped up
the crystal chandelier.

A cracked cup lay in the sink.
But we were fourteen,

and no way dust could hide
the expected glamour from us,

or teach us anything.
We whispered, we imagined.

It would be years before
we'd learn how effortlessly

sin blooms, then softens,
like any bed of flowers.

POCKET DEFINITIONS

Abecedarian Poem—Each line (or stanza) begins with a letter of the alphabet.

End-Stopped—Occurs when phrase, clause, and/or sentence punctuation occurs at the end of a line of poetry. See the lines in Alan Shapiro's poem.

Enjambment—Occurs when sentence syntax carries on from one line to the next (including movement from one stanza to the next). See the lines in William Carlos Williams' and Gwendolyn Brooks' poems for samples.

Full Rhyme—Full-rhyming words have different initial consonants, similar vowel sounds, and similar consonant sounds. This is a complicated way of describing how *moon* and *June* rhyme—*m* and *J* are different initial consonants, *oo* and *u* are similar vowel sounds, and *n* and *ne* are similar consonant sounds. In slant rhyme (also called half rhyme), the vowel sound is not exact: *cloth/growth, out/mouth*. Rhymes can come in one, two, or three or more syllables: *hit/sit, plastic/drastic, librarian/agrarian*. Three-syllable rhymes seem to move toward the humorous. See Adams, *Poetic Designs,* Appendix 1, "The Terminology of Rhyming" 198–202 for an extensive list of briefly illustrated definitions of rhyme, including perfect, imperfect, eye, identical, rich, assonant, consonant, macaronic, light, wrenched, one-syllable, etc.

Heroic Couplet—A closed couplet of rhymed iambic pentameter, most familiar as the final couplet of a Shakespearian sonnet.

Image—When you use descriptions that rely on the five senses—taste, sight, touch, sound, smell—you are creating a word picture, a mental construction of a felt experience, an image, or a representation of the natural world as you, the poet, experienced it. Contemporary poets rely on creating strong images as much as historical poets relied on rhyme and stanza structures. Visual images are most common, and images using our other senses often need to be intentionally developed. Examples from this chapter: "We sing sin"—sound image; "glazed with rain"—sight image; "I took the lake between my legs"—touch image; "we ate cherries by the pound for moisture"—taste image; "string of rotting apples"—smell image.

Slant Rhyme—See *Full Rhyme.*

4

ELEGIES AND AUBADES

Meditations on Loss and Longing

On My First Son
BEN JONSON

Farewell, thou child of my right hand, and joy;
My sin was too much hope of thee, loved boy:
Seven years thou wert lent to me, and I thee pay,
Exacted by thy fate, on the just day.
O could I lose all father now! for why
Will man lament the state he should envy,
To have so soon 'scaped world's and flesh's rage,
And, if no other misery, yet age?
Rest in soft peace, and asked, say, "Here doth he
Ben Jonson his best piece of poetry."
For whose sake henceforth all his vows be such
As what he loves may never like too much.

The elegy and aubade are thematic, meditative forms. The elegy grows from the desire—and the need—to memorialize and mediate human loss. In her villanelle "One Art," found in chapter 13, Elizabeth Bishop claims "The art of losing isn't hard to master." By the end of her poem, however, we understand that quite the reverse is true. Bearing up under loss of a loved one is difficult: Loss makes humans question their place in the universe; their relationship to their past, present, and future; and their beliefs in this life and any other. As Robert Frost puts it in the poem "In Hardwood Groves": "However it is in some other world/I know that this is the way in ours."

The elegy represents a complex tradition. Preparing and presenting elegies was a crucial part of ancient and historical burial rites and replicates the *process* of grieving as the poet moves from loss to consolation: experiencing loss and doing the work of mourning and reconciliation. This thematic form began, in fact, with a mourning for the very condition of humankind, mortality, represented by the change of seasons, the cyclical death and rebirth of nature, and humans in nature.

ELEGIAC MEDITATIONS: FROM GRIEF TO CONSOLATION

> Among the conventions [that elegies drew upon] . . . are the use of pastoral contextualization, the myth of the vegetation deity (particularly the secular elements of such myths, and their relation to the sexuality of the mourner), the use of repetition and refrains, the reiterated questions, the outbreak of vengeful anger or cursing, the procession of mourners, the movement from grief to consolation, and the traditional images of resurrection . . . the elegist's need to draw attention, consolingly, to his own surviving powers. —Peter M. Sacks, 2

Not unexpectedly, poets long after the Greek elegists continued to deal in themes of loss and love. For instance, Elizabethan court poets claimed, rightly, that their words would endure beyond their date of composition to commemorate a time, place, or person, particularly a person for whom the poet had experienced great love. "Nor shall Death brag thou wand'rest in his shade," writes William Shakespeare in Sonnet XVIII, "When in eternal lines to time thou grow'st./So long as men can breathe or eyes can see [these lines],/So long lives this [poem] and this gives life to thee."

Ben Jonson uses the elegiac poem to mourn the loss of his children. The fact that infant mortality was exceedingly high in England in the sixteenth century doesn't diminish his pain at the death of both his first son and first daughter.

On My First Daughter
BEN JONSON

Here lies to each her parents' ruth,
Mary, the daughter of their youth;
Yet all heaven's gifts being heaven's due,
It makes the father less to rue.
At six months' end, she parted hence
With safety of her innocence;
Whose soul heaven's Queen (whose name she bears)
In comfort of her mother's tears,
Hath plac'd amongst her virgin-train:
Where, while that sever'd doth remain,
This grave partakes the fleshly birth.
Which cover lightly, gentle earth.

But what exactly contributes to this meditative form we call an **elegy**? A lament, a consolation, and a tracing out and understanding of (a resolving of) strong emotions define an elegy. An admission that life is often tragic, that we can understand tragedy though contemplation of the occasions of loss, that we survive it, and that something or someone is reborn into the cycle of life and lives on are also expressed in an elegy. To convey this in a poem, we create a song—a wreath of words that mourn the passing of something or someone. In the process, we remember, console, and if we are lucky, begin to heal ourselves and those we share these words with. We survive.

Love poetry often apostrophizes the absent beloved, and elegies may address the dead person as if he or she were still alive." —Tom Furniss and Michael Bath, 128

An elegy may be about the death of a person, but it may also be about the death of love, growth, or possibility since it is possible to miss something one never had or wished one had or was. An elegy helps us make transitions as events begin and end in rapid, sometimes bewildering succession: relationships, families, feelings, jobs, countries, and communities, spinning in and out of our understanding and our control. The elegy helps the poet make sense of some of this activity, allowing him or her to take a photo instead of watch a movie, to freeze the frame, and to consider how one moment relates to another.

Elegy for My Sister
SHEROD SANTOS

Sketchbooks. Night fires. Aesop and Grimm.
An electric model of the Lipizzaner stallions
circling each other in her darkened room.
An empty schoolyard after a morning rain,
and a figure eight traced by bicycle tires,
over and over, without a flaw. Her vine-
borne flowering marginalia (flowering now

in the ever-widening margins of memory).
The up-early privacy of a house at dawn;
a jigsaw puzzle, disarranged, arranging
into evergreen leaves on a holly tree (the
quick bird-movements of her slender hands).
The window she'd look in each time
we'd pass the Home for Retarded Children.

A doll whose name changed day by day,
and an imaginary friend she called "Applause."
My feeling (no doubt hopelessly tinged
with how, were she here, her looks alone
would resist my attempts to say these things)
that all of this was already lost, even then.
The Palace of Nowhere. L'Hôtel de Dream.

The returns of writing an elegy are many: an elegy may engender deeper understanding, begin a process of consolation, or generate peace and acceptance for both the writer and the reader as "Elegy for My Sister" begins to do. Written in three seven-line stanzas, Sherod Santos' poem begins with fragments of memory—seven full stops (periods)—and builds—three full stops in the second stanza, four if you count the colon—to a longer, complicated, two-sentence final stanza with parenthetical explanation that tries to make sense of the loss of the speaker's sister. In a way, this poem's structural movement echoes how our memories work: examining bits and pieces of the past and assembling them into comprehensible wholes.

Elegies offer our explanations of the world to others. For instance, in "Spring and Fall," Gerard Manley Hopkins addresses a child who is just beginning to understand that life must coexist with death. In "When You Are Old," W. B. Yeats' speaker maintains that love or a lover's time on earth may be over, but the lover will always remember the loved one and the time of love, especially because this speaker has written love poems that commemorate Maud Gonne, the woman he is addressing. (Those not familiar with Yeats' poems will find it profitable—and romantic—to look up the poet and Maud Gonne in reference books or on the Web.) Robert Frost's poem "In Hardwood Groves" reminds us to consider the patterns of the life we live. You also see in these poems why the elegy is considered a thematic form. It can be cast in stanzas or in free verse, but the formal impulse at work is the movement from loss to consolation, even if present-day consolation takes the bleak ironic hues of contemporary experience. These poems map a portion of the emotional landscape that can trigger the redemptive powers of the elegy as we explore our desire to understand and reconcile ourselves to life.

Spring and Fall
GERARD MANLEY HOPKINS
To a Young Child

Margaret, are you grieving
Over Goldengrove unleaving?
Leaves, like the things of man, you
With your fresh thoughts care for, can you?

Ah! as the heart grows older
It will come to such sights colder
By and by, nor spare a sigh
Though worlds of wanwood leafmeal lie;
And yet you will weep and know why.
Now no matter, child, the name:
Sorrow's springs are the same.
Nor mouth had, no nor mind, expressed
What heart heard of, ghost guessed:
It is the blight man was born for,
It is Margaret you mourn for.

When You Are Old
WILLIAM BUTLER YEATS

When you are old and grey and full of sleep,
And nodding by the fire, take down this book,
And slowly read, and dream of the soft look
Your eyes had once, and of their shadows deep;

How many loved your movements of glad grace,
And loved your beauty with love false or true,
But one man loved the pilgrim soul in you,
And loved the sorrows of your changing face;

And bending down beside the glowing bars,
Murmur, a little sadly, how Love fled
And paced upon the mountains overhead
And hid his face amid a crowd of stars.

In Hardwood Groves
ROBERT FROST

The same leaves over and over again!
They fall from giving shade above
To make one texture of faded brown
And fit the earth like a leather glove.

Before the leaves can mount again
To fill the trees with another shade,
They must go down past things coming up.
They must go down into the dark decayed.

They *must* be pierced by flowers and put
Beneath the feet of dancing flowers.
However it is in some other world
I know that this is the way in ours.

Certainly three poems can't completely define the variations available to a thematic form; they just start our conversation. Since the elegy is meditative, it readily takes many shapes. But that's also what is freeing about the elegy: you can draft poems that are elegy-like, or you can even use your poem philosophically, to define the elegy as William Stafford and Donald Justice do.

A Lecture on the Elegy ❖
WILLIAM STAFFORD

An elegy is really about the wilting of a flower,
the passing of the year, the falling of a stone.
Those people who go out, they just accompany
many things that leave us. Death is only
bad because it is like sunset, or a long eclipse.
If it had a dawn for company, or came with
spring, we would need laws to keep eager people
from rushing into danger and thus depopulating the world.

So, I have turned the occasion for such sadness
around: those graceful images that
seem to decorate the poems, they are
a rediscovery of those elements
that first created the obvious feelings,
the feelings that some people cannot even sense
until they are built up from little losses
and surrounded with labels: "war," "catastrophe," "death."

An Elegy Is Preparing Itself ❖
DONALD JUSTICE

There are pines that are tall enough
Already. In the distance,
The whining of saws; and needles,
Silently slipping through the chosen cloth.
The stone, then as now, unfelt,
Perfectly weightless. And certain words,
That will come together to mourn,
Waiting, in their dark clothes, apart.

∽ READING INTO WRITING ∽

1. In contemporary western cultures, it's becoming increasingly rare that we die at home or that we become accustomed to or intimate with ceremonies for dealing with death. Do some freewriting about several of the following; after freewriting you might also choose to research burial rites in other cultures:

    a. the death of people, animals, and places in your life;

    b. funerals you've attended; ceremonies you've seen or learned about from other cultures that differ from your own culture's ways of marking death and loss;

    c. the way you've envisioned your own death—the notes you would leave to family telling them what to do and how to celebrate your passing;

    d. things that are mysterious to you or hard to understand—the death of a child, the loss of a father, and the movement away from you, perhaps unexplained, of a lover.

2. Consider the positive aspects of death, loss, change. Are there any? If so, what are they? If not, why do people say things like, "It's better this way" or "It was meant to be" or "He/she is happier now?" How can you reconcile the loss of someone or something with your own continued survival? How do you see yourself or others you know doing this?

3. When did you first understand death? When did you first understand that someone or something wouldn't return? How did you deal with this understanding, which you may still be trying to understand? List three moments of major loss in your life or your family's life. Are there recurrent patterns?

4. Think of consolation—as a concept and a practice. Where do you go for consolation? What do you need to have happen in order to feel consoled? Do you find it in nature, religion, another person? Do you find it in yourself, your understanding of history, biology, destiny, or evolution?

5. In a group, use this definition of an elegy to freewrite your own response to Stafford and Justice. How do the poets' definitions and the encyclopedic definition agree or disagree?

    > Traditionally the functions of the elegy were three, to lament, praise and console. All are responses to the experience of loss: lament by expressing grief and deprivation; praise, by idealizing the deceased and preserving her or his memory among the living; and consolation, by finding solace in meditation on natural continuances or on moral, metaphysical, and religious values.
    > —Alex Preminger and T. V. F. Brogan, 324

LOSING AND FINDING FAMILY

As a parent, I can imagine no worse loss than the loss of a child. And the loss of a family member (blood kin or family by marriage, adoption, or affection) strikes us dumb, makes us scream, and drives us to try to understand why *this* has happened to *us*. In the poem "Mid-Term Break," Seamus Heaney memorializes in an indirect manner, offering us puzzle pieces to the speaker's loss, whereas Sherod Santos' "Elegy for My Sister" addresses the loss more directly. You might ask yourself (as a technique to borrow for yourself) how you construct the person who has died from the clues Heaney provides. How does the distance created by this effect work on your understanding and emotions? Does the stanza format (tercets, which are discussed further in chapter 13) seem appropriate in any particular way for this poem? Consider also how Heaney uses off rhyme. Since the loss of a family member is a great but inevitable tragedy, all who discuss such loss risk oversentimentalizing their subject. How does that happen or get avoided in the poems you read in this section?

Mid-Term Break
SEAMUS HEANEY

I sat all morning in the college sick bay
Counting bells knelling classes to a close.
At two o'clock our neighbours drove me home.

In the porch I met my father crying—
He had always taken funerals in his stride—
And Big Jim Evans saying it was a hard blow.

The baby cooed and laughed and rocked the pram
When I came in, and I was embarrassed
By old men standing up to shake my hand

And tell me they were 'sorry for my trouble'.
Whispers informed strangers I was the eldest,
Away at school, as my mother held my hand

In hers and coughed out angry tearless sighs.
At ten o'clock the ambulance arrived
With the corpse, stanched and bandaged by the nurses.

Next morning I went up into the room. Snowdrops
And candles soothed the bedside; I saw him
For the first time in six weeks. Paler now,

Wearing a poppy bruise on his left temple,
He lay in the four-foot box as in his cot.
No gaudy scars, the bumper knocked him clear.

A four-foot box, a foot for every year.

Andrew Hudgins, on the other hand, prepares an elegy before the fact—one that explores loss before loss, allowing the speaker to explore his relationship to his and his father's beliefs. As you did with "Mid-Term Break," consider how the single stanza and line lengths and enjambment in this poem affect your reading.

Elegy for My Father, Who Is Not Dead
ANDREW HUDGINS

One day I'll lift the telephone
and be told my father's dead. He's ready.
In the sureness of his faith, he talks
about the world beyond this world
as though his reservations have
been made. I think he wants to go,
a little bit—a new desire
to travel building up, an itch
to see fresh worlds. Or older ones.
He thinks that when I follow him
he'll wrap me in his arms and laugh,
the way he did when I arrived
on earth. I do not think he's right.
He's ready. I am not. I can't
just say good-bye as cheerfully
as if he were embarking on a trip
to make my later trip go well.
I see myself on deck, convinced
his ship's gone down, while he's convinced
I'll see him standing on the dock
and waving, shouting, Welcome back.

The next three poems spend some time saying clearly whom they are about: a grandmother, a relative, and an aunt by marriage. You should also compare David Starkey's use of tercets to Seamus Heaney's and consider how Nora Roberts like Andrew Hudgins chooses not to break her poem into stanzas while Peter Stillman does. Where might Hudgins have chosen to make stanza breaks, and what would be the effect if Peter Stillman had not chosen to make stanza breaks?

Touched on the Cheek by the Tip of a Vulture's Wing
DAVID STARKEY

Even the best can't do it,
everyone told me, there's no way
to write about grandparents

without getting sentimental.
I was thinking that again
as I turned onto the country road

from Kisburg to Mars Bluff,
windows down, spring just hinting summer,
wild flowers blooming in the ditch—

white, purple, gold—my grandmother
gone for a half a year now.
I swerved slightly to miss

a 'possom crumpled on the asphalt
when a rack of feather,
big as a child, exploded

across my windshield
and circled back to the corpse,
so hungry for death

life itself was worth the risk.

John Edward's Wake
PETER STILLMAN
for Sergeant John E. Reynolds

Twice a week he walked the mile
up Woodward to Saint Joe's—
Saturdays confession, Sundays to receive—
until the final once they drove him there,
in the back door, out the front,
sun winking from the mica in the granite,
from the hearse, so this would be
a perfect day for it,
my aunts and cousins and their mothers
bright as tulips planted all around the grave,

and O I'd get to have my first glass ever
on his stoop and then another
fairy sounds beginning in my head
two uncles laughing, faces white as lilies.
Everybody then, the parlor bulged with it,
pearls flew up and down on women's chests,
my aunt Kathleen announced she'd taken off
her corset in the pantry, and the boom
of laughter made the curtains flutter.
Someone said he'd caught more crabs
than there were stars and everybody drank
to that.

He'd coast the skiff beneath the Boat Club pier
and you could see them, clinging to the pilings,
hear the timbers moan with the pull of tide,
the way the old take pain. Such grace, the net
slipped down, his knowing to the second when,
the deft flick of his wrists,
the crab encompassed by the rushing rim,
the silver wake of bubbles, drops of water stinging
my bare back. I thought about the rightness of
his name, John Edward,
how whoever lived here next, the place would be
no good without him napping on the couch.

Jane's Gifts
NORA RUTH ROBERTS

Jane gave the best gifts.
Every Christmas we would eagerly open the box.
Just the wrapping and the ties
took your breath away.
Inside on Christmas morning
would be leather wallets
when all you'd had was plastic
or a blouse you knew you'd wear for best.
She always remembered your favorite colors.
Or what set off your eyes.
Sometimes in a given year
Jane's gifts would be all I'd have
that didn't come from Sears.
She told me one Christmas
after the children had opened their just right gifts

that she and Ray had visited me
when I was three
boarded in a foster home.
They had seen my very neat little cot
with a very neat little bear
with a very neat little dresser.
They had wanted to take me in their arms.
But they hadn't.
They had talked about adopting me.
But they didn't.
For years my mother bad-mouthed
her so-called rich and uncaring doctor brother.
Quietly and thankfully I opened
Jane's richly and carefully tied gifts.
When my mother was alive, my mother was my mother.
I was not up for adoption.
Quietly, without words, now that she is gone
Jane and I have adopted each other.

➤ INVENTION EXERCISES ➤

When my father died, my sisters, stepbrothers, stepmother, and I surprised ourselves, sitting around the kitchen table, everyone with a cup of this or that, a crumbled piece of cake, and a fork, tines turned down, telling stories of "Bob" or "Dad." Suddenly, we were all laughing at a particularly good anecdote, and I remember looking around the 2 A.M. table in wonder after weeks of grief about cancer and futures. Reading Peter Stillman's poem, I experience similar waves of sweet and sorrowful emotion my family experienced that night. And in reading Andrew Hudgins' poem, I feel again the ambivalent confusion any human feels in trying to understand the future loss of a parent. You may have (or be willing to imagine) similar life experiences that will help you complete the following exercises:

1. Write your own poem with a description of a real funeral and/or wake (but invent the necessary details to make it vivid—if you don't know that anyone wore pearls, assume so-and-so did rather than say, "I can't remember").

2. If you've never been to a wake, invent one for a relative who deserved one but didn't get celebrated in this way.

3. Write an anti-elegy—what can't be mourned, or about what can't you be consoled?

4. Or send this person to heaven (your idea of heaven or a place that would be "heaven" to them) as in Hans Ostrom's poem.

5. If all this talk of loss and dying is getting you down, kick up your heels for a famous person, a hero, or a pop icon and write that person's elegy. As in exercises in other chapters, you may find his-

torical/context-setting details for this poem through an Internet
search.

6. Which path will you follow? Talking directly about a person com-
   mits you to recreating his/her life, person, or essence to some extent.
   Talking more obliquely, as Heaney does, allows the poet/speaker to
   focus on the self in relation to the loss or lost individual. Both methods surely have their uses. The following poem, about two enduring
   popular figures, gives the sense of how you might affectionately
   recuperate or celebrate the loss of people you never really knew:

Emily Dickinson and Elvis Presley in Heaven
HANS OSTROM

They call each other 'E.' Elvis picks
wildflowers near the river and brings
them to Emily. She explains half-rhymes to him.

In heaven Emily wears her hair long, wears
Levis and western blouses with rhinestones.
Elvis is lean again, wears baggy trousers

and T-shirts, a letterman's jacket from Tupelo High.
They take long walks and often hold hands.
But she prefers that they remain friends. Forever.

Emily's poems now contain naugahyde, Cadillacs,
electricity, jets, TV, Little Richard and Richard
Nixon. The rock-a-billy rhythm makes her smile.

Elvis likes himself with style. This afternoon
he will play guitar and sing "I Taste a Liquor
Never Brewed" to the tune of "Love me Tender."

Emily will clap and harmonize. Alone
in their cabins later, they will listen to the river
and nap. They will not think of Amherst

or Las Vegas. They know why God made them
roommates. It's because America
was their hometown. It's because

God is a thing without
feathers. It's because
God wears blue suede shoes.

7. For another way to get the feel of the elegy, try writing across, through, into (and maybe eventually out of) any of the elegies you've already read. Here's what happened when Jason Hooper responded to Nora Roberts' poem. He resees a relationship he had through the lens of Roberts' poem about Jane.

Ralph's Gifts*

Ralph gave the lamest gifts.
Every Christmas I would sigh and open the box.
Just the comic wrapping took the fun away.
Inside on Christmas morning
would be the latest cassettes
when I already had the CDs
or a shirt that said "Kill me!"
He never remembered my favorite color
or what he had gotten me the year before.
Sometimes, more often than not,
I'd have to return Ralph's gifts
back to the local Sears.
He told me one Christmas
after the children had disowned their just-wrong gifts
that he and Cynthia had visited me
when I was two
looked in my playpen.
They had seen my very neat little smile
with my very neat little curls
with my very neat little bib.
They had wanted children of their own.
But they couldn't.
For years my mother bad-mouthed
her so-called sick and unemployed vagrant sister.
Quietly but annoyingly I opened
Ralph's childish and last-minutely wrapped gifts.
When Ralph was alive, Ralph was Ralph.
I was never quite thankful.
Quietly, without words, now that he is gone,
Ralph and I have thanked each other.

(Imitation of Nora Roberts' poem "Jane's Gifts")

REMEMBERING TO REMEMBER

My poetry functions at times for me as a life diary. I can remember where I was sitting when I composed a certain poem, and hidden in the public text is a private text—my knowledge of what prompted me to write, how I felt, and who I thought I was at the time. In a way, an elegy can do the same work—allowing a writer to consider the implications of memory and loss. Elegies about people we've known less intimately than family members can teach us to remember to remember and teach us how not to forget, yet go on living with painful memories, as in the next three poems about a lost hunter, a lost pilot, and a lost driver. Even though accidents *do* happen, knowing about the accidental nature of our lives doesn't make accidents easier to bear—which is why, perhaps, we continue to try to understand such events through poetry. And, as in the fourth poem by Peter Meinke, people we know can live their lives like accidents about to happen—and then the accidents *do* happen. You'll notice that three of these poets choose stanzas of five or more lines, which is longer than the often-used quatrain or four-line stanza (discussed in chapter 10), while the fourth—Christianne Balk—chooses a long-lined repetitive form of the sort discussed in chapter 7.

Back by Noon
DARRELL FIKE

On the counter in the kitchen
beside a coffee cup and biscuit
with one bite gone, the note:
"Ducks are flying over Brandywine Chute.
Back by noon."

Noon, grey and blowing like January,
passed, but we laughed at our worry
sure that you were warm and dry
in your plaid hat with the ear flaps down
and your longjohns and lucky boots,
and that as soon as we began to call around
your truck would pull into the drive
with the dog barking and you home
with duck tales to tell.

But at three o'clock
the dog alone was there on the bank
looking out towards Arkansas,
and our panicked breath beat against the hardening air
as we called out across the water
your name and your name and your name.

The dog, at five o'clock, in the revolving
brightness of the emergency lights
could not tell us how the johnboat,
a shallow scoop of metal
pushing through the chute,
had lost the balance of air and water
and spilled you out,
with the wind slicing
the water into white capped peaks
like tiny mountains of ice
too slippery to climb.

And the dog could not say
if you cried out for us
and clutched at the sky,
or if you cussed and fought
against the cold stone weight
of your lucky boots
until in surrender,
while ducks were flying overhead
you hugged yourself once
and slipped below.

Elegy
CHRISTIANNE BALK

In Wainwright they say the plane went down in the Brooks Range,
    perhaps near Porcupine River, or perhaps in the Arctic Ocean;
It was spring, the rivers were breaking up, and the mist settled in for weeks.
The plane went down in March, when it rains one day and snows the next;
When the ice fields split into islands big enough to crush ships.
The plane went down in the early spring, when the snow still drifts
    in the wind, snow so fine it works into the tightest weave
    of a man's coat;
In the north, where the snow is hardened and serrated by winter
    winds, where metal sled runners wear out in days, and where men do not
    leave heel marks;
In the spring, when the winds begin to drop, when the snow turns
    soft and honeycombed, and cannot support a man's weight;
In the spring, when the winds leave, and the insects come, swarms of insects
    that can weaken a man until he cannot walk;
In the far north, where magnetic compasses are useless.

Snowshoe frames can be made of metal from plane keels, sleds
    built from wings, harnesses woven from shroud lines;
Cloudy streams of fresh water can be found; and salmon, tomcod,
    needlefish, and pike caught;
But the Brooks Range stretches from Cape Lisburne to
    Demarcation Point, and few of its mountains are mapped.
The plane went down in the north, where valley glaciers crack
    into crevasses above deep, granite beds;
In the spring, when rivers swell with melt water, when
    snowbridges are swept away, and debris dams up the streams;
In the north, where the overflow fills the flatland with shallow,
    swampy lakes.
Beaver, marmot, and ground squirrel can be trapped; and molting
    spruce grouse, arctic loon, and ptarmigan can be snared.
Bushes can be dug for the starchy roots; cup-fungus, bracken, and the inner
    white bark of willow, poplar, and birch can be eaten;
But the north is filled with rose-capped mushroom, water hemlock,
    baneberry, and amanita.
A plane crashed six years ago in the Bering Sea, in water so cold it paralyzed
    the pilot's hands, but he used his teeth to lash himself to a raft with
    ripcord.
A man went under for forty minutes in the Yukon River, but was pulled up
    breathing because the water had been just cold enough.
But masses of sea-ice crowd into the bays in the spring, colliding
    with each other and the coast, and the booming can be heard for miles.
A woman lifted an ice-wall in Kotzebue, fracturing her spine, but
    she held the ice up so her husband could crawl out.
A plane crashed near Eagle, and a woman dragged her husband from the
    fuselage, and she melted snow in her mouth, and brought it to him, until
    help came.
A Galena trapper was lost two years ago, but his wife waited, and
    pounded beef suet, berries, and bacon with a wooden mallet into
    pemmican, for his next trip out, and he was found;
But tundra streams wander aimlessly in the spring, and often lead
    to marshes filled with mosquitoes, midges, and blackflies.

*After Thunderstorms**
    Amorak Huey

On the seventh anniversary of your death,
it storms. It always rains this day,
purple-bruised clouds swelling, spitting
angry teardrops, slicing the air
with lightning. The night grows chill,

but it isn't until afterward that
the danger begins: Asphalt goes slick
as oil, ditches fill with water,
muddy, cold, rushing. After is when
dampness stalled your car, forced

you, late, to ask for a ride home.
And he said yes, goddamn him, goddamn
him because he was trying to be friendly
but he drove too fast, too fast
around that last curve before the turnoff.

Every year on this day I imagine
tires sliding, screaming, fighting, losing
their grip on the road, and that moment
when you must have known exactly
what was happening to you.

Elegy for a Diver
PETER MEINKE
—*for R. W.*

Jackknife swandive gainer twist
high off the board you'd pierce the sky
& split the apple of the devil sun
& spit in the sun's fierce eye.
When you were young you never missed,
archer-diver who flew too high
so everything later became undone.

Later everything burned to ash
wings too close to the sun broke down
jackknife swandive gainer twist
can't be done on the ground
and nothing in your diver's past
had warned you that a diver drowns
when nothing replaces what is missed.

Everything beautiful falls away
jackknife swandive gainer twist
muscles drop and skin turns coarse
even skin the sun has kissed.
You drank the sun down every day
until the sun no longer existed
, and only the drink had any force.

Only the drink had any force
archer-diver who flew too high
when you were young you never missed
& spit in the sun's fierce eye.

➤ INVENTION EXERCISES ➤

1. Choose a tragedy from the local newspaper or TV news or Internet
   news and write an elegy that respects this loss but teaches you
   and/or your reader and tries to reconcile you to life. Use the actual
   reported details to make meaning and to tell yourself what you think
   about this and similar events.

2. In Peter Meinke's poem we suspect the tragedy was long-coming and
   happened to someone the speaker knew well. Write your own elegy
   for someone you know whose life in your opinion might have been
   misspent. Before you do, look at the complicated way Meinke con-
   structs his poem: from informal punctuation (using "&" for *and*) to
   the invented words, repeating lines, short final stanza, and so on.

3. Explore any guilt you may feel about the loss of something or someone. (All of us have moments when we say, "If only I had averted
   this tragedy by . . . .") Perhaps you want to write a person out of an
   accident, take them down a different path, or . . . ? Before doing
   this, consider W. H. Auden's often-anthologized poem about suffering and tragedy and how they often happen just out of sight, as
   when the speaker of this poem contemplates a painting, *The Fall of
   Icarus*, by the Dutch painter Pieter Brueghel that portrays Icarus and
   his father Daedalus. (You might also look at the original myth and
   use it to read Meinke's poem or look for Web sites that list the poem
   and the painting.)

Musée des Beaux Arts
W. H. AUDEN

About suffering they were never wrong,
The Old Masters: how well they understood
Its human position; how it takes place
While someone else is eating or opening a window or just walking dully
     along;
How, when the aged are reverently, passionately waiting
For the miraculous birth, there always must be
Children who did not specially want it to happen, skating

On a pond at the edge of the wood:
They never forgot
That even the dreadful martyrdom must run its course
Anyhow in a corner, some untidy spot
Where the dogs go on with their doggy life and the torturer's horse
Scratches its innocent behind on a tree.

In Brueghel's *Icarus,* for instance: how everything turns away
Quite leisurely from the disaster; the plowman may
Have heard the splash, the forsaken cry,
But for him it was not an important failure; the sun shone
As it had to on the white legs disappearing into the green
Water; and the expensive delicate ship that must have seen
Something amazing, a boy falling out of the sky,
Had somewhere to get to and sailed calmly on.

4. Three of these elegies relate individuals to the landscape. Do the same in your own elegy as Pat MacEnulty does in "St. Mark's Elegy" about a day at a wildlife refuge near Tallahassee, Florida.

*St. Mark's Elegy**

St. Mark's Wildlife Refuge:
honeycomb hedge
in the middle of the path, yellow
and bright. The dog pants
hard behind us,
sniffing the heat.
Eastern kingbird,
black with white trim,
a clerical sort of bird,
keeps a watchful eye on us,
as we check to make sure
the alligator is still lodged
in the mud, and not edging
toward the dog
collapsing in the shade.
We stop to admire the
white bracketed sedge,
not morning glory
but a distant cousin.
The lyre-leaf sage
is everywhere,
small purple bursts of color.

A great blue heron rises
from the swamps
the dog wags his tail.
The alligator's eyes are closed,
or so we imagine.

It would have been
the perfect day
if not for the bird
that flew in front
of my fast-going truck
on the way home.

THE MOCK-SERIOUS ELEGY:
LOSING ANIMALS AND ATTRIBUTES

If you smiled when Hans Ostrom's poem paired Elvis and Emily in heaven, you're ready to move from the heavy-hearted elegy to the mock-serious elegy. We all know humor and sadness are closely related feelings (much like love and hate)—the woman who slips on the banana peel slips to make us laugh, and the man makes fun of his own phobias to make us laugh. In the same way, mocking our own tendency to despair, creating send-ups of our very strong feelings through humorous verse, can provide an effective means to defuse pain. The next four poets composed elegies on animate creatures (a canary, a mouse, snails, and caterpillars) and an attribute (the state of being innocent). In their poems, we continue to learn about the human condition, for there is always a kernel of seriousness in the mocking, light wordplay. We also learn that sometimes taking our medicine with sugar is necessary. As always, you'll want to spend some time thinking about the formal elements of these thematic poems: tercets, free verse, and in the case of Sandra McPherson's poem, a two-part poem. (For more on poems in parts, see chapter 6.)

Little Elegy
DONALD JUSTICE

Weep, all you girls
Who prize good looks and song.
Mack, the canary, is dead.

A girl very much like you
Kept him by her twelve months
Close as a little brother.

He perched where he pleased,
Hopped, chirping, from breast to breast,
And fed, sometimes, pecking from her mouth.

O lucky bird! But death
Plucks from the air even
The swiftest, the most favored.

Red are the eyes of his mistress now.
On us, her remaining admirers,
They do not yet quite focus.

—After Catullus

Mouse Elegy
SHARON OLDS

After he petted his mouse awhile,
Gabriel said "He's really still,
he doesn't move at all," running his
small finger over the tiny
luxurious black and white back,
and then in awe and shock he said "He's—
dead." I lifted him out of his cage in his
bed, a brown-rice box, and Gabey
turned and turned his chest as if
struggling to get unstrapped from something,
twisting and twisting from the waist up and then
trying to get ahold of me
several times as if he couldn't, as
if something was holding him by the body but
finally it broke, he came into my arms,
I said whatever you say then,
My darling, my sweetheart.
We got a hanky with roses on it and
laid it on the kitchen floor and laid
Blackie on it. He drifted there like a
long comma,
front paws, pink and tiny as
chips of broken crockery, held
up in wonder, like a shepherd at the Christ Child's
crèche; back paws strong as a jackrabbit's
thrust back in mid-leap; and the
thick whisker of the tail arrested in a
lovely male curve. We kneeled on

either side of the miniature head,
wedge-shaped and white, floating there with an
air of calm absence and demanding dreams.
I started to roll up the hanky, rocking the
light body a little, and one of his
ears unfurled, a grey petal
opening slowly in the night, and then we
wrapped Blackie in red roses and
paper towels, Gabe laid him in the glossy
black box lined with crimson
the champagne came in, we put it in the freezer
until we could take him to the country and crack the
frozen ground with axes so Blackie can
lie with the others in the earth, in a field of mice.

Elegies for the Hot Season
SANDRA MCPHERSON

1. The Killing of the Snails

Half the year has hot nights, like this,
When gnats fly thick as stars, when the temperature is taken
On the tongues of flowers and lovers,
When the just-dead is buried in warm sod.
The snail-pebbled lawns glimmer with slime trails, and the unworried,
Unhurried snail tucks into his dark knuckle, stockaded
With spears of grass, safe. When I first heard
The sound of his dying, it was like knuckles cracking.

The lightest foot can slay snails. Their shells break
More easily than mirrors. And like bad luck, like
A face in a mirror, they always come back.

Good hunting nights were stuffy as a closed room.
No moon shone but my father's flashlight.
As if it were Jericho, he circled the house,
And I'd hear all evening the thick crunch
Of his marching, the sound of death due
To his size 13 shoe.

In the morning I'd find them, little clots on the grass, pretend
They'd been singed by geranium fire-bursts, asphyxiated by blue
Iris flame, burnt to shadows under the strawberry blossom.
The fuchsias bled for them. White-throated calla lilies
Maintained appearances above the snail slum.

But the slow-brained pests forgave and fragilely claimed the garden
The next hot season, like old friends, or avengers.

2. The Killing of the Caterpillars

Today I watch our neighbor celebrating May,
Ringing round the besieged cherry-tree,
His haunted maypole, brandishing his arson's torch
Through the tents of caterpillars. He plays conductor,
Striking his baton for the May music.
And the soft, fingery caterpillars perform,
Snap, crackle, pop.

They plummet through a holiday of leaves like fireworks or shooting stars or
    votive candles
Or buttercups, under the hex of the neighbor's wand, first fruits of
    euthanasia,
Ripe and red before the cherries. And it is over,
Grown cold as a sunset. They lie on the grass
Still and black as those who lie under it.

It is night. Lights burn in the city
Like lamps of a search-party, like the search-beam
Of my father's flashlight, at every swing discovering
Death.

Elegy for My Innocence
STEPHEN DUNN

You always stumbled in,
came out smelling
not quite like a rose.

Your most repeated gesture:
the blush.
You didn't know how to hide.

I do not miss you, but experience
is the guest
who only knows how to stay.

You, at least, were built to go,
which is why you can be loved.
I remember everything you craved.

Interesting, how you were diminished
by whatever you got. Sex,
knowledge, you kept going up in flames.

Each year you became
a little more dangerous,
eyes wide, the same poor reflexes

for pain. I last saw you
in Texas, 1963. No need by then
for a goodbye. Yet I've heard

that at the end of a long passage,
a lifetime, something like you exists,
terrifying and desirable,

and that no one who hasn't sinned
ever arrives. Innocence,
we could be such friends

if that were so. I'd start out now
if I didn't know
the lies told in your name.

━ INVENTION EXERCISES ━

1. In a group make a list of attributes like innocence that you might
   want to elegize. Use the most provocative on the list and do so. Or
   everyone can agree on the same attribute and write poems for comparison.

2. In his poem, David Starkey claims that it's impossible to write about
   grandparents without getting sentimental. Some writers feel the
   same holds true for animals. Make a list of animals and pets you lost
   and then try to write a nonsentimental serious elegy and then a
   humorous version.

3. Another way to do this might be to elegize a normally maligned
   creature that you've just eradicated—the fly, the flea, the cockroach,
   or unexpected lifeforms such as the penicillin mold, or a lost and/or
   endangered plant or animal. If your poem is not directly humorous,
   you may find that irony serves you well here.

4. Stylistically, you might try the direct, second person "you" address
   of Dunn's poem or the complicated double vision of Olds and
   Justice—mother talking to/for son and/or ironic observer making
   affectionate fun over the grief of one little girl (or of grief itself).

5. In terms of technique these poets vary tremendously, from Justice's and Dunn's three-line stanzas to Olds' and McPherson's free verse—one without stanza breaks, the other in two parts with stanzas; one with short lines, one with long lines; one with a heavier reliance than the other on rhyme). Analyze each poem for its technical attributes and then choose three or four of the most striking techniques for this type of poem and incorporate them intentionally into your elegy.

MEDITATION ON LOVE: THE AUBADE

An **aubade** (also known as an alba) is a dawn song. Traditionally, the dawn song belonged to parting lovers, the poem expressing regret that dawn has come to part them, as in the parting of Romeo and Juliet. In some of the following poems, the morning parting has broadened to the more general sense of "after," as in after lovemaking, after being together, or after domestic intimacies. And the tenor of such a poem can fluctuate from sensual and celebratory to lost and tragic. The sense of time passing that is often accentuated in the thematic form of an aubade relates it to the elegy since an aubade is a celebration of what no longer is or can be, an attempt to reconcile the heart with changes of heart.

William Shakespeare's Romeo and Juliet are not only the world's most famous lovers, but they also have one of the most well-known scenes of parting. Their dawn song takes place in act 3, scene 5 as Romeo leaves Juliet. First Juliet tries to argue that it is not really dawn: "It was the nightingale, and not the lark,/That pierc'd the fearful hollow of thine ear." Then Romeo too resists the coming day, complaining that the dawn is jealous of their love: "what envious streaks/Do lace the severing clouds in yonder east." While he knows he must go, he offers to stay and die. Wanting him to stay, Juliet tries to convince herself again that it is not dawn. And Romeo, the eager lover, gives himself over to the self-deception: "Come, death, and welcome! Juliet wills it so./How is't, my soul? Let's talk; it is not day." Finally Juliet has to face the truth: it is dawn, and the lovers must part: "O now be gone! More light and light it grows." And Romeo replies, foreshadowing the coming tragedy: "More light and light, more dark and dark our woes!"

The seventeenth century aubade "The Sun Rising" by John Donne is far less tragic but ultimately no less moving. Wryly serious, the lover asks the sun to go away and let him and his love stay in the bedroom instead of calling them out to the work of the world. "The Sun Rising" also offers fine examples of several traditional poetic devices: **apostrophe**—direct address to the sun, **hyperbole**—she is all states and he is all the rulers of those states: no other loves are as important as their love; **metaphysical conceit**—used particularly often in seventeenth century poems like this one where the lover is in mock-battle with the power of the sun and is claiming, because of the strength of his love, that he has or should have dominion over the sun; **personification**—the sun is a court fool or jester and a "Saucy pedantic wretch"; and **synecdoche**—beams stand for the heat and force of the sun: "I could eclipse and cloud them," a claim that the poet's love eclipses the strength of the sun itself. Notice the complicated play of stanza and line lengths in this poem.

The Sun Rising
JOHN DONNE

> Busy old fool, unruly sun,
> Why dost thou thus,
> Through windows, and through curtains, call on us?
> Must to thy motions lovers' seasons run?
> Saucy pedantic wretch, go chide
> Late schoolboys, and sour prentices,
> Go tell court-huntsmen that the king will ride,
> Call country ants to harvest offices;
> Love, all alike, no season knows, nor clime,
> Nor hours, days, months, which are the rags of time.
>
> Thy beams, so reverend and strong
> Why shouldst thou think?
> I could eclipse and cloud them with a wink,
> But that I would not lose her sight so long:
> If her eyes have not blinded thine,
> Look, and tomorrow late, tell me
> Whether both the Indias of spice and mine
> Be where thou left'st them, or lie here with me.
> Ask for those kings whom thou saw'st yesterday,
> And thou shalt hear, all here in one bed lay.
>
> She is all states, and all princes I,
> Nothing else is.
> Princes do but play us; compared to this,
> All honor's mimic, all wealth alchemy.
> Thou, sun, art half as happy as we,
> In that the world's contracted thus;
> Thine age asks ease, and since thy duties be
> To warm the world, that's done in warming us.
> Shine here to us, and thou art every where;
> This bed thy center is, these walls thy sphere.

In Timothy Steele's poem "An Aubade," morning is implied at first by the lover waking and hearing the shower and then detailing the numerous particulars of the scene as dawn light makes clearer parts of the scene that will deliver him into another day. This is a classic aubade moment as he decides to delay rising in order to have one more view of his lover. Notice in this poem and those that follow the way stanzas are used: in Steele's a five-line stanza and in Richard Wilbur's and Marilyn Chin's a four-line stanza, one rhymed, one not, and in Marilyn Hacker's poem, no stanza breaks. How does line length, enjambment, and end-stopping play out in each narrative?

An Aubade
TIMOTHY STEELE

As she is showering, I wake to see
A shine of earrings on the bedside stand,
A single yellow sheet which, over me,
Has folds as intricate as drapery
In paintings from some fine old master's hand.

The pillow which, in dozing, I embraced
Retains the salty sweetness of her skin;
I sense her smooth back, buttocks, belly, waist,
The leggy warmth which spread and gently laced
Around my legs and loins, and drew me in.

I stretch and curl about a bit and hear her
Singing among the water's hiss and race.
Gradually the early light makes clearer
The perfume bottles by the dresser's mirror,
The silver flashlight, standing on its face,

Which shares the corner of the dresser with
An ivy spilling tendrils from a cup.
And so content am I, I can forgive
Pleasure for being brief and fugitive.
I'll stretch some more, but postpone getting up

Until she finishes her shower and dries
(Now this and now that foot placed on a chair)
Her fineboned ankles, and her calves and thighs,
The pink full nipples of her breasts, and ties
Her towel up, turban-style, about her hair.

Marilyn Hacker's aubade is loving and sensual, but the scene is more chaotic as the two women who are lovers sort through the tasks of taking care of their child and child's friend and still strive to maintain the erotic intensity that will deliver them to bed and to each other. The narrator lets us see this by alluding to two famous love poems (by W. B. Yeats and Omar Khayyam) and having the women share food. In a sense, this poem is about desire rather than satisfaction, as suggested by the title "Almost Aubade."

Almost Aubade
MARILYN HACKER

The little hours: two lovers herd upstairs
two children, one of whom is one of theirs.
Past them, two of the other sex lope down,
dressed for mid-winter cruising bars in brown
bomber-jackets—their lives as uncluttered
as their pink shaven cheeks, one of us muttered,
fumbling with keys. Yes, they did look alike.
Hooking their scarves and parkas on the bike,
the seven-year-old women shuck a heap
of velvet jeans and Mary Janes. They sleep
diagonal, instantly, across the top
bunk, while their exhausted elders drop,
not to the bliss breasts melt to against breasts
yet, but to kitchen chairs. One interests
herself in omelets, listening anyhow.
It's certain that fine women pick at food.
A loaf of bread, a jug of wine, and thou
shalt piecemeal total both, gripped in that mood
whose hunger makes a contrapuntal stutter
across connectives. Unwrap cheese, find butter,
dip bread crusts in a bowl of pasta sauce
saved from the children's supper. Tired because
of all we should stay up to say, we keep
awake together often as we sleep
together. I'll clear the plates. Leave your cup.
Lie in my arms until the kids get up.

Richard Wilbur's aubade develops in seven quatrains, rhyming *abba*. His use of rhyme, choice of first-person narration, and use of rhetorical questions emphasize the irony of this poem.

A Late Aubade
RICHARD WILBUR

You could be sitting now in a carrel
Turning some liver-spotted page,
Or rising in an elevator-cage
Toward Ladies' Apparel.

You could be planting a raucous bed
Of salvia, in rubber gloves,
Or lunching through a screed of someone's loves
With pitying head,

Or making some unhappy setter
Heel, or listening to a bleak
Lecture on Schoenberg's serial technique.
Isn't this better?

Think of the time you are not
Wasting, and would not care to waste,
Such things, thank God, not being to your taste.
Think what a lot

Of time, by woman's reckoning,
You've saved, and so may spend on this,
You who had rather lie in bed and kiss
Than anything.

It's almost noon, you say? If so,
Time flies, and I need not rehearse
The rosebuds-theme of centuries of verse.
If you *must* go,

Wait for a while, then slip downstairs
And bring us up some chilled white wine,
And some blue cheese, and crackers, and some fine
Ruddy-skinned pears.

Marilyn Chin's poem has a strongly elegiac feel to it. Note the long line that begins the third stanza and echoes the length of the horizon she is mentioning. Do you find this technique—where form aims to underline meaning—effective or not? You might compare her use of unrhymed quatrains to Wilbur's. Consider too what happens to you as a reader as you overhear the poem's speaker talk to a lover. How do you piece together this couple's history, and how do you read yourself into this poem (if you do)?

Aubade
MARILYN CHIN

The candle that would not burn
will never share its glory.

Waking is this easy:
Sunday; Haunauma Bay, your birthday,
and we—too comfortable to notice
the sea forging inward,

that before the picture window
our special pine, dwarfed and hunched
through decades of seastorm and salty air,
has uprooted to die in the rain.

And in our sleep, the years have proceeded toward the horizon
like a school of uninteresting driftwood
or tortoises plodding disconsolately
to find what lurks at the edge.

What lurks there might be disaster:
the charred aftermath of Rome and Cathay, or
more deceptive, a sea of new aquatic flora
bathed in eternal dawn light.

But today as clouds give way to sunshine,
we wake as tourists of yet another decade.
Our tongues stale with last night's lovemaking,
our eyes bleared with tomorrow's dreams.

For now, let each candle gutter, as they do
and celebrate earth's mundane surprises:
family, lovers, friends,
clams in the mudflat for the taking.

I composed "Dawn Song" to investigate the aubade right after I learned about this thematic form one day by skimming through a poetic dictionary. In the poem, I fit event to definition in order to explore a relationship, and the poem appears as a letter from the speaker to the lover, whom the speaker reluctantly leaves early one morning.

Dawn Song ❖
WENDY BISHOP
Capay Valley, California

Aubade, I read, any lyric
Suggesting morning,
So I write to you:

"It was hard to leave
so early and in the dark.
I lifted the covers and rose
Into the coatish weight
Of predawn: moist in nostril,
Heavy in bone, chains
On the dogs clinking
And raw snorts
As they waited outdoors
Eager to bay at the new sun.

"I waited too, propped up in bed,
Halfway in, halfway out,
Toes in the nether world,
Frosted still by sleep,
One hand benedicting your hair.
I heard the bats nesting
In gunny sacks, flat
And rotten, that hung
Along the ridgepole of the barn.
They chittered and flapped.
Darkness eased by a hue.

"It was hard to imagine
Bats nesting,
Folding and stroking
Their leaf-rough skin.
Passion: straw bones,
The clutch of attenuate hands.
'The only mammals
With the power of true flight.'
Giving up mammal heaviness
For a stringy dance,
A sonar loop-the-loop.

"When I started the car
And turned into the road,
Low beams on,
Bats flattened in the headlights,
Arrowheads without shafts.
I saw the skin cased fingers,
The free sweeping claws
Raised as if to say,
'Someday, you too.'
I saw them disintegrate,
Caught between the lamps
And the first flashes of morning.
They seemed to carry my heart
With them, into the day's shadows,
As I took the next curve."

Laurie McLeod composed an aubade with double vision: it is a poem about lovers parting, but in it the speaker is already aware that such partings often lead to distance. Readers are able to see that the kiss is not as simple as it seems and sounds.

*Nocturnal Tryst**

Afterwards in the kitchen
I drink a glass of water and you
put one hand on my neck.
Something is whispered
but I don't know what I said.
It is six a.m. and the sun is calling
as it creeps through
the line of the parted curtains.
I lean forward and you kiss me
and I walk down the hall to my bed.
I love this part because it is simple
and grey.
There are no colored lies
no morning afters,
not yet.

━ INVENTION EXERCISES ━

1. Imagine (and investigate) the dawn parting of (in)famous lovers in story and history: Samson and Delilah, Anthony and Cleopatra, the Duke and Duchess of Windsor, Gertrude Stein and Alice B. Toklas, Tarzan and Jane, Bonnie and Clyde, and so on. Write a dawn song for them, either as one character to another (first person) or as a

literary omniscient observer (third person). Since this exercise could so easily fall into parody, try a serious version first. Let your poem explore why these couples have remained vivid in popular imagination.

2. Write your real aubade about a moment of leaving a real scene of love. Of course, you don't always have to leave a lover to be shaped by the act of parting. You might transform the form by writing about leaving a landscape or a point in your life.

3. Again, turn expectation on its head, as Marilyn Hacker does, and write about women who love or about a parent who regrets parting with a child's youth, broadening your definition of love. Or write a dawn song about fraternal, maternal, paternal, or religious love, or about friendship. Also consider the love of learning, of language, of life. The dawn song form argues that all love has moments of turning away and time passing (and changing all love relations if only momentarily). Let your poem explore any of this.

This chapter closes with a bouquet of aubades that will offer you some drafting inspiration. These dawn songs talk about: finding your lover gone, happiness and praise, the moments we wake to our children's lives and both mourn and celebrate the passing of every growing cell that composes them, the times when lovemaking opens us into new life understandings, and the times when we stand marveling at what has just happened. All that and more happens in these poems. Because they are meditative and expansive thematic spaces, the elegy and the aubade present thirteen times thirteen options for forming your own poems. Make some of these discoveries and moves your own.

Aubade*
Michelle Liles

He left this morning, one sock
crumpled in palm as he filled the
buttonholes in his jeans.

She was asleep, not aware of
loss so silent and quick. The alarm
went off at eight, "Got to get you into

my life," it said until she slapped it,
warm with plugged-in music heat and hum.
Stretching,

pulling T-shirt over thighs, she thinks
he's making coffee. In the kitchen,
the pot's cold, parched, empty.

No note on pillow—just a brown sock
folded in on itself, nesting at the
foot of the bed, poking through covers.

French Quarter Kiss
        Darrell Fike

Sweet and sticky
beignets from the Cafe
du Monde do powder
our mouths with sugar,
French roast and chickory
sipped 2:00 a.m. tenderly, au lait.

On the curb at Jackson Square
a man with a fat telescope
hawks a $2 moon,
a buck more, a turn of the crank
and comet-kissed Saturn,
dizzy rings and all, comes into view.

From the river-licked levee
along Decatur a paddleboat splashes,
the smokestack light the only
star left to wish upon as day breaks,
and with pralines in our pockets
we share a last French Quarter kiss.

After Love
ROBIN BEHN

Tonight, after love, our bodies so recently
returned to us, we lie apart awhile

and let the cold touch us
along the sudden boundaries of skin.

I can almost see above us where the air holds on
to some idea of us, the shape of our clear bodies—.

Once, two starlings got into my room.
From under my bed I saw them printing

their hard bodies in the shafts of sun
till the room was gorged with the image of those wings;

then there was only air
rasping air, my father's cleared throat, the black

birds knocked down.
This air

lies down on us. The weight
of my body lies down in me, lies down.

You slide an old song from its paper sleeve
and hold the black coin to the lamp.

And before it circles beneath the diamond needle
I can hear a few bars, playing

far off, where what's marred
seems beautiful—

Then our window takes on the open-eyed stare
of a musician playing wholly for herself,

testing notes off the walls
to find the shape of that body she's entered

in the dark. In that other
filled room

the birds are shoveled out,
the walls scrubbed clean of blood.

Here, the music heals the air. Tiny veins
beneath your lids finally turn their blue backs:

I see you scanning the private
constellations as you sleep, connecting lamp

to lamp as your one body moves up the lighted street,
getting itself home before you wake.

My Place
STEPHEN SANDY

—My loft, and how
you came

over letting your coat go
as if it was your room

already! And what I was
doing there is

not clear
to me—now—nor

why I am
standing here dumb

lips shaping amazing words
that fall forth duds.

Breathless, my pulse
is doing a waltz

through this room
and very same

"bachelor apartment" air
where, O, you were.

POCKET DEFINITIONS

Apostrophe—A direct address, often to someone or something that is not there; originally a dramatic term that meant a turning away from the general audience to address a particular audience, present or absent.

Aubade—A poem, also called an alba, that is literally a dawn song where the lover regrets the coming of daylight and inevitable separation of the lovers. The aubade doesn't have a fixed form but can be in the form of a dialogue, or a speaker may address the loved one.

Elegy—A meditative commemorative poem on the loss of a loved one or to mark the passing of a person of fame or importance. Modern elegies can also mourn the death of love or possibilities, the loss of family members, landscapes, and, often more humorously, animals and personal attributes.

Hyperbole—Bold, often ironic exaggeration. We don't expect our claims to be taken literally, but we do expect our exaggeration to draw attention to our point rather ostentatiously, when we claim, for instance, that our love is the truest, deepest, best.

Metaphysical Conceit—John Donne, George Herbert, Andrew Marvell, and their seventeenth century contemporaries have been termed metaphysical poets because their metaphors are often highly intellectual and complicated and detailed, requiring meditation by the reader to unpack the metaphor's possibilities as in the John Donne poem "The Sun Rising" where the lover is in mock-battle with the power of the sun and claiming, because of the strength of his love, that he has, or should have, dominion over the sun.

Personification—A rhetorical technique where animals, concepts, or inanimate objects are given human attributes, such as when we claim a tree sways in the wind like a dancer or the sun is a hard taskmaster.

Synecdoche—One part standing for the whole: sunbeams, for example, standing for the heat and force of the sun, or an individual standing for a group.

5

GHAZALS AND PANTOUMS
Inhabiting Another Language

from *Ghazal VI*
GHALIB

Thousands of strangled urges lurk in my silence;
I am a votive lamp no one ever lighted.

from *Ghazal*
AGHA SHAHID ALI

The sky is stunned, it's become a ceiling of stone.
I tell you it must weep. So kneel, pray for rain in Arabic.

The **ghazal**, a Persian form that is also found in Arabic, Urdu, and Turkish literature, is generally composed of five to twelve loosely related couplets, often mystical and/or melancholy in tone, often on the subject of love, and traditionally united by the same rhyme at the end of each couplet. The form was taken up by German Romantic poets and then again by late twentieth century poets.

The **pantoum** (or pantun) was originally a couplet/quatrain form in Malayan poetry (with the rhyme scheme of *abab*) but was transformed into a repeating form in English after being popularized and regularized in France in the nineteenth century. Generally, English-language pantoums are composed in four-line stanzas; lines two and four become lines six and eight of the next stanza, and so on. The pantoum is generally at least four stanzas long, and there is no set rhyme scheme to the English version of this form.

from *Harmonie du Soir*
CHARLES BAUDELAIRE

Now is the hour when, swinging in the breeze,
Each flower, like a censer, sheds its sweet.
The air is full of scents and melodies,
O languorous waltz! O swoon of dancing feet!

Each flower, like a censer, sheds its sweet,
The violins are like sad souls that cry,

WRITING ACROSS CULTURES

Why try these forms? Anyone who has tried, successfully or not, to learn another language knows there is more to doing this than memorizing verb patterns and word definitions. To live, think, or dream in another language is to inhabit another universe, to become, in part, another person, and to explore another reality. While we're not all lucky enough to do this through travel or extensive study or immersion in another culture, we can inhabit other poetic forms in order to investigate new habits of thinking.

Robert Kaplan, working in an area called contrastive rhetoric, posits different organizing patterns for different cultures. If you learned to write a five-paragraph theme or organize a logical argument, you know that Western organizing structures value linearity, unity, and clarity. We have all been exposed to stereotypes about thinking in other cultures—some cultures are known for indirect expression, others for flowery exaggeration, others for delay. Such stereotypes are true to a point, as all stereotypes are partially true, including those about our own culture. Yet most stereotypes disintegrate in the particular. As we get to know people from other places, we value their individuality and the uniqueness of their way of seeing the world. Writing into another culture's poetic forms can offer you new ways to see your culture, your topics, and your feelings.

A writer who can value nonlinear thinking may thrive on the associational qualities of the ghazal or enjoy the slow addition of repetitions that build the pantoum. After such a composing experience, a new way of thinking can be added to the writer's repertoire. This certainly happened when Asian and African art influenced Parisian artists at the beginning of the twentieth century, leading to cubism and other new ways of rendering reality.

WRITING GHAZALS

The Persian ghazal took two directions: developing as a love poem (often of loss and longing) and as a mystical, religious poem. The form dominated as early as A.D. 1000 and flourished from 1100 through 1500. Contemporary American writers became interested in the ghazal and in translating this form. Through translation, William Stafford and Adrienne Rich have both composed their own poems in this form.

Ghazal VI
GHALIB

Even God's Paradise as chanted by fanatics
merely decorates the path for us connoisseurs of ecstasy.

Reflected among spangles, you flare into a room
like a sunburst evaporating a globe of dew.

Oh, buried in what I say are shapes for explosion:
I farm a deep revolt, sparks like little seeds.

Thousands of strangled urges lurk in my silence;
I am a votive lamp no one ever lighted.

Ghalib! Images of death piled up everywhere,
that's what the world fastens around us.
                    —trans. by William Stafford

Ghazal XII
GHALIB

I'm neither the loosening of song nor the close-drawn tent of music;
I'm the sound, simply, of my own breaking.

You were meant to sit in the shade of your rippling hair;
I was made to look further, into a blacker tangle.

All my self-possession is self-delusion;
what violent effort, to maintain this nonchalance!

Now that you've come, let me touch you in greeting
as the forehead of the beggar touches the ground.

No wonder you came looking for me, you
who care for the grieving, and I the sound of grief.
                    —trans. by Adrienne Rich

☙ READING INTO WRITING ❧

1. Apply the previous definition of a ghazal to the poems you've just
   read. You should have a better idea of the intentional sense of this

form, which is unlike the logic-oriented Western form of main point, supporting point, main point, supporting points. Look at the way the Stafford and Rich translations do or don't fit these definitions of a traditional ghazal.

> The rhyme scheme is *aa ba ca*, etc., and after the 12th century, the poet mentions his name toward the end of the poem. . . . The principal subject of the ghazal is earthly or mystical love, and the mood is melancholy. . . . —Alex Preminger and T. V. F. Brogan, 478

> The ghazal is a poem made up of couplets, each couplet wholly independent of any other meaning and complete in itself as a unit of thought, emotion, and communication. No two couplets have to be related to each other in any way whatever except formally (one may be about love, the next about the coming of a season; one about politics, the next about spring), and yet they can be parts of a single poem. . . . The unit of rhyme repeated at the end of each couplet may be as short as a single syllable or as long as a phrase of half a line. The convention is that a ghazal should have at least five couplets. Otherwise it is considered a fragment. There is no maximum length." —Aijaz Ahmad, *xvi*

2. Many of us don't apply the preferred modes of argument or thought of our cultures. Make some drawings of what you think that preferred mode is. Then make a drawing of how you think. Does your way of thinking or way of developing points change by genre? Draw how you think in different genres—prose, poetry, letter-writing, etc. It might help to draw the organization of a five-paragraph theme (as you learned that organization), to consider inductive and deductive development patterns and then to explore associational patterns. It may also help to do this thinking aloud with group members, pooling your resources.

3. If you are fluent in or familiar with another language, write about the experience of thinking in that language and thinking in English. What is similar and what is different? Can you/have you composed a poem in another language? What happens when you do?

Contemporary poets, not unexpectedly, have changed the form of the traditional ghazal to suit their needs and abilities. The following poems take you through some of those changes. In the first, Agha Shahid Ali provides insight into the ancient form because he is trilingual and his poem closely follows traditional form: a series of couplets, with the second line of each rhyming, in this case by repeating the word Arabic (the language of composition for some of the world's classic ghazals). In a sense, Ali uses the traditional form to consider the loss of tradition. In *What Will Suffice: Contemporary American Poets on the Art of Poetry,* Ali says of this poem and his poetry: "And my poetics? Lover and beloved at once, witness of three worlds, each from the beginning, mine: Hindu, Islamic, and Western. These I distill in exile" (2).

Ghazal ❖
AGHA SHAHID ALI

The only language of loss left in the world is Arabic—
These words were said to me in a language not Arabic.

Ancestors, you've left me a plot in the family graveyard—
Why must I look, in your eyes, for prayers in Arabic?

Majnoon, his clothes ripped, still weeps for Laila.
Oh, this is the madness of the desert, his crazy Arabic.

Who listens to Ishmael? Even now he cries out:
Abraham, throw away your knives, recite a psalm in Arabic.

From exile Mahmoud Darwish writes to the world:
You'll all pass between the fleeting words of Arabic.

The sky is stunned, it's become a ceiling of stone.
I tell you it must weep. So kneel, pray for rain in Arabic.

At an exhibition of Mughal miniatures, such delicate calligraphy:
Kashmiri paisleys tied into the golden hair of Arabic!

The Koran prophesied a fire of men and stones.
Well, it's all now come true, as it was said in the Arabic.

When Lorca died, they left the balconies open and saw:
his qasidas braided, on the horizon, into knots of Arabic.

Memory is no longer confused, it has a homeland—
Says Shammas: Territorialize each confusion in a graceful Arabic.

Where there were homes in Deir Yassein, you'll see dense forests—
That village was razed. There's no sign of Arabic.

I too, Oh Amichai, saw the dresses of beautiful women.
And everything else, just like you, in Death, Hebrew, and Arabic.

They ask me to tell them what "Shahid" means—
Listen: it means "The Beloved" in Persian, "Witness" in Arabic.

The Spanish poet Federico García Lorca (1899–1936) has composed his ghazal with much less attention to the traditional form beyond the long-lined couplets and associational qualities. He unifies his poem with the anaphoric echo of "I want" at the beginning of several stanzas in counterpoint to assertions of possibility ("if the oxen could only talk") or exception ("[b]ut don't let"). However, there is a ghazal sensibility in the loss and longing and the unusual jumps of imagery: Wind without mountain passes, worms dying from too much darkness, green poisonous sunsets. Lorca does come from a tradition of **surrealist** writing that promotes automatic writing, attention to dream states, and free-associational play. However, the play here is more intentional than the word *play* might predict, for the poem feels steeped in the sadness and mysticism of the ghazal. In this sample, then, we see a bridging of cultures.

Ghazal of the Terrifying Presence
FEDERICO GARCÍA LORCA

I want the water to go on without its bed.
And the wind to go on without its mountain passes.

I want the night to go on without its eyes
and my heart without its golden petals;

if the oxen could only talk with the big leaves
and the angleworm would die from too much darkness;

I want the teeth in the skull to shine
and the yellowish tints to drown the silk.

I can see the night in its duel, wounded
and wrestling, tangled with noon.

I fight against a sunset of green poison,
and those broken arches where time is suffering.

But don't let the light fall on your clear and naked body
like a cactus black and open in the reeds.

Leave me in the anguish of the darkened planets,
but do not let me see your pure waist.

In its contemporary form, the ghazal doesn't usually rhyme, poets don't
sign their name in the last couplet, and it isn't very often about love or
drinking. So you might wonder what's left of the original Persian form.
The two important features of the contemporary ghazal are the long-
lined couplets (sometimes unrhymed) and the often mystical thoughts
that are expressed. —Ron Padgett, 88

Using this definition of contemporary ghazals, Jim Harrison is more plain-
talking and regional, yet maintains strong elements of the original form in his
second-line repeats ("drink," "drinking") and his couplets, while his poem
starts to develop a narrative line similar to that of a good country and western song.

Drinking Song
JIM HARRISON

I want to die in the saddle. An enemy of civilization
I want to walk around in the woods, fish and drink.

I'm going to be a child about it and I can't help it, I was
born this way and it makes me very happy to fish and drink.

I left when it was still dark and walked on the path to the
river, the Yellow Dog, where I spent the day fishing and drinking.

After she left me and I quit my job and wept for a year and
all my poems were born dead, I decided I would only fish and drink.

Water will never leave earth and whiskey is good for the brain.
What else am I supposed to do in these last days but fish and drink?

In the river was a trout, and I was on the bank, my heart in my
chest, clouds above, she was in NY forever and I, fishing and drinking.

⬤ INVENTION EXERCISES ⬤

1. Write a close imitation of Ghalib's "Ghazal XII" or Lorca's "Ghazal of the Terrifying Presence." Do this by leaving the structural frame and inserting your own images. Example:

I want the. . . .
And the. . . .

  I want the . . .
and my . . . ;

  if the . . .
and the . . .

or

I'm neither the . . ;
I'm the . . .

You were . . . ;
I was. . . .

and so on

*Ghazal of Change**
    Richard Wade

I'm neither the sun nor the rain—
I'm the dark, fertile ground of change.

You were the warm west wind.
I was the driven leaf.

All that matters now is to remember
the sound of the rain falling on soft pine needles.

Now the caterpillar winds his cocoon
as summer follows spring follows winter.

No wonder I couldn't see the truth. You
who did tried to show me there is only change.

> Or imitate any of the ghazals presented so far. You might imitate rhetorical patterns or structural patterns or both. Mary Jane Ryals' ghazal is about writing and teaching, and she innovates by repeating

the end rhyme more often and in unexpected patterns of appearance and absence (she leaves out the word "students" in three lines). I was so impressed with the power of this continuous repetition that I imitated her in my ghazal, repeating the same end word ("light") in every line and signing my name obliquely in the second-to-last stanza. Both of us deviate from the form by lengthening lines to the point where one could argue we're writing tercets or quatrains in the form of couplets, especially in the case of "Wishing Spring." As I mentioned several times in the preface, purists will say my version is a failed ghazal, but an apprentice to the form like me will find this a way to learn the possibilities and difficulties of the ghazal. While writing other ghazals I've challenged myself to hold to a shorter line but released myself from the constraints of the end rhyme. Meanwhile, Hans Ostrom in "This Is The Gazelle Ghazal" intentionally writes couplets so long they push his poem toward tercet-like spacing, another form of experimentation with interesting results.

Ghazal for Undergraduate Writing Students * ❖
    Mary Jane Ryals

The least of my worries is my students.
I say these words to myself daily, my students.

Tonight, they read at a dark green bar. My students
know how every day is a Tragic God,

smoke cigarettes, the most shy of my students
turn up beers and shout with my students.

Some of them are not my students
yet. They read to Allen Ginsberg that they, too, my students,

have seen the best minds of their generations, my students',
destroyed by madness, starving hysterical naked.

Leaning into the microphone, one of my students
writes that her father told her "boys will be boys." My student

says she kept part of herself deaf. My students
clap and cheer. They listen to the story about the boy who

relishes wrinkled apricots offered by a dying woman. My students
sit at odd angles almost touching the shoulders of my students.

They laugh at the story about the storyteller who put no sex
in his story, "It must be a failure," he says. My students

laugh at Hollywood, my students
sway over the poem about the razor, how close we come, my students,

to the bone each day. My students
know every day chases them like a Tragic God, my students

feel Comic Dog pant and drool at Tragic God's heels. My students,
the least of my worries, my students.

*Wishing Spring: A Ghazal**
    Wendy Bishop

The cardinal shakes his cape of red blades in the morning light,
eclipses his mate, who falls from the roof-ridge halo of light

to the darkness of the cat's claws. Dull brown stays dull in porch light.
The squirrel on the fallen oak, freezes, stunned by morning-glory-light.

My son says—I had a dream, the sun passed the moon, blocked out light.
Daybreak fills with cardinal's whistle: worship and call. Light

won't warm spring eggs. It takes a mate. He needs to pull another into his light.
Tulips, despite the morning frost, unfurl meaty green leaves into thin light.

My daughter unfurls each morning, reluctantly, blinking at the lights
I turn on. I try to call her out of sleep, body growing lighter

with growing, lost in eclipses of sleep. Slow to greet the light
and then slow to let it go. The cat responds to longer light.

Her tawny fur clumps, ready to fly like dandelion seed into light
spring air. The cardinal wife escapes into the light

beyond all light, where sudden dead and newly born come to light.
What does "eclipse" mean and What does Bishop mean? my son says, alight

with the day's questions. It's a church office, I say. I bless this light.
Bless light rising and setting. Bless squirrels, cardinals, cats, children—light.

2. Use a popular magazine, instructions, bulletin board notices, newspaper headlines, music liner notes, or any found document to construct a *found* ghazal. Aim for five to six couplets. Decide if you want to try for rhyme or not. My poem comes from a *Mirabella Magazine* horoscope page. After reading the language there, I cut and pasted the predictions into this poem. After reading my poem, Jenny Harvey wrote her own ghazal using clichés. She also managed to sign her ghazal in the traditional manner, while I took the long-lined couplet to the extreme because I had so much found text to work from.

Horoscope Imperatives: A "Found" Ghazal*
    Wendy Bishop
  for G.L.C.

It is important to realize you are looking at others through fresh eyes.
We are here to add what we can to life, not to get what we want from it.

You feel your hands are tied. You are in the right place at the right time.
It would be a grave mistake not to act. Your are urged to settle your
    differences.

Continue to live according to the maxim: "We are here and it is now; further
    than that
All knowledge is moonshine." The Sun is challenged by your ruling planet.

Denotes joint financial arrangements, signifies a strange turn of events,
On no account should you issue an ultimatum to those in positions of power.

Venus, your ruler, needs to be watched like a hawk.
You would be well advised to take criticism in stride.

What occurs in an unusual manner around the 15th
Will accomplish what you have set your heart on achieving.

You do not have to compete to be noticed. July is about refusing to accept
What is second best. Finances are always a major consideration.

Planetary, July, The Sun, Pluto in Scorpio, on the 15th, rise above, you should,
Pay your dues, cannot fail, The Sun, your ruler, The Sun, aspected, imperative.

No doubt you are entitled to use others' deviousness as an excuse
Not to act. The 3rd, 12th, 15th, and 19th are likely to be days.

A word of warning: The Sun, passing over the mid-heaven point of your solar
    chart
And challenged by Uranus and Neptune. Spend a short time in a totally
    different setting.

Fortunately the Sun joins forces with Pluto and a windfall ought to save the day
When colleagues seem to turn against you around the 12th.

Once you have eliminated feelings of personal inadequacy, everything—
Personal and professional—should change for the better. After June.

Clichéd Ghazal*
        Jenny Harvey

I want the pride of a lion,
And the wisdom of an owl,

I want to be fit as a fiddle,
And the grass to be greener,

If love is blind
And money doesn't grow on trees.

Then why should I forgive and forget
When an elephant never forgets?

Nobody lives forever
Even with an apple a day.

So, pick up and go—
Be like Jenny and seize the day!

3. Look at the school report of another country. Search the Web for
   data and voices and discussions and use some of that information to
   write a cross-cultural ghazal. You can also fashion a found ghazal
   from these materials.

4. Write your own ghazal on love or some other strong emotional
   experience.

Brown*
      Natasha Clews

I want my skin burned to the color of melted brown sugar
and to walk on dirty shores through washed up brown beer bottles.

I want brown cardboard boxes filled with cobwebs of junk
and old books with torn and chewed brown edges.

If the leather on my coat and shoes are the brown of a dead animal
and the cracks and bubbles on my old car are that same brown rust

I can feel this brown in living tree trunks then
and it suffocating the white snow, with smears of brown.

I fight and tear my way from this brown shell of a house
and search for brownies, or chocolate bars, sweet brown smells.

But brown paper bags and too tall brown carpet grass keep me down
like a swamp or a net made of tangly, matted grey-brown hair.

Leave me in a brown ocean puddle of earth worm mud
but don't try to tell me brown's not my color.

4. Write a ghazal that includes your name in the last stanza.

This Is the Gazelle Ghazal
      Hans Ostrom

This is the piano which holds its black hat in its white hands.
This is the shovel that says excuse me and enters an important person's office
      and will not leave.

This is the pebble which politely intrudes. Like a hard brown seed it sprouts
      discomfort.
This is the important person, leveled by regret, desperate for hope.

This is the outside, which is rain, and the inside, which is dry.
This is the student, who wants to be older. This is the teacher, who wants to
      be younger.

This is the love affair, so raging it convinced itself it would last forever but
   ended.
This is the friendship, which began before it knew it began and will not end.

This is the gazelle that springs, tawny, onto the savanna of your mind as you
   read.
This is the name I write when I write my name to conclude the gazelle ghazal:
   Hans Ostrom.

5. Write a ghazal that obeys at least three or four of the classic definitions of the form: long-lined couplets, second line of couplet
   rhyming in each stanza, signing your name, earthly or mystical love
   as the subject, having a melancholy mood, couplets being able to
   stand on their own like proverbs or sayings and yet cohere, etc.

WRITING PANTOUMS

   . . . a pantoum is like a hawk with a chicken, it takes its time about
   striking. —Malayan proverb (Preminger 875)

An oral form that developed by the fifteenth century into a cornerstone of
Malayan literature, the pantoum is as engaging as the French villanelle in its
memorable repetition of lines. The pantoum is somewhat easier to compose
because, unlike the villanelle, it has no rhyming requirement, although the
translation of the Charles Baudelaire pantoum by Lord Alfred Douglas maintains an *abab* rhyme scheme. The French took up the form in the nineteenth
century, and contemporary American poets have adapted and inhabited it with
some interesting results.

Harmonie du Soir
CHARLES BAUDELAIRE

   Now is the hour when, swinging in the breeze,
   Each flower, like a censer, sheds its sweet.
   The air is full of scents and melodies,
   O languorous waltz! O swoon of dancing feet!

   Each flower, like a censer, sheds its sweet,
   The violins are like sad souls that cry,
   O languorous waltz! O swoon of dancing feet!
   A shrine of Death and Beauty is the sky.

The violins are like sad souls that cry,
Poor souls that hate the vast black night of Death;
A shrine of Death and Beauty is the sky.
Drowned in red blood, the Sun gives up his breath.

This soul that hates the vast black night of Death
Takes all the luminous past back tenderly,
Drowned in red blood, the Sun gives up his breath.
Thine image like a monstrance shines in me.
                    —trans. by Lord Alfred Douglas

The pantoum form repeats entire lines (either exactly or with slight variations, the former being more difficult, of course). You can write these in any
length as long as you use four-line stanzas with the second and fourth line of the
first stanza becoming the first and third of the next, the second and fourth lines
of the second stanza becoming the first and third of the third stanza, and so on.
You can end when you want or circle the pantoum by using lines three and one
as the second and fourth lines of the final stanza. Here's what a four-stanza
pantoum would look like:

Stanza 1   Line 1

            Line 2

            Line 3

            Line 4

Stanza 2   Line 2 above repeats as Line 5

            Line 6

            Line 4 above repeats as Line 7

            Line 8

Stanza 3   Line 6 above repeats as Line 9

            Line 10

            Line 8 above repeats as Line 11

            Line 12

Stanza 4   Line 10 above repeats as Line 13

            New line or Line 3 above repeats as Line 14

            Line 12 above repeats as Line 15

            New line or Line 1 above repeats as Line 16.

Atomic Pantoum
PETER MEINKE

In a chain reaction
the neutrons released
split other nuclei
which release more neutrons

The neutrons released
blow open some others
which release more neutrons
and start this all over

Blow open some others
and choirs will crumble
and start this all over
with eyes burned to ashes

And choirs will crumble
the fish catch on fire
with eyes burned to ashes
in a chain reaction

The fish catch on fire
because the sun's force
in a chain reaction
has blazed in our minds

Because the sun's force
with plutonium trigger
has blazed in our minds
we are dying to use it

With plutonium trigger
curled and tightened
we are dying to use it
torching our enemies

Curled and tightened
blind to the end
torching our enemies
we sing to Jesus

Blind to the end
split up like nuclei
we sing to Jesus
in a chain reaction

Notice how Peter Meinke's tight political stanzas tumble down the page. He starts each stanza with capitalization but offers no final period for stanza closure, causing each stanza to tumble into the next stanza, which echoes the way a chain reaction triggers other reactions. I'd suggest trying at least two of the inventions I list below, although you can certainly just jump right in and pour your ideas into this form. I like to begin pantoum writing by stealing others' lines for some or all of a poem. The following poem developed from quotations I kept from authors as I read them. (You might also look through poems in this book or other collections to borrow a line.) Equally, my classes and I sometimes hold a half-facetious contest to draft "great first lines," which we write on the board and then "auction" to whatever class member convinces the author of the line that he/she will come up with the best pantoum using that line as a starting place.

To compose "Pantoum on Lines by Wallace Stegner," I returned to some lines I had copied into my journal while reading his book of essays: *Where the Bluebird Sings to the Lemonade Springs: Living and Writing in the West* (Random House, NY: 1992). Some of those included:

- I was used to horizons that either lifted into jagged ranges or rimmed the geometrical circle of the flat world. I was used to seeing a long way. I was used to earth colors—tan, rusty red, toned white—and the endless green of Iowa offended me. I was used to a sun that came up over mountains and went down behind other mountains. I missed the color and smell of sage brush and the sight of bare ground (17–18).
- Sagebrush is an acquired taste, as are raw earth and alkali flats (53).
- The Westerner is less a person than a continuing adaptation. The West is less a place than a process (55).
- The principal invention of western American culture is the motel, the principal exhibit of that culture the automotive roadside (72).

Here is the poem constructed from those lines, followed by some drafting suggestions for your own found pantoums:

*Pantoum on Lines by Wallace Stegner**
    Wendy Bishop

Like raw earth and alkali flats,
sagebrush is an acquired taste.
The westerner is less a person
than a continuing adaptation.

Sagebrush is an acquired taste.
I miss the sight of bare ground
and the continuing adaptation
of earth colors—tan, rust, red.

I miss the sight of bare ground.
Bits of east, middle west, are buried here
in earth, colored tan, rust, red.
I'm used to sunrise over mountains.

Bits of east, middle west, are buried here
but west is never found in the east.
I'm used to sunrise over mountains
and sunset over other mountains.

West is never found in the east.
It's less a place than a process
like sun setting over mountains.
Western culture: automobiles, motels.

It's less a place than a process.
The endless greens of Iowa offended me.
Western culture: automobiles, motels,
to live in and be shaped by bigness.

The endless greens of Iowa offended me.
I missed the color and smell of sagebrush.
Living in and shaped by bigness
I was used to horizons, jagged ranges.

I missed the color and smell of sagebrush.
Like I missed the west, like a person
Of wide horizons, jagged ranges,
acquired taste of raw earth and alkali flats.

~~ INVENTION EXERCISES ~~

PANTOUM ON A METAPHORICAL CHARACTER EXERCISE

1. Complete the prompts for a metaphorical character exercise found at the end of Devan Cook's revision case study in the appendix.
2. Take this raw material and use it like you used the borrowed lines— that is, highlight your own best lines and start to shape a pantoum portrait of this person.

PANTOUM ON BORROWED LINES

1. Pick two lines (or four lines) that you like and start your first stanza. End-stopped lines may be easier to repeat. Your first stanza will set your line length, more or less. Try to keep each stanza approximately that many syllables long. In the poem below, William Snyder found a pantoum in an advertising brochure for Dodge trucks. Victoria Lan Sears found her text in quite a different place: Plato's *Symposium*. And Terri Sapp parodies magazine advice; she also removed the white space between her stanzas.
2. Finish your borrowed-line stanza by pulling down two lines and writing the lines that go in between (or, if you like borrowing lines, keep inserting new borrowed lines). Pull down, expand, pull down, expand, until you feel it's time to end—then decide if you want to repeat from the first stanza or open out with your own last new lines.

> ### *If This Doesn't Change Your Mind, Read It Again While Sitting in Your Old Truck: A Pantoum**
> WILLIAM SNYDER
>
> This is one comfortable truck:
> relax, you'll get used to it.
> Its cup holders will accommodate even Super Big Gulps.
> We designed each knob, button and switch.
>
> Relax, you'll get used to it—
> the ride is superior on potholed surfaces, and steering is excellent
> because we designed each knob, button and switch.
> Has any truck ever been so convenient?

The ride is superior, the steering excellent
and down the road you'll thank us.
Listen: has any truck ever been so convenient?
After all, we just wouldn't hear of making a noisy truck.

Down the road, you'll really thank us.
If you think style has nothing to do with beasts of burden,
think again, 'cause, we just wouldn't hear of making a noisy truck.
Our Ram has the biggest cab. See dealer for latest information.

If you think style has nothing to do with beasts of burden,
think again, and for serious torque, diesel is the only choice.
This Ram has the biggest. See your dealer for information.
Dodge delivers more hard working torque.

For serious torque, diesel is the only choice.
Our Magnum series engines wrote the book on power.
Dodge delivers more hard working torque—
(See Dodge's limited warranties, restrictions and details at dealer.)

Our cup holders will accommodate Super Big Gulps.
God fuckin' damn, this is one comfortable truck.

The Desire of One (based on Plato's Symposium)*
    Victoria Lan Sears

So ancient is the desire of one another
—making one of two—
to heal the state of man and
reunite our original nature.

Making one of two—
we seek more than what we have
to heal the state of man
and find a type of wholeness.

We seek more than we have,
but isn't that our nature,
to find a type of wholeness,
and cling to it as our truth?

But isn't that our nature,
to heal the state of man,
and cling to it as our one truth—
so ancient is the desire, one for another.

Pantoum*

    Terri Sapp

forget who's doing what to whom
sex is more of a headtrip than ever
can adultery save your marriage
men and women cheat differently
sex is more of a head trip than ever
men's infidelities are not merely forgiven, but admired
men and women cheat differently
the rules here in the "real world" have changed
men's infidelities are not merely forgiven, but admired
a menace to the moral fiber of the nation
the rules here in the "real world" have changed
virginity is a radical state
a menace to the moral fiber of the nation
can adultery save your marriage
virginity is a radical state
forget who's doing what to whom

The next two poets show the range of the pantoum subject. In the first poem, "In the Attic," Donald Justice provides a quietly unnerving view of childhood. He varies his lines—("And ceilings slope towards remembrance" becomes "Only, being stored up for remembrance") so that the pantoum form drifts to the background and we can almost imagine we're reading a quatrain, especially since his lines are fairly regular in length. Pamela Stewart, on the other hand, varies her lines somewhat less ("You'll wear blood jewels and last week's ochre bruise" becomes "last week's final bruise"), and she lets her hard-hitting, more often end-stopped lines spin out to greater length.

In the Attic
DONALD JUSTICE

There's a half hour towards dusk when flies,
Trapped by the summer screens, expire
Musically in the dust of sills;
And ceilings slope towards remembrance.

The same crimson afternoons expire
Over the same few rooftops repeatedly;
Only, being stored up for remembrance,
They somehow escape the ordinary.

Childhood is like that, repeatedly
Lost in the very longueurs it redeems.
One forgets how small and ordinary
The world looked once by dusklight from above . . .

But not the moment which redeems
The drowsy arias of the flies—
And the chin settles onto palms above
Numbed elbows propped on rotting sills.

Punk Pantoum
PAMELA STEWART

Tonight I'll walk the razor along your throat
You'll wear blood jewels and last week's ochre bruise
There's a new song out just for you and me
There's sawdust on the floor, and one dismembered horse

You'll wear blood jewels and last week's final bruise
I got three shirts from the hokey-man at dawn
There'll be sawdust on the floor and, ha, his dismembered horse:
Rust-stained fetlock, gristle, bone and hoof . . .

They'll look good hanging from the shirt I took at dawn.
Bitch, let's be proud to live at Eutaw Place
With rats, a severed fetlock, muscle, bone and hooves,
George will bring his snake and the skirt Divine threw out.

For now, I'm glad we live at Eutaw Place
Remember how we met at the Flower Mart last Spring?
George wore his snake and the hose Divine threw out—
Eating Sandoz oranges, we watched the ladies in their spats.

Remember how you burned your hair at the Flower Mart last May?
I put it out with Wes Jones' checkered pants,
The pulp of oranges and that old lady's hat—
I knew I loved you then, with your blistered face and tracks

That I disinfected with Wes Jones' filthy pants.
There's a new song out just for you and me
That says I'll always love you and your face. Let's make new tracks
Tonight, dragging the white-hot razor across our throats, and back . . .

⬭ READING INTO WRITING ⬭

As you read the next three poems, consider how each "is like a hawk with a chicken, it takes its time about striking"—remembering that some pantoum writers use the repeats to delay and play slow changes and some to explore listing and variation. Topics center generally on love and/or relationships although Melanie Rawls vaults us into the arena of science fiction while still honoring the requirements of the form. If you read the pantoums in this chapter aloud, you'll notice how pleasing the repetition is to the ear. Mary Swander's poem "Two Skulls" varies from the expected repeat-line pattern in a way that illustrates the effectiveness of letting a poem be informed by but not constrained by an originating form. Like the accentual-alliterative verse discussed in chapter 2, these repeats (as well as the rhyme pattern in the original form) would allow for easier memorization. However, this is less true to the degree that the poet chooses to vary the repeat lines or to shorten the lines. Having read these variations on the pantoum form, I hope that you'll create your own. Whether found, borrowed, or newly originated, the pantoum, like the ghazal, can allow you to create satisfying cross-cultural music.

Here*
    A. S. Kaufman

    Unlike me
    You prefer the pool
    To the sea
    Come here

    You prefer the pool
    To the heat
    Come here
    You whisper

    In the heat
    I shiver
    You whisper
    I slip into cold blue

I shiver
Float into your arms
Slip into cold blue
I crave you

Float into your arms
Only your mouth warm
I crave you
Sweet fervor

Only your mouth warm
Addictive oblivion
Sweet fervor
The only warm place

Addictive oblivion
You swallow me
The only warm place
Such a small space

You swallow me
You prefer safety
Such a small space
To the sea

You prefer safety
Unlike me
To the sea
Come here.

*Crash Site**
    Melanie A. Rawls

"Proceed to Delta Echo—aircraft down!"
A ball of light has arced across the sky
And plummeted—flare of violet, blue, and white
And thundering upward whirling spewing earth.

A ball of light has arced across the sky,
Trees fall flat, cliffs shudder, rivers steam.
And thundering upward whirling spewing earth,
Murking the air, briefly hiding the sun.

Trees fall flat, cliffs shudder, rivers steam.
What catastrophe has occurred behind this hill
Murking the air, briefly hiding the sun?
Are there survivors? What kind of—*thing* is this?

What catastrophe has occurred behind this hill?
What crashed in a glare of violet, blue, and white?
Are there survivors? What kind of—*thing* is this?
The ground is fused, white metal fragments scattered.

What crashed in a glare of violet, blue, and white?
What *are* these creatures tangled in the wreckage?
The ground is fused, white metal fragments scattered,
Smoking petals curled around—"Oh, God!"

What *are* these creatures tangled in the wreckage?
Lobed heads shattered, three lax fingers on each hand—
The ground is fused, white metal fragments scattered.
We huddle in groups, the universe undone.

Lobed heads shattered, three lax fingers on each hand—
And the silence of deep space cold behind this hill.
We huddle in groups, the universe undone.
"Proceed from Delta Echo—God! What next?"

Two Skulls
MARY SWANDER

We hope to sketch their bones, but do not want their meat,
the stench floating through our house for days.
So, tonight we open the cold October dirt
and the moon shines down through the scarecrow's eyes.

The moon shines down through the scarecrow's eyes
and the cow skulls lower into the garden holes.
Dug up in spring, flesh stripped worm-clean in the April haze,
the bones, cast in clay, become our vessels.

And the cow skulls lower into the garden holes,
their eyes staring through us, still in place, tongues bitten in two.
The bones, cast in clay, become our vessels,
our study of form, texture, color, tone.

Their eyes staring through us, still in place, tongues bitten in two—
in silence we lean against our spades—
our study of form, texture, color, tone—
then draw the dirt back over their eyes like shades.

POCKET DEFINITIONS

Ghazal—Generally ten to twenty-four lines in length and originally a Persian form, these long-lined couplets develop mystical and/or romantic themes. They may be monorhymed (*aa, ba, ca, da*) and/or include the poet's name in the last line.

Pantoum—Sixteen or more lines long, pantoums developed in Malayan literature as rhyming quatrains (*abab*) but developed in English as unrhymed quatrains with repeating lines: the second and fourth lines of each stanza repeat as the first and third lines of the next stanza.

Surrealism—A movement to free thought from reason through automatic writing, attention to dream states, and free-associational play. In poetry, well-known practitioners include Andre Breton, Charles Baudelaire, Arthur Rimbaud, Stephen Malarme, and Federico Garcia Lorca, and in the twentieth century, Robert Bly, John Ashbery, and James Tate. Artists Salvador Dali, Juan Miro, and René Magritte are representative of the breadth of surrealist painting.

6

HAIKU AND HAIKU-LIKE SEQUENCES

Making a Perfect Little Out of a Lot of Life

RICHARD WRIGHT
(1908–1960)

In the falling snow
A laughing boy holds out his palms
Until they are white.

NOBUKO KATSURA
(b. 1914)

Outside the window, snow;
a woman in a hot bath,
water overflowing.

Because it has been much borrowed, tossed off, and taken up, the **haiku** form has often been dismissed and oversimplified, but it's still a form that challenges, pleases, and instructs. When undertaken by Richard Wright and Nobuko Katsura, the form continues to cross centuries, cultures, and continents effectively. Contemporary poets generally cast haiku as small poems of 5, 7, 5 syllables. Growing out of Zen Buddhist philosophy (a version of Buddhism that began in India and then spread widely, in which believers seek enlightenment through introspection and intuition rather than through interpretation of a text or scripture), the haiku seeks to capture a moment of perception. Haiku turns on strong natural images and intense emotions, often leading to spiritual insights. The number of syllables does not have to be exact, although some American poets (and poetry contest rules for haiku-making) take pleasure in counting them precisely.

> The Japanese haiku began with poets who looked, deeply and apprecia-
> tively, at the world around them. That world consisted mostly of what
> we call "nature." But the "nature" of Basho's day also included para-
> sols, mosquito nets, and other paraphernalia of human affairs.
> —William J. Higginson, 94

Haiku were originally composed as part of a linked-verse form called a
Haikai no Renga—36, 40, or 100 stanzas together. Poets would gather and take
turns composing these stanzas. Each poet would vie to produce the "hokku"—
the stanza that starts a renga series. Only one was used so poets often had leftover hokku, which became haiku, starting verses that were then collected for
their own power and effect. Pleased with haiku (although Japanese meter never
translates purely into English syllabics), English-speaking poets also adopted the
tanka form—5, 7, 5, 7, 7 syllables, more or less. These short poems are also
moment or mood pieces, commenting on love, life, seasons, and often sadness.
(Only one is included in this chapter: "Cheetos" by Ann Turkle.)

POETIC SCRIMSHAW

> As a self-contained short poem, the haiku was used to distill the uni-
> verse through the juxtaposition of dissimilar elements while creating
> unity through the use of a seasonal word (kigo). As seasons are tied to
> the life cycle, seasonal references give the poem vitality and rhythm . . .
> anything can offer the opportunity to achieve enlightenment. The haiku
> poet, although working with commonplace imagery and experience, can
> nevertheless evoke profound feelings and sensibility. —Leza Lowitz,
> Miyuki Aoyama, and Akemi Tomiko, 17

Distillation. A perfect little life. Scrimshaw. If you've ever seen scrimshaw, you
don't forget the impressive craft of etching into bone or shell or ivory. Sailors
in New England once created complicated scenes on whale bone. When I lived
in Alaska, I saw detailed demonstrations of Native American craft as individuals carved and incised walrus bones and shells. It seems as if the polar bear has
just succeeded in its fishing, a swipe of the paw catching a fighting salmon.
Scrimshaw is like haiku, and haiku is like scrimshaw: to succeed in either, the
artist distills the universe. The carver incises the bone, the haiku writer crafts
plain and odd observations into the smallest of verse spaces. The craft of each
impels admiration, for the smaller the bone canvas, the greater the art, just as
the less said in the compacted form of the haiku, the greater the reverberations.
    I suspect haiku are popular because the form is congruent with several of the
values held most dear to contemporary poets, as can be seen in these "rules"
from the poet Basho, who wrote three hundred years ago:

- One need not be a haikai poet, but if someone doesn't live inside ordinary life and understand ordinary feelings, he's not likely to be a poet.
- The bones of haikai are plainness and oddness.
- When we observe calmly, we discover that all things have their fulfillment.
  —Basho (Robert Hass 233–238)

These rules match the contemporary poet's interest in the local, the personal, and the carefully observed details of the world. Basho, along with poets Buson and Issa (whose joint years of composing cover the years 1644 to 1827) are the most well-known of the Japanese haiku poets. Basho is known for his ability to capture nature in his stunning, small lyrics. Buson, who was a well-known painter, is considered by some to be more objective than Basho, while Issa is the most humorous of the three. Insects and the smaller creatures of the world populate Issa's poems. The following selection includes one poem by each poet and then two versions of the same poem by Issa to highlight the problems (and pleasures) of translation. (For more on translation issues, look at *Nineteen Ways of Looking at Wang Wei* by Eliot Weinberger and Octavio Paz. These poets guide you through many translations of a four-line Japanese poem.) Following are more haiku by each poet from a volume by translator/poet Robert Hass. Then I ask you to play with these poets and imitate them or turn them into influences for composing your own contemporary haiku, etching your words as precisely into print as the scrimshaw artist does with knife and ink onto a delicate shell.

Poems by three haiku masters:

MATSUO BASHO
(1644–1694)

    This road—
no one goes down it,
    autumn evening.
—trans. by Robert Hass

TANIGUCHI BUSON
(1716–1783)

The piercing chill I feel:
    my dead wife's comb, in our bedroom,
    under my heel . . .
        —trans. by Harold G. Henderson

KOBAYASHI ISSA (1763–1827)

Cricket, be
careful! I'm rolling
over!
—trans. by Robert Bly

Two versions of the same haiku by Issa:

The old dog bends his head listening . . .
I guess the singing
of the earthworms gets to him.
                —trans. by Robert Bly

   The old dog—
listening for the songs
   of earthworms?
—trans. by Robert Hass

∽ READING INTO WRITING ∽

1. Try recasting each haiku as a prose passage of your own and then
   share your passage with others. Have you each interpreted the poem
   differently or fairly similarly? What happens to the tension of the
   poem when you turn it into prose?

2. Compare the two dog haiku by Issa. Which version do you like best
   and why? Try to compose your own version that is a mixture or
   interpretation of the two versions. Share your version with those
   written by other group members.

3. How do these haiku match your previous expectation of haiku writing? Do you feel let down or freed by the fact that few translators
   worry about the 5-, 7-, 5-syllable rule?

Before composing your own haiku (or while you're trying to do so), read this
small collection of haiku by the three Japanese masters, Basho, Buson, and Issa,
all translated by Robert Hass.

BASHO

   Harvest moon—
walking around the pond
   all night long.

Fleas, lice,
a horse peeing
 near my pillow.

Misty rain,
can't see Fuji
 —interesting!

BUSON

Coolness—
the sound of the bell
 as it leaves the bell.

That snail—
one long horn, one short,
 what's on his mind?

Escaped the nets,
escaped the ropes—
 moon on the water.

The end of spring— ❖
the poet is brooding
 about editors.

ISSA

The man pulling radishes
pointed my way
 with a radish.

These sea slugs,
they just don't seem
 Japanese.

Writing shit about new snow ❖
for the rich
 is not art.

Fiftieth birthday:

From now on,
it's all clear profit,
 every sky.

His death poem:

> A bath when you're born,
> a bath when you die,
>   how stupid.

At this point, let me encourage you to play anthropologist. Given this small selection, and assuming that's all we have left of these writers, what conclusions would you/can you draw about the art of each? What subjects predominate? What patterns can you see within an artist's work and across the work of all three? You might make three columns and write down attributes of each.

> Conventions arise because many people do the same thing. Many
> people wrote poems on frogs in the spring, when their singing was first
> noticed, and therefore most noticeable. Soon it was the fashion to write
> of frogs in the spring. People who observed—and observe—this fashion
> do not deny the existence of frogs in the summer. But they express their
> membership in a special community of human perception by writing of
> frogs in the spring. —William J. Higginson, 94–95

Now look at some contemporary Western haiku writers. First, Ezra Pound's poem "In a Station of the Metro" is renowned for reviving interest in the form just past the turn of the twentieth century (1917, to be exact). His reading and translations of Chinese and Japanese poetry highly influenced his work with image. Contemporary poet Gary Snyder has also spent many years studying both poetries, has lived in Japan, and continues to study and practice Zen Buddhism as well as devote himself to poetry writing that is strongly influenced by his Asian studies. Both of these poets place their haiku in unexpected locations (the Paris metro and the California Sierras), which will encourage you, I hope, to find your own images wherever you may be by noticing the oddness (uniqueness) in the ordinariness of your everyday life. The last haiku, by Richard Brautigan, makes some fun of the form as imported into the contemporary American scene. Finally, you might return to the Richard Wright and Nobuko Katsura haiku that open this chapter.

In a Station of the Metro
EZRA POUND

The apparition of these faces in the crowd;
Petals on a wet, black bough.

On Climbing the Sierra Matterhorn Again After Thirty-One Years
GARY SNYDER

Range after range of mountains
Year after year after year.
I am still in love.

4X40086, On the summit

Haiku Ambulance
RICHARD BRAUTIGAN

A piece of green pepper fell
off the wooden salad bowl:
so what?

➤ INVENTION EXERCISES ➤

1. Walk out into your backyard or to a nearby park, school yard, or campus lawn. Look at that world until you observe something—an ant, a snail, a bird, kids on roller blades—in action. Write a short haiku-like passage that tries to capture that scene at that moment: the natural world intersecting with your perception. Then reshape this into your haiku. Recast the haiku three times in the manner of Basho, then Buson, then Issa (as you understand that manner from your reading and analysis of their poems shared above). You might title these "Basho in My Backyard," "Buson in My Backyard," and "Issa in My Backyard." Compare the four versions to see which you like best, and compose a fifth, a composite of the best images of each.

2. Like Issa above, make up several occasional haiku. (His are on his fiftieth birthday and his death.) You might write about your six-teenth or twenty-first or fiftieth birthday or your marriage, gradua-tion, first child, etc. You can also write about the future, your retirement, or your death, as Issa obviously does to some degree with his death poem. Then, as a change from haiku seriousness, try haiku irony, as Richard Brautigan does.

3. Read the following two contemporary haiku and use them as a springboard for your own. Kim Wheatley engages southern themes—heat and watermelon—and mixes them with love. Devan Cook looks around a workplace and also speaks of love, and her poem assures you that despite haiku's origin in observations about

the natural world, nature doesn't always get highlighted in contemporary haiku—at least not outdoor nature. Here Devan Cook looks at human nature.

Kim Wheatley*

Love was hotter and
sweeter than watermelon.
We overlooked the seeds.

Working Saturday Night
Devan Cook

These stamps are virgins—
not even licked yet. Date night
alone at my desk.

4. Contemporary meditations: Make your own haiku-like inventions after reading Terry Ehret's poem based on Egyptian hieroglyphics. Maybe your modern symbols are found in the computer symbol (✳ ➤ ❦ ❖) sets.

from *Papyrus*
TERRY EHRET

A lake. A night without moon. Distant memory of what the sun looks like rising. The darkness blows across the water like a wind. Passions that cool with age.

5. Enter with care. The Web has a number of haiku sites. There are haiku societies, associations, and listings of classic and contemporary works. A search for "pantoum" will leave you yearning, whereas a search for "haiku" will overwhelm you. Scan the sites and read the journals, and you'll see why this has been both a valued and a trivialized form (at least in Western culture). A good exercise for such a search is to write your best and your worst haiku and then look through these sites to see which would publish your best and which would publish your worst attempt. Spend some time writing in a journal or with classmates your own guide to writing art haiku and popular haiku.

LINKED HAIKU

You may find it productive to write sequences of haiku: two or more haiku that can stand alone yet also gain power when read together. Rex West completed a composing statement that explains why he practices this form.

Haiku*
REX WEST

Leningrad Station's marble halls
lined with flowers
smell of toilets

woman loses an earring
whispers her name
in English.

Ironically, I always think of a haiku as a kind of syllogism, that is, the first two lines need to set up premises, while the third line acts like the conclusion, giving the haiku closure. Of course poetry isn't math, but a haiku does have that logical, linear quality: something needs to be asserted; some connection between images beyond conventional observation needs to be demonstrated. Put another way, I often think of the third line of a haiku like the punch line of a joke: it's got to push the reader, not to laughter, but to thought.

This is all possible because the haiku form tells us to bring particular expectations to the page. Form, then, defines not only the writing, but the mindset necessary to get anything from the form, that is, conventions and expectations. The form itself is (usually) defined by three lines and abbreviated language. In writing haikus I often drop articles, conjunctions, punctuation, and verbs to achieve the tone I think works best. As I understand it, the haiku should give the reader the images, spare—even stark—so nothing gets in the way of the "Zen" connection. The haiku poet does not explain, but offers. What's important is to remember that the haiku is not some abstruse form whose subject is limited to wild flowers and pond frogs. Instead, as Earl Miner says in his book *Japanese Linked Poetry*, the haiku "abounds in things of daily use." Thus, the form's brevity implies something about intimacy too.

I like haiku sequences because the poet has more of an opportunity to develop some sort of narrative, however brief. For instance, in only two stanzas, I've said as much as I might say in a hundred line free verse poem about the Leningrad train station.

I guess I turn to haikus for relief. When longer poems aren't working out, and I'm frustrated because I can't finish a poem, I'll work on a haiku to feel that satisfaction of finishing something. I don't want to suggest haikus are easy. But even revising a haiku nine times takes less time than revising a longer work.

However hesitant we are to admit it, we all need to feel that success surge ("Yes! it's finished, done!"). The haiku can provide that. I also find myself using haikus to warm up. Writing a haiku sequence on a given subject helps me get some initial images down, which I can go back to and embellish later.)
—Rex West

Like Rex, I don't find haiku an easy form, and I also find them to be exquisite practice for learning how to get the most mileage out of my images and statements. For my own linked haiku, I decided to write about the four seasons (and then added a time of day as a fifth season of sorts) and shared these with my class. Scott Dias and Abby Anderson both write response seasonal haiku sequences.

*Five Colors, Five Animals, Five Reasons**
   Wendy Bishop

   Winter's scurrilous
   breath, red-tail hawk never looks
   down, flaps twice, then lifts

   Hoot-owl calls spring moon
   all manner of names. Moon turns
   gold, quarter by quarter.

   Green lizard
   holds green dragon-fly
   in his summer mouth.

   Black dog meets fall leaf
   carries it across her nose,
   knocks it free, then runs.

   Bat slices sideways
   between day and dusk, between
   night and a blue dawn.

*The Seasons**
   Scott Dias

   Summer:
      I feel the sun's warmth
      rubbing slowly at my ear
      until it falls off.

Winter:
>   Don't hate the blizzard
>   'cause he whistles in your ear.
>   Hate him 'cause he's cold!

Spring:
>   The Kodiak Bear
>   can't bear to open her eyes,
>   and neither can I.

Autumn:
>   Her name was Autumn.
>   She rode the bus with me once,
>   then she moved to Tampa.

*Four Louisiana Haiku**
>   *Abby Anderson*

Rains dampen cotton
blankets left too long into
Southern afternoons.

Shimmering highways
draw armadillos away
from burrowed safety.

The first chill, an end
to shrimp season—boat motors
abruptly quiet.

Spanish moss hanging.
Icy wind knocks thin tendrils
into still bayous.

⟩ INVENTION EXERCISES ⟨

1. Compose your own four-seasons haiku inspired by any of the poem
   sets you've just read. Equally, you can use other ideas to create
   haiku sets: haiku on numbers, haiku on five locations in a place
   that's important to you, haiku on different times of day at the same
   location (the beach at dawn, noon, and dusk, for instance), haiku
   sets on people in your family, and so on. In a group, expand this list
   of possible sets and draft your own haiku series. As always, it helps

if you go to that location, observe during that time of day, look at that person, and really consider the particulars as you compose.

2. Write some anti-haiku—haiku that break with the tradition in every way except the number of syllables. Write urban haiku, still-life haiku, technology haiku, etc.

COLLABORATIVE HAIKU

Haiku are a very social form: they are immediate, portable, shareable, and collaborative. In the following example, you'll read a tape script—haikus composed by two authors, Lara Moody and Ann Turkle, and then interwoven as a performance piece. Each author retains authorship by marking her work with initials after the title. However, you may want to take your own composing a step further and compose the single haiku units together. Also, you'll notice that Ann's poem "Cheetos" is in the tanka tradition. The last section of the tape was recorded as a round: one author started her haiku and the next started hers as the first was still speaking, overlapping sounds and lines.

*Tape Script: Food Haiku**
    Lara Moody and Ann Turkle

> All six pieces are written in Asian forms: haiku, double haiku or tanka (with liberties). We alternately read through the series of six, including titles the first time, then begin an informal round, allowing our voices to overlap, interspersed with some solo reading. We are accompanied by The Dixie Dregs, a bluegrass band; their song is "The Riff Raff."

FRIDAY MORNING—LM
    Seven bananas
    stolen from the Chinese fair
    ripen on the sill.

    Brown dapples yellow
    like the necks of young giraffes,
    stretching, ripening.

PICKING BERRIES—AT
    Sun-hot strawberries
    scent the air. Garter snake green
    on yellow straw. We
    eat more berries than we pick.
    Weigh the kids! the farmer yells.

FRENCH PASTRY SHOP—LM

    Little almond boats
    of raspberries and sweet cream
    float in the window.

    I'll take three of those.
    Give me a few eclairs, too,
    and that kiwi tart.

RASPBERRY HAIKU—AT

    In summer rain, red
    raspberries jewel green stems,
    flavor for my eyes.

BEDTIME AT PUCKY'S—LM

    My grandma stirred quick
    until the powder and cream
    became chocolate milk.

    A tiny snowstorm
    of soft, sugary brown flakes
    sifted through my glass.

CHEETOS—AT

    Salty, fat, neon
    orange, precisely what I don't
    need. I savor them,
    fingers pollinated by
    cheese twigs. Timid rebellion.

    See, Mother, I eat what I like!

➤ INVENTION EXERCISES ➤

Write your own tape script, tape it, and play it for your class or listeners of your choice. Like Lara Moody and Ann Turkle, you may want to set a theme, such as food, and compose separately and then weave your texts together, or you may want to sit in the same room like studio musicians and compose until you have what you want. You'll want to decide whether to record this a cappella or with background sounds or music—and why.

HAIKU SEQUENCES AND IMITATIONS

Contemporary poets take up forms but often turn them this way and that until the title—the label—is the main clue we have to the formal inspiration. This seems to be the case with John Ashbery's poem "37 Haiku," which places each haiku on a single line, and the connections between lines and to the originating form are sometimes hard to trace—but fascinating to try to trace. Devan Cook showed me the following poem and her own imitation, "21 Summer Haiku," in which I think you'll see more linear, interconnected thinking. While Ashbery takes huge linguistic leaps, Cook's leaps are more dreamlike as she works around the subject of summer. My imitation of Devan's imitation is also more themed, about the suburbs. Instead of leaving each haiku as a single line, I run mine into a prose paragraph, marking divisions between haiku with asterisks.

37 Haiku
JOHN ASHBERY

Old-fashioned shadows hanging down, that difficulty in love too soon
Some star or other went out, and you, thank you for your book and year
Something happened in the garage and I owe it for the blood traffic
Too low for nettles but it is exactly the way people think and feel
And I think there's going to be even more but waist-high
Night occurs dimmer each time with the pieces of light smaller and squarer
You have original artworks hanging on the walls oh I said edit
You nearly undermined the brush I now place against the ball field arguing
That love was a round place and will still be there two years from now
And it is a dream sailing in a dark unprotected cove
Pirates imitate the ways of ordinary people myself for instance
Planted over and over that land has a bitter aftertaste
A blue anchor grains of grit in a tall sky sewing
He is a monster like everyone else but what do you do if you're a monster
Like him feeling him come from far away and then go down to his car
The wedding was enchanted everyone was glad to be in it
What trees, tools, why ponder socks on the premises
Come to the edge of the barn the property really begins there
In a smaller tower shuttered and put away there
You lay aside your hair like a book that is too important to read now
Why did witches pursue the beast from the eight sides of the country
A pencil on glass—shattered! The water runs down the drain
In winter sometimes you see those things and also in summer
A child must go down it must stand and last

Too late the last express passes through the dust of gardens
A vest—there is so much to tell about even in the side rooms
Hesitantly, it built up and passed quickly without unlocking
There are some places kept from the others and are separate, they never exist
I lost my ridiculous accent without acquiring another
In Buffalo, Buffalo she was praying, the nights stick together like pages in an
     old book
The dreams descend like cranes on gilded, forgetful wings
What is the past, what is it all for? A mental sandwich?
Did you say, hearing the schooner overhead, we turned back to the weir?
In rags and crystals, sometimes with a shred of sense, an odd dignity
The boy must have known the particles fell through the house after him
All in all we were taking our time, the sea returned—no more pirates
I inch and only sometimes as far as the twisted pole gone in spare colors

21 *Summer Haiku**
     Devan Cook
     (after John Ashbery)

Skin the color of toast, air like warmed milk. Torn sheets.
Eclipse. The hoot owl's bad luck can't fill overturned shoes.
Starlight faint as snail trails on a skirt of galaxies and facts.
Cemetery, angels mold between heavy grass and low clouds, flying.
The dog nudges my right hand. The left is cupped, empty.
Breeze slips from the river past bridge, waterwheel, factory.
Beyond dunes, three whiting in a tide pool. A paper boat.
Nuns' orchids in damp woods, brown as habits. Space between.
Mockingbird dreams written down, made up. Hands stick to paper.
Sun between clouds like the yolk of an old blue egg, peeled.
Bread rises fast and light, but the house is too hot to bake.
Whack bean rows to scare snakes. Dirt rolled flat as corn bread.
Cotton bolls burst to thread, spines, grasshoppers like finches.
Dogs bark at heat lightning, raindrops on leaves. Breeze first.
Zinnias and marigolds in a quart jar shed petals, stamens, ova.
The neighbors play *Goldberg Variations* and bridge, windows open.
I never expected it: I didn't know it would be so soon.
Corn in the field—a conservative process. Not kissing, sleep.
The day we climbed past the tree line, stars became rocks.
Porch chairs rock empty in yellow air. Sheets tear like rain.
What's coming leaves me behind; I keep walking through ghosts.

12 Suburban Haiku*
WENDY BISHOP
(after Devan Cook)

* ceiling fan sows confetti of cooler air * alerted, statue of rabbit stares down headlights of slow moving car * the pulse of sleeping children, four legs growing, four arms * cat wails rounder and rounder moons into each window frame—tight fit * stack of books, read, unread, page by page, slides down, * chlorine, ozone, must, rose, oleander, dream sweat, Gulf air, breath * now, again, now, now clumped dried grass drops from lawn mower engine * slight green frog balanced on lip of the hot tub: alluring steam and death * like an expensive dress folded in tissue paper, cotton sheets layer new sleep * wind plays a mariachi of blinds— same tune, one leads, one follows, one strays, catches up * sun ignites woodpecker, cardinal, mockingbird, dampens owl * spoon on white bowl, again, milk smell, pungent, almost sour? again, almost sweet? *

➤ INVENTION EXERCISES ➤

1. Write your own series of haiku after one of these series. Make up your own lineation rule—one haiku to a line, run-on haiku, or boundaries marked by whatever you choose.

2. Write a series of six haiku that make no sense, which isn't an easy thing to do, and then run the haiku together. Looking at Ashbery's poem, can you see more (il)logical connections now that you've tried to create none yourself?

3. Write a series of haiku that attempt to capture the way your mind circles, leaps, and moves around a subject. It might help to draw your pattern first.

HAIKU-LIKE SEQUENCES—
POEMS IN CONNECTED SECTIONS

In the preface to this book, I mention that some readers consider Wallace Stevens' poem "Thirteen Ways of Looking at a Blackbird" to be a haiku sequence. I'm of that way of thinking myself because haiku attributes seem encoded in his poem: the poet is trying to become one with the blackbird by placing himself in the blackbird's place and perspective. The poem reverberates beyond itself in the sense that I can never see a blackbird on a branch without thinking of the ways Stevens sees this bird.

Stevens' poem echoes the idea of scrimshaw, incising a particularly reverberant small vision of the world. "It was Wallace Stevens who asserted that 'Poetry is the Subject of the Poem.' Indeed, the whole of Stevens' work—The Whole of Harmonium, as he wanted to call his *Collected Poems*—is devoted to that subject and thus amounts to a grand ars poetica, each part of which illustrates or explains how "'The poem refreshes life'" (Buckley and Merrill xi). I find that haiku, and more particularly the haiku sequence, "refreshes life" due to the way it juxtaposes images in unexpected, arresting ways. The same is true of the following haiku-like sequences.

Gary Snyder takes us into a Japanese bath house; Linda Pastan writes her beliefs in a poem titled "Ars Poetica"; Charles Simic's series on trees seems influenced by poets like Wallace Stevens and John Ashbery because the units of thought connect but don't exactly say things about trees at night; while Raymond Patterson's "Twenty-Six Ways of Looking at a Blackman," shared in part in the preface and completely here, responds to both Stevens and the haiku tradition. In each of these haiku-like sequences, terseness and tension is maintained, but the haiku form is expanded, seeming more like a series of snapshots or cinema stills with each adding to the preceding shot and each necessary to create the whole.

The Public Bath
GARY SNYDER

the bath-girl
    getting dressed, in the mirror,
        the bath-girl with a pretty mole and a
    red skirt is watching me:
        am I
           different?

the baby boy
    on his back, dashed with scalding water
    silent, moving eyes
    inscrutably
    pees.

the daughters
    gripping and scrubbing his two little daughters
        they squirm, shriek at
          soap-in-the-eye,
    wring out their own hair
        with grave wifely hands,
    peek at me, point, while he
    soaps up and washes their
        plump little tight-lip pussies
    peers in their ears,
        & dunks them in hot tile tub.
        with a brown-burnt farmboy
        a shrivelled old man
        and a student who sings *silent night.*

—we waver and float like seaweed
pink flesh in the steamy light.

the old woman
    too fat and too old to care
       she just stands there
          idly knocking dewy water off her
            bush.
the young woman
    gazing vacant, drying her neck
       faint fuzz of hair
       little points of breasts
          —next year she'll be dressing
            out of sight.
the men
    squatting soapy and limber
    smooth dense skin, long muscles—

I see dead men naked
tumbled on beaches
    newsreels, the
       war

Ars Poetica ❖
LINDA PASTAN

   1. THE MUSE
You may catch
a butterfly
in a net
if you are swift enough

or if you keep
perfectly still
perhaps it will land
on your shoulder.

Often
it is just
a moth.

   2. WRITING
In the battle
between the typewriter
and the blank page

a certain rhythm evolves,
not unlike the hoofbeats
of a horse groomed for war
who would rather be
head down, grazing.

    3. REJECTION SLIP
Darling, though you know
I admire your many
fine qualities
you don't fill all my needs
just now, and besides
there's a backlog
waiting to fit
in my bed.

    4. REVISION
The tree has been green
all summer, but now
it tries red . . . copper . . .
even gold. Soon
leaf after leaf
will be discarded,
there will be nothing
but bare tree, soon
it will be almost time
to start over again.

    5. ARS POETICA
Escape from the poem
by bus, by streetcar—
any way you can,
dragging a suitcase
tied together with twine
in which you've stuffed
all your singular belongings.

Leave behind
a room
washed by sun
or moonlight.
There should be a chair
on which you've draped a coat
that will fit anyone.

Trees at Night
CHARLES SIMIC

Putting out the light
To hear them better
·

To tell the leaves
Of an ash tree
Apart from those
Of a white birch.
·

They would both
Come closer,
They would both whisk me away
·

Images of birds
Fleeing from a fire,
Images of a lifeboat
Caught in the storm.
·

The sound of those
Who sleep without dreams.
·

Being taken hold of
By them.
Being actively taken hold of,
Being carried off
In throes.
·

At times also like the tap
Of a moth
On a windowscreen.
·

A flurry of thoughts.
Sediments
On the bottom of night's ink,
Seething, subsiding.
·

Branches bending
To the boundaries
Of the inaudible.
·

A prolonged hush
That reminds me
To lock the doors.

•

Clarity.
The mast of my spine, for instance,
To which death attaches
A fluttering handkerchief.

•

And the wind makes
A big deal out of it.

Twenty-Six Ways of Looking at a Blackman
RAYMOND PATTERSON
For Boydie & Ama

   I
On the road we met a blackman,
But no one else.

   II
Dreams are reunions. Who has not
On occasion entertained the presence
Of a blackman?

   III
From brown paper bags
A blackman fills the vacancies of morning
With orange speculations.

   IV
Always I hope to find
The blackman I know,
Or one who knows him.

   V
Devouring earthly possessions
Is one of a blackman's excesses.
Exaggerating their transiency
Is another.

   VI
Even this shadow has weight.
A cool heaviness.
Call it a blackman's ghost.

VII
The possibilities of color
Were choices made by the eye
Looking inward.
The possibilities of rhythms
For a blackman are predetermined.

VIII
When it had all been unravelled,
The blackman found that it had been
Entirely woven of black thread.

IX
Children who loved him
Hid him from the world
By pretending he was a blackman.

X
The fingerprints of a blackman
Were on her pillow. Or was it
Her luminous tears?
. . . An absence, or a presence?
Only when it was darker
Would she know.

XI
The blackman dipped water
From a well.
And when the well dried,
He dipped cool blackness.

XII
We are told that the seeds
Of rainbows are not unlike
A blackman's tear.

XIII
What is more beautiful than black flowers,
Or blackmen in fields
Gathering them?
. . . The bride, or the wedding?

XIV

When it was finished,
Some of the carvers of Destiny
Would sigh in relief,
But the blackman would sigh in intaglio,
Having shed vain illusions in mastering the stone.

XV

Affirmation of negatives:
A blackman trembles
That his thoughts run toward darkness.

XVI

The odor of a blackman derives
No less from the sweat of his apotheosis,
Than emanation of crushed apples
He carries in his arms.

XVII

If I could imagine the shaping of Fate,
I would think of blackmen
Handling the sun.

XVIII

Is it harvest time in the brown fields,
Or is it just a black man
Singing?

XIX

There is the sorrow of blackmen
Lost in cities. But who can conceive
Of cities lost in a blackman?

XX

A small boy lifts a seashell
To his listening ear.
It is the blackman again,
Whispering his sagas of drowned sailors.

XXI

At the cradle of Justice were found
Three gifts: a pair of scales, a sword,
And a simple cloth. But the Magi had departed.
Several who were with us agreed
One of the givers must have been
A blackman.

XII
As vines grow towards light,
So roots grow towards darkness.
Back and forth a blackman goes,
Gathering the harvest.

XXIII
By moonlight
We tossed our pebbles into the lake
And marveled
At the beauty of concentric sorrows.
You thought it was like the troubled heart
Of a blackman,
Because of the dancing light.

XXIV
As the time of our leave taking drew near,
The blackman blessed each of us
By pronouncing the names of his children.

XXV
As I remember it,
The only unicorn in the park
Belonged to a blackman
Who went about collecting bits
And torn scraps of afternoons.

XXVI
At the center of Being
Said the blackman,
All is tangential.
Even this laughter, even your tears.

⬳ INVENTION EXERCISES ⬱

1. Undertake a series of linked haiku or linked short observations, as
   Melanie Rawls does here with the insects and animals noted in her
   house one day. Find connections between snapshots of your regular,
   repeating life motions and moments, looking for rituals and significance in what occurs and reoccurs.

*Housekeeping**
    Melanie A. Rawls

When I discovered moths in my rice,
I set the uncapped jar out of doors
so they could fly away.

Small spiders and I
employ diplomacy:
mutual non-acknowledgment.

Large spiders I herd
onto a flyswatter,
rush, trembling,
to the door,
flip them out.

Roaches? I smack.
Or pursue with clouds of
noxious spray around
sticky glasses on the
kitchen counter, down crevices
back behind the sink,
both parties quick and desperate.
Only now I cry,
"All you had to do was
stay outside!"

Ants—two, three, or four ONLY—
okay: "There's sugar on the counter.
Help yourself."

A lizard lived with me once.
It was all unmoving grace:
Aztec brooch pinned
to the living room wall,
needlepoint on a window screen.

2. Like Linda Pastan above and Rita Dove and Archibald MacLeish in the preface, write your ars poetica-based aspects of the poetic life you've discovered in drafting poems from *Thirteen Ways*.

3. Like Raymond Patterson, you may choose your central image for its social and political significance. The linkages here can create tension, point to inequities and assumptions, contrast scenes, and highlight issues.

COMPOSING PERSPECTIVES—GENDER AND AGE

While reading Robert Hass' collection *The Essential Haiku,* I was intrigued by the absence of women haiku writers, which is due to the fact that haiku writing was primarily a man's art. I wondered what it would mean to recuperate the haiku for women. I found my answer in a collection of translations, *A Long Rainy Season,* the work of contemporary women poets, gathered together by another poet who had actively asked the same question.

As you read four haiku by these Japanese women poets, play anthropologist once again and ask if you can sense where they stay with—and where they stray from—the tradition, for, as the editors say in their preface: "many modern and contemporary women poets have found the strict rules of haiku composition stifling and the hierarchical atmosphere of haiku contests intimidating" (18). In these poems, though, the poets seem to have transcended their sense of constraint and intimidation, turning the form to their own uses and interests.

NOBUKO KATSURA
(b. 1914)

The nuisance
of breasts—
a long rainy season.

KIMIKO ITAMI
(b. 1925)

The wedding reception in progress:
a fake view
of the Pacific Ocean.

KIYOKO UDA
(b. 1935)

Window in the
pleasure quarters!
Glint of flying fish.

Dead fireflies—
the night skies have cleared
beautifully.

These writers clearly felt a need to break from traditions even as they acknowledged them. As you do the same, you jazz up haiku, jumping off from other haiku. Ever the advice giver, Basho warns you:

To a prospective student: ❖

> Don't imitate me;
> it's as boring
>   as the two halves of a melon.
>   —trans. by Robert Hass

But I argue that, depending on the way you create, and depending on your attitude toward influence and homage, the two melon halves each have something unique to offer. Imitation in the best sense is an act of reverberation: something in a powerful poem sets up an appreciative response in the reader-who-would-be-writer. And this is far different from rote imitation. Compare, for instance, the ninth haiku in Etheridge Knight's often-anthologized sequence to Issa's haiku.

9 ❖
ETHERIDGE KNIGHT

Making jazz swing in
Seventeen syllables AIN'T
No square poet's job.

ISSA

> Writing shit about new snow ❖
> for the rich
>   is not art.
>   —trans. by Robert Hass

As the quotation from Basho earlier suggests: "The bones of haikai are plainness and oddness." Perhaps you hear a seemingly inevitable honoring of influence that links haiku writers across time and cultures.

"Japanese society, after all, considers that haiku poets do not begin to develop their true talents until age 65, and the average age of famous haiku poets today is over 50" (Lowitz et al. 18). Clearly, the art of achieving insight through haiku writing is part of a lifetime poetic journey.

POCKET DEFINITIONS

Haiku—Growing out of Zen Buddhist philosophy, this is a three-lined poem of 5, 7, 5 syllables; haiku writers seek to capture a moment of perception. Haiku turns on strong natural images, using a word called the *kigo*, that indicates the season, and relays intense emotions, often leading to spiritual insights. Contemporary haiku writers may drop the three-line requirement (often writing the poem as a single line) and/or the syllable count and/or the kigo.

Tanka (also called *waka* or *uta*)—A traditional Japanese poem that is rendered in English in five lines of 5, 7, 5, 7, 7 syllables. Historically, tankas were combined with prose, linked together, and/or published to include exchanges of verse between poets. Subjects vary but often center on travel, love, and the seasons. As with haiku, in Japan today there are regular tanka competitions and a continuing appreciation of this form.

7

LISTING AND REPETITION

Cataloging, Complicating, and Syncopating

Driving at Dawn
VAN K. BROCK

A dead rabbit by the roadside,
Sunlight turning his ears to rose petals.

A new electric fence,
Its five barbed wires tight
As a steel-stringed banjo.

The feet of a fat dove
On a high black line
Throbbing to the hum
Of a thousand waterfalls.

A flock of egrets in a field of cows.

Three Great Blue Herons like hunchbacked
    pelicans in a watering pond.

The red leaves of a bush
Burning inside me.

A swamp holding its breath.

Most of us have driven at dawn and seen the world unrolling beside us, coming alive in the returning light of morning. Like Van K. Brock, we may have looked, listed, and enumerated. When we name what we see, we see it again more fully.

Humans repeat words, sentences, lines. We repeat sounds through assonance and alliteration. We repeat and elaborate on images and themes: flower names in a list of summer flowers in a field include wild iris, wild rose, purple vetch, dandelion, fireweed. And we can list the ways we love or don't love someone. We can number roadkill and celebrate the birds who flock and fly whether we see them or not. We listen for regularity (the woodpecker knocking repetitively on a dry tree trunk) and variation (the moment when he launches into the air, leaving the world empty yet meaningful after the bird's bright presence). We're regulated by sound (heartbeat and breathing), and we like to make noise and to imitate (you clap, I clap). You hum a tune and a day later, I'm humming the same tune. And we learn pledges because elements in them repeat, songs because their refrains repeat, and poems because the rhymes and lines repeat.

> *Repetition is a basic unifying device in all poetry.* Various aspects of form all involve some kind of recurrence of equivalent elements, differing only in what linguistic elements are repeated. —Alex Preminger and T. V. F. Brogan, 1035 (emphasis mine)

Certainly our physical existence is steeped in repetitive motions (in walking we chant, "left, right . . . left, right, left"). And our lives are regulated by repetition (brushing our teeth before we leave the house to go to school or work), while our language echoes, supports, and creates complicated rhythm and syncopation in our lives. Repetition often leads to listing (or is it the reverse?): We list what we need to do today, what to buy at the store, what we hope we'll get for our birthday, our goals, and our promises. List and repetition poems are very tempting to imitate because they are so familiar and comfortable. This chapter provides a limited catalog of such catalogs (since it is by listing we sometimes catalog the world as being a little bit of this and this and this).

One of the list and repetition poems you may be familiar with already is the blues song: "Blues are more than sad songs about lost love and loneliness. They exist as instrumental and vocal music, as psychological state, as lifestyle, and as psychological stance. . . . The blues entered the literary canon as 'folk poetry' in anthologies such as *The Negro Caravan,* and as 'literary poetry' or poems in the folk manner in collections such as Langston Hughes' *The Weary Blues,* where the title poem is not, strictly speaking, blues at all but a lyric framework with narrative elements" (Preminger 142). Those narrative elements rely on repeated lines, variation, and listing, full rhyme, and other familiar song elements, some of which you may have identified when you completed the song/poetry exercise in chapter 1.

The Weary Blues
LANGSTON HUGHES

Droning a drowsy syncopated tune,
Rocking back and forth to a mellow croon,
    I heard a Negro play.
Down on Lenox Avenue the other night
By the pale dull pallor of an old gas light
    He did a lazy sway. . . .
    He did a lazy sway. . . .
To the tune o' those Weary Blues.
With his ebony hands on each ivory key
He made that poor piano moan with melody.
    O Blues!
Swaying to and fro on his rickety stool
He played that sad raggy tune like a musical fool.
    Sweet Blues!
Coming from a black man's soul.
    O Blues!
In a deep song voice with a melancholy tone
I heard that Negro sing, that old piano moan—
    "Ain't got nobody in all this world,
    Ain't got nobody but ma self.
    I's gwine to quit ma frownin'
    And put ma troubles on the shelf."

Thump, thump, thump, went his foot on the floor.
He played a few chords then he sang some more—
    "I got the Weary Blues
    And I can't be satisfied.
    Got the Weary Blues
    And can't be satisfied—
    I ain't happy no mo'
    And I wish that I had died."
And far into the night he crooned that tune.
The stars went out and so did the moon.
The singer stopped playing and went to bed
While the Weary Blues echoed through his head.
He slept like a rock or a man that's dead.

As Hughes does in this poem, there are many ways to repeat and return, including quoting a blues song's lyrics within a blues poem. Writers launch a poem and then return to opening lines, or use **refrains** to close the poem with a satisfying thud or a lighter sense of closure. When a single line is repeated in altered form, it is called a **repetend,** and when the repetend returns to the original form, we know the piece has finished. In some cases, here again a poem by Langston Hughes, the repetend is the initial line of each stanza, while another repetend forms the second line that appears in the first and third stanzas but is changed in the second stanza, leaving the third and fourth lines of each stanza to carry the story. (You'll find more on the shaping of quatrains like these in chapter 10.)

Song for a Dark Girl
LANGSTON HUGHES

Way Down South in Dixie
   (Break the heart of me)
They hung my black young lover
   To a cross roads tree.

Way Down South in Dixie
   (Bruised body high in air)
I asked the white Lord Jesus
   What was the use of prayer.

Way Down South in Dixie
   (Break the heart of me)
Love is a naked shadow
   On a gnarled and naked tree.

Repetition is one of the oldest poetic techniques and the one that is most familiar to many of us. The King James translation of the Bible includes memorable passages of lyrical repetition, from the Old Testament genealogies to the New Testament's Sermon on the Mount, as "begats" and "blesseds" structure the verses. Native American **chants** name the world and create it in words by repeating, varying, elaborating, repeating, and finally closing. "Repetition connects my poetry with the oral tradition," says Lenore Keeshig-Tobias. "I'm Native, so that's my background. . . . Repetition takes place in a number of ways in the oral tradition—repetition of sounds, words, incidents, and events" (Finch 107).

Well-known uses of repetition and listing in the Western poetic tradition include Christopher Smart's poems "Jubilate Agno" (turning on the repeat "Let . . .") and "For I Will Consider My Cat Jeoffry" (turning on the repeat "For he . . .), both written around 1760. The long-lined repeating and listing form was used extensively by Walt Whitman in the last century and by Allen Ginsberg in the 1950s, and Ginsberg's poem "Howl" was influenced by his reading of Whitman and Blake. The pleasures and prevalence of litany and listing continue into present-day poetry.

Gerrit Henry's poem below takes a dark, ironic turn: the author, who really is an art critic, is making fun of the writing and art lives and personas he knows, including his own. In his notes to the poem "The Confessions of Gerrit," Henry says: "The poem is in five stanzas of five lines each—it's a kind of overgrown ballad. Or course, I could have 'confessed' to far graver sins than I did. But this is poetry, and it's always good to hear people laugh." The litany-like, highly repetitive form, even if divided into stanzas, is appropriate for a poem that will be read aloud because the form makes it easier for the writer to dramatize and for the audience to apprehend on first listening.

The Confessions of Gerrit ❖
GERRIT HENRY

I drink a lot of skimmed milk.
I use Lysol Spray in the bathroom.
I stare long and hard at pretty faces.
I'm afraid to ask for the real price of my work.
I write poems, high, after midnight, *well* after.

I stay home alone on Saturday nights.
I have laid in a good supply of Tucks.
I've gotten fat to ward off AIDS.
I've used diet pills to help me work—and think.
I don't exercise anymore, except coming up the stairs.

I was bored by *A Clockwork Orange*, the movie.
I pore over the *National Enquirer*.
I've read about 30 pages of Proust's novel(s).
I like Peggy Lee better than Ella Fitzgerald.
Doesn't that say something awful about me?

My parlor palm is dying, frond by yellowing frond.
I think I'm running out of things to confess.
I'm no Augustine, or even Christina Crawford.
I usually feel like an ass-hole.
I say "Hi, guys!" to dogs tethered on the street.

I write art criticism faster than I can read it.
I don't always enjoy Henry James.
Maybe Geraldine Page is my favorite movie star,
If I could just think of a few movies she starred in.
I hope I am very ambitious.

∽ READING INTO WRITING ∽

Look at the poems presented so far in this chapter and try to make your own catalog of ways a poet can use listing and repetition in a poem. Share this list with your writing group and/or your class. As you continue to read through this chapter, add to and refine this catalog. (You can find list and repetition poems, like Christianne Balk's "Elegy," by consulting the index.) Also, be sure to consider how these writerly choices work with the sense/content/overall delivery of each poem as you interpret and experience it.

REPETITION TO UNIFY

Two Worlds
RAYMOND CARVER

In air heavy
with odor of crocuses,

sensual smell of crocuses,
I watch a lemon sun disappear,

a sea change blue
to olive black.

I watch lightning leap from Asia as
sleeping,

my love stirs and breathes and
sleeps again,

part of this world and yet
part of that.

In the poem "Two Worlds," Raymond Carver uses repetition vertically down
the poem's stanzas, repeating the word "crocuses." Even though no other exact
words repeat across the first three stanzas, the *s* and *c* alliteration does: crocuses, sensual smell, sea, crocuses and change. He links stanzas 4 and 5 with
"sleeping" and "sleep" and stanzas 5 and 6 with repetition of the word "part."
The *s* sounds continue in the last three stanzas: Asia as, sleeping, stirs, breathes
and sleeps. The *t* sounds links together the lines of the final couplet, creating a
sense of closure with "this" and "that." Although this is a couplet poem, the
sounds and repeated words ring down the lines randomly but satisfyingly. The
poet is playing by ear—but with a highly trained ear. Consider Oliver Ruiz's
poem: does he/how does he use repetition to unify his poem? How and how
well does he borrow Carver's techniques?

*Key West**
    Oliver Ruiz

  In the tropic air
  full of coconut smell,

  sweet coconut smell
  I watch the sun go down
  changing my world
  to a fiery red and orange

  A fiery sky, that burns
  in my love's aquatic eyes

  as our heads melt together
  and we breathe the ocean air.

  Land and sea, day and night
  we walk on the beach.

In Hans Ostrom's poem "Fortuitous Twos," the number "two" is used to
unify thematically (each description tries to help us define the essence of
twoness) and audibly. He also casts the poem in couplet form, emphasizing
twoness. To keep the repetition from becoming too predictable, and thus less
engaging, Ostrom includes the word "two" once in the title and once in stanzas 1, 4, and 6; twice in stanzas 4 and 5; and not at all in stanzas 2 and 3. You
can also look back at Van K. Brock's poem that opens this chapter and see how
numbering adds unity to that catalog. Lauri Bohanan, writing her poem after
reading Ostrom's, uses the unifying number "three" differently—as a refrain—
changing the second line of each couplet to provide needed variation that helps
us piece together a possible story. In her poem, we look for the first line to be

repeated, and we're refreshed and urged on when the second line supplies more information, changing both the sound and sense of the poem.

Fortuitous Twos
　　　Hans Ostrom

A pair of spats. Two herons,
early in the morning bending

their necks into water. Windows
on either side of a carved door.

Cells dividing in a newborn baby.
A mother and a daughter

singing two-part harmony.
Two lovers waking up near

the ocean. Two moons circling
one planet. Two old men

golfing in a thunderstorm.
Two minutes before midnight.

Horns on a moonlit skull
two miles from the water hole.

*When I Count to Three**
　　　Lauri Bohanan

When I count to three,
the toys better be picked up.

When I count to three,
the quarter will disappear from my fist.

When I count to three,
your butt better be in the car.

When I count to three,
I'll have calmed down.

When I count to three,
the swats will end.

When I count to three,
the world will explode.

When I count to three,
the pain will be gone.

➤ INVENTION EXERCISES ➤

1. Hans Ostrom has written a series of poems on the numbers zero to
   nine. Try writing your own poem that captures the essence of a different number as it's used and manifested in your everyday life.
   Think about how (and if?) you'll repeat the number and how you'll
   achieve closure.

2. Like Lauri Bohanan, you might draft a poem that uses numbers as
   they're manifested in clichés or sayings yet makes us rethink those
   expected ways of using them: three to get ready; one, two, three, go;
   a stitch in time saves nine, and so on. Try making a list of "number
   sayings" in a group and then choose a few and freewrite on them to
   decide which one is most productive for you.

3. Write a poem that uses exploration and repetition of a color to
   unify. There are many poems that do this. The following is one of
   my favorites. (Lawrence's poem will open up to you if you read it
   with a dictionary to learn about the holiday of Michaelmas, the
   gentian flower, and the myths associated with Dis and Pluto and
   Demeter.

BAVARIAN GENTIANS
D. H. LAWRENCE

Not every man has gentians in his house
in soft September, at slow, sad Michaelmas.

Bavarian gentians, big and dark, only dark
darkening the day-time, torch-like with the smoking blueness of Pluto's
   gloom,
ribbed and torch-like, with their blaze of darkness spread blue
down flattening into points, flattened under the sweep of white day
torch-flower of the blue-smoking darkness, Pluto's dark-blue daze,
black lamps from the halls of Dis, burning dark blue,
giving off darkness, blue darkness, as Demeter's pale lamps give off light,
lead me then, lead the way.

Reach me a gentian, give me a torch!
let me guide myself with the blue, forked torch of this flower
down the darker and darker stairs, where blue is darkened on blueness
even where Persephone goes, just now, from the frosted September
to the sightless realm where a darkness is awake upon the dark
and Persephone herself is but a voice
or a darkness invisible enfolded in the deeper dark
of the arms Plutonic, and pierced with the passion of dense gloom,
among the splendour of torches of darkness, shedding darkness on the lost
    bride and her groom.

Other places to work with, through, and about color include flower
catalogs, bird books, music evoking moods that can be cast in
colors, kitchen utensils, clothes, a car lot, times of day and the colors
of nature at those times, and so on. All these spectrums provide
ideas for talking about objects and the colors they have as well as
the feelings, emotions, and thoughts those colors evoke.

4. In a group, think of other sets and categories that can be used to
   create unity through repetition in a poem—letters of the alphabet,
   traffic signs, types of plants, animals, objects, and so on. Choose one
   and draft a poem that uses one set of these repeats.

LISTING AND REPETITION THAT CATALOGS AND NAMES

Theme for English B ❖
LANGSTON HUGHES

The instructor said,

> *Go home and write*
> *a page tonight.*
> *And let that page come out of you—*
> *Then, it will be true.*

I wonder if it's that simple?
I am twenty-two, colored, born in Winston-Salem.
I went to school there, then Durham, then here
to this college on the hill above Harlem.
I am the only colored student in my class.
The steps from the hill lead down into Harlem,
through a park, then I cross St. Nicholas,
Eighth Avenue, Seventh, and I come to the Y,
the Harlem Branch Y, where I take the elevator
up to my room, sit down, and write this page:

It's not easy to know what is true for you and me
at twenty-two, my age. But I guess I'm what
I feel and see and hear, Harlem, I hear you:
hear you, hear me—we two—you, me, talk on this page.
(I hear New York, too.) Me—who?

Well, I like to eat, sleep, drink, and be in love.
I like to work, read, learn, and understand life.
I like a pipe for a Christmas present,
or records—Bessie, bop, or Bach.
I guess being colored doesn't make me not like
the same things other folks like who are other races.
So will my page be colored that I write?

Being me, it will not be white.
But it will be
a part of you, instructor.
You are white—
yet a part of me, as I am a part of you.
That's American.
Sometimes perhaps you don't want to be a part of me.
Nor do I often want to be a part of you.
But we are, that's true!
As I learn from you,
I guess you learn from me—
although you're older—and white—
and somewhat more free.

This is my page for English B.

In "Theme for English B," an often-anthologized poem by Langston Hughes, the speaker writes about himself for an English teacher. While the poem is memorable for its social and political content, it is also technically impressive as Hughes collages in an instructor's note (in a rhymed quatrain) and then has his speaker ask questions and reply to them. Hughes also lets us see the physical landscape as he lists the speaker's passage down into Harlem, through a park to the YMCA, and into his room. He tells us what he likes—pipes and records—and contemplates the act of writing and what it means for a black man to write his life across a white page. Hughes also underlines his repetition with unexpected and pleasing rhythms and half rhymes that sometimes develop across the distance of several lines: *Salem/Durham, page/age,* and *life/pipe.*

Form to me does not just mean European forms such as the sonnet. It also means forms suggested by the blues or jazz, soul music, call and response communal talk, vernacular speech. It's important to understand the logic to those shapes, as well, and to think about the various syntactic, rhythmic, and organizational logics available to writers who are listening and looking for a multiplicity of forms. —Elizabeth Alexander (Finch 9)

Elizabeth Alexander offers a perspective similar to that which underlies *Thirteen Ways*. To find what forms can do, we have to play with them and work with them to understand their logic. And the logic of the list and repetition poem requires that we examine the rhythms of speech, the decisions of line length and line break, and the syncopated tonal palette that repeat words and rhymes can offer us. We have to remember that we can reiterate, emphasize, play off, and play against ideas as well as with sounds and consider how loudly or softly we want to exhibit all these effects.

In the poem "Nineteen," Elizabeth Alexander repeats less than she returns: each of the three stanzas is a recontemplation of her life at nineteen (and also a continuation of the story of who she was). In the first stanza, she lists the things she eats and drinks. She reminds us of the shape of her narrative by opening the second stanza with a repeat of the words "At nineteen." The repetition in this stanza emphasizes the man she's remembering: "*his* eyes, *he'd* say, *He* brought, *he* learned, *he* said." The third stanza shares the speaker's many questions, reminds us of the "white" foods of the first stanza, and ends with the man—"*he* said"—even though what is important in what he said is all he cannot tell her and all she learns from knowing him. The difference in these two poems is great, but the predisposition to catalog—through list and rhyme and repetition in the case of Hughes and mainly through listing in the case of Alexander—makes me want to imitate them both.

Etheridge Knight's poem, "The Idea of Ancestry," reminds us that one way to catalog, examine, praise, and understand our lives may be to look at the family we are a part of: what composes them, composes us, or as Knight puts it, "I am me, they are thee." That refrain almost demands that we reverse the equation and explore: if these are mine (experiences for Hughes and Alexander, kinfolk for Knight), what parts of them are in me? For all of these poets, race, class, and gender also play a part in the poetic composition and the dramatic effects of the poems.

Nineteen
ELIZABETH ALEXANDER

That summer in Culpeper, all there was to eat was white:
cauliflower, flounder, white sauce, white ice-cream.
I snuck around with an older man who didn't tell me
he was married. I was the baby, drinking rum and Coke
while the men smoked reefer they'd stolen from the campers.
I tiptoed with my lover to poison-ivied fields, camp vans.
I never slept. Each fortnight I returned to the city,
black and dusty, with a garbage bag of dirty clothes.

At nineteen it was my first summer away from home.
His beard smelled musty. His eyes were black. "The ladies love my hair,"
he'd say, and like a fool I'd smile. He knew everything
about marijuana, how dry it had to be to burn,
how to crush it, sniff it, how to pick the seeds out. He said
he learned it all in Vietnam. He brought his son to visit
after one of his days off. I never imagined a mother.
"Can I steal a kiss?" he said, the first thick night in the field.

I asked and asked about Vietnam, how each scar felt,
what combat was like, how the jungle smelled. He listened
to a lot of Marvin Gaye, was all he said, and grabbed
between my legs. I'd creep to my cot before morning.
I'd eat that white food. This was before I understood
that nothing could be ruined in one stroke. A sudden
storm came hard one night; he bolted up inside the van.
"The rain sounded just like that," he said, "on the roofs there."

The Idea of Ancestry
ETHERIDGE KNIGHT

I

Taped to the wall of my cell are 47 pictures: 47 black
faces: my father, mother, grandmothers (1 dead), grand
fathers (both dead), brothers, sisters, uncles, aunts,
cousins (1st & 2nd), nieces, and nephews. They stare
across the space at my sprawling on my bunk. I know
their dark eyes, they know mine. I know their style,
they know mine. I am all of them, they are all of me;
they are farmers, I am a thief, I am me, they are thee.

I have at one time or another been in love with my mother,
1 grandmother, 2 sisters, 2 aunts (1 went to the asylum),
and 5 cousins. I am now in love with a 7 yr old niece
(she sends me letters written in large block print, and
her picture is the only one that smiles at me).
I have the same name as 1 grandfather, 3 cousins, 3 nephews,
and 1 uncle. The uncle disappeared when he was 15, just took
off and caught a freight (they say). He's discussed each year
when the family has a reunion, he causes uneasiness in
the clan, he is an empty space. My father's mother, who is 93
and who keeps the Family Bible with everybody's birth dates
(and death dates) in it, always mentions him. There is no
place in her Bible for "whereabouts unknown."

        II
Each Fall the graves of my grandfathers call me, the brown
hills and red gullies of mississippi send out their electric
messages, galvanizing my genes. Last yr / like a salmon quitting
the cold ocean—leaping and bucking up his birthstream / I
hitchhiked my way from L.A. with 16 caps in my pocket and a
monkey on my back, and I almost kicked it with the kinfolks.
I walked barefooted in my grandmother's backyard / I smelled the old
land and the woods / I sipped cornwhiskey from fruit jars with the men /
I flirted with the women / I had a ball till the caps ran out
and my habit came down. That night I looked at my grandmother
and split / my guts were screaming for junk / but I was almost
contented / I had almost caught up with me.
The next day in Memphis I cracked a croaker's crib / for a fix.

This yr there is a gray stone wall damming my stream, and when
the falling leaves stir my genes, I pace my cell or flop on my bunk
and stare at 47 black faces across the space. I am all of them,
they are all of me, I am me, they are thee, and I have no sons
to float in the space between.

ᗡ READING INTO WRITING ᗡ

1. Read the following two poems, "Nineteen" and "Shopping with
   Freud." Andrea Monroe directly imitates Elizabeth Alexander's
   poem, and William Snyder's poem "Shopping with Freud" offers a
   personal catalog through an analysis of the junk mail the speaker
   has received. Snyder's poem offers an interesting counterpoint to

Hughes', because Snyder's poem considers consumerism in a way reminiscent of how Hughes considers race. Write an analysis of the way repetition and listing is used in each.

Nineteen*
> Andrea Monroe
(Imitation of Elizabeth Alexander's Poem "Nineteen")

That winter in Tallahassee, Christ was in the air. "Christ!" I'd swear as the preachers threw hellfire and brimstone at the students calmly eating in the student union. We ate pizza, bagels with cream cheese, and subs, our saviors for the moment. I ran around with a rebel religion student who didn't tell me he secretly wanted goodness and God. I was a sheep, he told me, because my friends were Christians and Christian Scientists. I tiptoed with him on rooftops where we stared at the stars. When I saw my first shooting star there, it wasn't a revelation.

At nineteen, all I knew was that I wanted to know more. His eyes were black. He reminded me of the mean-spirited gecko which ran free around his apartment, preying on insects. I watched a demonstration of how the gecko can bite down, hard, and never let go. He knew everything about religion, about Bertrand Russell, two creation stories, and contradictions. He had three framed pictures of Jesus on his wall, a mask of the devil above his door, and an iguana which roamed in the Garden of Eden aquarium.

I asked and asked about his youth as a Christian, about his questions never answered by the minister, about his first love who used to say "fishhh" softly when she was two. Those were the best years of his life because he was blind, was all he said, and tried to kiss me. I'd leave at midnight, feeling for my shoes in the dark. At home, I'd eat leftover pizza from the fridge. This was before I understood that I was the Good and the God, with a gecko biting into my neck. One night, as I felt for my shoes in the dark, he sat up and said, "Please stay. Please stay. Please." His eyes were soft like the face in the painting above his head, but I left. He said, "I'll remember this" as I slipped out the door.

Shopping with Freud
WILLIAM SNYDER

A good haul in the mail today—the rejection
note, the sign-up card
for AARP notwithstanding—my box was crammed
with catalogues. Sales. I scan
them this evening over stir-fry and Gallo. Campmoor,
New Year 1996. My weakness: packs particularly, and travel,
but nothing new. Bean's *Spring Thaw 1996.* Sale. An olive
baseball jacket looks good
at $19.95 but I just bought two anoraks, on sale.
And Lands End, but nothing
there except their *Pima Perfected,* and photographs
of men sorting Andean-heaps of cotton. "Soil
and climate," says Senor Fialo who farms
four hectares. But I harvested up
a stack of pants, and shirts and a charcoal herringbone
just before Christmas, so I only skim. *A New Beginning, 1996:*
75 Days of Winter Still to Come and J. Crew's in moss, mushroom,
bark, chili, mineral, pond and their thick, knobby, solid, brown
leather shoes. I would buy an Unconstructed Jacket
in wool melton, probably black,
or maybe loden, if not for my herringbone. I scrape
the bowl with a cold, green,
cabbage ribbon, savor a last hit of wine, turn
to Routledge, *Lit. and Cultural Studies, 1996.* The
Constraints of Desire. Shopping
with Freud. Selves in Discord. In my wallet, in my backpack,
in the livingroom, my VISA, aroused,
tingles its leather sheath. While I scrub
the dishes, and the ink left on my fingers.

2. Etheridge Knight's poem plays with form typographically—emphasizing numbers, using shorthand spellings ("yr" for "year") playing
   with double-voice (parenthetical remarks)—and with the way the
   lines are broken. He uses the traditional method of indicating poem
   line breaks when prose discussions quote poems, that of inserting a
   slash mark, but he uses the slash mark within the lines of his poem.
   How do you read the slash marks in the second stanza of his poem
   (as well as all his other technical, list, repetition, and structural decisions)? What might you borrow for your own work?

1. To write a personal catalog, use the fifteen-sentence portrait prompts found in Devan Cook's Revision Case Study in the appendix. Instead of answering these for someone you know, answer them for yourself. Shape the resulting answers into a first draft.

2. To write a metaphorical personal catalog, answer the following questions about yourself: If you were a time of day, what time of day would you be? (Ask yourself the same question, substituting an animal, a car, a period in history, a piece of clothing, a metal, a plant, an emotion, a landscape, a type of wood, a food.) Take some of this freewriting and begin to shape a self-catalog poem that includes metaphors and similes.

3. Like Hughes, walk yourself from where you live to your classroom and then examine who you are and what you bring to this location at this time in your life. Or like Knight, look through a collection of family photographs and use them as triggers to explore your ancestry.

4. Like Snyder, examine the physical artifacts of your life and use them to define you. You might do this by describing yourself through: all the items on your desk, in your room, in your wallet, and in a junk drawer of odds and ends; or through your mail, the books and newspapers and magazines on your shelves, your sports equipment, and so on. Pick two of these artifact clusters and literally go through them and describe them. Shape the freewrites into a poem draft.

5. Like Alexander and Monroe, go back to an important age your life. First, you might make a list of times that are usual rites of passage, such as puberty, sixteenth birthday, graduation, reaching driving or drinking or voting age. Or, choose ages that are personally significant in your life. Freewrite about several until you find a story unfolding. Follow it into a poem.

GRAMMATICAL OR STRUCTURAL REPETITION FOR NARRATING, NAMING, EXPLAINING— OR THEME AND VARIATION

I Go Back to May 1937
SHARON OLDS

I see them standing at the formal gates of their colleges,
I see my father strolling out

under the ochre sandstone arch, the
red tiles glinting like bent
plates of blood behind his head, I
see my mother with a few light books at her hip
standing at the pillar made of tiny bricks with the
wrought-iron gate still open behind her, its
sword-tips black in the May air,
they are about to graduate, they are about to get married,
they are kids, they are dumb, all they know is they are
innocent, they would never hurt anybody.
I want to go up to them and say Stop,
don't do it—she's the wrong woman,
he's the wrong man, you are going to do things
you cannot imagine you would ever do,
you are going to do bad things to children,
you are going to suffer in ways you never heard of,
you are going to want to die. I want to go
up to them there in the late May sunlight and say it,
her hungry pretty blank face turning to me,
her pitiful beautiful untouched body,
his arrogant handsome blind face turning to me,
his pitiful beautiful untouched body,
but I don't do it. I want to live. I
take them up like the male and female
paper dolls and bang them together
at the hips like chips of flint as if to
strike sparks from them, I say
Do what you are going to do, and I will tell about it.

In "I Go Back to May 1937," Sharon Olds looks not at her own life but at her parents' life, re-narrating the moment they first meet as she imagines it and informed by her knowledge of their subsequent years. Olds considers them as college students and young lovers and works to understand how that moment of meeting has impacted her entire life and how she will testify against and for them.

In "She Had Some Horses," Joy Harjo chooses third-person narration and moves from looking at a particular person to creating a composite of the lives lived by Native Americans today. The poem forces readers to look at cultural stereotypes and see how such typings are both true and false. Harjo—in her chant-type list poem—takes us through the paradoxes and pains and beauties of life for contemporary Native Americans. Both poets use structural repetition to organize their poems. In Sharon Olds' poem, "I see" repeats, and then later in the poem "you," and "her," and then "his," repeats, the pronouns taking on an unexpected importance. In Harjo's poem, the mesmerizing **anaphoric** repeat of "She had some horses" makes us savor the variations in the second half of each line while we remain involved in the first half as we participate, repeating "She had some horses" over and over with the poet.

She Had Some Horses
JOY HARJO

She had some horses.

She had horses who were bodies of sand.
She had horses who were maps drawn of blood.
She had horses who were skins of ocean water.
She had horses who were the blue air of sky.
She had horses who were fur and teeth.
She had horses who were clay and would break.
She had horses who were splintered red cliff.

She had some horses.

She had horses with long, pointed breasts.
She had horses with full, brown thighs.
She had horses who laughed too much.
She had horses who threw rocks at glass houses.
She had horses who licked razor blades.

She had some horses.

She had horses who danced in their mother's arms.
She had horses who thought they were the sun and their
bodies shone and burned like stars.
She had horses who waltzed nightly on the moon.
She had horses who were much too shy, and kept quiet
in stalls of their own making.

She had some horses.

She had horses who liked Creek Stomp Dance songs.
She had horses who cried in their beer.
She had horses who spit at male queens who made
them afraid of themselves.
She had horses who said they weren't afraid.
She had horses who lied.
She had horses who told the truth, who were stripped
bare of their tongues.

She had some horses.

She had horses who called themselves, "horse."
She had horses who called themselves, "spirit," and kept
their voices secret and to themselves.
She had horses who had no names.
She had horses who had books of names.

She had some horses.

She had horses who whispered in the dark, who were afraid to speak.
She had horses who screamed out of fear of the silence, who
carried knives to protect themselves from ghosts.
She had horses who waited for destruction.
She had horses who waited for resurrection.

She had some horses.

She had horses who got down on their knees for any saviour.
She had horses who thought their high price had saved them.
She had horses who tried to save her, who climbed in her
bed at night and prayed as they raped her.

She had some horses.

She had some horses she loved.
She had some horses she hated.

These were the same horses.

Thomas Lux's list poem "He Has Lived in Many Houses" is also written in the third person and presents a catalog of options—the types of places any of us may have and may still call a *house*. By poem's end, we see that the narrator has embarked on an inspection of these habitations that helps him to define what would for him truly be home out of the many possibilities of life and a life's journey.

He Has Lived in Many Houses,
THOMAS LUX

furnished rooms, flats, a hayloft,
a tent, motels, under a table,
under an overturned rowboat, in a villa (briefly) but not,
as yet, a yurt. In these places
he has slept, eaten,
put his forehead to the window glass,
looking out. He's in a stilt-house now,
the water passing beneath him half the day;
the other half it's mud. The tides

do this: they come, they go,
while he sleeps, eats, puts his forehead
to the window glass.
He's moving soon: his trailer to a trailer park,
or to the priory to live among the penitents
but in his own cell,
with wheels, to take him, when it's time
to go, to: boathouse, houseboat
with a little motor, putt-putt,
to take him across the sea
or down the river
where at night, anchored by a sandbar
at the bend,
he will eat, sleep, and press his eyelids
to the window
of the pilothouse
until the anchor-hauling hour
when he'll embark again
toward his sanctuary, harborage, saltbox,
home.

⟶ INVENTION EXERCISES ⟵

1. To write a poem about your parents (working from a real or made-up story), turn to William Snyder's Revision Case Study in the appendix. You'll see how he clusters on the idea and then freewrites and then shapes his writings into a quatrain poem. Follow the same process to write your own. You can also use this technique to re-create the life of any family member or ancestor, from as far back on your family tree as you're willing to go.

2. All of us have complicated backgrounds based on our race, class, and gender. Make a list of who you are. For instance, I'm a heterosexual, white female of 50 percent Norwegian descent who was raised in a lower-middle-class home and now inhabits a professional white-collar niche in the university system. I was raised Methodist and consider myself an agnostic, and politically I'm a democrat and a liberal. While these labels don't really tell you much about my life, I can use them to compose a poem in the manner of "She Had Some Horses" in which I try to analyze "people like me." Here is Rosa Soto's analysis in the same vein. After you read her poem, make your own list about yourself, and then consider several list poem options. You might be gay or Christian or Lebanese or Catholic or blue-collar and want to investigate one or more of those life aspects. Or, more simply and perhaps less politically and/or socially charged, you might want to investigate a current role: being a student, a worker, a writer, etc.

*We Are America**
   Rosa Soto

We don't hang out on street
corners,
We don't stoop in the fields
of our imaginations,
We don't steal the crumbs
of our economy,
We don't drop out of our
schools of knowledge.
We live in the homes
of our people.
We work with our thoughts
and imaginations.
We give to our economy.
We live for the school
who teaches.

We are known as Hispanics.
We are Mexicans, Chicanos,
Puerto Ricans, Cubans, Venezuelans,
Argentineans, and most importantly
we are Americans.

To America we bring
money and poverty, new
attitudes, and old prejudices,
problems and traditions.
We are part of the
American society with
our dreams and lives.
We are like others, we
are doctors, nurses, lawyers,
sport stars, bankers, politicians,
and we are Americans.
In my eyes and in the eyes of our world,
we can say there are
liberals, conservatives,
patriots, and separatists.
We can be the civic minded, the
apathetic, the ambitious
and the beaten.
We Are Americans.

3. Like Thomas Lux use literal descriptions and categories, subcategories, and variations of place to explore a concept. Lux lists types of houses on the way to defining "home." You might do the same. You might use places in a town to define your sense of community or use items and situations in a workplace to define the work that goes on there. Use the third person and a title that works the same way Lux's does. For example, you might title this poem "She Goes Home" or "He Walks through His Town" or "She Works in the Hospital."

Why I Take Good Care of My Macintosh ❖
GARY SNYDER

Because it broods under its hood like a perched falcon,
Because it jumps like a skittish horse
     and sometimes throws me
Because it is poky when cold
Because plastic is a sad, strong material
     that is charming to rodents
Because it is flighty
Because my mind flies into it through my fingers
Because it leaps forward and backward,
     is an endless sniffer and searcher,
Because its keys click like hail on a boulder,
And it winks when it goes out,

And puts word-heaps in hoards for me,
     dozens of pockets of
     gold under boulders in streambeds, identical seedpods
     strong on a vine, or it stores bins of bolts;
And I lose them and find them,

Because whole worlds of writing can be boldly layed out
     and then highlighted and vanish in a flash
     at "delete"   so it teaches
     of impermanence and pain;
And because my computer and me are both brief
     in this world, both foolish, and we have earthly fates,
Because I have let it move in with me
     right inside the tent
And it goes with me out every morning
We fill up our baskets,   get back home,
Feel rich,   relax,   I throw it a scrap and it hums.

Gary Snyder relied on anaphora as do the poets who wrote the next three poems. They used the strong structural repeat to organize our reading of the listing variations that follow. Gary Snyder uses the subordinating conjunction "Because" while Raymond Carver defines "fear" by starting with that word in each line. Hans Ostrom's "Infinitives for the Waitress" explains the speaker's feelings through different infinitive phrases ("to come," "to walk," "to have") that show the speaker's loneliness and need. My poem repeats the subject and verb "I remember" to guide the reader back through the speaker's memories.

Each poem takes a different form. Snyder spins out each "Because" phrase many times in the first stanza and then varies the form in the last two stanzas, using typography—extra spacing—in the last line to emphasize his meaning. Carver's listing of fears is more dense and relentless, the word "Fear" in a line down the left-hand margin, which creates a feeling more like a chant or incantation, similar to Joy Harjo's poem. Ostrom's poem does a little of both: a new infinitive begins each line, and "To" is set out at the left-hand margin so the eye sees a row of "To" going down the page. But each infinitive phrase is varied in length, and Ostrom has cut his lines short to make a narrower poem than Snyder's. My poem "A Life" is in off-rhymed couplets, a reminder that poets can control and let loose across a page their lists, repetitions, and variations.

Fear
RAYMOND CARVER

Fear of seeing a police car pull into the drive.
Fear of falling asleep at night.
Fear of not falling asleep.
Fear of the past rising up.
Fear of the present taking flight.
Fear of the telephone that rings in the dead of night.
Fear of electrical storms.
Fear of the cleaning woman who has a spot on her cheek!
Fear of dogs I've been told won't bite.
Fear of anxiety!
Fear of having to identify the body of a dead friend.
Fear of running out of money.
Fear of having too much, though people will not believe this.
Fear of psychological profiles.
Fear of being late and fear of arriving before anyone else.
Fear of my children's handwriting on envelopes.
Fear they'll die before I do, and I'll feel guilty.
Fear of having to live with my mother in her old age, and mine.
Fear of confusion.
Fear this day will end on an unhappy note.
Fear of waking up to find you gone.
Fear of not loving and fear of not loving enough.

Fear that what I love will prove lethal to those I love.
Fear of death.
Fear of living too long.
Fear of death.
　　I've said that.

Infinitives for the Waitress
　　Hans Ostrom

To come in after work and see
　the blouse slightly unbuttoned.
To walk rudely but speak politely.
To have less than a hundred dollars
　to your name, not counting the pickup
　and the tools.
To not know what "to your name" means.
To look at her hands. To look at her
　look at your hands. To hold the cup
　she held. To taste the bitter bad
　familiar good coffee.
To feel thunderheads stacking up, just
　as if they were leaning against
　the cafe's glass.
To feel the long day's sweat dry.
To worry what the rain will do
　to the house you're building.
To forget about the house you're building.
To watch her re-tie her apron.
To feel empty and full, strong and little,
　lost and found.
To want to ask. To want to hold.
To want to run away from work from life.
To watch her lean against the jukebox,
　hip against chrome.
To watch her drop the quarter in.
To watch her tuck the hair behind her ear.
To leave a big tip and get up and face
　the music of thunderstorms
　and overdue bills. Or
To get up, walking rudely, talking
　politely, holding her, dancing
　with her whose name you do not
　know, the cafe holding its breath,
　the big drops of rain splotching
　the window, her dirty apron against
　your dirty jeans, forever or never.

A Life
WENDY BISHOP

> There is an extravagance in the means my sanity took to rescue their madness
> that makes the one look uncommonly like the other.
> —Rebecca West, "Parthenope"

I remember the sister who fed me soap saying it was food.
I remember falling heavy against the child I said I loved.

I remember amnesiac fists of electricity at my temples.
I remember the chalky powdered diet drinks, change was simple.

I remember an eye of red wine in an arid household.
I remember his deceptive chest, the way his arms pulled.

I remember my voice deep in a well of bed clothes.
I remember the breath-held Sundays, the way the sun rose.

I remember the juggle of accounts, the Christmas sewing machine.
I remember his heart exploding, the way my children screamed.

I remember parties where I was scalded with coffee.
I remember adulthood like work in a munitions factory.

I remember letters I wrote about the facts he altered.
I remember the smell of bolting awake. I remember darkness.

I remember insisting "I am just like everyone else,"
I remember thinking much later that maybe I was.

➤ INVENTION EXERCISES ➤

1. Like Michelle Liles, write a close imitation of any of the preceding
   four poems.

*Why I Miss the Midwest**
   Michelle Liles

Because it is flat space, stretching nowhere,
Because it is simple house, shag carpet,
  and crumbling Victorian turret, hardwood scar,
Because it is wood and brick and fireplace and basement,
Because weather is kinder—
  breeze that turns smoothly chill, quiet snow,
Because it is dark rains that last from morning to night,
Because it is country—buffers of empty grain spread between sharp towns,
Because it is boredom, the stretch of endless clear days that lays a mind flat,
And we push through the storefronts that mirror us,

And it puts upon us the burden of entertainment—
  riding bikes through town,
  ordering plates of fried breading at the fish store for a quarter,
  standing in the freezer doors at Krogers to cool off—
And the days tick over slowly,

Because there's nowhere to go
  no traffic   no beach
  to get tans at   so we explore the terrain
  in which we live, familiar with pockets of epiphany
And because this land holds me
  tightly down, I smell the earth, deep coffee pungency and thick black growth,
Because living was easier and more of a thrill
  then, I remember,
And it goes with me out every morning,
Yet we live separately,   removed,
Alone,   in quiet,   yet the same.

2. Use the structural form to write a looser imitation of any of these poems. After Snyder, you might write about why you value something, but you might choose a stanza form and less obviously repeat words. Following Carver, you might investigate another emotion: hunger, rage, etc. You might try a title with that word but never mention the word again in the poem. Or you might hold off using the defining word entirely until the last stanza.

3. Write a poem back to any of these poems. You might explain why you hate a Macintosh or computers in general. You might be the waitress offering infinitives to the customer or someone else remembering the life the narrator remembers in "A Life" although you see this life quite differently.

4. In a repetition poem, it can be difficult to achieve closure. Often your hardest writing decision to make is determining when and how the poem ends. Look at the techniques used by all the poets so far in this chapter, and make a list of options. Try some on poems you're in the process of drafting. Close a poem in two different ways and share them with a partner to see which method seems to be the most satisfying and effective.

SOUND AND THEME IN COLLUSION

If you try reading Lawson Fusao Inada's poem "To Get to Fresno" aloud, you'll find that the repeated word "Fresno" starts to feel odd in your mouth. It is both object and subject of this poem. Amorak Huey's use of the word "slip" reminds us of the many ways we take a seemingly simple word for granted. He shows us literally how many slippages we can find in the very word *slip*. Read his poem aloud to hear the musicality of the word and its ironic variations. The repeated line in Jane Kenyon's poem, "It might have been otherwise," is insistent in a different way, focusing our reading of that poem. Like most poems—but even more than most poems—list and repetition poems gain from oral readings.

To Get to Fresno
LAWSON FUSAO INADA

To get to Fresno,
you need to turn left
in New York City.

To get to Fresno,
you need to
pop a U-turn
in Tucson.

To get to Fresno,
you need to go up to people
in the marketplace
in Lima, Peru,
and just say "Fresno"
several times.

They'll give you directions,
but be sure you don't settle for
Fresnillo, Mexico—
because you want
the *Real Thing:*

    Fresno, California,
    West Coast,
    U.S. of A.

To get to Fresno,
you have to be
dancing in Zimbabwe
and ask some people
through the music and the heat;

They won't lose the beat,
and from there you can
dance back to Fresno.

To get to Fresno,
you have to go
around and around
the traffic circle
in Berlin, Germany,
around and around
some historical statue
and after you get tired of that
you have to tell some policeman
that it's *Fresno* you're after—
not Paris, not London,
certainly not Rome,

but over there, you know,
beyond all that,
beyond the ocean,
both continents,
and over to F Street, you know,
and the old fish store.

To get to Fresno,
you have to get into, somehow,
the Golden Arches of Moscow,
where they'll tell you to
make a right
at the Ukraine K-Mart
and keep on a-going.

To get to Fresno,
you have to walk along the Ganges
at dusk,
and then just wade in up to your waist,
soaking your robe
as you recite
"Fresno Fresno Fresno"
over and over,

and from there, really,
any direction will get you to Fresno.

To get to Fresno,
you have to look at your watch
at the edge of the Bering Sea,
overlooking the ice floe;
your watch is set
to Fresno time,
so you wave good-bye
to whales, polar bears, seals,

and set out
south through the tundra.

To get to Fresno,
you have to know
where you're getting,

you have to know
what you're getting.

To get to Fresno,
you have to
live in Fresno,

you have to
be in Fresno
for a long time;

you have to
drive all around Fresno
over and over;

you have to
walk all around Fresno
through all the seasons;

you have to
talk about Fresno,
think about Fresno,
ask about Fresno,
know about Fresno;

and just about the time
you think you're
familiar with Fresno,

think that you
finally know Fresno,
really know Fresno,
the *real* Fresno,

someone will ask you,
or you will ask yourself:

> "*Where* is Fresno?"
> "*Who* is Fresno?"
> "*What* is Fresno?"

and despite all of your knowledge,
all of your maps,
all of your facts—

all the certificates and documents
and photographs
you have as proof—

Fresno, as you *think* you know it,
Fresno, as you *know* you know it,

this it, this thing, this place
called "Fresno"

will disappear before your very eyes,

gone forever,
as if it never
existed—

and when you blink your eyes again,
you will be standing in line
or driving through traffic,

startled back to your senses,
to life as you know it, accept it,

and say to yourself:

> "*Welcome back, Fresno.*
> *Welcome back home.*"

Slip*

> Amorak Huey

The way a stranger slips
up to your eight-month-old
in the instant you leave her
to carry the clothes to the car,
knowing you have left
that instant unguarded
but for Christ's sake
you can barely carry the hamper.

The way you slip a love letter
from a woman in another state
between the pages of your book
when your wife walks in.

The way a cartoon oaf slips on a banana peel.

The way time slips away
in the morning and suddenly
you're late and sorry but sorry
doesn't make you on time.

The way you almost call the wrong name.

The way the sun slips and drips
in the afternoon window and lulls
you to sleep. The way her voice,
her eyes, her face, her flesh
slip around you like a net,
draw you in until you forget
who you are.

Otherwise
JANE KENYON

I got out of bed
on two strong legs.
It might have been
otherwise. I ate
cereal, sweet
milk, ripe, flawless
peach. It might

have been otherwise.
I took the dog uphill
to the birch wood.
All morning I did
the work I love.

At noon I lay down
with my mate. It might
have been otherwise.
We ate dinner together
at a table with silver
candlesticks. It might
have been otherwise.
I slept in a bed
in a room with paintings
on the walls, and
planned another day
just like this day.
But one day, I know,
it will be otherwise.

➤ INVENTION EXERCISES ➤

1. If you've ever asked someone how to get from here to there (across a town, to the next post office) or how to assemble something (from a stereo to a Mexican dinner), you know there's more to each of these acts than meets the eye. Lawson Fusao Inada tells you how to get to a real and a mythic city of Fresno. Think of places you might give directions to: how to get to a physical home or how to "go back home" in the sense of return (or combine both ideas in one poem). You can also tell a reader how to make or do something, from how to act on a first date or after a divorce to how to get through college or make a birthday cake. Sketch out some of the things you're expert at (or have a strong opinion about or want to even make fun of perhaps) and decide which one or two has the most levels of possibility. That is, making a birthday cake could also be about how you want a loved one to celebrate your arrival on earth, while how to assemble a stereo could offer literal directions but provide a subtextual commentary on technology (or your lack of skill with the same). Or, you might want to start with a simple celebration of directions like Richard Wade does in his poem "Jambalaya," working for down-to-earth details, and then go on to write a second poem (on the same or a different subject) that plays with levels of meaning.

*Jambalaya**
   Richard Wade

Cook rice until steaming then
heat oil in a Dutch oven.

Add sausage and brown, then
add chicken cubes and continue cooking

until the chicken is white, then
stir in ham then stir in Cajun

seasonings, onion, green pepper and celery, then
cook and stir for five minutes then stir

in tomato sauce and heat to boiling, then
pour over cooked rice and stir to combine.

2. Amorak Huey's poem plays on the meanings of a single word, *slip*. In a group come up with a list of words that could function this way for you in a poem. Choose one such as *drive* and list its meanings: drive a car, drive someone crazy, drive-in movie, driving rain, etc. Then take each phrase and freewrite from there. See if you can assemble these pieces into a poem that tells a story or has a moral (or immoral) twist like Huey's poem.

3. For Inada, Kenyon, and Huey, the subject of the poem is the title of the poem, and the subsequent lines investigate the meaning of that word. Do some free-associating by listing words that have verbal or emotional or content power for you. Start your poem by typing one of your words on your computer screen. Then turn off the screen so you can't see what you're doing and start to investigate the word, using all the techniques you've observed in poems in this chapter: categories, repeats, themes, directions, naming, and so on.

4. Find one of your freewrites from this chapter and shape a poem like Jane Kenyon does. Repeat a phrase but embed the repeats in the poem, away from the left-hand margin. Like Kenyon, you might want to create closure by varying the phrase just slightly.

5. Inada and Huey cast their poems in the second person, telling "you" what to do. This is common when giving directions. In fact, the "you" can be left out as in Wade's poem. Take a poem you've worked on for this chapter and change it from first or third person to second person. How does that change the force and feeling of the poem?

6. Look up one of these poets at your bookstore, in the library, or on the Internet. Read at least one complete collection of poems and then explore how representative the poem in this chapter is to poet's general use of listing and repetition. Is it a technique he or she relies on or uses seldom? Imitate another one of his/her poems that use these techniques in ways you appreciate.

POCKET DEFINITIONS

Anaphora—Initial repetition. This can be a repeated word or phrase ("blessed are they," "a time to"), sentence, or entire line. Used often in biblical verse and many modern list and repetition poems. After a poem is composed in this manner, it is sometimes more effective to drop the originating repetition. Anaphora offers structure and parallelism to a poem and can also help the poet to memorize the verse. Walt Whitman, of course, uses the device in remarkable and memorable ways as do—in variation—authors of hymns, ballads, and poems that use refrains.

Chant—A verbal presentation that is a mixture of speech and song and is aided by repetition, accompaniment, recurring rhyme, and/or syntactic patterns. A chant is performed by a single or several performers.

Refrain—A regular, nearly exact repeat of a phrase or line, often at the end of a stanza.

Repetend—An irregular repeat of a word, phrase, or line in a poem.

8

ODES AND PRAISE SONGS

When Poets Look Up

A Noiseless Patient Spider
WALT WHITMAN

A noiseless patient spider,
I mark'd where on a little promontory it stood isolated,
Mark'd how to explore the vacant vast surrounding,
It launch'd forth filament, filament, filament, out of itself,
Ever unreeling them, ever tirelessly speeding them.

And you O my soul where you stand,
Surrounded, detached, in measureless oceans of space,
Ceaselessly musing, venturing, throwing, seeking the spheres to connect
   them,
Till the bridge you will need be form'd, till the ductile anchor hold,
Till the gossamer thread you fling catch somewhere, O, my soul.

Too often, perhaps, we imagine poets as doomed romantic creatures, speaking of lost love and deep sadness. Or isolated in a vast universe, as is the speaker of Walt Whitman's poem in the "measureless oceans of space." Images from movies certainly help nurture this vision. In one of my classes, one of my students said, "I can only write poems when I'm depressed." Knowing that a long tradition of poetic celebration does exist, ranging from odes to certain types of verse written to commemorate a particular event, I took this student's statement as an example of accepted but unchallenged stereotypes and replied jokingly, "I hope you won't have to be depressed all term." Still, these cultural beliefs about poets and sadness, madness, and depression made me think it was time to include more celebration poems when teaching poetry to show its positive virtues as a vehicle of affirmation, appreciation, and humor. We can use poetry to create that delicate filament of connection that the spider and soul in Whitman's poem create. The writers whose drafts appear next took my challenge to look up, celebrate, and praise, even if ironically, in their poems.

Ode on Mountains of Haiti*
    Mitshuca Beauchamp

> O I climbed, climbed the hill tops!
>   Bare feet, I hurt, but I climbed on.
> O I climbed my beloved mountain to reach stars!
>   I shaped my mountain in a staircase.
> O I climbed the trees with joyful awareness of my youth!
>   Playing hide-and-seek while I ate mangoes.
> O I climbed high into the woods whereas,
>   I heard Mama calling me, "Shuca!"
> O I climbed and I yelled, "The birds are making too
>   Much noise, I can't hear you."
> O I climbed frightened to reach the top!
> O I climbed, climbed the hill tops!

In Praise of Henry James*
    Richard Wade

> Henry James
> with a turn of the screw
> turned one story into two.
> We can't ask the governess, because of her psychosis.
> We can't ask the children, because of their sweetness.
> We can't ask Mrs. Gross, because she is illiterate.
> We can't ask the Lord, because he lives in London.
> So the questions still remain,
> was the governess insane,
> or was it truly something supernatural?

ODES

To celebrate, commemorate, and meditate on people or events, you might chose to write an **ode**. Originally, these were formally structured and written for choruses in Greek plays to sing or chant. (You may remember how the movie *The Mighty Aphrodite* by Woody Allen makes fun of this tradition.) In *Pindaric odes,* the chorus on stage speaks and moves left, speaks again and moves right, and finishes with a third response. The left (strophe) and right (antistrophe) movements take the same stanza form, while the final response (epode) differs from these two. The celebratory Pindaric ode evolved into the more meditative *Horatian ode* like this one by John Keats. Using five ten-lined, generally pentameter, mostly end-stopped stanzas, Keats develops his philosophical theme.

Ode on a Grecian Urn
JOHN KEATS

I

Thou still unravish'd bride of quietness,
    Thou foster-child of silence and slow time,
Sylvan historian, who canst thus express
    A flowery tale more sweetly than our rhyme:
What leaf-fring'd legend haunts about thy shape
    Of deities or mortals, or of both,
        In Tempe or the dales of Arcady?
    What men or gods are these? What maidens loth?
What mad pursuit? What struggle to escape?
    What pipes and timbrels? What wild ecstasy?

II

Heard melodies are sweet, but those unheard
    Are sweeter; therefore, ye soft pipes, play on;
Not to the sensual ear, but, more endear'd,
    Pipe to the spirit ditties of no tone:
Fair youth, beneath the trees, thou canst not leave
    Thy song, nor ever can those trees be bare;
    Bold lover, never, never canst thou kiss,
Though winning near the goal—yet, do not grieve;
    She cannot fade, though thou hast not thy bliss,
    For ever wilt thou love, and she be fair!

III

Ah, happy, happy boughs! that cannot shed
    Your leaves, nor ever bid the spring adieu;
And, happy melodist, unwearied,
    For ever piping songs for ever new;
More happy love! more happy, happy love!
    For ever warm and still to be enjoy'd,
        For ever panting, and for ever young;
All breathing human passion far above,
    That leaves a heart high-sorrowful and cloy'd,
        A burning forehead, and a parching tongue.

IV

Who are these coming to the sacrifice?
 To what green altar, O mysterious priest,
Lead'st thou that heifer lowing at the skies,
 And all her silken flanks with garlands drest?
What little town by river or sea shore,
 Or mountain-built with peaceful citadel,
  Is emptied of this folk, this pious morn?
And, little town, thy streets for evermore
 Will silent be; and not a soul to tell
  Why thou art desolate, can e'er return.

V

O Attic shape! Fair attitude! with brede
 Of marble men and maidens overwrought,
With forest branches and the trodden weed;
 Thou, silent form, dost tease us out of thought
As doth eternity: Cold Pastoral!
 When old age shall this generation waste,
  Thou shalt remain, in midst of other woe
Than ours, a friend to man, to whom thou say'st,
 "Beauty is truth, truth beauty,"—that is all
  Ye know on earth, and all ye need to know.

Reading this romantic, lovely (though to the modern ear possibly somewhat archaic) poem, the author's language may sound stilted to us. And it's not hard to see how the form could easily lend itself to parody and irony since we don't regularly walk around saying, "Thou shalt remain, in midst of other woe." Famous odes, like those of John Keats, are also easy to parody because we live in a more fragmented social climate—that of video, soundbites, freeways, and malls.

Ode on a Grecian Urn Summarized ❖
DESMOND SKIRROW

Gods chase
Round vase.
What say?
What play?
Don't know.
Nice, though.

The term "ode" has a checkered history, in part because it is derived from a Greek word for "song" and differs little in root meaning, therefore, from "sonnet," "hymn," "carmen," "cantata," "canzone," and countless other terms. Appealing to usage does not clarify matters as much as one could wish because poets have often seemed to use the word so indiscriminately that most readers pay no attention to its presence in a title. —Paul Fry, 4

Consider your own developing definition of *ode* as you read these two translations of a Horatian ode—Ode 1 (out of eleven)—from the Latin.

Horace to Leuconoe
EDWIN ARLINGTON ROBINSON

I pray you not, Leuconoe, to pore
With unpermitted eyes on what may be
Appointed by the gods for you and me,
Nor on Chaldean figures any more.
'T were infinitely better to implore
The present only:—whether Jove decree
More winters yet to come, or whether he
Make even this, whose hard, wave-eaten shore
Shatters the Tuscan seas to-day, the last—
Be wise withal, and rack your wine, nor fill
Your bosom with large hopes; for while I sing,
The envious close of time is narrowing;—
So seize the day, or ever it be past,
And let the morrow come for what it will.

Horace Coping
JOHN FREDERICK NIMS

Don't ask—knowing's taboo—what's in the cards, darling, for you, for me,
what end heaven intends. Meddle with palm, planet, séance, tea leaves?
—rubbish! Shun the occult. Better by far take in your stride what comes.
Long life?—possible. Or—? Maybe the gods mean it your last, this grim
winter shaking the shore, booming the surf, wearying wave and rock.
Well then! Learn to be wise; out with the wine. Knowing the time so short,
no grand hopes, do you hear? Now, as we talk, huffishly time goes by.
So take hold of the day. Hugging it close. Nothing beyond is yours.

For many of us, it's hard to find appropriate moments and methods for exploring the meaning(s) of life. Often, we find it easier to provide cultural commentary in a wry or ironic voice (as Richard Wilbur's poem "Junk" in chapter 2 does). One of the more famous twentieth century odes, "Dulce et Decorum Est" by Wilfred Owen, takes its title and closing lines from Horace. "Dulce et decorum est pro patria mori" translates as "It is sweet and fitting to die for one's country" and gives us the real sense of the hellishness of war (in this case World War I). Following it is what seems to be a parody of war odes (until the final two lines), Peter Meinke's "Ode to Good Men Fallen Before Hero Come." Reading these, you see that practicing poets will benefit from making time for writerly meditations. Writing odes intentionally is one way to do this philosophical work. Owen writes two rhymed octets (eight-line stanzas) with a regularizing pattern of *a b a b c d c d* followed by a third stanza of twelve lines. He also uses alliteration (*backs, boots, blind, behind*) and repetition (*fumbling, stumbling, drowning, drowning*), emphasizing line endings. Meinke's poem is also in octets with slant end rhymes in more irregular patterns, as he adds unexpected spacing to the lines of his third stanza.

Dulce et Decorum Est
WILFRED OWEN

Bent double, like old beggars under sacks,
Knock-kneed, coughing like hags, we cursed through sludge,
Till on the haunting flares we turned our backs
And towards our distant rest began to trudge.
Men marched asleep. Many had lost their boots
But limped on, blood-shod. All went lame; all blind;
Drunk with fatigue; deaf even to the hoots
Of tired, outstripped Five-Nines that dropped behind.

Gas! Gas! Quick boys!—An ecstasy of fumbling,
Fitting the clumsy helmets just in time;
But someone still was yelling out and stumbling
And flound'ring like a man in fire or lime . . .
Dim, through the misty panes and thick green light,
As under a green sea, I saw him drowning.
In all my dreams, before my helpless sight,
He plunges at me, guttering, choking, drowning.

If in some smothering dreams you too could pace
Behind the wagon that we flung him in,
And watch the white eyes writhing in his face,
His hanging face, like a devil's sick of sin;
If you could hear, at every jolt, the blood
Come gargling from the froth-corrupted lungs,
Obscene as cancer, bitter as the cud
Of vile, incurable sores on innocent tongues,—
My friend, you would not tell with such high zest
To children ardent for some desperate glory,
The old Lie: Dulce et decorum est
Pro patria mori.

Ode to Good Men Fallen Before Hero Come
PETER MEINKE

In all story before hero come
good men from all over set forth
to meet giant ogre dragon troll
and they are all killed every one
decapitated roasted cut in two
their maiden are carted away and gobbled like cupcake
until hero sail across white water
and run giant ogre dragon troll quite through

and of course explode into rejoicing
and king's daughter kisses horny knight
but who's to kiss horny head of slaughtered
whose bony smile are for no one in particular
somewhere left out of story somebody's daughter
remain behind general celebration
combing her hair without looking into mirror
rethinking life without Harry who liked his beer

I sing for them   son friend brother
all women-born men like one we know
ourselves   no hero they no Tristan
no St. George Gawain Galahad Sgt. York
they march again and again to be quartered and diced
and what hell for them never attempt to riddle
I'm talking about Harry Smith caught in middle
who fought pretty bravely for nothing and screamed twice.

The ode differs from elegy . . . chiefly in coming upon death while
meaning to talk about birth; whereas in the typical movement of an
elegy it is the other way around. —Paul Fry, 4

Having read several odes, reconsider them in light of Paul Fry's definition. In
what way do they come upon death while talking about birth? (You'll also want
to consider if the reverse seems true in regard to the elegy, discussed in chapter
4.) Consider, too, how this definition might prove true in the odes you draft
using any of the following inventions.

➤ INVENTION EXERCISES ➤

1. Find an artifact—a painting, a relic, a family treasure, a sculpture, a
   piece of old town architecture, a gravestone—and contemplate it for
   some time. Make notes on the actual physical details of what you
   see.

a. Freewrite regarding the object from the perspective of the person/persons you imagine putting it there or constructing it.
b. Freewrite regarding the object from your own contemporary perspective.
c. Freewrite about what you've learned from these two exploratory perspectives.

Shape these freewrites into a modern Pindaric ode in three parts. To do this:

- Choose a simple stanza or syllabic pattern for freewrites a and b. (These patterns should be identical.) Choose a looser or different syllabic pattern for freewrite c.
- Your poem might consist then of one stanza of syllabic verse (eight syllables per line times ten lines) and a second following the same pattern.
- The final verse might be in longer lines (fourteen syllables). Continue on until you've completed your thoughts.
- Title the poem "Ode on a. . . ." (Or like Natasha Clews create your own form but retain the title to indicate the source of your poem.)

*Ode to a Reliable Thing**
  Natasha Clews

The yellow sheets lay wrinkled around you.
The stale air of sleeplessness and beer hung over you.
In the hard dark of early morning I heard you.
I lay silent for a moment, then touched you.

You felt cold and smooth.
You had a glowing face.
You were familiar to my touch.
You had a tattooed side.
(initialed S.O.N.Y.).

At first I threw you.
I tried to ignore you.
Then again I heard you
Eventually I pleased you
(jumped out of bed)

You, who bring me into each new day.

2. Write an ode that deals with war by memorializing a person known or unknown who gave her or his life; by commenting on nationalism; or by presenting your response to a movie on war you've seen (such as *Saving Private Ryan* and *The Thin Red Line*). You can look up reviews and responses to these movies on the Internet and get a

sense of the controversies these portrayals have raised—some of
which you might want to explore in your ode.

Some modern poets write odes that, while humorous, do commemorate the
beauty they find in unexpected places. In doing this, they move from the
Horatian ode to the *Cowleyan ode* pattern. By freeing the ode from formal constraints, they've turned the ode into a genre of writing, a type of text that celebrates, praises, and even teases. In fact, today almost any meditative or
celebratory poem can be labeled an "ode" if the poet so chooses. In the first of
the following odes, the poet uses free verse, and in the second and third, the
poets follow a regular—but not traditional Pindaric or Horatian—stanza pattern. The poets, Pablo Neruda, Mary Swander, and Donald Hall, uncover the
praiseworthy in the plain as Neruda speaks of watermelon, Swander of okra,
and Hall of cheeses. In fact it's easy to see that odes require an exclamatory attitude of discovery and appreciation. Each poet has used a strikingly different
verse form for composing their odes: Neruda choosing short-lined free verse,
Swander alternating tercets and quatrains of differing line lengths, and Hall
using fairly regularized long-lined quatrains.

Ode to the Watermelon
PABLO NERUDA

The tree of intense
summer,
hard,
is all blue sky,
yellow sun,
fatigue in drops,
a sword
above the highways,
a scorched shoe
in the cities:
the brightness and the world
weigh us down,
hit us
in the eyes
with clouds of dust,
with sudden golden blows,
they torture
our feet
with tiny thorns,
with hot stones,
and the mouth

suffers
more than all the toes:
the throat
becomes thirsty,
the teeth,
the lips, the tongue:
we want to drink
waterfalls,
the dark blue night,
the South Pole,
and then
the coolest of all
the planets crosses
the sky,
the round, magnificent,
star-filled watermelon.

It's a fruit from the thirst-tree.
It's the green whale of the summer.
The dry universe
all at once
given dark stars
by this firmament of coolness
lets the swelling
fruit
come down:
its hemispheres open
showing a flag
green, white, red,
that dissolves into
wild rivers, sugar,
delight!

Jewel box of water, phlegmatic
queen
of the fruitshops,
warehouse
of profundity, moon
on earth!
You are pure,
rubies fall apart
in your abundance,
and we

want
to bite into you,
to bury our
face
in you, and
the soul!
When we're thirsty
we glimpse you
like
a mine or a mountain
of fantastic food,
but
among our longings and our teeth
you change
simply
into cool light
that slips in turn into
spring water
that touched us once
singing.
And that is why
you don't weigh us down
in the siesta hour
that's like an oven,
you don't weigh us down,
you just
go by
and your heart, some cold ember,
turned itself into a single
drop of water.
          —trans. by Robert Bly

Ode to Okra
MARY SWANDER

Mumbo, jumbo, pot-full-of-gumbo, o sweet okra,
red stem, pink blossom, only plant in the garden
to survive this summer's heat, wilt, grasshopper drought.

And there is no cure for this plague:
guinea hens, traps, sprays, hand-picking won't stop
these insects from stripping leaves,
chewing through the screen door.

Rain fifteen inches down, their eggs never drowning,
these bugs just keep on fucking—two, three, four
generations at once hovering on the fence,
waiting to begin their chomping.

And there is no help for the poor
tomatoes, potatoes, lettuce, turnips, squash.
They've all collapsed into mush.

All but my beautiful, ugly okra.
Seed pods: sliced, diced, rolled in corn meal,
fried in a pan. Cut up and dropped into soups,
stew pots in the winter to stretch further.

Take me in, sweet meat, teach me the secret
of your stalks, eye high by the Fourth of July.
Heal me with the nod of your leaves,

the deep veins and lobes, bundles of fibers,
the thin layer of skin covering your bud scars,
the shimmer of each new flower.

O Cheese
DONALD HALL

In the pantry the dear dense cheeses, Cheddars and harsh
Lancashires; Gorgonzola with its magnanimous manner;
the clipped speech of Roquefort; and a head of Stilton
that speaks in a sensuous riddling tongue like Druids.

O cheeses of gravity, cheeses of wistfulness, cheeses
that weep continually because they know they will die.
O cheeses of victory, cheeses wise in defeat, cheeses
fat as a cushion, lolling in bed until noon.

Liederkranz ebullient, jumping like a small dog, noisy;
Pont l'Evêque intellectual, and quite well informed; Emmentaler
decent and loyal, a little deaf in the right ear;
and Brie the revealing experience, instantaneous and profound.

O cheeses that dance in the moonlight, cheeses
that mingle with sausages, cheeses of Stonehenge.
O cheeses that are shy, that linger in the doorway,
eyes looking down, cheeses spectacular as fireworks.

Reblochon openly sexual; Caerphilly like pine trees, small
at the timberline; Port du Salut in love; Caprice des Dieux
eloquent, tactful, like a thousand-year-old hostess;
and Dolcelatte, always generous to a fault.

O village of cheeses, I make you this poem of cheeses,
O family of cheeses, living together in pantries,
O cheeses that keep to your own nature, like a lucky couple,
this solitude, this energy, these bodies slowly dying.

In the poetry group I belong to, we're all fans of food poems, and that's probably why I'm so fond of these food odes. In addition, there's plenty of room for truly contemporary celebrations, poems that praise or at least explore the miracles (or terrors) of technology. Gary Snyder, who often writes poems about the natural environment, tells us in a poem why he takes care of his Macintosh computer despite its nonnatural being. This poem, shared in chapter 7, is a list poem as well as an ode, just as Donald Hall's poem "O Cheese" is also a list and repetition poem. In fact, to write in praise of something, we may begin by listing the noteworthy attributes of that person, place, or thing, paying homage to the wise and meditative ranges of the ode. For instance, look back at the opening poem by Walt Whitman, who uses his observations of a spider to consider an element in our lives that no science can explain.

⬝ INVENTION EXERCISES ⬝

1. Make the following lists:
   a. foods you love
   b. animals you love
   c. plants you value
   d. special places (locations or landscapes) in your life
   e. technologies you admire
   f. famous people you admire (or infamous people you admire)
2. Choose two of these categories and write (at least semi-) serious odes on the object, person, or place. For one ode, follow your own free verse pattern. For the second ode, follow any sort of stanza pattern you care to set up.
3. Choose the most unlikely object, person, or place on your list. Cluster about the connections you can make and explore the unlikelihood of this as an object of meditation. Form this cluster into a free verse parody of an ode that comments on the subject of the poem and on you, the writer.

*Ode to a Pancake**
  Mindy Kemman

Saturday morning
The table's already set
Baby's prancing around the kitchen
Sporting a blue checkered apron
I sip my coffee
And listen to the sticky lick
Of batter spilling onto a hot pan.
Oil's heavy effervescence
Banging and chanting until
The edges are crisp and brown.
It's delivered to my plate with pleasure
A full moon. . .
Now with yellow butter . .
Now overripe with maple syrup . .
A slow, sweet halo forms around
My pancake.

PRAISE SONGS AND POEMS OF PRAISE

The [African] bard, who himself may play a musical instrument, is accompanied by a small group of musicians . . . and eventually by one or more apprentices, one of whom may act as the most active listener, encouraging the bard through praises and helping him when he has a problem. The text may be sung in its entirety, or recited with interspersed songs. Some performances include dramatic action during the recitation, the bard, enacting, often, some action in which the hero is involved. In most groups, the bard is also dressed, painted, and provided with appropriate paraphernalia for the occasion; for example, he may hold certain objects that suggest the power of the hero's possessions. —Alex Preminger and T. V. F. Brogan, 14

As mentioned earlier, we often think of poets as expressing strong but often overwrought emotions: depression, sadness, loss, longing, unrequited love, etc. While this is sometimes true, it is not universally so. When I lived for a year in Nigeria, every festival had several praise singers. These were individuals—often religious men in this predominantly Moslem area—who sang songs praising the family who hired them. Payment was made by running up to the sweating singer and letting currency stick to his wet forehead, for his sweat showed the sincerity and strength of his **Praise Song**. When the praise singer would begin, everyone at the festival would circle around and participate in the moment of celebration. My poem is written in the persona of a boy who accompanies a blind praise singer, a holy man:

Praise Song
Kano, Nigeria

I was the blind man's begging boy,
Guide and crutch. Touching my arm,
He tugged like a shirt in the breeze.
He was pleased to wander while I worked
To turn him from traffic to alleys
And safe pathways. He waited in shade
Outside the school where I copied Koran.
Later, with my bowl, I'd beg for us both
From strangers and friends as he
Walked along singing praise for Allah
Beneath fierce Kano skies. I was that
Blind man's son. I grew up in this town
And passed through the streets at his side.
How he sang on hot mornings his praise songs!

Writing this poem and considering this genre of writing, I realized that certain poems—often odes and sometimes poems labeled song, **psalm**, or containing the word *praise*—were a special type of verse I valued. These poets found beauty and wonder in the world, often in the natural world. I present some here. In some ways these are less exclamatory and more meditative poems than the odes above, yet they share a careful attention to the details of the world and offer readers a poet's sense of devoted celebration.

Pied Beauty
GERARD MANLEY HOPKINS

Glory be to God for dappled things—
    For skies of couple-colour as a brindled cow;
        For rose-moles all in stipple upon trout that swim;
Fresh-firecoal chestnut-falls; finches' wings;
    Landscape plotted and pieced—fold, fallow, and plow;
        And all trades, their gear and tackle and trim.

All things counter, original, spare, strange;
    Whatever is fickle, freckled (who knows how?)
        With swift, slow; sweet, sour; adazzle, dim;
He fathers-forth whose beauty is past change:
                    Praise him.

Poem Made of Water ❖
NANCY WILLARD

Praise to my text, Water, which taught me writing,
and praise to the five keepers of the text,
water in Ocean, water in River, water in Lake,
water in cupped hands, water in Tears. Praise
for River, who says: Travel to the source,
poling your raft of words, mindful of currents,
avoiding confusion, delighting in danger
when its spines sparkle, yet keeping
your craft upright, your sentences alive.
You have been sentenced to life.

Praise for Ocean and her generous lesson,
that a great poem changes from generation to generation,
that any reader may find his treasure there
and even the landlocked heart wants to travel.
Praise for that heart, for its tides,
for tiny pools winking in rocks
like poems which make much of small matters:
five snails, two limpets, a closely watched
minnow, his spine a zipper,
and a white stone wearing the handprints of dead coral.

Praise for Tears, which are faithful to grief
not by urns but by understatement.
Praise for thirst, for order in the eye and in the ear
and in the heart, and for water in cupped hands,
for the poem that slakes thirst
and the poem that wakes it.
Praise for Lake, which bustles with swimmers at noon.
I have been one, busy under the light,
piling rocks into castles, not seeing
my work under the ruffled water.

And later—the lake still sleepy in the last light—
the castle squats like the rough draft of a prayer,
disguised as a castle, which tells me
to peer into the dark and interpret shapes in the ooze:
the row boat rising like a beak, the oil drum rusting,
the pop bottles fisted in weeds, every sunken
thing still, without purpose, dreamed over
till the fisherman's net brings up—
what? a bronze mask? a torso of softest marble?

Go deep. Save, sift, pack, lose, find again.
Come back as snow, rain, tears, crest and foam.
Come back to baptize, heal, drown.
Come back as Water. Come back as Poem.

The Plum Trees
MARY OLIVER

Such richness flowing
through the branches of summer and into

the body, carried inward on the five
rivers! Disorder and astonishment

rattle your thoughts and your heart
cries for rest but don't

succumb, there's nothing
so sensible as sensual inundation. Joy

is a taste before
it's anything else, and the body

can lounge for hours devouring
the important moments. Listen,

the only way
to tempt happiness into your mind is by taking it

into the body first, like small
wild plums.

August
MARY OLIVER

When the blackberries hang
swollen in the woods, in the brambles
nobody owns, I spend

all day among the high
branches, reaching
my ripped arms, thinking

of nothing, cramming
the black honey of summer
into my mouth; all day my body

accepts what it is. In the dark
creeks that run by there is
this thick paw of my life darting among

the black bells, the leaves; there is
this happy tongue.

Praise the Tortilla,
Praise the Menudo,
Praise the Chorizo
RAY GONZÁLEZ

I praise the tortilla in honor of El Panzón,
who hit me in school every day and made me see
how the bruises on my arms looked like
the brown clouds on my mother's tortillas.
I praise the tortilla because I know
they can fly into our hands like
eager flesh of the one we love,
those soft yearnings we delight in biting
as we tear the tortilla and wipe the plate clean.

I praise the menudo as visionary food that it is,
the tripas y posole tight flashes of color
we see as the red caldo smears across our notebooks
like a vision we have not had in years,
our lives going down like the empty bowl
of menudo exploding in our stomachs
with the chili piquin of our poetic dreams.

I praise the chorizo and smear it
across my face and hands,
the dayglow brown of it painting me
with the desire to find out
what happened to la familia,
why the chorizo sizzled in the pan
and covered the house with a smell
of childhood we will never have again,
the chorizo burrito hot in our hands,
as we ran out to play and show the vatos
it's time to cut the chorizo,
tell it like it is before la manteca runs down
our chins and drips away.

Happiness
RAYMOND CARVER

So early it's still almost dark out.
I'm near the window with coffee,
and the usual early morning stuff
that passes for thought.
When I see the boy and his friend
walking up the road
to deliver the newspaper.
They wear caps and sweaters,
and one boy has a bag over his shoulder.
They are so happy
they aren't saying anything, these boys.
I think if they could, they would take
each other's arm.
It's early in the morning,
and they are doing this thing together.
They come on, slowly.
The sky is taking on light,
though the moon still hangs pale over the water.
Such beauty that for a minute
death and ambition, even love,
doesn't enter into this.
Happiness. It comes on
unexpectedly. And goes beyond, really,
any early morning talk about it.

➤ INVENTION EXERCISES ➤

1. List ten instances when you felt a moment of exquisite happiness. Freewrite on two of those occasions, trying to catch the physical details: where were you, what were you wearing, who else was there, what was occurring, why was the happiness unexpected or expected, and so on. Then write a poem titled "Happiness" (for now—you may change the title later) that paints a picture of that moment and by doing so, evokes the sense of happiness and makes the reader experience some of your happiness. Try not to be vague or general (look at how Raymond Carver paints his scene: "the moon still hangs pale over the water") because you're aiming to make your reader have a physical reaction, like goosebumps, to your words.

*Senses of Happiness**
   Natasha Clews

Echoes of Barr Harbor
its sea cities
dancing with the ocean
crystal conversation
of the seal, seagull and seagrass.

Smells of
steaming pancakes
homemade batter
sweet maple syrup
late mornings
of flap-jacks, firewood and family.

Sights of
night planes
passing the world
synthesizing stars
awakening eyes
on long drives, the locust and lovers.

Touches of
shaved legs
rubbed slowly together
still warm
the long shower
water's spray, a soft towel, and silken body.

Tastes of
a tangerine
its bursting capsules
erupting in the mouth
an orange ocean
a sweet sea, sugar brushed, sense of happiness.

2. List individuals in your life who have helped you become the person you are (or the person you want to be). Choose one of these individuals and list what things you learned about and from the person: how to dress, how to speak, how to deal with a situation, how to fix ice cream sundaes, how to repair a flat tire, how to love a difficult situation or person, and so on. Tell how you learned through watch-

ing this person in the world. Then shape that writing into a praise poem. Try not to be sentimental but think of sharing the poem with that person and how you'd really like him or her to learn about things you've never shared before. Make the poem exclamatory but leave off the exclamation points.

3. Close your eyes a minute and put yourself in your favorite natural scene. Better yet, go to that physical location.

    a. Write a physical description of everything that makes this place special, using all your senses. What does it smell like, look like, feel like, sound like, taste like? Now, let moments when you've experienced peace in this location play through your mind like a slide show and take notes as you do these mental or physical rememberings.

    b. Write a praise song that uses the location in the title: "In Praise of the Gazebo at Lake Ella" or "The Shore of St. George Island in February: a Praise Song."

4. You might try a praise song of a natural environment that praises a single element, like Hopkins does when he praises spotted and freckled and dappled things. You might praise elements of flying things (at a bird refuge) or aquatic things (found on a reef) or whatever you choose. Like Ray González you might praise the foods (and in doing so, the culture) of your youth to explore what you felt then and what you know now.

After trying some of these inventions, you may find that the praise song suits your contemporary sensibility more than the ode. Praise songs often rely upon listing and repetition, so you may want to revisit chapter 7 as you compose yours. While the ode has quite a bit of historical weight behind it, making poets feel they must wrench themselves to exhalted heights or they'll dip into silliness or irony, meditative, praiseful poems are rare, challenging, and very satisfying to compose. And they may just make us see the world in ways that change us all, for the better.

POCKET DEFINITIONS

Odes—These poems celebrate, commemorate, and meditate on people or events and were originally structured and written for choruses in Greek plays to sing or chant. In *Pindaric odes* the chorus on stage speaks, and moves left, speaks again and moves right, and finishes with a third response. The left (strophe) and right (antistrophe) movements take the same stanza form, while the final response (epode) differs. The Pindaric ode evolved into the more meditative *Horatian ode* that is composed in regular stanzas (having the same length, number of lines per stanza, and rhyme scheme, if any rhyme is used). The *Cowleyan ode* is composed in free verse although it retains the lyrical, serious qualities of the ode in general.

Praise Song—In many African societies, tribal bards recite traditional epics of praise and celebration at festivals and coronations and perform these epics in rhythmic prose and verse, often accompanied by percussionists.

Psalm—A song sung to the accompaniment of a plucked instrument; a Near Eastern form best known today as the Book of Psalms in the Bible.

9

PROSE POEMS

Redefining the Line

When Boswell asked Johnson, 'What is poetry?' Johnson answered:
'Why, Sir, it is much easier to say what it is not. We all *know* what light
is; but it is not easy to *tell* what it is.' —Paul Fussell, 4

It is just as hard to *tell* a reader about prose poetry. When is a poem effective,
active prose poetry and not ineffective poetry that has relaxed into a flat, prosy
line? Once a fiction writer told me that he didn't know if he "believed" in the
prose poem. This comment has amused me ever since because this form has a
tradition going back at least as far as the French poet Baudelaire, whose *Petits
Poemes en Prose* was published in 1869. Many poets write prose poems that are
qualitatively different from the pieces they call short stories and those they call
poems. Still, for many poets, a sense of measured line is an essential part of their
definition of poetry. Perhaps in this chapter we won't be able to *tell* what prose
poems are until we've read and experienced—gotten to *know*—some work in
this form.

A block-shaped, usually paragraphed text, the prose poem relies on **imagery**
and condensed, rhythmic, repetitive, often rhymed language. Prose poems often
make a point via metaphor, analogy, or association, but they also use fictional
techniques like character building, plot, and dialogue. However, when a prose
poem's lines get shorter and drift toward narrative verse or when they get
longer and drift toward a short short story or microfiction, then defining the
form is more complicated—and contentious.

Shorter-lined prose poems are often laid out by the clause or the phrase,
each clause or phrase being allocated its own line. This construct is
called line-phrasing, and it occasionally omits punctuation at the ends
of lines entirely, the end of the line serving as sight punctuation.
—Lewis Turco, 7

To some degree, we accept as prose poems those poems the poet labels or
presents to us as such, for, in fact, at the edges of any genre distinction, an

author's intention may be the best guide we have for distinguishing a form. Not surprisingly, then, in this form called "prose poem" we'll find great variation in theme and format. Since it is the goal of this text to explore theme and variations, we'll do well to spend some time on this form. James Tate titles one of his poems "Prose Poem," and the second, "Man with Wooden Leg Escapes Prison," I categorize as a prose poem because of its shape, its prosaically presented content, and because of its apparent difference from poems in stanzas in the same collection of his poems.

Prose Poem
JAMES TATE

I am surrounded by the pieces of this huge
puzzle: here's a piece I call my wife, and
here's an odd one I call convictions, here's
conventions, here's collisions, conflagrations,
congratulations. Such a puzzle this is! I
like to grease up all the pieces and pile
them in the center of the basement after
everyone else is asleep. Then I leap headfirst like a diver into the wretched confusion.
I kick like hell and strangle a few pieces,
bite them, spitting and snarling like a mongoose.
When I wake up in the morning, it's all fixed!
My wife says she would not be caught dead at
that savage resurrection. I say she would.

Man with Wooden Leg Escapes Prison
JAMES TATE

Man with wooden leg escapes prison. He's caught.
They take his wooden leg away from him. Each day
he must cross a large hill and swim a wide river
to get to the field where he must work all day on
one leg. This goes on for a year. At the Christmas
Party they give him back his leg. Now he doesn't
want it. His escape is all planned. It requires
only one leg.

In the first prose poem, the speaker is looking at a puzzle. The first piece is, rather surprisingly, what he calls his wife, and then suddenly the image of the puzzle takes on a new, poetic meaning: the puzzle pieces are not physical but metaphysical—"collisions, conflagrations, congratulations"—and we're not even sure if "congratulations" fits the list or was simply added (as poets sometimes do) to complete an alliterative sequence. Tate's poems often work this way, with the ordinary word tipped upside down and turned inside out. The poet jumps and associates ideas in unexpected, strange, sometimes disturbing—certainly surreal—ways. The poet forces his insights on the momentarily unwary reader.

The speaker of "Prose Poem" continues to treat conceptual "pieces" as real, and, absurdly, to grease them, throw them in a heap on the basement floor, and dive into them. Then the pieces, as if in a dream, take on physical attributes— or the narrator treats them as biteable, spitting and snarling like a mongoose. The simile comparing person to mongoose makes us pause to consider: What manner of person is this? What is this scene really about? The story is over, abruptly, as is often the way in prose poems. It's morning (was the scene a dream or not?); the wife says she wouldn't "be caught dead" in the same situation ("that savage resurrection"); and now we see the "huge puzzle" may be the speaker's married life or his entire life. When he closes out the prose poem by claiming, "I say she would," we're left to ponder the meanings of this conclusion. This is a story and it is not: that is, it is ironically a puzzle. It is half human and half beast, half prose (with characters: man and wife and reported dialogue: "my wife says") and half poetry ("I leap . . . like a diver into the wretched confusion," "snarling like a mongoose").

Tate's second poem, "Man with Wooden Leg Escapes Prison" looks like a paragraph: a short rectangle with a half-length last line. It's more of a parable than a narrative and exhibits Tate's trademark disconcerting humor. In this prose poem there are fewer poetic effects beyond condensed, compacted language. "Man with wooden leg escapes prison" is terse and telegraphic; and the poet is economical, using no extra words: not "The man" but "Man." And what alliteration or repetition there is seems included to drive the plot rather than to ornament the music of the lines.

Lest you think James Tate's poems are accidental oddities of the prose poem's narrative wildness, consider his work side-by-side with the following prose poems by Russell Edson. Edson works almost exclusively in this form, and reading his collections gives one a sense of a unified voice and vision, of a poet who sees the world in surreal, often dark-humored vignettes.

Oh My God, I'll Never Get Home
RUSSELL EDSON

A piece of a man had broken off in a road. He picked it up and put it in his pocket.

As he stooped to pick up another piece he came apart at the waist.

His bottom half was still standing. He walked over on his elbows and grabbed the seat of his pants and said, legs go home.

But as they were going along his head fell off. His head yelled, legs stop.

And then one of his knees came apart. But meanwhile his heart had dropped out of his trunk.

As his head screamed, legs turn around, his tongue fell out.

Oh my God, he thought, I'll never get home.

A Death
RUSSELL EDSON

Even if newspapers are the washclothes of the world, we read them for signs, as the hunter reads dung.

So he taught his car a few tricks, like playing dead, or how to sit up and beg a cup of gasoline.

He pretends not to think too much of his remarkable machine, and reads a newspaper as if nothing were more important than a moment of murder, or a simple reversal of current trends.

Roll over, roll over. And his car rolls over and crushes him. (Naturally the car will have to be destroyed.) But he's in luck because the paper boy is just arriving to wipe him up with his evening paper.

My Head
RUSSELL EDSON

This is the street where my head lives, smoking cigarettes. I pass here and see it lying half asleep on a windowsill on my way to school where I study microbiology, which I finally give up because it all seems too small to have very much meaning in a world which I attempt to live in.

Then I begin my studies in advanced physics, which entails trying to understand atoms and subatomic particles. I give this up too when I finally realize that I have entered a world even smaller than microbiology.

I think then that I should become an astronomer and open myself to the largest view, but see only dots, which the professor says anyone of which might have taken millions, or perhaps billions, of years to reach only recently evolved optic nerves; and that in fact any star whose light we accept might be long perished, leaving only a long wistful string of light. And I wonder what this has to do with me or the world I attempt to live in. So I give up astronomy.

I come here now, into this street, looking up at my head lying half asleep on a windowsill, smoking cigarettes, blinking, and otherwise totally relaxed in the way men become when they have lost all hope . . .

⌘ READING INTO WRITING ⌘

Write out your "reading" of the Edson poems as I wrote out my "reading" of the Tate poems. Share these readings with other class members.

In the next three prose poems, Robert Hass, Robin Becker, and Darrell Fike tell longer stories in paragraph length stanzas (or is that stanza length paragraphs?).

The Harbor at Seattle
ROBERT HASS

They used to meet one night a week at a place on top of Telegraph Hill to explicate Pound's *Cantos*—Peter who was a scholar; and Linda who could recite many of the parts of the poem that envisioned paradise; and Bob who wanted to understand the energy and surprise of its music; and Bill who knew Greek and could tell them that "Dioce, whose terraces were the color of stars," was a city in Asia Minor mentioned by Herodotus.

And that winter when Bill locked his front door and shot himself in the heart with one barrel of a twelve-gauge Browning over-and-under, the others remembered the summer nights, after a long session of work, when they would climb down the steep stairs that negotiated the cliff where the hill faced the waterfront to go somewhere to get a drink and talk. The city was all lights at that hour and the air smelled of coffee and the bay.

In San Francisco coffee is a family business, and a profitable one, so that members of the families are often on the society page of the newspaper, which is why Linda remembered the wife of one of the great coffee merchants, who had also killed herself; it was a memory from childhood, from those first glimpses a newspaper gives of the shape of the adult world, and it mixed now with the memory of the odor of coffee and the salt air.

And Peter recalled that the museum had a photograph of that woman by Minor White. They had all seen it. She had bobbed hair and a smart suit on with sharp lapels and padded shoulders, and her skin was perfectly clear. Looking directly into the camera, she does not seem happy but she seems confident; and it is as if Minor White understood that her elegance, because it was a matter of style, was historical, because behind her is an old barn which is the real subject of the picture—the grain of its wood planking so sharply focused that it seems alive, grays and blacks in a rivery and complex pattern of venation.

The back of Telegraph Hill was not always so steep. At the time of the earthquake, building materials were scarce, so coastal ships made a good thing of hauling lumber down from the northwest. But the economy was paralyzed, there were no goods to take back north, so they dynamited the side of the hill and used the blasted rock for ballast, and then, in port again, they dumped the rock in the water to take on more lumber, and that was how they built the harbor in Seattle.

The Accident
ROBIN BECKER

Because you were in Navaho Nation, which is a nation within a state within a nation, there is nothing you can do. He stood silent, eyes averted, waiting, and when the authorities came, he did not give his name, address, or reason for slamming you clear across the highway from behind. You've gathered clay from every country in the state and trusted the magic of feathers, bone, deer hoof, animal hair. At the pueblos, in the terrible heat, you listened to the drums, penitent, sweat pouring down your face.

But he has no insurance, and the tribal elders and the lawyer from the BIA explain that everyone needs a car or truck in New Mexico, insurance isn't mandatory, you were on Indian land. When you tell me the story, you've changed the point of view. No longer victim, you've become a witness to the accident, to the slaughter of the Indians, to the years of food stamps and lousy jobs. In Shiprock, New Mexico, you stand in his shadow, the only shaded spot for miles.

The Letters of Sun Gee
DARRELL FIKE

Mingled in with the bills and advertisements that daily crowd the narrow postbox, letters for Sun Gee keep coming, from a lover, a sister, a mother, sky-blue envelopes addressed in a woman's careful curving hand, English alphabet and dancing characters spelling his name twice beneath the thumb-long stamps. Once a week she sends a letter halfway around the world to these quiet rooms where Sun Gee used to stand reading on the stairs, dark eyebrows furrowed or his wedge of a mouth grinning, or so the neighbors say; he couldn't wait to read her words, letting the pages drift to his feet like fallen petals; and once a mysterious box wrapped in red tissue like fire-crackers came and left in the care of the widow next door, which Sun Gee bowed to receive and then hurried away, back later with a porcelain bowl of steaming soup and tiny cakes in thanks of the neighbor's kindness and to her surprise.

On moving day there was hardly any trace of him: In a drawer a single sheet with equations and formulae and an unfinished sketch of a face, and on a high shelf in the hall closet a bow tie, unclipped and tossed in glee, forgotten perhaps the night the champagne bottle under the sink was uncorked and raised. Though others were dutifully marked "No longer at this address" and returned, new letters come. I keep them, just in case, for a week, propped on the desk while I busy through my days, then with the offers to sell and pleas for help that make up my mail, I throw them out, these blue letters of Sun Gee.

∞ READING INTO WRITING ∞

1. Using the prose poems by Robert Hass, Robin Becker, and Darrell Fike, list the elements of each that seem more prose-like and those that seem more poetic, as I did for the James Tate poems. In addition, consider the paragraphs in each: how do they work? Are they like or unlike stanza breaks in a poem?

2. Consider, as I have when working with these poems, how typography influences your reading and how the poet allows paper size and margin conventions to shape his or her lines. How much do the line breaks of the poems you see in this chapter affect your reading of those poems?

3. In a group, speculate why the poet chooses this form for this content. Is there anything about what is being said in each poem that might require this shape and this form? To figure this out, you might find it worthwhile to recast one or more of these prose poems as a free verse poem. Cut it into smaller lines, removing extra words if needed. Read each version aloud. In fact, it's worth comparing how several members of a group would cast the same prose poem into free verse lines.

4. Of the eight prose poems presented so far, which best fits the definition? Defend your choice using details from the poem. First, though, since the definition is itself almost a prose poem in intensity and compactness, talk through the definition and rewrite it in your own words.

> With its **oxymoronic** title and its form based on contradiction, the prose poem is suitable to an extraordinary range of perception and expression, from the ambivalent (in content as in form) to the mimetic and the narrative (or even anecdotal). . . . Its principal characteristics are those that would insure unity even in brevity and poetic quality even without the line breaks of free verse: high patterning, rhythmic and figural repetition, sustained intensity, and compactness. —Alex Preminger and T. V. F. Brogan, 977

5. In the following two prose poems by Alys Culhane, consider how her work fits your growing definition of a prose poem. (You might compare her truck with Edson's car.) Also, what can you say about this writer's signature style, if anything? I mentioned that both of James Tate's poems and all three of Russell Edson's poems use ironic humor in similar ways. What writing strategies would you expect to find in any prose poem Alys Culhane writes?

Truck
ALYS CULHANE

It will not start. We will not travel. I give it gas. It gives me gas. Mornings like this seem endless. I coerce, beg, plead, get down on my hands and knees and pray to a God that exists only when my truck does not move.

I lift the hood and study what's underneath. Mud, dried oil, and ice coat metal, rubber and plastic. Nothing looks different to me.

I think that what is good for me when I can't run is good for it. I spoon ice cream, B-vitamins and Coca Cola syrup into the gas tank.

It will not turn over.

If my truck is not dead, I think that it should be. I lift a maul and let it fall on the top of my truck's flat top. One dent becomes two, three, four . . . .

When the mirror shatters, the sound of breaking glass is a song that rings in my ears. In the shards, I see myself, fragmented.

I pick the keys out of the rubble and hitchhike to work. All day, I pretend that nothing is wrong.

Breaking the Mirror
ALYS CULHANE

Her head splinters into a thousand pieces and goes places she has never been before. The shadow of her lower lip trembles on the edge of a sill; her cornea transplanted, wedges itself in the slippery smooth complexion of a bar of soap; a sliver of eyelash finds seclusion in the sink drain.

Running her hands through thin air, the place where her hair used to be, she thinks, "This is no way to travel," and falls onto the slick, cold, floor that knows her feet so well.

With fingers splayed, she feels for other women who are also in her position: headless, hapless, and unable to cry because their tear ducts are someplace beyond reach, maybe to the left of the right knee. No. Maybe to the right of the left knee. Taking a mole between thumb and forefinger she asks, what am I going to do with crows feet? moles? facial imperfections? Am I obligated to put these blemishes back?

Piecing together fragments, she begins reclaiming what she knew was never lost. As her left eye orbits blue around jagged edges, she takes in the new shape of her former self.

6. For each of the prose poem poets you've read so far, make a list of their basic techniques and then decide which of those techniques you might like to adopt, borrow from, or let yourself be influenced by.

7. Read the following poem by Peter Stillman and make an argument for (a) this being a prose poem or (b) this being a poem that uses prose techniques. For either position, what would you expect to see happen if the author decided to redraft the poem away from the form you think it is and toward the form you think it isn't yet?

Culley's Dog
PETER STILLMAN

Culley's dog is dead. I come down the mountain on
a Friday night to shoot a little pool, and quote
the-best-damn-friend-I-ever-had is dead again.
He says its father was pure wolf. Our wolves
don't have to breed; they've been flowing thin
and trackless for a hundred years out there beyond
the farthest light. Only liars see them,
except when they come in for easy kills,
when Culley's tears begin to smell like blood,
and then they lope out of the shadow of
the woods and cross the country road and crouch
outside the Rainbow door.

"You make me sick," he tells the stool his son
abandoned half an hour ago. He turns back to
the smoky light, the Country Renegades packing up
their instruments, and sets the story loose
a final time, the ghost of a hound by now,
bounding up and down the bar with Culley's heart
clamped in its jaws.

Then someone says, "You shot that goddam dog
ten years ago," and Culley spins around
half-falling off his stool, his face the wet-gray
color of a lie, and I see wolf
breath rising past the window in the door.

LET US COUNT THE WAYS ... OF THE PROSE POEM

The following four prose poems differ greatly, but each should work as a powerful prompt for drafting your poems. Etheridge Knight raises racial politics; Jane Kenyon looks at childhood fears of abandonment; Carolyn Forché examines the violence of political terror; and David Lee uses working-class speakers to discuss writing aesthetics. In these ways, each prose poem capitalizes on the oxymoronic nature of the form and uses it to comment on contradictory issues, sometimes surprisingly and disturbingly juxtaposing scenes and subjects.

Rehabilitation & Treatment in the Prisons of America
ETHERIDGE KNIGHT

The Convict strolled into the prison administration building to get assistance and counseling for his personal problems. Inside the main door were several other doors proclaiming: Doctor, Lawyer, Teacher, Counselor, Therapist, etc. He chose the proper door, and was confronted with two more doors: Custody and Treatment. He chose Treatment, went in, and was confronted with two more doors: First Offender and Previous Offender. Again he chose the proper door and was confronted with two *more* doors: Adult and Juvenile. He was an adult, so he walked through that door and ran smack into two *more* doors: Democrat and Republican. He was democrat, so he rushed through that door and ran smack into two *more* doors: Black and White. He was Black, so he rushed—*ran*—through that door—and fell nine stories to the street.

My Mother
JANE KENYON

My mother comes back from a trip downtown to the dime store. She has brought me a surprise. It is still in her purse.

She is wearing her red shoes with straps across the in-step. They fasten with small white buttons, like the eyes of fish.

She brings back zippers and spools of thread, yellow and green, for her work, which always takes her far away, even though she works upstairs, in the room next to mine.

She is wearing her blue plaid full-skirted dress with the large collar, her hair fastened up off her neck. She looks pretty. She always dresses up when she goes downtown.

Now she opens her straw purse, which looks like a small suitcase. She hands me the new toy: a wooden paddle with a red rubber ball attached to it by an elastic string. Sometimes when she goes downtown, I think she will not come back.

The Colonel ❖
CAROLYN FORCHÉ

What you have heard is true. I was in his house. His wife carried a tray of coffee and sugar. His daughter filed her nails, his son went out for the night. There were daily papers, pet dogs, a pistol on the cushion beside him. The moon swung bare on its black cord over the house. On the television was a cop show. It was in English. Broken bottles were embedded in the walls around the house to scoop the kneecaps from a man's legs or cut his hands to lace. On the windows there were gratings like those in liquor stores. We had dinner, rack of lamb, good wine, a gold bell was on the table for calling the maid. The maid brought green mangoes, salt, a type of bread. I was asked how I enjoyed the country. There was a brief commercial in Spanish. His wife took everything away. There was some talk then of how difficult it had become to govern. The parrot said hello on the terrace. The colonel told it to shut up, and pushed himself from the table. My friend said to me with his eyes: say nothing. The colonel returned with a sack used to bring groceries home. He spilled many human ears on the table. They were like dried peach halves. There is no other way to say this. He took one of them in his hands, shook it in our faces, dropped it into a water glass. It came alive there. I am tired of fooling around he said. As for the rights of anyone, tell your people they can go fuck themselves. He swept the ears to the floor with his arm and held the last of his wine in the air. Something for your poetry, no? he said. Some of the ears on the floor caught this scrap of his voice. Some of the ears on the floor were pressed to the ground.

Loading a Boar ❖
DAVID LEE

We were loading a boar, a goddam mean big sonofabitch and he jumped out of the pickup four times and tore out my stockracks and rooted me in the stomach and I fell down and he bit John on the knee and he thought it was broken and so did I and the boar stood over in the far corner of the pen and watched us and John and I just sat there tired and Jan laughed and brought us a beer and I said, "John it ain't worth it, nothing's going right and I'm feeling half dead and haven't wrote a poem in ages and I'm ready to quit it all," and John said, "shit young feller, you ain't got started yet and the reason's cause you trying to do it outside yourself and ain't looking in and if you wanna by god write pomes you gotta write pomes about what you know and not about the rest and you can write about pigs and that boar and Jan and you and me and the rest and there ain't no way you're gonna quit," and we drank beer and smoked, all three of us, and finally loaded that mean bastard and drove home and unloaded him and he bit me again and I went in the house and got out my paper and pencils and started writing and found out John he was right.

⚊ INVENTION EXERCISES ⚊

1. Like Etheridge Knight, shape a prose-writing into a political parable or commentary. Start by listing issues that concern you. What have you always wanted to speak out about but haven't? (Try to list at least ten issues.) Next, explore two of these: Why are they important to you? What has kept you (or still keeps you) from talking about this issue? Who needs to hear from you on this issue? Or write back to Knight's prose poem, taking another position or viewpoint. Equally, once you've written your own prose poem—parable or commentary—write back to yourself, playing devil's advocate.

2. Like Jane Kenyon, tell a family story in snapshots. First, imagine five or six snapshot scenes that come to mind when you say the word *family* with your eyes closed. For me, there's a photo of my grandmother, mother, and four daughters, all in dresses with Peter Pan collars, all lined up by age on a bench. If you can, start with a deck of actual photos. Choose one to start a literal, descriptive freewrite and then add three or four photos that take place just before or after the photo you're working from. It can be equally interesting to take the photographer's position: who was snapping the photo? What did he/she have to do with these people? Think about them. Notice how Jane Kenyon starts her three central paragraphs with the same word, "She." Use a repetition device across your paragraphs to link them together. Also, try being descriptive in the main paragraphs and reveal only a fear, emotion, or secret in the last stanza or even in the last line as Jane Kenyon does.

3. Although Carolyn Forché's poem is a powerful political indictment of a dictatorship, the poem also turns on the horror of the unexpected. Make a list of times in your life when normal expectations of any kind were overturned dramatically. The tendency will be to list tragic overturnings, but I encourage you to explore unexpected happinesses also. Then begin your paragraph with one of these lines (or a variation on one of these lines):

   "You'll never believe"

   "I have to tell you"

   "At that time"

   "Because"

4. Both Carolyn Forché and David Lee mention poetry or poets in their prose poems. Write a prose poem where you explain to someone why you write but embed your explanation in an everyday activity or an analogy. For David Lee, loading the boar created the occasion

to think about what the themes of poetry might really be. Like Lee, be oblique on one hand and straightforward on the other.

5. Imitate any of the prose poems you've read so far. For instance, Sean Carswell's draft has the everyday feel of Lee's poem. What would be your everyday, everyperson scene of life?

The Moment You Know You Would've Been a Cowboy*
Sean Carswell

When you walk into a west Oklahoma bar with a thousand miles of road dust on your jeans and New Orleans gumbo still churning in your gut and the silence is so loud the door swings to a crash and every eye wants to know what you want with this town so you slam a shot of whiskey and drop a quarter in the juke to play some Waylon and turn to a face so bushy you don't know where the beard ends and the hair starts and say, "What the hell, buddy, Dallas gonna take this Super Bowl or what?" and you and your beer go to his table where a story about the cop three hundred miles southeast who was so sure you were armed he wouldn't frisk you without backup and he still didn't find the ounce you had under the seat gets you in so good that the pitchers start to roll in for free and your arm is around a local old enough to be your mother but only because she looks like she gave birth at fourteen and probably to her uncle's kid but she's still kind of pretty in the way that if you don't find her warm bed tonight you'll spend another night in the snow covered tent where sleeping is just a way to make it to the morning alive or make it to heaven painlessly.

When you jump back into your truck and it feels like the bench under your ass breathes the hot breath of a Toro and you know you've got to point west and ride this one to Colorado or get a horn in your back trying.

6. Take any prose poem you've written so far and try it two or more ways. (You'll find an example of this type of transformation in chapter 1.)

a. Recast it as free verse.

b. Change the point of view, from first person to third person, or put the narrator in dialogue with a second-person listener. ("What you have heard is true.")

c. Include dialect or regionalisms: "you ain't got started yet and the reason's cause. . . ."

d. Take a single paragraph prose poem and break it into several smaller paragraphs or combine smaller paragraphs into a rollicking long-breathed single paragraph, making changes where necessary. (Sean Carswell's first paragraph is a good example of long-breath drafting.)

    e. Experiment with the differences between direct and indirect speech: "The colonel told it to shut up" versus "John it ain't worth it."

    f. Add more **similes** and **metaphors**: "small white buttons, like the eyes of fish" and "like dried peach halves."

THE FOUND PROSE POEM AND THE LONG PROSE POEM

Poets find language so engaging that they often decide to adopt someone else's words, phrases, and sentences and cut these into their own lines, producing a **found poem**.

Order in the Streets
DONALD JUSTICE
(*From instructions printed on a child's toy, Christmas 1968,
as reported in the* New York Times.)

1. 2. 3.
Switch on.

Jeep rushes
to the scene
of riot

Jeep goes
in all directions
by mystery action.

Jeep stops periodically
to turn hood over

machine gun appears
with realistic
shooting noise.

After putting down riot,
jeep goes
back to the headquarters.

    As in Donald Justice's poem, the found poem can be created from the absurdity of directions or the glut of advertisement language. You can also discover one in the table of contents of a book, the collage of notices found on a campus bulletin board, or from any type of specialized text—from an academic lecture to diary entries to computer programming instructions to letters, as in the following poem that I "found" in my father's World War II V-mail letters to my mother. Reading across many of these, I saw that letter-writing conventions (writing about the weather) and current obsessions (buying some fox furs as a present for my mother, absence from family, longing for intimacy) created language patterns that I cut and pasted into this prose narrative. The poem is in block capitals as Army censors required the V-mails to be written.

V-Mail
WENDY BISHOP

Passed by Base 083 Army Examiner

Somewhere in Iceland
1940–1943

Today

TWO YEARS AGO AT SIX IN THE MORNING I BROUGHT THE FIRST WORKING PARTY ASHORE IN ICELAND. WE WENT OVER THE SIDE OF THE TRANSPORT ON LANDING NETS AND USED LANDING OR HIGGENS BOATS TO COME ASHORE. IT WAS IN POURING RAIN AND WAS ONE OF THE MOST UNCOMFORTABLE DAYS I HAVE EVER PUT IN.

TODAY IS CLEAR AND THE SUN IS SHINING BUT THE WIND IS COLD.

TODAY IT IS RAINING LIKE THE DEVIL.

TODAY IT IS SNOWING AND RAINING AT THE SAME TIME.

IT IS RAINING PITCHFORKS TODAY.

IT IS A VERY DEPRESSING DAY ANYWAY, DARK, AND RAINING, AND THE RAINY SEASON IS HERE AGAIN SO WE WILL PROBABLY REVERT TO BEING DUCKS.

TODAY I START MY THIRD YEAR IN ICELAND.

I HAD HOPED TO HAVE A LETTER FROM YOU TODAY.

Getting the Silver Fox

THE MINK SKINS IF I GET THEM WILL BE THE WHOLE SKIN.

I AM GETTING SEVEN SILVER FOX SKINS FOR SURE.

THE FELLOW THAT WAS GOING TO GET ME THE BABY SEAL SKINS GOT THERE TOO LATE.

BY THE WAY, I CAN GET THE BABY SEAL SKINS AFTER ALL. AS SOON AS THE SKINS ARE TANNED I'LL SEND THEM TO YOU.

ABOUT YOUR SEAL SKINS, THEY ARE ON THE WAY, AND YOU CAN HAVE THEM MADE INTO ANYTHING YOU WANT.

I AM QUITE SURE THAT I CAN GET ENOUGH MINK SKINS FOR A COAT. IF YOU WANT THEM SAY SO RIGHT AWAY.

BY THE WAY, IF YOU CAN'T USE THE SEAL SKINS FOR A COAT OR IF YOU DON'T WANT TO, JUST KEEP THEM UNTIL I GET THERE AND WE WILL FIND A SUCKER TO UNLOAD THEM ON OR TRADE THEM FOR SOMETHING YOU CARE FOR.

This Letter

THIS LETTER IS BEING INTERRUPTED VERY FREQUENTLY.

I AM HAVING MORE DIFFICULTY WRITING LETTERS.

THE LAST LETTER I WROTE YOU HAD A NOVEMBER DATE. PLEASE DISREGARD THE SAME.

I AM WAITING FOR THE LETTERS YOU SAID YOU WERE GOING TO SEND. I THINK YOU HAD BETTER KEEP WRITING THROUGH NOVEMBER.

THERE ISN'T MUCH IN THIS LETTER BUT IT BRINGS YOU MY LOVE.

I JUST SAW THEM UNLOAD TWENTY-SIX HUNDRED BAGS OF MAIL. IN A DAY OR TWO I SHOULD HAVE A LETTER.

NOW MAYBE I CAN WRITE YOU A MORE INTERESTING LETTER.

IT TAKES ME THE BETTER PART OF AN HOUR TO TYPE A LETTER. YOU PROBABLY DO YOURS IN FIFTEEN MINUTES.

I ALMOST FORGOT TO USE CAPITALS FOR THE CENSORS WHEN WRITING LETTERS.

TODAY IS A RED LETTER DAY.

I JUST READ THIS LETTER OVER.

SO FAR TODAY I HAVE RECEIVED FOUR LETTERS.

I IMAGINE THAT I REPEAT MYSELF IN THESE LETTERS BUT SOMETIMES MY MEMORY GOES BACK ON ME AND I FORGET WHAT I WRITE TO YOU.

I OWE ALMOST EVERYONE LETTERS.

AFTER MY LONG LETTER THE OTHER DAY I REALLY AM AT A LOSS FOR SOMETHING TO SAY.

THE COLONEL WAS JUST IN. HE FOUND ME WRITING THIS LETTER BUT HE DIDN'T SAY ANYTHING. ALL OF THE CLERKS IN HIS OFFICE WERE DOING THE SAME.

I HAVE JUST RUN OUT OF WORDS FOR THIS LETTER.

WELL, HERE IS ANOTHER DAY AND ANOTHER LETTER.

I WISH I KNEW WHAT I WAS GOING TO PUT IN THIS LETTER TO FILL UP THE PAGE.

I'M VERY HAPPY THAT YOU ENJOY MY LETTERS. IF I EVER STOPPED TO PROOFREAD THEM, YOU PROBABLY WOULD NEVER GET THEM.

DARLING, I DON'T ALWAYS FEEL LIKE THIS LETTER.

Cross Your Fingers, Don't Worry

DON'T WORRY ABOUT YOUR RING.

I DON'T KNOW OF A THING THAT YOU CAN DO BEFORE I GET THERE.

TO ME YOU ARE GETTING BETTER LOOKING IN EVERY PICTURE THAT YOU SEND. I'LL BE GLAD TO MEET ALL OF YOUR NEW FRIENDS.

YOU SOUND AS THOUGH YOU ARE GETTING JITTERY ABOUT MY COMING HOME.

DON'T WORRY. WE ARE GOING TO DO PLENTY OF DANCING AND ANY THING ELSE THAT WE DARN PLEASE.

I HAVE BEEN DREAMING ABOUT WALKING IN ON YOU ONE OF THESE EVENINGS AND TRYING TO FIGURE OUT WHAT THE REACTION WILL BE.

I WOULD GIVE A LOT TO BE ABLE TO GO OUT TO THE LAKE WITH YOU AND SPEND

A WEEK-END THERE DOING NOTHING BUT MAKING LOVE, AND IF THERE WERE A NICE BIG FIRE IN THE FIRE PLACE AND RAIN ON THE ROOF SO MUCH THE BETTER.

YOU WILL JUST HAVE TO BE PATIENT AND WAIT UNTIL I GET THERE THERE IS NOTHING THAT WILL HURRY ARMY PROCEDURE.

YOU ARE NOT TO OPEN IT UNTIL I GET THERE. DO YOU UNDERSTAND?

SHE IS CERTAINLY A FINE HEALTHY LOOKING LITTLE GIRL. SHE WILL CERTAINLY HAVE TO GIVE UP SLEEPING WITH YOU.

I HAVEN'T THE SLIGHTEST IDEA OF WHAT IS GOING ON IN THE STATES. I STILL THINK I'LL JUST WALK IN ON YOU.

I LOVE YOU LIKE CRAZY. DON'T LET ANYONE TELL YOU ANY DIFFERENT.

CROSS YOUR FINGERS AND NOTHING CAN GO WRONG THIS TIME.

━ INVENTION EXERCISES ━

1. Use the Internet to import a variety of found texts into your computer. Cut and paste and shape a poem from some of these. This is where you may want to embark on concrete or illustrated poetry. How does adding an illustration or image change your developing definition of a prose poem? How might you define a new form called the "collage poem" or the "3-D poem"? (Hint: hypertext writers are already going much further into questions like these.)

2. A tradition of **letter poems** goes back to Horace and Ovid. The most well known twentieth century letter poem is probably Ezra Pound's loose paraphrase of a poem by the eighth century Chinese poet Li Po (Rihaku) called "The River-Merchant's Wife: A Letter" (shared below). In "V-Mail" the letter poem and prose poem forms combine. Find a set of letters you or someone you know has kept and write a similar prose poem where you look for the patterns and combine them into separate paragraphs. Or take the letters and steal the best lines for a composite letter—a prose poem.

3. Follow these prompts and then shape the resulting text into a letter prose poem.
   a. Choose someone you know well, with whom you've shared past experiences, and to whom you would like to write a letter. This may be someone you've fallen out of touch with and never would really send a letter to, yet you still long to communicate with this person.
   b. Address the person as you would in a letter (or use a fictitious name if it makes you feel more comfortable).
   c. Write for three or four minutes on the following suggestions. (If one doesn't work for you, skip it and go to another. There is no set order to how you should try these.)
      • Describe today's weather.
      • Describe where you imagine this person is when he/she gets your letter.

- Remind him or her of an event or moment you experienced together.
- Describe your relationship or feelings for this person in a metaphor, but do not explain the metaphor.
- Ask a question or two.
- Describe how you're now living or what you're now doing that you wish he or she could know about.
- Say something you've always wanted to say to the person but didn't have the courage to, or were afraid to, or too shy to, or didn't know for sure at the time but do now, etc.
- Remind the person of the best advice he/she ever gave you: quote this person.
- Tell the person how you've changed, physically and/or emotionally, since last you met or communicated.
- Say you have to stop writing now but next time you write you'll tell him/her about: _____.

    d. Now, take a moment and record your feelings for this person after writing to him or her.

    e. Use any of this material to write a letter prose poem. Rearrange and shape it to make it have a true prose poem feeling rather than a prose letter feeling.

4. In a group, look at Tina Cassel's draft and use the response techniques in the last section of this chapter to discuss how she might make her letter prose poem even more poetic in her next draft. You'll see that she drafted this text from some of the letter-writing prompts in exercise 2.

*Saturated Summer**
    Tina Cassel

Dear Dan,

    This evening the rain came only like the light spray of a shower and I watched as the steam rolled off the hot pavement, smelling of tar and oil mixed with fresh rain. It was like fog, hovering above the road and around the building tops so that everything seemed gray. My damp clothes clung to me and even though I tried to put my hair up, those little pieces around my neck still stuck to my skin. The afternoon saw temperatures over 100 degrees. The rain only released the stored heat from the ground. At least my plants are enjoying the weather. My little potted gardenia bush was dying inside, so I replanted it in the yard and it is thriving. The tag said it needed humidity, but this is ridiculous. You know how the bathroom is all steamy after you take a shower and you can see the air, even feel it when you move? That's how it feels outside. So when I sweat because it is 98 degrees outside, it just stays on me, dripping between my shoulder blades and down my stomach. There is no breeze. All is completely still. It's hard to breath with the weight of the atmosphere on my chest. I'm not a fish, I need unsaturated air.

O.K. so I'll stop complaining and tell you what's good about summer. Well, like I said, the gardenia bushes flourish in weather like this. The bush outside of my front door is full of blooms. Every time I open my door to walk out the strongly perfumed aroma from the bush rushes at me, nearly toppling me because it makes me dizzy.

5. As a less-structured exercise, reply to Ezra Pound's poem below with a poem from the River-Merchant's husband, writing back to his wife in a prose poem of your own. Equally, you could find any letter from a family member or historical figure and respond in turn. The second poem that follows, "Listen Mr Oxford Don," shows the Guyana-born poet John Agard talking back to a composite figure in his life about acculturation and language. If you choose to transform your prose response into structured free verse, studying the line breaks in both poems will give you some ideas for making such a change. At the same time, considering what would happen to each poem if the lines were run into prose paragraphs can tell you something else about the poetic choices leading to prose poem rhythms. For instance, in stanzas 3 and 6, Agard (as did Etheridge Knight in his list and repetition poem "The Idea of Ancestry" found in chapter 7) begins to play with slash marks, indicating new considerations and complications of line lengths and line breaks.

The River-Merchant's Wife: A Letter
EZRA POUND
(after Rihaku)

While my hair was still cut straight across my forehead
I played about the front gate, pulling flowers.
You came by on bamboo stilts, playing horse,
You walked about my seat, playing with blue plums.
And we went on living in the village of Chokan:
Two small people, without dislike or suspicion.
At fourteen I married My Lord you.
I never laughed, being bashful.
Lowering my head, I looked at the wall.
Called to, a thousand times, I never looked back.

At fifteen I stopped scowling,
I desired my dust to be mingled with yours
Forever and forever and forever.

Why should I climb the lookout?
At sixteen you departed,
You went into far Ku-to-yen, by the river of swirling eddies,
And you have been gone five months.
The monkeys make sorrowful noise overhead.

You dragged your feet when you went out.
By the gate now, the moss is grown, the different mosses,
Too deep to clear them away!
The leaves fall early this autumn, in wind.
The paired butterflies are already yellow with August
Over the grass in the West garden;
They hurt me. I grow older.
If you are coming down through the narrows of the river Kiang,
Please let me know before hand,
And I will come out to meet you
  As far as Cho-fu-sa.

Listen Mr Oxford Don ❖
JOHN AGARD

Me not no Oxford don
me a simple immigrant
from Clapham Common
I didn't graduate
I immigrate

But listen Mr Oxford don
I'm a man on de run
and a man on de run
is a dangerous one

I ent have no gun
I ent have no knife
but mugging de Queen's English
is the story of my life

I don't need no axe
to split/ up yu syntax
I don't need no hammer
to mash/ up yu grammar

I warning you Mr Oxford don
I'm a wanted man
and a wanted man
is a dangerous one

Dem accuse me of assault
on de Oxford dictionary/
imagine a concise peaceful man like me/
dem want me serve time
for inciting rhyme to riot
but I tekking it quiet
down here in Clapham Common

I'm not a violent man Mr Oxford don
I only armed wit mih human breath
but human breath is a dangerous weapon
So mek dem send one big word after me
I ent serving no jail sentence
I slashing suffix in self-defence
I bashing future wit present tense
and if necessary

I making de Queen's English accessory/ to my offence

You certainly should consider how important the idea of the poetic line is to you: When do you want to measure and meter your lines and when are you willing to loosen them into the fluid, shifting container of the prose paragraph? Does that willingness change with experience or subject? To what degree do you still believe the line is the basic tool of the poet? Alfred Corn claims, "In the very best poems, each separate line strikes us as a special entity, something with its own living character, worth examining in isolation from the rest" (8). To what degree do you agree with Alfred Corn? And to what degree do you sympathize with the more expansive prosody of Bill Ransom in the poem "The Woman Who Plays Imaginary Piano for Her Potato," which is much longer than the prose poems that opened this chapter? The poem is also striking for its unabashedly magical, associational, metaphor-and-image-crammed qualities. The poet partakes greedily of poetic devices and yet tells a coherent (if an oddly unexpected and even dreamlike) story. After you read this poem, you may ask yourself "What just happened to me?" and "What was that?"—and find it useful to write a journal entry responding to this text, as you continue to develop your own answers to the questions about form that this chapter raises.

The Woman Who Plays Imaginary Piano for Her Potato
BILL RANSOM

spends her days cooking bland food for a British archeologist at Luxor. At night, the archeologist drinks wine and plays a Yamaha keyboard for his friends, while the woman sits in her nearby room and unrolls across her lap a shawl that she has knitted up with the forbidden image of the black-and-white keys. She feels the counterpoint strong in her thighs, where her fingers tap out patterns of love, and she sees herself playing for the All-Knowing-One on a black-lacquered piano in a great hall of stone and blue tile. Her potato with the single sprout balances in a white demitasse that she bought one cacaphonous afternoon in Cairo. She pinned to her potato a likeness of the baldheaded archeologist and tonight, long after his keyboard stops, she patters out the syncopation of her dreams, her spirit and her complicated heart.

squats at the tiller of her boat, steers with her left armpit and plays her life out on a well-carved transom. Both legs blew into mist on a paddy-dike when she was twelve, so she keeps her blunt fingers twice busy. A red-haired medic gave her mother medicines, dressings and a bag of potatoes, but he had no news of her father. Now the young woman sells potatoes from her boat, as far downriver as Da Nang, while searching for word of her father. Her seed potato crouches atop its damp dishrag in the bow. It watches for snags while she plays the old french waltzes her mother loves and her grandmother hates so much. Her french grandfather died at Dien Ben Phu for stubbornness and for stupidity, so her grandmother says. Her mother married a black-skinned man whom the Kennedy sent to vaccinate her village. They killed the Kennedy a few months later and after the girl was born her father left them for the Montagnards. He spoke a kind of French from the south of America, so she plays the French waltzes for him now, fingers oiling the mahogany transom, plays hard enough that the breeze carries her music downriver and across the unforgiving sea. Soon he will waltz back on the wind to her mother, who has never taken herself another man. The seed potato nods with the chop of the river, or with the rhythm of her callused fingers, and with all those extra eyes, it never looks back.

is a painter from Tierra del Fuego, educated in Paris, her supple fingers trying out tones instead of hues, her husband asleep on the veranda. She made her fortune in oysters and sheep, and her husband, who married for money, learned to stay for love. And for love of a sleeping man she abandons her grandmother's piano in the parlor for the ebony desktop that her grandfather shipped around the horn. The lump of potato that hunches in front of her fingers grew in the servants' garden out back. Lupita scrubbed it blind until the starchy white of its soul shone through. If the artist were playing at the real piano, she would play Satie. Here, at the ebony desk, her fingers play the surf breaking in from Antarctica, the glitter of the Southern Cross, the huddle of shorn sheep against the leeward wall of a lambing shed. Her blue silk shift blows about her in the breeze from the veranda, and the sibilant caress of her fingers on the desktop wakes something symphonic in the dreams of her husband. He sweeps the paper keyboard aside and lifts her shift and loves her there as he has not loved her in years, and she lets her faithful blind potato watch.

   is not a woman yet but a village girl from Nebaj with black sapphire eyes, a muddied slat across her knees, two octaves marked out with stick-scratches and charcoal. She hums a scrap of tune to the *pitta-ta pitta-ta* tapping of fingertips on thin white pine. The small potato between her bare feet stands on end on the ground. More than half of its eyes watch the flicker of her fingers and the tight purse of her chapped lips. She frowns at the potato, and the potato trembles with the pulse of blood through her feet or with joy from the thrill of her playing. This girl from Nebaj heard piano for the first time on her uncle's radio that he bought at Chichi that time the army fought the army in the Church of God's Grandmother. Her uncle and old witch-woman from La Libertad hid from the fighting behind a carving of God's Mother, and the *bruja* sold him that little radio while they waited for enough soldiers to be dead to stop shooting. The girl's wide, dark eyes focus on the music within, never see the desperate potato trying to applaud without hands.

   loves a deaf man from Nanaimo, and doesn't need a piano. Some nights, when he is away driving truck, she wants him to call and sometimes he feels this and he does call. He speaks to the same silence whether she answers or not. But those other nights she waits up, tired but sleepless after waiting tables, and practices deaf piano for him in the kitchen, where she has drawn a keyboard on the yellow formica with a blue felt pen. Mu used to jump onto the table and bat at the flurry of her fingers, but he died Monday morning on the highway out back. Saturday night one unwashed Idaho spud rocks in a basket on the tabletop, oblivious to everything but those long, black fingers marking time until the woman's deaf man drives up at dawn for his sausage, his eggs over easy and his plate of fresh hash browns.

⟿ INVENTION EXERCISES ⟿

1. Make a list of all your favorite fairy tales, tall tales, and myths. Try writing a long (perhaps updated) version of one of these in prose poem form. For example, write about Norse Gods or Persephone or Paul Bunyon and Babe the Blue Ox. Or try to turn Babe the Blue Ox into a Florida tale, inventing a swamp-dwelling, alligator-wrestling hero of mythic proportions.

2. Take an urban legend that you know—or a campfire horror story— and cast it into an exuberant prose poem. In this case, the universal will be found in the specific. There are the lovers parked on lovers' lane who hear a scratching on the car roof, drive off suddenly, and

find the attacker's hooked hand caught in the door. You might have heard that one, but don't let it be any lovers, any lovers' lane, any place: make us re-experience the slumber party terror of first hearing this story by making it real in your prose using poetic techniques—images, metaphors, specific details. Like Bill Ransom, you might want to go a little wild with alliteration and see if you can pull it off without sounding too corny.

3. The following exercises are intended to help you explore **sensory details**. Do some of them for the poems they might lead to in their own right but then come back to your exuberant, long prose poem drafted from exercise 1 or 2 and see if you can't add more telling details to your tale.
   a. *Smell and Scent Exercise:*
   Find something that smells! Yes, *choose a strong, powerful, memory-evoking smell:* old gym clothes, musty books, wet earth, a lemon peel, a clove, incense, etc. This should be something:
   • that reminds you of a story in your life
   • that can be transported to class in a lunch-sized brown paper bag
   First, write a prose paragraph evoking the smell and telling the story it reminds you of. Bring the scent-filled bag to class. In groups of five, share the bags by circulating them to your left. Without looking at the contents, each person should smell a new bag and write a prose response to the smell: write memory pieces, triggered by the shared smell. Although I've listed smells that come easily to mind, push your mind to think of a very evocative scent before you take it to class.

   Here are two freewrites completed by a class writer on the smells that wafted up to her from brown bags holding cinnamon, a granola bar, an herbal tea bag, and popcorn. Reading these, I think you'll see how easily a scent leads to a story and how that story can be condensed into a prose poem.

Cinnamon*

Pumpkin pie, spice cake, apple strudel—holidays. The color of the neighbor's dog by that name, but not the odor. Arriving at my grandmother's house, her special desserts just coming from the oven. She died when I was 10, and many of my memories of her are related to aromas—drugstore dust powders in ornate round canisters, sweet and musky. Her compact of face powder and a smaller circle of red rouge. Tide detergent in her wringer washer, the smell changed later by drying in the sun. Stiff sheets on fresh made beds. There was some kind of tooth brushing powder in an oval can with a red top that she used. It almost burned your mouth and you couldn't get away from the smell the rest of the day.

*Herbal Tea Bag**

Boiling Chinese tea before the sweet and sour delight, delft blue teapot, "short and stout." Can almost inhale the steam that reminds me of a wildflower meadow somewhere in the northwest where I stopped during travel one spring. Surprising how sometimes I cannot remember important particulars of my life—but I seem always able to recall that yellow meadow. The flowers looked like miniature black-eyed Susans, with fewer petals. When they blew in the breeze it really did look like waves of yellow.

b. *Alternatives:*
This exercise can, of course, be adapted to other senses:
- *For taste,* bring in enough pieces of a favorite candy from your past for group members to sample. After each taste, everyone in the group freewrites and shares the stories evoked by that taste. My secret failing is a need to eat candy corn each Halloween, and my freewrite told me why:

*Original Sin—Halloween, 1960**

There are so many ways to eat it. By dissolving under tongue, leaving that sweet sediment, that crumbling-building taste. By eating first the tips—baby teeth-white, all of them; then the second layer of hard orange; then the last fat wedges of boiled yellow corn color. I try to decide if each layer tastes differently, but the wash of one cancels the memory of the last as a coating of grit turns the inside ridges of my teeth into shellacked shells. The metal filings in my molars taste sour. If I throw a whole handful in and chew hard, fast, the lump turns into a satisfying cud of memory, of last year, the year before. Finding candy corn in the school Halloween basket, snitching one into my mouth even though Mrs. Proby says "Wait." Seeing Brian put two on his dog-teeth and smile like a smooth-cheeked vampire. Seeing Vanessa impale ten with her long dirty finger nails, waving her claws at me, inviting me toward her altered, black-masked face. Our partial costumes—Superman cape for Keith, torn net and wire angel wings for JoAnn—are wrinkled and our laps are full of small packaged candies, wrappers crackling between fingers like bat sonar. I'm indifferent to the Mars and Musketeers because Halloween doesn't begin without an overdose of mouth-melted corn syrup that erupts in my stomach all night long as a dull ache. I run across a lawn, fling toward friends the dark rattle of my sack, pull linty and smashed candy corn out of my pocket and suck my way through the night. Triangles of molded sugar like mock antacid tablets for kids, for whom sunset was so long coming—but came at last.

You might use these freewrites to practice shaping a prose poem using the advice at the end of this chapter for revising an invention into a prose poem. Each group member can do this, and you'll find it instructive to read your revisions out loud and to compare changes you each chose to make.

- *For touch,* bring in an object with an unusual texture—one that makes you squirm or swoon or just makes you curious, such as the bumps on a summer squash, the teeth-gritting feel of cheap polyester, etc. Each person in the group passes around the object, feels it, writes about it, feels the next, writes about it, and continues doing this for all the objects. Share your responses aloud.
- *For sight,* become more precise and obsessed about the colors of the world. For instance, take an object to a paint store and match it to different color strips; look at the new fall colors in a catalog; look at the colors in a crayon box; collect artist's paint colors and flower catalogs. Using these observations, take old passages of prose or poetry and revise them to include new and detailed and precise colors. Use colors repetitively to unite a passage of prose. (See D. H. Lawrence's poem "Bavarian Gentians" in chapter 7 for a sample of this.)

SUGGESTIONS FOR TURNING PROSE INTO PROSE POETRY

Writing prose poems involves you in an act of definition, deciding how much poetry and how much prose to mix into your paragraph(s). Equally, revising a prose poem asks you to revisit your initial decisions. This chapter ends with some advice one of my classes generated for helping you move from the freewrite of an exercise into the first draft of a prose poem, for responding to a peer's prose poem, and for revising your poem.

REVISING AN INVENTION INTO A PROSE POEM

1. Eliminate extra words, particularly articles (*a, an, the*) and prepositions (*on, toward,* etc.).
2. Turn "to be" verbs to active verbs: "The dog was going" becomes "The dog pranced," or use "to be" verbs in patterns.
3. Substitute specific detail for general words: instead of "spider," use "black-striped banana spider.")
4. Re-order sentences to increase rhythm and repetition.
5. Alternate sentence lengths: short and long, simple and complex.
6. Include or add metaphors and similes.
7. Add references to the senses: sight, sound, taste, touch, smell.
8. If the poem is conceptual, focus on grammatical/syntax variation and reader interest; if the poem is descriptive, focus on specific

detail, comparisons, and senses (and then grammatical/syntax variation and reader interest).

RESPONDING TO A PROSE POEM

1. Underline the most powerful images.
2. Bracket words the poet could cut: [ ].
3. Circle words the poet could make more specific and list some examples in the margin.
4. Identify the center of gravity of the poem: tell the poet what it seems
   most to be about and what sentence in particular makes you think
   this.
5. Identify what is almost said but not yet/quite said, What do you
   sense about the poem?

REVISING A PROSE POEM TO INCLUDE MORE
REPETITION AND/OR LISTING

1. Repeat a word, phrase, or line several times within the poem.
2. End the poem on the same sentence you begin it with.
3. Intentionally add modifiers to every other sentence with a comma
   and *ing* listing word or phrase.
4. Repeat one word from each sentence in the sentence that follows.
   This sentence, for instance, repeats the word *sentence*. And this one
   repeats the word *word*.
5. Use a phrase or sentence as a refrain to begin, end, or repeat
   between prose paragraphs.
6. Repeat a color, a place name, a person's name.
7. Repeat sentence patterns in expected ways (subject-verb-object followed by a question, then subject-verb-object followed by a question, etc.).
8. Repeat modifiers in expected or unexpected ways: "The quick
   brown fox meets the old red hen" and "The soft yellow chick or the
   brown quick fox meets the red old hen and the yellow soft chick."
9. Begin each sentence with the same word or words. *Because . . .,
   When . . ., I saw . . . .*
10. Use related words, such as beach words (*sand, sandpiper, sea oats,
    seaweed*) or desert words (*red rock, cactus shadows, jumping cholla,
    sandstone, ocotillo, salt flats*).

POCKET DEFINITIONS

Found Poem—Originally a poem that represents only a slight change or substitution from words encountered in the environment—from signs, advertisements, notices, and so on. In a slightly broader sense, a found poem is any poem assembled from borrowed words that are then shaped into lines.

Imagery—Images may be incorporated into a poem through metaphor or simile or a symbol, as well as through concrete and specific description which evokes a corresponding mental image in the reader's mind. Poems may be composed of a number of images—moon-rise, rain on gardenias, a red wheelbarrow—which provoke vivid sense impressions for readers and can be considered together or alone. The imagistic word or phrase (or entire poem) leads us to imagine or reimagine a similar, visually striking moment, feeling, or effect.

Letter Poem—As ancient as biblical epistles and Horace's epistles, contemporary letter poems are often in free verse but perform the same act of allowing readers to peer into private thoughts made public as the speaker addresses a listener, setting up a dramatic monologue situation. Epistolary literature (prose or poetry) narrates in the form of letters exchanged between characters.

Metaphor—A figure of speech, a comparison of one thing to another. If the words *like* or *as* are used to complete the comparison, the writer has produced a different figure of speech, the **simile**.

Oxymoronic—An oxymoron is a figure of speech that joins or yokes together two seemingly contradictory or opposite things, often ironically: "nonworking mother," for instance, or "cafeteria cuisine." It's oxymoronic when a car rolls over like a dog as in the Russell Edson poem.

Prose Poem—A block-shaped, usually paragraphed text that relies on the poetic techniques of imagery and condensed, rhythmic, repetitive, often rhymed language and often makes its point via metaphor, analogy, or association, yet still may partake of fictional techniques like character building, plot, dialogue, and so on.

Sensory Details—These are usually developed by carefully evoking the five senses of sight, sound, touch, taste, and smell. Writers tend to rely more on sight and sound, but attention to touch, taste, and smell can turn ordinary observations into vivid expressions of the poet's world.

10

QUATRAINS

Compounding the Options in Line and Rhyme

Old Home Week
DONALD HALL

Old man remembers to old man
    How bat struck ball upon this plain,
Seventy years ago, before
    The batter's box washed out in rain.

Watermelons
CHARLES SIMIC

Green Buddhas
On the fruit stand.
We eat the smile
And spit out the teeth.

The **quatrain,** four lines of rhymed or unrhymed verse, is one of the most flexible stanza shapes in poetry, with short or long lines that can contain one small image or story as in Donald Hall's and Charles Simic's poems. However, these stanzas can also be added together to develop lyric insight or to narrate as in some of the poems shared below. Because most speakers of English have extensive experience with quatrains, from nursery rhymes to hymns to popular songs, we delayed examining the quatrain until after we'd explored less familiar forms like the ghazal or praise song. Now we can return anew, refreshed by the possibilities of form instead of committed solely to the one we know best.

Most of the actual poems that ordinary people remember (and recite) are written in quatrains, as are most common mnemonic verses, nursery rhymes, rhymed saws and proverbs and admonitions, hymns, and popular songs. The unsophisticated person's experience of poetry is almost equivalent to his experience of quatrains, which tends to suggest that there is something in the four-line stanzaic organization (or in the principle of alternate rhyming) that projects a deep and permanent appeal to those whose language is English. —Paul Fussell, 133

Once we see how fundamental this stanza form is and how favored by readers, we can realize the potentials of playing with and against the formal regularity of the quatrain. "By using such a stanza for highly sophisticated and knowing or sardonic purposes, as Emily Dickinson frequently did and as Eliot does . . . a poet can cause the bare stanza itself to contribute mightily to his irony" (Fussell 134). Emily Dickinson wrote almost exclusively in ballad- and hymn-influenced quatrains, and most English-speaking poets have used both rhymed and unrhymed quatrains during their careers.

The primary purpose of this chapter is to share examples of poets who make effective changes on the quatrain form in order to encourage you to experiment with it as an organizing principle for some of your own poems. May Swenson, for instance, takes that deceptively sardonic and ironic turn in her quatrains about a cat.

The Secret in the Cat
MAY SWENSON

I took my cat apart
to see what made him purr.
Like an electric clock
or like the snore

of a warming kettle,
something fizzed and sizzled in him.
Was he a soft car,
the engine bubbling sound?

Was there a wire beneath his fur,
or humming throttle?
I undid his throat.
Within was no stir.

I opened up his chest
as though it were a door:
no whisk or rattle there.
I lifted off his skull:

no hiss or murmur.
I halved his little belly
but found no gear,
no cause for static.

So I replaced his lid,
laced his little gut.
His heart into his vest I slid
and buttoned up his throat.

His tail rose to a rod
and beckoned to the air.
Some voltage made him vibrate
warmer than before.

Whiskers and a tail:
perhaps they caught
some radar code
emitted as a pip, a dot-and-dash

of woolen sound.
My cat a kind of tuning fork?—
amplifier?—telegraph?—
doing secret signal work?

His eyes elliptic tubes:
there's a message in his stare.
I stroke him
but cannot find the dial.

Quatrain rhyme patterns are various. A few have names:

the *envelope quatrain* rhyme runs *abba*;

the *couplet quatrain* runs *aabb*;

the *alternating quatrain* runs *abab*;

the *monorhyme quatrain* runs *aaaa*.

Of course there are many possibilities for mixing unrhymed lines in with rhymed lines (*abac*) or (*abcb*) or (*aaab*) and so on. Rhyme patterns are usually repeated from one stanza to the next—*abab, abab, abab*—although it would be possible and pleasurable to link the rhymes from one stanza to the next: *abab, bcbc, cdcd,* and so on.

⌘ READING INTO WRITING ⌘

1. Donald Hall and Charles Simic use single stanza poems that tell stories through imagery. Write out your version of each and investigate why and how the image supports the story. Share your version with others in a group.

2. Quatrains can be of any line length, metered or not metered, rhymed or not rhymed. What rhyme pattern do you find or not find in these single quatrain poems? In the longer poems by Yeats and Dickinson below? Which do you prefer, if either, and why?

3. Use the Internet to collect some examples of ballads and hymns and nursery rhymes that you can compare with the quatrain poems in this chapter. Do you agree or disagree with Paul Fussell's suggestion that these are poems for "ordinary" folks? What assertions about class and taste does his claim imply? Do you see technical aspects of these forms of quatrains that you can use to refute or support his point? What makes us think one quatrain is more or less sophisticated than another quatrain?

4. As you read the next four poems—one a well-known long-lined quatrain poem by William Butler Yeats and four shorter-lined quatrain poems by Emily Dickinson—write out the rhyme patterns and consider the way line length and subject matter interact.

The Lake Isle of Innisfree
WILLIAM BUTLER YEATS

I will arise and go now, and go to Innisfree,
And a small cabin build there, of clay and wattles make:
Nine bean-rows will I have there, a hive for the honeybee,
And live alone in the bee-loud glade.

And I shall have some peace there, for peace comes dropping slow,
Dropping from the veils of the morning to where the cricket sings;
There midnight's all a glimmer, and noon a purple glow,
And evening full of the linnet's wings.

I will arise and go now, for always night and day
I hear lake water lapping with low sounds by the shore;
While I stand on the roadway, or on the pavements grey,
I hear it in the deep heart's core

EMILY DICKINSON

The Wind—tapped like a tired Man—
And like a Host—"Come in"
I boldly answered—entered then
My Residence within

A Rapid—footless Guest—
To offer whom a Chair
Were as impossible as hand
A Sofa to the Air—

No Bone had He to bind Him—
His Speech was like the Push
Of numerous Humming Birds at once
From a superior Bush—

His Countenance—a Billow—
His Fingers, as He passed
Let go a music—as of tunes
Blown tremulous in Glass—

He visited—still flitting—
Then like a timid Man
Again, He tapped—'twas flurriedly—
And I became alone—

EMILY DICKINSON

Wild Nights—Wild Nights!
Were I with thee
Wild Nights should be
Our luxury!

Futile—the Winds—
To a Heart in port—
Done with the Compass—
Done with the Chart!

Rowing in Eden—
Ah, the Sea!
Might I but moor—Tonight—
In Thee!

EMILY DICKINSON

The Bat is dun, with wrinkled Wings—
Like fallow Article—
And not a song pervade his Lips—
Or none perceptible.

His small Umbrella quaintly halved
Describing in the Air
An Arc alike inscrutable
Elate Philosopher.

Deputed from what Firmament—
Of what Astute Abode—
Empowered with what Malignity
Auspiciously withheld—

To his adroit Creator
Ascribe no less the praise—
Beneficent, believe me,
His Eccentricities—

EMILY DICKINSON

As imperceptibly as Grief
The Summer lapsed away—
Too imperceptible at last
To seem like Perfidy—
A Quietness distilled
As Twilight long begun,
Or Nature spending with herself
Sequestered Afternoon—
The Dusk drew earlier in—
The Morning foreign shone—
A courteous, yet harrowing Grace,
As Guest, that would be gone—
And thus, without a Wing
Or service of a Keel
Our Summer made her light escape
Into the Beautiful.

In a way, Yeats has pushed the quatrain form: his lines could well be trimmed, and he'd have a form with less visually declared regularity. In fact, you might try restructuring this into a more regular free verse poem with internal rhymes to see how that could take place. In his poem, the rhyme adds strong closure, especially in the short final line "I hear it in the deep heart's core."

Dickinson, on the other hand, is eccentric with her quatrains in a different way. She never titles poems, she often punctuates with dashes, and she sometimes runs her meaning across stanza breaks. Editors have often taken great liberties with her poems, conventionalizing her eccentricities to meet the grammatical conventions of the time. In fact, "As imperceptibly as Grief" appeared in one "edited" collection as quatrain stanzas even though Dickinson had compressed the quatrains into the single stanza poem you find here.

Most poets prefer Dickinson in her original manuscript form. She's also the artist of half rhyme, telling her stories with slant rhymes. Yeats' *free/bee* and *slow/glow* and *shore/core* are artful but ring far more soundly than Dickinson's *flitting/flurriedly* and *Man/alone* (which end the first poem) or *Article/perceptible* and *Air/Philosopher* (of the bat poem). In fact, it can take some reading and rereading aloud to capture the regularity of her patterns at all. Also, while Yeats seems to be noting the actual or metaphoric particulars of a place, Dickinson tends to personify nature freely: wind is a "tired Man" and summer is a "her" making an escape.

➤ INVENTION EXERCISES ➤

1. Compose a single stanza love poem. Then like Hall and Simic write a single stanza poem that captures a scene and comments on it. You might want to write this first in an unrhymed quatrain and then see if you can work in rhyme. Conversely, casting your thought into a preconceived rhyme scheme will take your observation to a new place. Try developing a quatrain both ways.

2. Write a quatrain poem in several regular stanzas, choosing an approximate syllabic line length and one full rhyme (no second rhyme) per stanza. If you choose the rhyme scheme of *abac,* your poem will close with less of a slamming door than if you choose the rhyme scheme of *abcb.* Like Yeats, you might want to write about a particularly memorable place that you one day hope to return to.

3. Like Dickinson, cast your quatrain poem in short, slant-rhymed quatrains. For one of your quatrain poems, take out the stanza spaces. For another, try dashes and your own regular but unconventional punctuation. (You might want to compare an original and an edited version of Dickinson's work before doing this.) Then you might draft a poem on the same subject using Yeat's longer-lined stanzas, cutting your lines where you stop your breath.

4. For your Dickinson-like poem, you might want to try to observe an aspect of nature by personifying it; when doing this it's easy to fall

into clichéd thinking: wind always wails, the moon always sails overhead like a boat. So, you'll want to work hard—as Dickinson always does—seeing how a bat is a philosopher of air. You can tease out one personification across the whole poem or tumble your animal or natural object through a series of comparisons.

In the next quatrain poem by Thom Gunn, a poet who regularly writes in both free and formal verse, you'll see an example of looser, intuitive line structure than found in his poem "The Bed" (chapter 1). His stanzas here fall into regular eight- or nine-syllable lengths with, generally, an accented line of four beats. Compare the effects the two quatrain types have. Which do you prefer? Next, look at Kelly Cherry's poem "Reading, Dreaming, Hiding" and see if you find—and how much you find—a formal pattern of line, beat, and rhyme.

A Map of the City
THOM GUNN

I stand upon a hill and see
A luminous country under me,
Through which at two the drunk must weave;
The transient's pause, the sailor's leave.

I notice, looking down the hill,
Arms braced upon a windowsill;
And on the web of fire escapes
Move the potential, the gray shapes.

I hold the city here, complete:
And every shape defined by light
Is mine, or corresponds to mine,
Some flickering or some steady shine.

This map is ground of my delight.
Between the limits, night by night,
I watch a malady's advance,
I recognize my love of chance.

By the recurrent lights I see
Endless potentiality,
The crowded, broken, and unfinished!
I would not have the risk diminished.

Reading, Dreaming, Hiding
KELLY CHERRY
You asked me what is the good of reading the Gospels
in Greek. —Czeslaw Milosz, "Readings"

You were reading. I was dreaming
The color blue. The wind was hiding
In the trees and rain was streaming
Down the window, full of darkness.

Rain was dreaming in the trees. You
Were full of darkness. The wind was streaming
Down the window, the color blue.
I was reading and hiding.

The wind was full of darkness and rain
Was streaming in the trees and down the window.
The color blue was full of darkness, dreaming
In the wind and trees. I was reading you.

⚊ INVENTION EXERCISES ⚊

1. While Thom Gunn's poems tell fairly explicit "stories," the story in
   Kelly Cherry's poem is more mysterious. Look at these two imitations and see if it helps you understand the movement of her work
   any better. You might want to write your own imitation of her
   poem or of either of these two imitations.

Loving, Living, Falling (Imitation)*
   Ed Flagg

We were loving. Sky was living
The color blue. The snow was falling
In the valleys and ice was forming
Between us, clear, thick, and cold.

Ice was living in the valleys. We
Were clear, thick, and cold. Snow was forming
Between us, the color blue.
Sky was living and falling.

Snow was clear, thick, and cold and ice
Was forming in the valleys and between us.
The color blue was clear, thick, and cold, living
In the snow and valleys. Sky was loving us.

Writing, Drinking, Humming (Imitation) * ❖
  Ellen Schendel
  I can't write without doing something else: eating or drinking, listening to
  the hum of a fan. —Eric's midterm writing process memo

You were writing. I was drinking
thick red wine. The fan was humming
in the window and water was boiling
on the stove, ready for your tea.

Water was drinking in the window. You
were ready for tea. The fan moves steam
from the stove, stirring smells of thick red wine.
I was writing and humming.

We were ready for tea, and water
was boiling in the window and on the stove.
Tasting thick red wine, drinking in
the fan and window, I was writing you.

2. The speaker and listener in "The Bed" and "Reading, Dreaming, Hiding" are not gendered. How do you read these? How do you reread either poem if you consider that the speaker and listener may be of the same sex? How do you read a speaker's gender when you look at a poem by a new author? Does it matter? If not, why? If so, how? Write a love poem quatrain where you make it gender specific and then recast it more ambiguously (or vice versa). How does that affect the poem?

3. Take one of your quatrains from any draft you're working on and cast it in syllabics or metered verse (counting the strong accents as Thom Gunn does in "A Map of the City"); consider how such a change makes you change your meaning. If you like what's happening, continue to cast a poem as an unrhymed but syllabic or metered quatrain poem.

QUATRAINS ON LANGUAGE AND WRITING

Language and/or writing is highlighted in the following five poems as each poet explores his or her relationship with and to language.

The Thought-Fox ❖
TED HUGHES

I imagine this midnight moment's forest:
Something else is alive
Beside the clock's loneliness
And this blank page where my fingers move.

Through the window I see no star;
Something more near
Though deeper within darkness
Is entering the loneliness:

Cold, delicately as the dark snow,
A fox's nose touches twig, leaf;
Two eyes serve a movement, that now
And again now, and now, and now

Sets neat prints into the snow
Between trees, and warily a lame
Shadow lags by stump and in hollow
Of a body that is bold to come

Across clearings, an eye,
A widening deepening greenness,
Brilliantly, concentratedly,
Coming about its own business

Till, with a sudden sharp hot stink of fox
It enters the dark hole of the head.
The window is starless still; the clock ticks,
The page is printed.

Hold a Page Up to Your Lips and Blow ❖
DARRELL FIKE

Spiraling to the floor do dizzy
consonants and wobbly vowels
skip and scatter
sticking to the soles of your shoes as you pace?

Or do articles and prepositions, perhaps
an or in or a the, lift and soar
nouns left behind
heavy and dumb like your boots by the door?

Or do the fonts and faces collapse
into a heap of jagged and cracked
alphabet bones
leaving the page silent and bare?

Or do commas and serifs sift
slowly through the library yellow air
as the book closes
and you doze sock-footed in your afternoon chair?

Or does your timid breath
linger over your lips,
your tongue poised to strike
and your mouth full of myths?

Night Songs ❖
WENDY BISHOP

My daughter sings herself older in her bedroom
before sleeping. This is the sound of her self-flute:
tones float through a darkened house, loose
lean counterpoint to my evening's journey.

Sleep-awake myself, I leaf through anthologies,
throw I-Chings of poetry. Craft can frame
old messages a new way, blow longings secretly
into bottles: they drift along the inland waterways

of personal history. Enough densely scored songs,
enough possibility, and she falls to dreams. I have
that one we all have: float high above the city—not waving
not worried—assume I've finally pinched myself awake.

Read This Poem from the Bottom Up ❖
RUTH PORRITT

This simple cathedral of praise.
How you made, from the bottom up,
Is for you to remember
Of Andromeda. What remains

Until you meet the ancient light
With your sight you can keep ascending
Its final transformation into space.
And uphold

The horizon's urge to sculpt the sky
Puts into relief
Your family's mountain land
Upon the rising air. In the distance

A windward falcon is open high and steady
Far above the tallest tree
Just beyond your height.
You see a young pine lifting its green spire

By raising your eyes
Out onto the roof deck.
You pass through sliding glass doors
And up to where the stairway ends.

To the top of the penultimate stanza
Past the second story,
But now you're going the other way,
Line by line, to the bottom of the page.

A force that usually pulls you down,
Of moving against the gravity of habit,
While trying not to notice the effort
And feel what it's like to climb stairs

The Last Word ❖
JIM SIMMERMAN

You can have the bright
face of the full moon
if I can have the dark
one it keeps out of sight.

You can have the circles
we chased ourselves in
if I can have the empty
tunnels inside.

You can have the past
and the future to boot
if I can have the nick
of time in between.

You can have the warmth
from the bridges we burned
if I can have the ashes
drifting downstream.

You can have the music
that marshaled the waltz
if I can have the echo
that died in the rafters.

You can have the last
word, whatever it is,
if I can have
the silence thereafter.

➤ INVENTION EXERCISES ➤

1. Like Ted Hughes, you might want to write about the actual act of
   writing. Of course, Hughes does this metaphorically, turning thinking into the thought fox of inspiration and actualization. Take a
   minute and list some metaphors for writing. Use the simple formula
   of "For me, writing is like . . ." (for a simile) or "Writing is a . . ."
   (for a metaphor). Don't stop at one or two. Examine writing from
   many different angles and then start drafting your quatrains.

2. Like Darrell Fike, you might want to write about language itself.
   Also like him, you might want to cast your stanzas with a
   refrain/line and/or a rhetorical question. What do you want to know
   about language? You can also draft a poem about a language part—
   words, commas, or the alphabet. What happens if you let your qua-

trains join into a free verse poem? What would happen if any of these poets took out the white space between quatrains?

3. My poem mixes narrative and thinking about writing. Draft some scenes of you writing: Where are you? Are you up late at night? Are you drafting right before a deadline? Who is there with you? What are you doing? Then write about your ideal scene of writing: Where would you be? When? Doing what? Turn one or both of these into a poem.

4. Sometimes using a poetry game—word or line play—pays off. Ruth Porritt creates a poem that could be read backward from the bottom line up to the top line, and you might find it instructive to try to construct a backward poem in the same manner.

5. Or like Jim Simmerman, you might want to look at opposites: What is it about the world, about language, about writing that you want, and then what is the opposite that you'll leave for others? Who do you think the "you" in this poem is? How do his rhymes work for you? Note how some words rhyme fully or as half rhymes down the stanzas.

CONTEMPORARY NARRATIVE QUATRAIN POEMS

The next four poems highlight the narrative flexibility of the quatrain. Seamus Heaney weaves a mythic story around the remains of a woman found buried for untold years in an Irish bog, and Alma Luz Villanueva contemplates the life of one of the students in her poetry-writing classes. The topic choice of both poets is unusual, and the line length of each quatrain is shorter and faster moving than in the poems by Robert Pack and Lynn Emanuel that follow.

Punishment
SEAMUS HEANEY

I can feel the tug
of the halter at the nape
of her neck, the wind
on her naked front.

It blows her nipples
to amber beads,
it shakes the frail rigging
of her ribs.

I can see her drowned
body in the bog,
the weighing stone,
the floating rods and boughs.

Under which at first
she was a barked sapling
that is dug up
oak bone, brain-firkin:

her shaved head
like a stubble of black corn,
her blindfold a soiled bandage,
her noose a ring

to store
the memories of love.
Little adulteress,
before they punished you

you were flaxen-haired,
undernourished, and your
tar-black face was beautiful.
My poor scapegoat,

I almost love you
but would have cast, I know,
the stones of silence.
I am the artful voyeur

of your brain's exposed
and darkened combs,
and your muscles' webbing
and all your numbered bones:

I who have stood dumb
when your betraying sisters,
cauled in tar,
wept by the railings,

who would connive
in civilized outrage
yet understand the exact
and tribal, intimate revenge.

Crazy Courage ❖
ALMA LUZ VILLANUEVA
To Michael B.

Why do I think of Michael . . .
He came to my fiction class
as a man (dressed in men's
clothes); then he came

to my poetry class
as a woman (dressed in women's
clothes; but he was still
a man under the clothes).

Was I moved in the face of
such courage (man/woman
woman/man) . . .
Was I moved by the gentleness

of his masculinity; the strength
of his femininity . . .
His presence at the class poetry
reading, dressed in a miniskirt,

high boots, bright purple tights,
a scooped-neck blouse, carrying
a single, living, red rose, in a
vase, to the podium (the visitors,

not from the class, shocked—
the young, seen-it-all MTV crowd—
into silence as he's introduced,
"Michael . . .") And what it was, I think,

was his perfect dignity, the offering
of his living, red rose to the perceptive,
to the blind, to the amused, to the impressed,
to those who would kill him, and

to those who would love him.
And of course I remember the surprise
of his foamy breasts as we hugged
goodbye, his face blossomed

open, set apart, the pain of it,
the joy of it (the crazy courage
to be whole, as a rose is
whole, as a child is

whole before they're
punished for including
everything in their
innocence).

Reading the envelope quatrains of Robert Pack's "The Pardon," we learn a childhood story of great power. And in Lynn Emanuel's unrhymed quatrain poem "The Planet Krypton," we feel we're with the speaker in the town of Ely, Nevada. Emanuel in particular chooses a long-lined stanza to provide building blocks of some thickness—including the particulars of the time and place by mentioning the Philco, the taffeta clothing, the McGill smelter, the Tonapah Artillery and Gunnery Range. It would be productive to write a journal entry exploring the narrative elements of each of these quatrain poems before you undertake a longer poem of your own.

The Pardon
ROBERT PACK

My dog lay dead five days without a grave
In the thick of summer, hid in a clump of pine
And a jungle of grass and honeysuckle-vine.
I who had loved him while he kept alive

Went only close enough to where he was
To sniff the heavy honeysuckle-smell
Twined with another odor heavier still
And hear the flies' intolerable buzz.

Well, I was ten and very much afraid.
In my kind world the dead were out of range
And I could not forgive the sad or strange
In beast or man. My father took the spade

And buried him. Last night I saw the grass
Slowly divide (it was the same scene
But now it glowed a fierce and mortal green)
And saw the dog emerging. I confess

I felt afraid again, but still he came
In the carnal sun, clothed in a hymn of flies,
And death was breeding in his lively eyes.
I started in to cry and call his name,

Asking forgiveness of his tongueless head.
. . . I dreamt the past was never past redeeming:
But whether this was false or honest dreaming
I beg death's pardon now. And mourn the dead.

The Planet Krypton
LYNN EMANUEL

Outside the window the McGill smelter
sent a red dust down on the smoking yards of copper,
on the railroad tracks' frayed ends disappearing
into the congestion of the afternoon. Ely lay dull

and scuffed: a miner's boot toe worn away and dim,
while my mother knelt before the Philco to coax
the detonation from the static. From the Las Vegas
Tonapah Artillery and Gunnery Range the sound

of the atom bomb came biting like a swarm
of bees. We sat in the hot Nevada dark, delighted,
when the switch was tripped and the bomb hoisted
up its silky, hooded, glittering, uncoiled length;

it hissed and spit, it sizzled like a poker in a toddy.
The bomb was no mind and all body; it sent a fire
of static down the spine. In the dark it glowed like the coils
of an electric stove. It stripped every leaf from every

branch until a willow by a creek was a bouquet
of switches resinous, naked, flexible, and fine.
Bathed in the light of KDWN, Las Vegas,
my crouched mother looked radioactive, swampy,

glaucous, like something from the Planet Krypton.
In the suave, brilliant wattage of the bomb, we were
not poor. In the atom's fizz and pop we heard possibility
uncorked. Taffeta wraps whispered on davenports.

A new planet bloomed above us; in its light
the stumps of cut pine gleamed like dinner plates.
The world was beginning all over again, fresh and hot;
we could have anything we wanted.

⟶ INVENTION EXERCISES ⟶

1. List up to ten family stories in the vein of Robert Pack's ten-year-old
   speaker's memory of his dog dying or Lynn Emanuel's memory of
   atomic bomb testing. What are the little yet powerful events of your
   life and the bigger and public events of your life? For instance, I
   remember the moment I first saw my mother cry and the day John F.
   Kennedy was shot. Either memory could lead me into a narrative
   quatrain poem. After you make your list, sit at a computer and
   freewrite about your memories. Then go back and decide which one
   is richest for a poem. Like Lynn Emanual, try to populate your narrative with the vivid details of that time period. (If you can't remember, call a parent or a friend.) Look at maps of the area for place
    names. Look up a newspaper or magazine from that time period for
   headlines or product advertisements. Use the Internet for similar
   research. As you revise, investigate the history of your own life and
   share it with readers.

   In this poem, Rhain Capley remembers the death of a childhood
   friend:

Blue-Boxed Boy*
    Rhain Capley

Billy Boy, I remember the time we
went swimming down at Sander's Pond
we had stripped off our cut-offs
and leapt into the icy-blue water.

Only early March, there were still
clumps of snow on the ground
we nearly froze in half-thawed water
until we climbed into an old refrigerator box, to escape the wind.

And inside we held each other close
our teeth chattering loud like the airplanes up above
so cold, your skin seemed blue, and then you said,
"I am the blue-boxed boy."

We laughed because it was true, because at
sixteen we thought it was the closest we could come to blue
all our focus was on the fascination of your blue skin
inside our box, under the wide oak, cold and alive.

The funeral was a mess, your mother cried, naturally,
about the pills, her blue ones, she had said
that you took, and that brought you here
and in this coffin-box, you were a shade more blue.

2. Like Jennifer Wheelock and Darrell Fike in the two poems that
follow, you might want to go back to a more recent memory and
narrate the humor or absurdity of some simple event: List ten
moments that made you pause in the last year. Then freewrite on
one until you decide to turn the moment loose into rhymed or
unrhymed quatrains.

Feeding Francis Bacon
    Jennifer Wheelock

I tried this experiment:
fried a pound package of bacon.
While it was fresh, the smell pungent,
I took it to the pig pen

for Francis. I dropped it in
his tin slop bucket and waited.
(I could have sworn I saw him grin
like he knew I had baited

him.) But then, that helpless hog
I saved from slaughter—from the knife—
that litter runt, the underdog,
as though his whole stinking life

he had not heard of sin or ham,
devoured some relation's meat,
dug a hole, scratched, and burped and ran
his muddy snout across my feet.

Birthday
    Darrell Fike

This morning in the mirror
I was given my father's hair:
the slicked peak and swept back sides
flowing right out of the comb.

In the closet I found instead of mine
double-pocket work shirts and pants
that fit and felt like forever,
and steel-toed boots.

At dusk I sat mute
at the dinner table, gravy stubbled
on my chin, chewed small bites,
swallowing hard.

After the news, rain
splashed on the porch cement;
my shoulder ached and I rubbed rubbed
without relief.

Later, with dead fingers
I tightened the tick of the brass clock key
and to my father in the sleepless dark
said goodnight.

3. In the next four drafts, poets experiment in interesting ways with the quatrain form. You might try what they try or use their explorations to help you develop your own way of using the quatrain shape. In the first poem, "Not in My Room," Rhain Capley drops the fourth line, making us question whether this is a quatrain poem or tercets with single lines between them. He's made the reader's decision even harder because he doesn't punctuate his lines. Does his ending quatrain convince you this is a dropped-line quatrain poem? You might consider alternating quatrains and couplets, quatrains and tercets, as he does.

*Not in My Room**
        Rhain Capley

I've never slept with anyone in my room
It's a private place, just for me
A place I'm not willing to share with any man

I won't pretend, I won't play charades in my room

I've slept with men in nice cars and on worn, green velour couches
In mildewed showers and on dark quiet beaches
In black closets in rooms other than my own

I won't play power games in my room

Outside my room, I am a superman with no emotions, no regrets
No inhibitions and no secrets
But in my bed, in my room, I am only me, I have no masks
Unloved, except for the love of the cat who knows who I am

Richard Wade, in imitating a poem by Delores Kendrick titled "Note to the Ophthalmologist," mixes the quatrain poem with the letter poem (also discussed in chapter 9). Using this example, you might want to write an ironic poem to any specialist (from your medical doctor to your teacher to . . .) whose work you have mixed feelings about.

*Note to the Orthopedic Specialist**
        Richard Wade

Thank you for your kind
attention. Thank you (especially)
for the anesthetic. Bone-grind
and cartilage-pop told me—

almost immediately,
that my collarbone had snapped.
You and your x-ray machine proved it conclusively.
And we stood there and gazed at my image.

As if to encourage
me, you said in a warm voice, "You're lucky—
it's a clean break."
And your soothing anesthetic

flushed and flooded
each cell and tissue.
And as you gazed intently
at the hairline fissure,

I gazed at my image as it will appear
forever, as I lie silently in my grave.
"Be glad you didn't tear
a ligament," you said (you scientists are so objective).

I can't remember what I said then,
but I think you made it clear,
if I have something to say—say it now.
So thank you again.

Sincerely,

Richard Wade.
(based on "Note to the Ophthalmologist" by Delores Kendrick)

Brent Morris plays with line indentation, creating a staircase effect as his poem moves down the page, beginning at the title, running through four undulating quatrains, and ending with a period. Do you see any reason for his choices? Can you imagine a topic that might require some of this onomatopoeic textual movement? Try a quatrain poem that calls attention to how the lines are indented.

Ate Pimento on a Date*
    Brent Morris

dodged sand spurs
   like land mines
      coming from aquamarine
         waters back to the car

      after playing coquettishly
   in the surf like two platypi
on the chase in the oldest
city in America.

Then crossed the Bridge
   of Lions, over to the fort
      and sat squat on the thin
         green grass under the world's

      largest bonsai tree mangled
   and disfigured into beauty
by the wind. Imagining we lived
back when Indians gazed

from thin prison windows
   to watch the surf,
      and ate pimento sandwiches
         in St. Augustine.

*1990**

  A. S. Kaufman

Today I stared at
tiny powdered
sugar donuts
like we

shared on the way
to school
with your marijuana
cigarettes.

You'd pour
vodka in my juice
and say
no worries, no regrets.
I lay

in the back of the
Camaro
with all you long-haired boys
just to show

you that I wasn't scared.
We all
wore black even though
in fall

it was as hot as July.
Today I
remembered where I
lost the high.

To some degree, the more simple the form, the more room there is for you as poet to complicate it. You can make a great number of changes on the durable quatrain form as you've seen from the poems in this chapter. In part, poetry is the music of numbers: couplets turn to quatrains turn to octets. Play with doubling and dividing the number and lengths of your lines, and as you use the quatrain to sharpen your insight and strengthen your narratives, you'll learn quite a bit about the space words take up and the spaces you can place around words.

POCKET DEFINITIONS

Quatrain—A stanza consisting of four lines of verse, rhymed or unrhymed. The *envelope quatrain* rhyme runs *abba;* the *couplet quatrain* runs *aabb;* the *alternating quatrain* runs *abab;* and the *monorhyme quatrain* runs *aaaa.*

11

SESTINAS

A Cat's Cradle of Word Patterns

house, grandmother, child, stove, almanac, tears, home, roared, pass, alone, plant, baby, letters, king, light, rail, black, windows, sing, right, means, left, luminous, glass, says, work, hunger, hate, love, need, spreads, green, pairs, false, shave, wait, move, house, pipe, love, child, leave, serves, me, her, words, more, speak, said, English, closed, words, *nombres,* Spanish, wanted, glass, knobs, weighing, weight, walk, world, dog/God, cold, red, something, one, two, three, four, five, six, red, purple, blue, green, yellow, orange —Repeat words from the sestinas in this chapter

Forms go in and out of style in the world of poetry-writing like styles in clothes. This year bell-bottoms may come back and next year disco shirts. Hemlines go up and down, and tie widths increase and then decrease. The same is true of poems, although most of the forms in this book have shown impressive staying power, several crossing centuries and cultures. The **sestina**, attributed to French troubadour Daniel Arnout, who wrote around the year 1190, became popular again in Germany in the seventeenth century, in England in the nineteenth century, and in the United States in the second half of the twentieth century. The sestina captured the interest of contemporary poets perhaps because the form emphasized the repetition of words at a time when full rhyme and intricate verse patterns were felt to be too constraining.

The sestina requires that six end words be repeated in a set pattern across six stanzas and that all six words be used—again, in pattern—in a three-line final stanza, called an **envoi**—literally, a farewell or conclusion. Certainly these are constraints. But what seems at first like a game—an impossible mathematical equation—soon helps you create an intriguing pattern of sound as you knit word repeats up and down a ladder of seven stanzas. Although seeming not to be a rhymed form, the sestina is one in that exact rhymes (the same words) sound and resound, as in Elizabeth Bishop's sestina.

Sestina
ELIZABETH BISHOP

September rain falls on the house.
In the failing light, the old grandmother
sits in the kitchen with the child
beside the Little Marvel Stove,
reading the jokes from the almanac,
laughing and talking to hide her tears.

She thinks that her equinoctial tears
and the rain that beats on the roof of the house
were both foretold by the almanac,
but only known to a grandmother.
The iron kettle sings on the stove.
She cuts some bread and says to the child,

It's time for tea now; but the child
is watching the teakettle's small hard tears
dance like mad on the hot black stove,
the way the rain must dance on the house.
Tidying up, the old grandmother
hangs up the clever almanac

on its string. Birdlike, the almanac
hovers half open above the child,
hovers above the old grandmother
and her teacup full of dark brown tears.
She shivers and says she thinks the house
feels chilly, and puts more wood in the stove.

It was to be, says the Marvel Stove.
I know what I know, says the almanac.
With crayons the child draws a rigid house
and a winding pathway. Then the child
puts in a man with buttons like tears
and shows it proudly to the grandmother.

But secretly, while the grandmother
busies herself above the stove,
the little moons fall down like tears
from between the pages of the almanac
into the flower bed the child
has carefully placed in the front of the house.

> *Time to plant tears,* says the almanac.
> The grandmother sings to the marvelous stove
> and the child draws another inscrutable house.

As with any form, it's best to write more than one poem in this manner to gauge the form's usefulness and complexity. Each time I write a sestina, I learn a little more about the form's possibilities. As you'll see later in this chapter, poets also innovate within the form, collapsing the stanzas into seemingly free verse or near prose poems, disguising the end words by moving the repeat words to the interior of the line or to the beginning of the line (a head rhyme) or by substituting the same word in another language in different stanzas. These techniques expand the form while they allow poets to maintain the feel of the sestina because the repeat words always add texture and pattern to the poem no matter how much the stanzas are disguised or subverted.

ENTERING THE SESTINA

First choose six end words. It's useful if some are **homonyms**—words having the same pronunciation but different meanings and spellings, like *son/sun,* or if some can be both noun and verb as in "Throw the *pass*" versus "I *passed* her car." Number the words in the first stanza consecutively. In "Sestina for Summer 1970" by Devan Cook the six repeated words are:

1   roared
2   Alone
3   baby,
4   Plant
5   pass
6   home

Each subsequent stanza begins with the last word of the previous stanza and then uses the top word to end line 2, goes down for the next-to-last word to end line 3, goes back up to the next-to-top word, etc., until all six words are used. (Numbers and letters in the following chart will help you count.)

STANZA 1	STANZA 2	STANZA 3	STANZA 4	STANZA 5	STANZA 6	ENVOI
1 A	6 F	3 C	5 E	4 D	2 B	1,2 A,B
2 B	1 A	6 F	3 C	5 E	4 C	3,4 C,D
3 C	5 E	4 D	2 B	1 A	6 F	5,6 E,F
4 D	2 B	1 A	6 F	3 C	5 E	
5 E	4 D	2 B	1 A	6 F	3 C	
6 F	3 C	5 E	4 D	2 B	1 A	

The envoi repeats two end words within each line (A,B C,D E,F in contemporary versions) or three end words (usually 5,3,1 E,C,A or 1,3,5 A,C,E in older versions) using the other end words where possible, all in three lines. Poets often modify the envoi, breaking the repeat pattern or even dropping it entirely as in Mary Jane Ryals' sestina below.

This is how Devan's repeat words run:

STANZA 1	STANZA 2	STANZA 3	STANZA 4	STANZA 5	STANZA 6
roared	home,	baby	pass,	plant	alone.
Alone	roared	home.	baby.	pass	plant
baby,	pass.	plant	alone.	roared	home.
Plant	alone	roared	home)	baby,	pass.
pass.	plant	alone.	roared.	home	baby
home.	baby.	pass,	plant.	alone.	roared.

ENVOI

Alone roared

pass home baby

planted plant.

I've included the punctuation for Devan's poem to show that a sestina writer will often work hard at enjambment, running sentences across line endings as well as stanza endings, to fold the repeating words more naturally into spoken syntax. "Sestina for Summer 1970" is followed by Devan's composing statement; she mentions that Elizabeth Bishop's sestina helped her write her own poem.

Sestina for Summer 1970*
DEVAN COOK

The rain hissed in the chimney and roared
down the gutters to the garden. Alone
late at night, except for a sleeping baby,
I read *In Watermelon Sugar* and *Please Plant*
This Book. Seeds grow; times pass.
I waited for my husband to come home.

That spring I made a tent, a warm home,
to shield the melons from the wind that roared
down from Three Sisters through the pass.
I'd never started a garden alone
before, but I wanted to plant
the book, and read, and feed the baby.

The garden kept me warm. The baby
wasn't cold; to her, outside was home.
It was a cold summer, too cold to plant
corn or melons. The Northern Lights roared
and each star was separate and alone.
I waited for each night to pass,

and I waited for a man to make a pass,
and no one did. I read to the baby.
She liked it; she chewed the book, alone.
We hiked (we didn't stay home)
to where the canyon waterfall roared.
At home we ate, we read, we planned to plant.

One night I had a dream to plant
something to make the cold days pass
beside the place where the wind roared
and the water fell a sheet: the baby,
in the fir needles a soft pillow home
where she could be what she liked, alone.

The next day I went there alone.
I wanted to stay there, to plant
myself there, make it my home.
I'd got tired, waiting for time to pass.
I had some books and a baby
and a river, wind and sky that roared.

Alone I threw my ring in the river that roared
down the pass. I went home. The baby
and I planted the book it said to plant.

This is how I came to write the sestina: it was assigned. The assignment was to write either a sestina or a villanelle; first I tried the villanelle because it was shorter, and I had, as usual, put off the work on what I considered the most difficult part of the course's work until the night before (that was when I was still working for the post office. I would never, never do such a thing now).

The villanelle was a wash; I couldn't come up with one good line to repeat, and I needed two. So the poem had to be a sestina. We workshopped two very funny sestinas in class—one based on an interplay between sex and the fact that sestinas are built on six lines, sex in Italian—so I wasn't too frightened by the form any more. When I sat down to write, I didn't have a repetition scheme for the sestina with me, so I put a copy of Elizabeth Bishop's sestina next to the computer so I could figure it out.

Now it seems to me that her poem influenced me: there's a sadness in both, and the subtext of an abandoned child. I had been writing about the canyon in Oregon where the poem is set for several years off-and-on, and since it's probably my favorite place in the whole world, it pleased me to have it show up again. And my husband and I had recently argued about something that happened that summer, the summer of 1970. I was still angry about it, and the poem reveals my emotional state, both in memory and at the time I wrote it. The events it narrates are fiction; the feelings are not.

It wasn't hard to write. "Just write something," I told myself, and wrote the first six lines on the computer screen. "Oh, so those are the words," I told myself. "I'll try them." Then I went down the screen and arranged lists of those six words in the proper order for the six six-line stanzas, and I thought of words to go before them. —Devan Cook

∞ READING INTO WRITING ∞

1. How much of Elizabeth Bishop's influence do you see in Devan Cook's poem, including and beyond what Devan herself points out? To figure this out, you might tell the story of each poem in a sentence or two. You might also look for phrases and/or line breaks and even descriptive sections where you hear echoes (if you do).

2. Freewrite on either or both poems. What family story comes out of your contemplation? Look at this freewrite and highlight a set of end words and/or the first stanza. You might want to borrow one or two words from these poets' poems. Try drafting a first stanza.

These forms such as the sestina were really devices at getting into the remoter areas of consciousness. The really bizarre requirements of a sestina I use as a probing tool rather than as a form in the traditional sense. I have once told somebody that writing a sestina was rather like riding down hill on a bicycle and having the peddles push your feet. —John Ashbery (Packard 90)

As you read the next three sestinas and their authors' composing statements, you'll see that a lot of thinking goes into getting started. As it is for John Ashbery, the sestina form is an exploratory tool for these writers. Poets often follow where the first stanza's story leads them, all the while, aiming for the required end words for each new stanza. As you work on your own sestina, keep a process log so you can write a similar statement later to compare with the ones you're reading now.

King Edward Hotel*
MICHAEL TRAMMELL

The huge letters
of the King
Edward Hotel shined red light
that didn't reach the railroad tracks across the street. Black
birds nested in the hotel windows.

Staring out of the car window
I drew the letters
with white crayon on black
construction paper. My mother, thinking
I was tired, playfully railed
me; turned off my flashlight.

We paused at a traffic light;
I looked into the hotel windows
and saw the balcony rail
reflecting in the glass. Red letters
were painted on the wall marking
a broken window. A black

face appeared wearing a black
leather hat. In the dim light
I saw faces playing, maybe King
of the Hill, and smiling from the window
at me. I now recall sending you a letter
about this and the rail-

way. You told me the rails
were bent by black
men without letters
or light.
In the hotel windows
I saw the men breaking

the glass and chucking
wood over the rail
to the sidewalk. The car window
was black
with dirt from the street. The light
changed; I flipped my paper and lettered

"KING." I found the black
crayon and drew rails across the word. Dim light
flickered in the window: shrinking, red letters.

The "triggering subject" of the poem is a childhood memory of a huge (to me
as a kid at least), vacant hotel in the middle of downtown Jackson, Mississippi. My
grandmother lived in Jackson, so we always drove through the middle of the city
a couple of times on each trip. As we cruised through town, I'd lean against the
passenger door window of my parents' car so that I would get a clear glimpse of
the gigantic red, neon light letters that stood on top of the building. Those letters
always struck me with a strange mixture of fear and awe.

During the writing of the rough draft of the sestina, I recall that at the
halfway point I'd hit a roadblock. In the fourth stanza, I kept trying to take the
poem in a direction that explored more of my memories of Jackson and our
summer visits there. But this tack felt wrong for me. I kept rewriting and rewriting the fourth stanza and then just gave up for a while.

Then this "you" jumped into the poem. I think I had a specific "you" in mind,
but at the same time I knew the "you" was entirely fictional. This turn at the
sestina's midway point helped me to finish the next stanzas fairly quickly. I think
the addition of the "you" helped me to find the poem's "generated subject" (as
Richard Hugo would say), and added a greater level of complexity I hadn't
expected when initially rethinking the memory. —Michael Trammell

Sestina: Jeopardy ❖
DONNA LONG

In the hospital I think birds sing
in the bones of my hands, the right
one bandaged in thick white gauze means
I may never write again, the left,
useless until my wrist heals, is luminous,
the veins visible as though through glass.

I remember best the windshield glass
not breaking but buckling—and singing:
no one turned the radio off. An absence of light,
a ridiculous thought about writing
my mother, the sound of dry leaves
in the gutter where I landed. This means,

perhaps, I was close to death or means
nothing: the facts: blood in my eyes, glass
manufactured not to shatter, leaves
fall in this season, a favorite song
of my long-dead mother, the illegal right
the Buick made was made—I was light

compared to it, and my bike invisible as light
by day. My bills, which I have no means
to pay, the driver says she'll pay. She writes
care of the hospital: I have your glasses.
I'll drop by. And apologize? A singer,
I decide she drinks before she leaves

for the bar each evening. I picture her left
then right handed, I associate light
with a thin whine—not true song—
of anesthesia wearing thin. I mean
to ask for a mirror as soon as my glasses
are ready. I've felt the scars, like Braille

or some other tactile language, right
through the gauze, reading what's left.
I'm a patient, etherized upon a glass
surface, one vein plugged in, body dawning
with antibiotics, softening any meanness
I feel to a persistent liquid singing—

My right hand floating, a white light,
a smooth left, ambidextrous. I mean
to return loud as glass, clear as song.

I began thinking about writing a sestina, rather than thinking about writing a poem. My poems usually begin after lots and lots of writing—sometimes in lines, sometimes not. I read back and see if I have a poem lurking anywhere. The sestina began a little more "mechanically"; I knew my end words needed to be words I could get multiple meanings out of. I made lists of words and tried to see how many meanings I could get out of each one. I decided the narrative needed to be something fictitious, so I could bend and shape it as needed. I'm not sure where the idea to do a bike accident came from, except that since I ride a bike everywhere, I worry plenty about being hit by a car.

I wrote, "In the hospital I think birds sing/in the bones of my hands" first. I knew when I wrote it that I could write the whole poem, even though I wasn't sure what would happen next. That line had the resonance that I know means I have a poem. I knew I could place myself in the frame of mind that would bring up the images and fears and strange thoughts that come just before/during/after an auto accident. . . . I almost never write by hand. My poems usually start on a typewriter and, when I am almost "finished," I move to a computer. But the sestina form lent itself, for me, to writing by hand. I was writing toward the end words rather than for meter (my usual formal strategy). And I allowed myself to kind of dream it into being, to capture the surreal sense of an experience like this. Nonetheless, I am least happy with the envoi. I would like to come up with three sharp lines that don't use my end words at all—I feel a little boxed in by the envoi as it is now. —Donna Long

The Sestina of an Unmarried Mother ❖
MARY JANE RYALS

"You're looking for a husband," he says
perched on a stool watching you work
at feeding your pregnancy's hunger.
It's his cutthroat kidding you hate,
the delicious pain of possibility you love.
You would not keep just anyone's fetus. Need?

No. Want. This ham and cheese sandwich you need
but not his summer sleepy eyes that say
in an evergreen way "I love
you" or "Why are you angry now?" Your work
is his—rejections, revisions, a hate
of imperfect story, obsession with language, hunger

for the sound of ocean, of bodies cresting. Hunger
with need. You don't want need, fear need.
Can he know how a pregnant woman might hate
to reply No to marriage? To say
Yes can mean death even as a tiny life works
to feed itself on both your loves.

Sometimes you lust for his voice, his love
faulty, musical, lazy, hungering
to fill up a juice glass. He's seeped into this work.
What is it that a woman needs—
not wants like old Freud would say?
You get so sick of grocery dailiness, hate

paying bills, buying the hated
car part when what you'd love
is to buy silk clothes that say
see this beautiful bulge, body that some women hunger
after, at times even think they need.
They don't know how it hinders or helps work.

You long for him like work.
His long legs, his laughter. Hate
your empty space, lonely bed and broken need.
When he taunts you about a husband, love
his boyish hands under his chin bringing back hunger
that flares into an answer you simply cannot say.

This poem came first out of experience. I was pregnant and in love with the father of the baby, but I had been married and have a child from that marriage. The marriage ended badly and I have a hard time trusting men now as partners and fathers. One thing I learned is that I have to trust myself first, and know that I can take care of myself and a child. So I didn't really want to get married but I wanted the baby. I'm sure lots of people think that's insane. Others think it's the only sane way to approach it.

Anyway the scenario you read in the first stanza is what happened. He was teasing but it cut to the quick, because I have this argument with myself all the time about want and need.

Okay. So I read this sestina by a woman who was pissed off that a guy she loved had leaked into her poem. I think she used five of the six end words I use in her poem. I can't remember. These are easy words, because they pretty much sum up the human condition—except for the word "say" which is a writer's need. I didn't have an envoi because the poem was over at "you simply cannot say." Oh well, I just can't really follow forms without breaking them. — Mary Jane Ryals

∞ READING INTO WRITING ∞

1. What do you think of the poems? Read them aloud. Does the form create one type of sound or does the way each poet writes a sestina change the music? Can you verbalize what you're hearing as the words repeat? Which seems best to fuse content and form? Why and how? What might you steal from that author in particular that will help you in your sestinas?

2. Make a list of the questions these poets ask themselves as they compose, noting all the techniques they use to get their sestinas drafted. Since this type of poem does turn on end words, sestina drafts can be hard to revise in the sense of reseeing or substantially changing content. Still, most sestina writers I know work hard to regularize (even if they don't meter) the line length and to make the syntax more natural once they've developed the sense of the poem and have lined up the repeat words where they need to be. So for this form, having a list of questions/initial drafting suggestions can help you write your best initial draft. If you still can't redraft very easily, you might try substituting the most difficult two of your six words and draft a new, second sestina.

The next two sestinas illustrate the ways two poets drafted poems that open with the same word ("October") and then progress to different emotional and physical places, the same season, and two different kinds of love.

Sestina for Indian Summer
ENID SHOMER

October, and the kudzu still spreads
the pines and oaks with green
skirts wide as tents, still pairs
shack and shrub in a false
harmony, still resists the shave
of autumn's cool blade. Wait

for me like that. Wait
like heat rising under a spread
wing, like the cautious glide of a shaver
over skin or the slow greening
of bronze. Time is a false-
bottomed chest, a basket of pears

that never ripen, a clock pared
down to a single *tick*. Wait
as the orchard did, its false
rigging of blossoms spread
windward, then snagged on the green
slope where today tractors shave

the dropped leaves to dust. Say *a close shave*,
meaning you escaped a dangerous pair:
proximity and severance, green
belief and the final *no*. Wait
somewhere between the two, spreading
the words apart the way waterfalls

chisel through stone. The false
colors of autumn are summer's shavings,
bits of sun and lake spread
in the trees, fluttering above the pair
of lovers who recur but do not last. Wait
until they're replaced by the green

thrust of kudzu, that greenery
that does not flame before it falls.
Seasons always bring the pasts we waited
for, when the calendar was shaved
to a strip narrow as a paring
of light glimpsed through a lover's spread

hand. We were the green pair who spread
the season thin, waiting and counting on
autumn's sheaves. We were the false summer.

Sestina for the House
RONALD WALLACE

October. They decide it is time to move.
The family has grown too large, the house
too small. The father smokes his pipe.
He says, I know that you all love
this house. He turns to his child
who is crying. She doesn't want to leave.

Outside in the large bright yard the leaves
are turning. They know it is time to move
down onto the ground where the child
will rake them together and make a house
for her dolls to play in. They love
the child. A small bird starts to pipe

his song to the leaves while the pipe
in the father's hand sputters. The father leaves
no doubt that he's made up his mind. He loves
his family; that's why they must move.
The child says, this is a wonderful house.
But nobody listens. She's only a child.

The father continues to talk. The child
cries, staring out at the Indian pipes
in her backyard, wondering if the birds of this house
will pack up their children, their nests, and leave
the old yard. Do birds ever move?
Do they know her sadness, her love?

Her father is smoking and talking of love.
Does he know what it's like being a child?
He knows she doesn't want to move.
She hates him sitting there smoking his pipe.
When has he ever been forced to leave
something he loved? He can't love this house.

The father sits by himself in the house
thinking how painful it is to love
a daughter, a house. He's watched her leave
saying she hates him. She's just a child
but it hurts nonetheless. Smoking his pipe
he wonders if he is wrong about the move.

Outside the bird pipes: Don't move. Don't move.
The bright leaves fall on the wonderful house.
And the child sits crying, learning about love.

Edith Shomer like Devan Cook narrates her poem in the first person. In Shomer's poem, summer changes to fall and a false summer creates, perhaps, false hopes. This poem too is about time and change, but lover speaks to lover instead of father to daughter. Here, kudzu, a plant that grows wildly and destructively in the south, symbolizes the "false summer" of these lovers. Despite details about the natural world, the reader has to read and read again to build an understanding of the relationship between these two lovers. Notice how Shomer chose a homonym in *pair/pare/pear*. She alternates *shave* with *shavings* to move from verb to noun. Finally, Shomer's poem enjambs, like the trailing, tangling kudzu vine: in five out of six stanzas the repeat word *Wait* is poised alone at the end of a line and then runs into the next sentence. (Wallace's poem has more full stops and perfect matches between line breaks and sentence boundaries.)

It feels as if Ronald Wallace's poem may have been influenced by Elizabeth Bishop's sestina. His poem evokes a Northern fall, where, by October, leaves are turning, only small birds are left, and there are Indian pipes in the backyard. Like the Gerard Manely Hopkins' poem "Spring and Fall" in chapter 4, this poem is about change, loss of innocence, and growing older. Notice how the word *pipe* has multiple meanings (a plant, a sound, an object for smoking) as does the word *leaves* (what we rake up, how we go away). Wallace has also chosen two repeat words with slant rhyme: *move/love*. The speaker of the poem uses the third-person singular voice, and like the speaker of Elizabeth Bishop's poem, is distant, observing this father and daughter.

I regard the end of a line, the line break, as roughly equivalent to half a comma. . . . Sometimes the sentence becomes broken, sometimes the sentence is never finished, often the sentences are complete. But articulations have joints, they can bend—occur. These occur within the rationale of the syntax, and the line break is a peculiarly sensitive means of recording those things —Denise Levertov (Packard 60–61)

These two sestinas, and the sestina form in general, call attention to line length, end-stopping, and enjambment decisions the poet makes as he/she weaves the repeat words as fluently as possible into each line's syntax.

➤ INVENTION EXERCISES ➤

1. Choose four of Enid Shomer's and/or Robert Wallace's repeat words and add two of your own to write an October sestina. Try to capture the landscape you live in now or one you're drawn to: October in the South, the Southwest, the Northeast, and the Pacific Northwest vary greatly. Of course, you may want to write about love, time, change, and things seasonal, too. But you don't have to. You might find it challenging to write about an urban October— cold wind in the city streets, and so on.

2. Write a sestina in first person or third person and then recast it in the other voice to see what happens to your meaning. For Ronald Wallace's poem, such a transformation works this way:

father's point of view, 1st person

> I am smoking and talking of love.
> As if I don't know what it's like being a child.
> I know she doesn't want to move.
> She hates me sitting here smoking my pipe.
> She wonders if I've ever been forced to leave
> something I love, thinks I can't love this house.

daughter's point of view, 1st person

> He is smoking and talking of love.
> Does he know what it's like to be a child?
> He knows I don't want to move.
> I hate him sitting there smoking his pipe.
> When has he ever been forced to leave
> something he loved? He can't love this house.

> Changing a poem in this way shows me that the current voice supports the child's perspective because I had to change less to move to

the child's first-person voice than I did moving to the father's first-person voice. At the same time, I feel the speaker of this poem is an adult because I was forced to have the child say things I don't think a child would really say: the current vocabulary and syntax is too mature for a child. Before you try such a transformation with your own sestina draft, you might want to experiment on a stanza from any of the other earlier sestinas. For instance, try moving Devan Cook's or Enid Shomer's first-person narrator into a third-person perspective.

3. In a group pick a topic and generate repeat words. Each group member writes his/her own sestina using all six words (or you can agree on rules that allow you to substitute but try not to go below four repeat words in common if you want to hear the effect). You should also as a group make all the initial drafting decisions you can. For instance, should the stanzas be more or less regular in length or should the poet feel free to vary line lengths whenever possible, as Michael Trammell did, in order to work the repeat words in comfortably?

4. Forget imitating or writing off of someone else's poem. Think of a topic/subject/feeling that you've been wanting to explore and just play with the words but do so in clusters. If you want to write about never wanting to live away from the ocean (or never having traveled to the ocean), cluster ocean words. Or cluster words about a time of year, particular landscape, a person or animal (for a portrait sestina), colors, or one of your senses (which will lead to a color, sound, or smell sestina). Pick three sets of six words that are powerful for you (include one or two words in these sets that have multiple meaning possibilities) and draft three first stanzas. Then follow the most provocative one into a poem.

CHALLENGING THE FORM: CHANGING STANZAS, MULTIPLYING WORD MEANINGS, MOVING REPEAT WORDS

Six sestinas that challenge and play with the traditional format end this chapter. As always, I'd suggest reading these aloud to see how alternate ways of structuring the sestina affect its verbal music. In the first, Alberto Ríos removes the stanza breaks between the first three and the second three stanzas, giving his sestina the look and breath of a free verse poem. In the first stanza of eighteen lines, the speaker introduces his grandmother and sets the scene, considers her life in the second stanza, another eighteen lines, and ends with an envoi that says farewell to the reader by letting us know the scene is continuing on, with the grandmother serving her grandson as she always has and seemingly always will. Although repeat words in this modified sestina still fall at the ends of the lines, they call much less visual attention to themselves than in the traditional sestina.

Nani
ALBERTO RÍOS

Sitting at her table, she serves
the sopa de arroz to me
instinctively, and I watch her,
the absolute mama, and eat words
I might have had to say more
out of embarrassment. To speak,
now-foreign words I used to speak,
too, dribble down her mouth as she serves
me albondigas. No more
than a third are easy to me.
By the stove she does something with words
and looks at me only with her
back. I am full. I tell her
I taste the mint, and watch her speak
smiles at the stove. All my words
make her smile. Nani never serves
herself, she only watches me
with her skin, her hair. I ask for more.

I watch the mama warming more
tortillas for me. I watch her
fingers in the flame for me.
Near her mouth, I see a wrinkle speak
of a man whose body serves
the ants like she serves me, then more words
from more wrinkles about children, words
about this and that, flowing more
easily from these other mouths. Each serves
as a tremendous string around her,
holding her together. They speak
nani was this and that to me
and I wonder just how much of me
will die with her, what were the words
I could have been, was. Her insides speak
through a hundred wrinkles, now, more
than she can bear, steel around her,
shouting, then, What is this thing she serves?

She asks me if I want more.
I own no words to stop her.
Even before I speak, she serves.

While Alberto Ríos evokes his past in part by using a few words in Spanish—
nani, sopa de arroz, albondigas—his main focus is on the people and the scene.
Julia Alvarez uses Spanish words differently. Because her poem looks at the two
languages she speaks, Spanish and English, she chooses one telling repeat word,
nombres (*names* in Spanish), and uses many more Spanish words and sentences to create her poem, titled "Bilingual Sestina." Sometimes Alvarez translates the Spanish words, repeating them in English, and sometimes she relies on
context to provide the translation readers might need. Her lines are longer, perhaps because she's working conceptually—talking about language use, telling as
much as or more than showing, although in her telling she's careful to use a
poet's full palette of details: "snowy, blonde, blue-eyed, gum chewing English,"
for example.

Bilingual Sestina ❖
JULIA ALVAREZ

Some things I have to say aren't getting said
in this snowy, blonde, blue-eyed, gum chewing English,
dawn's early light sifting through the *persianas* closed
the night before by dark-skinned girls whose words
evoke *cama, aposento, sueños* in *nombres*
from that first word I can't translate from Spanish.

Gladys, Rosario, Altagracia—the sounds of Spanish
wash over me like warm island waters as I say
your soothing names: a child again learning the *nombres*
of things you point to in the world before English
turned *sol, tierra, cielo, luna* to vocabulary words—
sun, earth, sky, moon—language closed

like the touch-sensitive *morivivir* whose leaves closed
when we kids poked them, astonished. Even Spanish
failed us then when we realized how frail a word
is when faced with the thing it names. How saying
its name won't always summon up in Spanish or English
the full blown genii from the bottled *nombre*.

Gladys, I summon you back with your given *nombre*
to open up again the house of slatted windows closed
since childhood, where *palabras* left behind for English
stand dusty and awkward in neglected Spanish.
Rosario, muse of *el patio*, sing in me and through me say
that world again, begin first with those first words

you put in my mouth as you pointed to the world—
not Adam, not God, but a country girl numbering
the stars, the blades of grass, warming the sun by saying
el sol as the dawn's light fell through the closed
persianas from the gardens where you sang in Spanish,
Esta son las mañanitas, and listening, in bed, no English

yet in my head to confuse me with translations, no English
doubling the world with synonyms, no dizzying array of words,
—the world was simple and intact in Spanish
awash with *colores, luz, sueños,* as if the *nombres*
were the outer skin of things, as if words were so close
to the world one left a mist of breath on things by saying

their names, an intimacy I now yearn for in English—
words so close to what I meant that I almost hear my Spanish
blood beating, beating inside what I say *en inglés.*

The language changes in this poem mask some of the repetition, shifting the reader's attention to waiting for the next Spanish word to fall and in that way taking some of the focus off the repeat words.

In the next sestina, Sandra Teichmann takes Alberto Ríos' strategy to the extreme, collapsing and combining stanzas but also running the repeat words into the text so they disappear visually. She still has three stanzas, but her lines are approaching prose (and look a lot like the beat line of Allen Ginsberg's "Howl"). Unlike Ríos, Teichmann doesn't keep the envoi separate, so the words themselves need to lend necessary poetic closure. Her poem is notable also for how she uses prose narrative conventions to develop plot and character.

Three Hundred Forty-Two Fifth Street Sestina*
Sandra Teichmann

Gladys wanted glass door knobs for her bedroom, wanted them enough to
  steal from Day's hardware store while Jim Blackwood waited on Mike Cane,
  weighing a pound of finishing nails.
A restive bargain nailed, Gladys lifted two glass knobs into her pockets,
  weighing her skirt.
One hour she wanted before Sam came from the wood lot for lunch. Time to
  just daydream on their bed. (Glass, like a day star, scattering fire, nailing
  symmetry to lacquered wood.)

Gladys needed only two knobs for the closet's two doors, wanted things nice
  inside, not weighty, demanding praise—praise weighing decisions and Sam's
  days, his musings.
He wanted her happy, more money, nails pounded by hired labor, knobs
  turning with ease in fine wood.

Mornings, for work, Gladys would rearrange their things: weighting the village's
inbred distance or Sam's tie for Thursday, moving boots missing hobnails to a
low shelf. She wanted to feign things were honed, wanted the inside fine like
the wood skin of the door, free of nails, the glass handholds weighing only the
full star of daylight or light bulb.
Yes, the knobs were all she wanted, weighing down the wood, gathering
daydreams nailed inside. Just two knobs.

In the next sestina, I've underlined the repeat words. The challenge in this
poem was to keep the stanza forms, which say to the reader "six stanzas and a
three-line seventh stanza—must be a sestina," but also confound that expectation somewhat by taking the repeat words out of the right-hand margin. At
some point, I decided to allow myself to alternate the word *dog* with its reversed
spelling word *God,* to produce even more flexibility.

*Mid-Life**
    Wendy Bishop

Huck just moves on. Alice just wakes up. —Adam Gopnik

<u>Walking</u> one morning
the <u>world</u> has changed,
the <u>dog</u> lunges at her line
as <u>colder</u> wind teases trees,
as <u>red</u> cloud-light lines the horizon.
<u>Something</u>, It's time to decide—

<u>something</u>. Adrenaline and age.
I <u>walk</u> faster when I start thinking.
<u>Red</u> chrysanthemums in dawn light
open the <u>world</u> to speculation.
<u>Cold</u> snaps pumpkin vines, crimps leaves.
<u>God</u> balances on an old spider web.

The <u>dog</u>, recently adopted, knows
<u>something</u> about moving *and* about waking,
works the night's <u>coldness</u> from her legs,
<u>walks</u> with nippy grin, smells
the whole <u>world</u> with her lank
<u>red</u> tongue out, and then does it again.

<u>Red</u> heartbeats. I can feel them:
<u>God's</u> fist hammering into my
<u>world</u> this morning. I tell myself
<u>something</u> has to change. I
<u>walk</u> myself into perfect attention:
<u>cold</u> is like school lessons: Tuck in safely

<u>cold</u> toes. Keep head covered,
and <u>red</u> cheeks and nose. Take
a <u>walk</u>, morning, evening. Invigorating.
The <u>dog</u> is adept in ways of waiting.
This says <u>something</u> about
her <u>world</u>. It comes rushing up—

the <u>world</u>—each morning,
<u>cold</u> globe in a singular orbit. Tell her
<u>something</u>, the dog. Throw
the <u>red</u> ball. Tell her she's good,
the <u>dog</u>. How *she* takes *you* for
a <u>walk</u>. Tethers you to this earth.

where you <u>walk</u>, the dawning <u>world</u> offers
regular instruction, in <u>God's</u> <u>cold</u> skies,
in her <u>red</u>-leafed falls. And this, this is <u>something</u>.

While I found it difficult to get the repeat words in my poem in true head-rhyme position, Florence Cassen Mayers does so in the next poem by writing a commentary on American life—combining a sestina strategy with a list poem strategy as she places a different number—one, two, three, four, five, six—in the initial position in the line but then continues this across stanzas in the expected sestina configuration. Her poem is followed by Devan Cook's imitation of the same effect, only this time using colors in the initial position instead of numbers.

All-American Sestina
FLORENCE CASSEN MAYERS

One nation, indivisible
two-car garage
three strikes you're out
four-minute mile
five-cent cigar
six-string guitar

six-pack Bud
one-day sale
five-year warranty
two-way street
fourscore and seven years ago
three cheers

three-star restaurant
sixty-
four-dollar question
one-night stand
two-pound lobster
five-star general

five-course meal
three sheets to the wind
two bits
six-shooter
one-armed bandit
four-poster

four-wheel drive
five-and-dime
hole in one
three-alarm fire
sweet sixteen
two-wheeler

two-tone Chevy
four rms, hi flr, w/vu
six-footer
high five
three-ring circus
one-room schoolhouse

two thumbs up, five-karat diamond
Fourth of July, three-piece suit
six feet under, one-horse town.

Good-bye to the American West in Six Colors:
A Sestina After Florence Cassen Mayers'
*All-American Sestina**
        Devan Cook

red-headed woodpeckers
purple kool-aid
blue moon
green cheese
yellow journalism
orange you glad?

orange juice from Florida, better
red than dead
yellow peril
purple haze
Green River
blue highways

blue roses
orange julius
green corn
red wagon
purple-tie-dye
yellow-belly

yellow fever
blue Monday
purple rain
orange poppies
Red Emma
green grass of home

green eggs and ham
yellow ribbon
red tide
bluebird of happiness
orange speed bumps
purple mountain's majesty

purple orchids
green light
agent orange
yellow dog
blue morning
red Indians

and Custer: one
  yellow-hair
blue steel
red-blooded
dead boy

➤ INVENTION EXERCISES ➤

1. Write your own bi- or trilingual sestina. Choose two or more repeat words from another language. You could also consider slang or a regional dialect for variety and use several slang words or dialect words as your repeat words. When I wrote a bilingual sestina, I translated the English word into its Spanish equivalent to give me an excuse to vary the form.

2. Like Sandra Teichmann, after composing collapse your sestina: write it out as a prose poem and read it aloud. Does it work better or worse this way? Why? Do you read it differently? If so, why and how? To decide, you may need to tape record yourself reading both versions.

3. Take one of your sets of repeat words generated earlier and compose a sestina where the words fall anywhere but at the end of the line. Or take a sestina you already have, cut half a line from the beginning, restructure it so the repeats are internalized, and then end by adding a new half line. Again, compare the two versions. The beginning of Alberto Ríos' poem would change like this when the repeat words are moved to the left:

   She <u>serves</u> the sopa de
   arroz to <u>me</u> instinctively, and I
   watch <u>her</u>, the absolute mama,
   and eat <u>words</u> I might have had
   to say <u>more</u> out of embarrassment.
   To <u>speak</u> now-foreign words

4. Like Mayers and Cook, draft a poem where the initial words come from a sequence: numbers, colors, flower names, makes of cars, etc. Generate possibilities in a group and choose the one everybody likes best, each drafting his/her own version.

5. Think of someone you know who has an obsession (also, newspaper articles of strange human occurrences or a stroll through the more esoteric and original Web sites are good for this) and use that obsession for generating repeat words; then tell that person's story (as Sandra Teichmann tells Gladys') in either a first- or third-person narration. Maybe you know someone who runs a snake farm, studies the moon, salvages sunken ships, collects tacky figurines, or has opened a private museum. Mine stories such as these for your sestina.

POCKET DEFINITIONS

Envoi—Final lines of a poem—notably, the final three-line stanza of a sestina. The word literally means a farewell or conclusion.

Homonyms—Words having the same pronunciation but different meanings and spellings, like *son/sun*.

Sestina—This poetic form requires that six end words be repeated in a set pattern across six stanzas and that all six words be used—again, in pattern—in a three-line final stanza, called an envoi.

12

SONNETS

Exploring the Possibilities of Fourteen Lines

Desire
MOLLY PEACOCK

It doesn't speak and it isn't schooled,
like a small foetal animal with wettened fur.
It is the blind instinct for life unruled,
visceral frankincense and animal myrrh.
It is what babies bring to kings,
an eyes-shut, ears-shut medicine of the heart
that smells and touches endings and beginnings
without the details of time's experienced *part-
fit-into-part-fit-into-part.* Like a paw,
it is blunt; like a pet who knows you
and nudges your knee with its snout—but more raw
and blinder and younger and more divine, too,
than the tamed wild—it's the drive for what is real,
deeper than the brain's detail: the drive to feel.

The **sonnet.** Students of poetry love it and hate it. They think it is a more rigid a
form than it really is, and for this reason perhaps they find it less generative than
they might. At the same time, the sonnet is the poem we recognize most readily
as *poetry*—the type of poem found in anthologies and the type of poem written
by Shakespeare, the most venerated poet in the English poetic firmament (but you
can see in Molly Peacock's contemporary sonnet that the form is alive and well
today). Poets claim the sonnet has lost force and relevance, but secretly most want
not only to try their hand at it but also to succeed at saying something important
within its confines and its lines. The sonnet is composed in variations on combinations of several other stanza forms: couplets, tercets, and quatrains.

THE CLASSICS (ENGLISH AND ITALIAN)

The sonnet is a small, often passionate or philosophical song. Perfected in the sixteenth century, the English sonnet consists of fourteen lines of **iambic pentameter** verse: three **quatrains** and a closing couplet with the rhyme scheme of *abab, cdcd, efef, gg*. Although the sonnet came to England from Italy, the Italian sonnet is harder for English speakers to compose since it repeats the same rhyme more often: an octave rhyming *abbaabba* and a sestet rhyming *cdcdcd*. English is a less rhyme-rich language, so English sonneteers adapted the form. In fact, it doesn't take much reading of the form to find that poets have always adapted this structure, observing most consistently only its fourteen-line length. Over time we have moved from the numerical and religious significances of the form to a more secular contemporary version.

> . . . four represents this world, while three represents divinity.
> Moreover, the sum of these integers, seven, represents the entire range
> of human experience from lowest to highest. Of course, seven has been
> assigned special meaning in most systems of number symbolism. . . .
> The proportion 4/3, then, encapsulates the relation of body to soul,
> reflecting the relation between the mundane and celestial in the macro-
> cosm. And as readers proceed through the [Italian] sonnet, passing from
> quatrain to tercet (or from octave to sestet in the fourteen line scheme),
> they proceed from this world toward heaven. . . . So the sonnet carries
> its readers along this trajectory toward blessedness . . .
> —S. K. Heninger, Jr., 77

A sonnet can be written in **couplets** (see Weldon Kees' sonnet below) or with a personal rhyme scheme and then labeled a nonce sonnet. (Tom Heise labeled his sonnet—shared in chapter 1—a nonce sonnet.) There are sonnet sequences too. For instance, a crown of sonnets includes seven Italian sonnets that never repeat a rhyme chain from one to the other, uses the end line of the previous sonnet as the opening line of the next, and uses the opening line for the seven-sonnet poem as the last line of the last sonnet, creating a complete circle, a crown of great complexity. It's possible to try to write a monorhymed sonnet, and some poets have written double sonnets, poems of twenty-eight lines in length.

My poetry dictionary lists two other versions of the sonnet: the reversed Shakespearean sonnet, which has a couplet followed by three quatrains, and the retrograde sonnet that somehow reads the same backward as forward. Contemporary poets, of course, may decide to drop the rhyme scheme entirely, moving to slant rhyme or nonce patterns of slant rhyme. Likewise, they play with line length and shorten lines greatly, creating skinny fourteen-line vertical rectangles instead of the more traditional box of fourteen lines. But the fourteen lines remain the dependable way (other than a poet's naming a sonnet as "sonnet") to detect a sonnet. Count out a poem in fourteen lines and you've got, inevitably, the echo of the sonnet's song.

That time of year thou mayst in me behold
WILLIAM SHAKESPEARE

That time of year thou mayst in me behold
When yellow leaves, or none, or few, do hang
Upon those boughs which shake against the cold,
Bare ruined choirs, where late the sweet birds sang.
In me thou see'st the twilight of such day
As after sunset fadeth in the west;
Which by and by black night doth take away,
Death's second self, that seals up all in rest.
In me thou see'st the glowing of such fire,
That on the ashes of his youth doth lie,
As the deathbed whereon it must expire,
Consumed with that which it was nourished by.
    This thou perceiv'st, which makes thy love more strong,
    To love that well which thou must leave ere long.

Shakespearean: three quatrains of *abab, cdcd, efef*
and a couplet of *gg*

My mistress' eyes are nothing like the sun
WILLIAM SHAKESPEARE

My mistress' eyes are nothing like the sun;
Coral is far more red than her lips' red;
If snow be white, why then her breasts are dun;
If hairs be wires, black wires grow on her head.
I have seen roses damasked red and white,
But no such roses see I in her cheeks;
And in some perfumes is there more delight
Than in the breath that from my mistress reeks.
I love to hear her speak, yet well I know
That music hath a far more pleasing sound;
I grant I never saw a goddess go:
My mistress, when she walks, treads on the ground.
    And yet, by heaven, I think my love as rare
    As any she, belied with false compare.

Later [Renaissance] poets, however, recognized that the formal properties of the sonnets and its actual language constitute two different systems; and while they can be coordinated—harmonized and synchronized—they may also be differentiated and opposed. So later sonneteers learned to play off one system against the other. The subtext of form becomes a counterpoint to what the words themselves might say. Although the form of the sonnet remains unrelentingly optimistic, promising salvation after the divagations and tribulations of this world, the language of the sonnet might very well express doubt, questioning the faith that characterizes the orthodox culture. The resulting tension between the subtext of form and the verbal system energizes the poem, producing two possibilities of interpretation. —S. K. Heninger, Jr., 79–80

Sonnets from the Portuguese, 43
ELIZABETH BARRETT BROWNING

How do I love thee? Let me count the ways.
I love thee to the depth and breadth and height
My soul can reach, when feeling out of sight
For the ends of Being and ideal Grace.
I love thee to the level of everyday's
Most quiet need, by sun and candle-light.
I love thee freely, as men strive for Right;
I love thee purely, as they turn from Praise.
I love thee with the passion put to use
In my old griefs, and with my childhood's faith.
I love thee with a love I seemed to lose
With my lost saints—I love thee with the breath,
Smiles, tears, of all my life!—and, if God choose,
I shall but love thee better after death.

Italian sonnet : an octave of *abbabba*
and a sestet of *cdcdcd* (sestet variations include
cdecde and *cddcee*)

Design
ROBERT FROST

I found a dimpled spider, fat and white,
On a white heal-all, holding up a moth
Like a white piece of rigid satin cloth—
Assorted characters of death and blight
Mixed ready to begin the morning right,
Like the ingredients of a witches' broth—
A snow-drop spider, a flower like a froth,
And dead wings carried like a paper kite.

What had the flower to do with being white,
The wayside blue and innocent heal-all?
What brought the kindred spider to that height,
Then steered the white moth thither in the night?
What but design of darkness to appall?—
If design govern in a thing so small.

Italian octave: *abbaabba*
Nonce sestet: *acaacc*

The Oven Bird
ROBERT FROST

There is a singer everyone has heard,
Loud, a mid-summer and a mid-wood bird,
Who makes the solid tree trunks sound again.
He says that leaves are old and that for flowers
Mid-summer is to spring as one to ten.
He says the early petal-fall is past
When pear and cherry bloom went down in showers
On sunny days a moment overcast;
And comes that other fall we name the fall.
He says the highway dust is over all.
The bird would cease and be as other birds
But that he knows in singing not to sing.
The question that he frames in all but words
Is what to make of a diminished thing.

Nonce form: *aabc, dece, ffgh, gh*
or *aabcdece, ffghgh*

∞ **READING INTO WRITING** ∞

1. No doubt you've encountered several of these sonnets in your school readings. Still, you may not have spent much time puzzling out their meanings and their structures. Since I've sketched the rhyme scheme for each sonnet, with group members work out your reading of each. Who is being spoken to, by whom, about what? Puzzle out the archaic language and imagery. For instance, what is "[d]eath's second self"?

2. In what ways is the second Shakespeare sonnet a send-up of the sonnet tradition? Again, look at the language in this poem. What color is dun? What does the poet mean by "[a]s any she"?

3. Elizabeth Barrett Browning's sonnet continues the tradition of talking about love. Although she's addressing the loved one as "thee," does her poem seem more modern in any ways? If so, how? If not, why not?

4. Frost moves from love to philosophy. Write out interpretations of his poems and see if you can agree in your group about the points he's making in each sonnet. Because his language is much less archaic, are his sonnets easier to understand? Do you prefer the movement away from love poems to a contemplation of the natural world? Why or why not?

5. As you read the following sonnet, analyze both form and content. To understand the content, you'll need to research Greek myths, and the Internet can be a tool for doing so along with reference books. The swan in Yeats' poem is the Greek god Zeus, who took the form of a swan to rape Leda, who would become the mother of Helen of Troy. Further reading into this myth will open the poem's story to you.

Leda and the Swan
W. B. YEATS

A sudden blow: the great wings beating still
Above the staggering girl, her thighs caressed
By the dark webs, her nape caught in his bill,
He holds her helpless breast upon his breast.

How can those terrified vague fingers push
The feathered glory from her loosening thighs?
And how can body, laid in that white rush,
But feel the strange heart beating where it lies?

A shudder in the loins engenders there
The broken wall, the burning roof and tower
And Agamemnon dead.
                            Being so caught up,
So mastered by the brute blood of the air,
Did she put on his knowledge with his power
Before the indifferent beak could let her drop?

6. Return to each sonnet with imitation or homage in mind. List some
   people or subjects you might write about that are triggered by each
   fourteen-line contemplation.

➤ INVENTION EXERCISES ➤

To steal and recirculate end rhymes, write a poem of fourteen lines that fits the
end words you choose from other poets' end words listed below. (All poems are
in this chapter.) While drafting, you may change any two of the fourteen words
to make the poem better. You may work with a ten-syllable line or move to
lines of any length. You might want to: read the words stripped from the poem
and write a poem about any subject they suggest; return to the original poem
and look at the rhetorical/subject patterns; write a straight love poem or an anti-
love poem; write a poem that "counts" the ways of your love; look at a small
corner of the natural world; and so on.

Sample end rhymes from William Shakespeare:

sun, red, dun, head, white, cheeks, delight, reeks, know, sound, go, ground, rare,
compare

Sample end rhymes from Robert Frost:

heard, bird, again, flowers, ten, past, showers, overcast, fall, all, birds, sing,
words, thing

Sample end rhymes from Floyd Skloot:

wide, legs, hide, begs, mirror, hucklebone, her, grown, know, being, grow, freeing, thirst, first

Sample end rhymes from Marilyn Hacker:

wrong, lean, seventeen, belong, school, image, rummage, drool, dropping, in,
Insulin, ambulance, hands, shopping

Sample end rhymes from Robert Pinsky:

back, slap, dock, clamber, top, remember, lake, same, cheek, color, name, her,
over, her

For example, to write my draft from the rhyme words from Robert Frost's sonnet "The Oven Bird," I lined up the end words vertically on the right-hand margin of my computer screen and drafted toward them, with this result:

*Reveille**
  Quiet breathing in a morning bed, I heard
  The dew-eaves dripping and the mocking-bird
  Braced on his roof-vent tower start again
  To fling the sunrise up, to syncopate the flowers'
  Colors into dawn, flood the neighborhood with his ten
  Variations on ten uxorious seasons from the past.
  It seemed boast enough to hold back showers:
  A weaving, a knitting, an under and overcasting
  Of jumbled sounds. His shadow high and so far to fall
  If the resident cats could stalk him well, and all
  The jays forgot to harry these tigers out of trance. Bird
  Choruses knot sleeping shadows into next day's dreams, sing
  Hunter and hunted, crescendo in clear sky. My words
  Call cats from trees. Finally awake, we study spring.

SONNETS ABOUT SONNETS

> After [writing] hundreds of sonnets . . . I honor the sonnet, its ability to reduce a novel to a single paragraph, that play within a rhythm so natural to the English language. It's been a transformative vehicle for me, a joy, satisfying the way all discovery can be. —Maureen Seaton (Finch 208)

The following sonnets are about sonnet-writing. What form does each of the poets choose to write in? How much liberty has each taken with line and meter? After reading these poems that capture the perils and pleasures of the sonnet-writing process, you might consider writing a sonnet about your pleasure or lack of pleasure in reading sonnets or about your process of trying to write a sonnet.

Nuns Fret Not at Their Convent's Narrow Room ❖
WILLIAM WORDSWORTH

  Nuns fret not at their convent's narrow room;
  And hermits are contented with their Cells;
  And students with their pensive citadels:
  Maids at the wheel, the weaver at his Loom,
  Sit blithe and happy; bees that soar for bloom,

High as the highest Peak of Furness-fells,
Will murmur by the hour in foxglove bells:
In truth, the prison, unto which we doom
Ourselves, no prison is: and hence for me,
In sundry moods, 'twas pastime to be bound
Within the Sonnet's scanty plot of ground;
Pleased if some Souls (for such their needs must be)
Who have felt the weight of too much liberty,
Should find brief solace there, as I have found.

July 19, 1979 ❖
MARILYN HACKER

I'll write a sonnet just to get in form,
allowing fifteen minutes by the clock
to build gratuitously block by block
of quatrains. Almost six, pale sunlight, warm
(last night we thought there'd be a thunderstorm).
The crickets fiddle buzz-saws without vowels.
I've had thrice-daily bouts of runny bowels,
which seems, on travels south, to be the norm.
I must avoid the self-indulgent stance
of lovesick troubadours—that isn't wise,
in spite of being in the South of France
with a capricious woman whose blue eyes
invest the genre with some relevance.
She says they're green. I've done my exercise.

Sad Stories Told in Bars: The "Reader's Digest" Version ❖
WILLIAM MATTHEWS

First I was born and it was tough on Mom.
Dad felt left out. There's much I can't recall.
I seethed my way to speech and said a lot
of things: some were deemed cute. I was so small
my likely chance was growth, and so I grew.
Long days in school I filled, like a spring creek,
with boredom. Sex I discovered soon
enough, I now think. Sweet misery!
There's not enough room in a poem so curt
to get me out of adolescence, yet
I'm nearing fifty with a limp, and dread
the way the dead get stacked up like a cord
of wood. Not much of a story, it is?
The life that matters not the one I've led.

The Bad Sonnet ❖
RONALD WALLACE

It stayed up late, refused to go to bed,
and when it did it sang loud songs instead
of sleeping, disturbing its siblings—couplets, quatrains
in their small rooms, began caterwauling—
and soon the whole neighborhood was awake.
Sometimes it got in petty trouble with the law,
shoplifting any little thing it saw
that caught its fancy: happiness and heartache

slipped neatly in its pocket. It joined a gang
that forged currency, bombed conventions, and finally
tried to bump off all its competition.
Through a sequence of events, luckily
it was caught, handcuffed, and taken off to jail
where it would not keep quiet in its cell.

➤ INVENTION EXERCISES ➤

1. Use the sonnet shape to write a self-portrait. Like William
   Matthews, you might comment on the sonnet form. Or, like Beth
   Lashley in "Posing at Three and a Half," you might look at a photo
   of yourself at an earlier age and write in the vein of "The poet at
   three" (or fourteen or thirty-three or forty, etc.). Your main concern
   here is to measure your self-observations into the shape of fourteen
   boxy lines to get your initial feel for what can be done and said in
   that space of poetry.

Posing at Three and a Half *
   Beth Lashley

Pug nose, chubby cheeks, in a navy blue
dress, a gingham pinafore, lacy socks
and black patent leather Mary Janes, like a
little doll. The poet age three and a half.
sitting: on the laps of mom and daddy.
Like statues, faces frozen, in fake smiles.
Mom in her 1978 green blouse,
Dad in his picture perfect goofy grin.
Brown eyes focused on looking ahead, on
looking happy—I think I was happy
to be the center of attention, naive
mind full of questions, still full of promise.
Hair thin and ashen brunette, not thick curls,
not brown and tangled. Calm and in control.

2. Using the encyclopedia description of the sonnet form, you can draft your own poem about this poem after reading Marilyn Hacker's poem on sonnets and as an exercise to try to learn the sonnet form.

> During the past century, sonnet themes in both Europe and America have broadened to include almost any subject and mood, even though the main line of development has remained remarkably stable. . . . alternatives to exact rhymes have replenished the stock of rhyme-pairs and have sophisticated acoustic relationships; and a more natural idiom has removed much of the artificiality that had long been a burden. This adaptability within a tradition of eight centuries' standing suggests that there will be no diminution of interest in and use of the form in the foreseeable future, and that the inherent difficulties that have kept the numbers of truly fine Shakespearean sonnets to an extremely small percentage of those written will deter neither versifier nor genius from testing for her- or himself the challenge of what Rosetti called "a moment's monument,—/Memorial from the Soul's eternity." —Alex Preminger and T. V. F. Brogan, 1170

Alternatively, you might cut the rather alliterative language in the encyclopedia definition into a found poem on the theme of "The Sonnet in the Next Century."

3. Like Marilyn Hacker, write a sonnet to a lover about writing a sonnet to that lover. This time, you might pick a rhyme scheme but opt for half rhymes. Once you've picked an initial *a* and *b* rhyme, you might want to make a half-rhyme list and have it handy to enlarge your choices as you turn the corner of each line. Here's a list one of my students made: *home, some, come, rum, bum, loom, boom, carom, loam, foam, poem, gem, whim, him, dim, slim, doom, fume, room, gnome, comb, dumb, qualm, calm, sum, hum, pompom, roam, ram, tomb, womb.* You might also have fun dipping into a rhyming dictionary for help.

CONTEMPORARY (SEMI-TRADITIONAL)

In the following sonnets, five contemporary poets compose within the sonnet form. To get a sense of how the form has continued into the current century, read each and match it to what you now know about the traditions of the form. Is the sonnet Shakespearean, Italian, or a recognizable variant? Does the poet use full or slant rhyme or both? Is the topic the traditional one of love or a more contemporary exploration? Does the poem take a traditional turn between octave and sestet? Is the poet relying on regular meter, syllabics, masculine or feminine rhyme? Which sonnet do you find most satisfying and why?

My Daughter Considers Her Body
FLOYD SKLOOT

She examines her hand, fingers spread wide.
Seated, she bends over her crossed legs
to search for specks or scars and cannot hide
her awe when any mark is found. She begs
me to look, twisting before her mirror,
at some tiny bruise on her hucklebone.
Barely awake, she studies creases her
arm developed as she slept. She has grown
entranced with blemish, begun to know
her body's facility for being
flawed. She does not trust its will to grow
whole again, but may learn that too, freeing
herself to accept the body's deep thirst
for risk. Learning to touch her wounds comes first.

One Morning, Shoeing Horses
HENRY TAYLOR

I hold a shank while the blacksmith nails a shoe
in place, and think about how many years
I've worked at this—watching the horse's ears
for signs of what he might decide to do,
touching his neck, turning his head to coax
a little weight away from the lifted hoof,
the flywhisk light and always on the move,
the soothing whispers tuned to hammer strokes.

But I've been unsteady at it since a day
like this, some ten years back, when a driven nail
got under the blacksmith's wedding ring, unclinched.
There was a kind of roaring scream, the horse flinched
and snatched his hoof, and there the finger lay,
twitching a little, beside the water pail.

Poem Not to Be Read at Your Wedding
BETH ANN FENNELLY

You ask me for a poem about love
in lieu of a wedding present, trying to save me
money. For three nights I've lain under
glow-in-the-dark stars I've stuck to the ceiling
over my bed. I've listened to the songs
of the galaxy. Well Carmen, I would rather

give you your third set of steak knives
than tell you what I know. Let me find you
some other store-bought present. Don't
make me warn you of stars, how they see us
from that distance as miniature and breakable,
from the bride who tops the wedding cake
to the Mary on Pinto dashboards
holding her ripe red heart in her hands.

On the Grand Canyon's North Rim
ALAN MICHAEL PARKER

An amateur astronomer, a lay
ventriloquist, the Ranger leads his night
hike to a four-foot ledge, eight thousand feet
above sea level. Swaying there, he says
Be careful, folks. We lose a kid or two
each year. He turns and teeters, grins, then throws
his voice behind a crag behind the crowd
—a *woo* through Devil's Beak—as thirty souls,
all told, leap up in thirty gasping throats.
The crowd is his: black holes and quasars, quarks
and super novae, all the stars like sparks
inside a giant firefly—until one thought
escapes our thirty trillion molecules:
He could crush our hopes, we are that small.

Fourteen
MARILYN HACKER

We shopped for dresses which were always wrong:
sweatshop approximations of the lean-
lined girls' wear I studied in *Seventeen*.
The armholes pinched, the belt didn't belong,
the skirt drooped forward (I'd be told at school).
Our odd-lot bargains deformed the image,
but she and I loved Saturday rummage.
One day she listed outside Loehmann's. Drool
wet her chin. Stumbling, she screamed at me. Dropping
our parcels on the pavement, she fell in
what looked like a fit. I guessed: Insulin.
The cop said, "Drunk," and called an ambulance
while she cursed me and slapped away my hands.
When I need a mother, I still go shopping.

⬬ INVENTION EXERCISES ⬬

1. Now that you've read and analyzed these five sonnets, choose one to imitate. You can do this in one of several ways. You can adopt, borrow, or steal the end words as suggested in an earlier invention exercise. You can decide to write about the same subject, using your own rhyme scheme or no rhyme scheme, creating an unrhymed homage. You can do what students in my class did—what I call loosely writing across, over, and through another sonnet so that quite a few of the bones of the original remain when the prompt sonnet and the homage/imitation are compared. You'll have to decide to what degree this poem becomes your own or needs to be attributed to the poet—better to be safe than sorry and accused of plagiarism. (When making this decision within a tradition of imitation and borrowing, ask yourself: if the poet saw my poem, would he/she expect to be acknowledged?)

   Before you complete your own "experiment," read over the following six paired sonnets—the originals by poets Denis Johnson, Weldon Kees, and Rita Dove and the close responses by LaTrell Houston, Joseph Tuso, and A. S. Kaufman. Decide how they wrote over, across, and into the original sonnet. Then choose any sonnet in this chapter and write your own close imitation.

Sway
DENIS JOHNSON

Since I find you will no longer love,
from bar to bar in terror I shall move
past Forty-third and Halsted, Twenty-fourth
and Roosevelt where fire-gutted cars,
their bones the bones of coyote and hyena,
suffer the light from the wrestling arena
to fall all over them. And what they say
blends in the tarantellasmic sway
of all of us between the two of these:
harmony and divergence,
their sad story of harmony and divergence,
the story that begins
I did not know who she was
and ends *I did not know who she was.*

Sing Sway*
  LaTrell Houston

Since I find you will no longer sing,
from bar to bar in terror, I shall laugh
from Fifty-third and Seaway, Thirty-fourth
and Esther Rolle where old men drink
rusting their bones away with hot liquor,
suffer the light from night changed to day
to start all over. And what they say
makes no sense, absolutely none to me
because they don't use their minds in talking
but the alcohol scent from their breath
sways around my nose and eyes before I
can walk away. I don't know why you won't
sing. I promise, I will not laugh at you.
I don't want to deal with the drunks today.

For My Daughter
WELDON KEES

Looking into my daughter's eyes I read
Beneath the innocence of morning flesh
Concealed, hintings of death she does not heed.
Coldest of winds have blown this hair, and mesh
Of seaweed snarled these miniatures of hands;
The night's slow poison, tolerant and bland,
Has moved her blood. Parched years that I have seen
That may be hers appear: foul, lingering
Death in certain war, the slim legs green.
Or, fed on hate, she relishes the sting
Of others' agony; perhaps the cruel
Bride of a syphilitic or a fool.
These speculations sour in the sun.
I have no daughter. I desire none.

*For My Nephew**
    Joseph Tuso

When I look into my nephew's eyes I can see
That his fading smile has been replaced by fear.
He lies in pain, fighting what doctors cannot see;
The cause of the affliction is not clear.
Cold sweats and fever drench his pink flesh;
The IV line, piercing his little vein.
I feel his heart beat in his tiny chest
As he lies in bed, curled up, crying from his pain.
His frail body does as much as it can
To fight this hard and uncertain bout;
But he is much too young to comprehend
Some things, or to know what sickness is all about.
When I look into my nephew's eyes I can see
That both love and fear have taken over me.

Persephone Underground
RITA DOVE

If I could just touch your ankle, he whispers, *there
on the inside, above the bone*—leans closer,
breath of lime and peppers—*I know I could
make love to you.* She considers
this, secretly thrilled, though she wasn't quite
sure what he meant. He was good
with words, words that went straight to the liver.
Was she falling for him out of sheer boredom—
cooped up in this anything-but-humble dive, stone
gargoyles leering and brocade drapes licked with fire?
Her ankle burns where he described it. She sighs
just as her mother aboveground stumbles, is caught
by the fetlock—bereft in an instant—
while the Great Man drives home his desire.

*Europa Exposed**
    A. S. Kaufman

*If you would just ride me, he murmurs,
through these dry sands, across the water,* his
nostrils flare, *I know you could be free.* She lets
the bull's strong white flanks slip between her thighs,

feels thick, solid muscle ripple as he gets
going. Warm air rushes through her, she sighs.
He takes her, hot and full, moves like lava through
the earth's core, then salty splash of rushing sea. Wild,
she grasps horns for balance, feeling his hooves
trample her tangled curls. Sated, he leaves her on the isle,
alone and strangely empty with the memory of blue eyes,
more human than bovine. She looks for him in the tide,
ignoring thundering blasts of venom ravaging the skies
with a woman's voice, warning, *That was your last ride.*

2. Write more than one sonnet. Because we have so many preconceived ideas about sonnets, it's easy to give up after the first draft of our first one. Like Kris Bigalk, write two or more sonnets on a related theme. Or like Devan Cook, who often composes in unrhymed sonnet forms, see what happens to your "voice" when you write several sonnets on diverse topics. What is constant? You or the form? Neither or both? You'll also find two related sonnets by Devan Cook in her revision case study in the appendix. Ask yourself about these sonnets (and your own, once they're composed) whether one sonnet is stronger than or superior to the other (and if so, why?).

Minnesota April*
Kris Bigalk

The mud is cracking, oozing through the crust
of snow which coats the ground; the rain
beats holes through the ice, and footprints rusty
brown crunch across the peppered white terrain,
promising the last frost is coming. The trees hold
their budding leaves in tight; even child fingers
can't pry them open yet. Crocus leaves, the finest gold
begin to pop up in footprints, and the smell of mud mingles
with the heavy scent of coming rain, cold and clean.
Children break open the mudpuddles, feet breaking the ice glass
with a whipcrack, throwing the shards on the pavement, sheen
exploding into pieces of water, and the last
Christmas lights are gathered from the outdoor trees
and put away. The snow turns from bright to dull, piece by piece.

*Minnesota in October**
    Kris Bigalk

The sunset ripens like golden plums blush,
turning cheeks to the horizon until the juice
runs out, scattering purple in the trees and underbrush,
navy blue night rising in the east, meeting west like a bruise.
Fields' fall perfumes rise musky, cornstalks
rattling dry in the wind. This weather apples cheeks,
makes grapes taste frosty. Cider ripens hard in crocks,
leaves scuttle around heavy leather shoes; Shriek-owls
nestle in barn eaves, waiting for dark. Snow
comes soon, the taste is in the air cold as mint
on a warm tongue. Smoke plumes echo in the sky, indigo
mist over the stars, perfuming the air with tints
of oak and maple, poplar and elm; a night for lone
contemplation; red moon rising, blood on bone.

Lunch Counter
    Devan Cook

Steam pillows billow from the coffee pot;
the grill splatters greasy volcanoes. Heat
in chrome and red leatherette. Cheeseburger,
ketchup only, lettuce and tomato.
My tea arrives unassembled: squat pot,
styrofoam cup, tea bag. Two sugar lumps
to unwrap—a sweet sound. My lipstick leaves
ridged prints on the cup, as if my mouth were
fading to hollows. I hurry to meet
you, glance down to check my blouse for stains, wet
the napkin and polish a spot on my
shoe. Watching you cross the street glancing at
your watch, I grab a minute at the mirror
by the door to lick off ketchup, slick on
lipstick, push out on a happy red wave.

Seeking a Vegetable Body
    Devan Cook

This poem is for Jim S_____, who carved bok choy
into fantastic shapes, got stoned with his wife,
started to eat a popsicle, made love on the kitchen floor,
and awoke at four, vegetables pressed against his spine—

turnip fleurs-de-lis, carrot doubloons bearing the face
of Charles V, parsnip dragons waving slivers of bean
hair. Eggplant blooms opened to roses or revelation
of his skill as the source of a garden, an Eden.

He said the experience was like enlightenment—
sticky and sweet as the fudgesicle melting beneath them,
yet floating beside the kitchen cabinets, an ethereal egg
he could almost penetrate—his last vision before a sleep
like Adam's. I'm envious: bought a cleaver to slice
a vegetable creation, and grind it sharp on my frustration.

3. Sometimes the best warm-up for getting in the sonnet mood and
   way of thinking is to draft several of what I've come to call a 10 ×
   14 poem on a subject that means something to you, each line being
   ten syllables in length and the full poem having exactly fourteen
   lines. Here's a sample of how that can be done: Freewrite about possible topics, freewrite on the chosen topic, cut the freewrite by ear to
   the 10 × 14 shape, and then cut it more ruthlessly by counting syllables and retaining meaning. Finally, draft and redraft, aligning
   meaning and shape. Here's a sample from my notebook.

   a. Freewrite (in class)

   Choices (things I know I could describe):

   Making Pasta
   How to Clean the Pool
   How to Write a Sonnet

   The snake like plastic pool cleaner lifts into intestinal segments, sucks the
   breath from a cold morning. Leaves make a Braille on the water's surface. Plastic lines reflecting fake tiles. It's all a matter of optics. The way
   my hand enlarging and turns paler underwater as if a dryad is reaching
   up to grasp me back. We meet over a leaf, tannin-colored water, a centipede casing, spiders finding falls safety on a floating thermometer. I pull
   handfuls of leaves and better not mentioned insects from the trap. Drop
   in chlorine pellets the size of toxic hockey pucks. Remember my son the
   first day screaming his cannonball into the deep end and down to push
   off, swim the first length. The cleaning takes on ritual dimensions, the
   dog runs her static around the edges, smelling the full rotting smell of
   oak leaves in the blue mesh net. The gurgle of pool pumps soaks into
   my daughter's dreams. We groom this acre of water as if it were a
   hearth, a reminder of the way water is the solution—to my mother's
   death, the children in summer's heat.

b. First Notebook Draft (in class)—lined by ear

Pool Cleaning	syllables per line
1. It's all a matter of optics. Leaves make	10
2. a Braille on the water's surface. My hand	10
3. enlarges, turns pale reach down	7
4. for a leaf, oak leaves stain with tannin	9
5. spider seeks safety on a thermometer casing	13
6. that bobs and twirls. I pull out	7
7. handfuls of leaves, centipede casings	9
8. and drop in toxic chlorine tablets the size	11
9. of hockey pucks. Remember my son the first	11
10. day, cannonball into the deep end and swim	11
11. the first time toward me. The gurgle	9
12. of the pump soaks into my daughter's dreams.	10
13. We groom this acre of water, liquid	10
14. hearth for the long summer's heat.	9

c. Typing a Shaped Draft (about five drafts went into this draft)

Pool Cleaning

Oak leaves float in Braille on water's surface.
It's a matter of optics. My hand enlarges
turns pale, swims after leaf edges that stain
the cold waters brown with their tannin. Spider
finds safety on the plastic thermometer
that bobs and twirls. Dizzying. I empty traps—
more leaves, centipede casings—and I drop
in three horse-sized, toxic chlorine tablets,
rub rough fingers dry on jeans. The throbbing
pool pump outside her bedroom window floods
my daughter's dreams. I groom water with caution,
with regard for summer's heat while I recall
how my son—that first day—cannon-balled in,
swam for the first time, and safely, toward me.

d. A Revision after Writing Group responses (three more drafts went into this one)

Pool Cleaning in April*
    Wendy Bishop

Oak leaves float in Braille on water's surface.
It's a matter of optics. My hand enlarges
turns pale, swims after leaf edges that stain
the waters brown with their tannin. A spider
finds safety on the plastic thermometer
that bobs and twirls. Dizzying. The throbbing pool
pump outside her bedroom window floods my
daughter's dreams. I empty the traps—more leaves
centipede casings—drop in three horse-sized,
toxic chlorine tablets, rub rough fingers
dry on jeans. I groom water with caution,
with regard for summer's heat while I recall
how my son—that first day—cannon-balled in,
swam for the first time, and safely, toward me.

REDEFINING THE SONNET SPACE

What I wanted from the sonnet was the tradition that it offered as well
as the structure. The sonnet tradition was one in which women were
caged in golden cages of a beloved, in perfumed gas chambers of stereo-
type. I wanted to go in that heavily mined and male labyrinth with the
string of my own voice. I wanted to explore it and explode it too. I call
my sonnets free verse sonnets. They have ten syllables per line, and the
lines are in a loose iambic pentameter. But they are heavily enjambed
and the rhymes are often slant-rhymes, and the rhyme scheme is pecu-
liar to each sonnet. One friend read them and said "I didn't know they
were sonnets. They sounded like you talking!'" —Julia Alvarez (Finch
16–17)

The contemporary sonnet writer, as Julia Alvarez points out about her own
work, often breaks with tradition and toys with our expectations, as is especially true in the sonnets that follow. I'm not sure I would have noticed at first that
Robert Pinsky's poem was a sonnet had he not so titled it since he's substituted
tercets for quatrains by redividing the twelve lines that precede the final couplet.
Elizabeth Alexander's "House Party Sonnet: '66" includes the refrain "where did
our love go." Simic's sonnet title contradicts the content (this is romance?), and
he, like Pinsky, innovates in his stanzas, choosing two quatrains followed by two
tercets. Peter Meinke's sonnet makes a traditional turn in line 9, but his line
lengths are short, his humor dark, and his language and subject very contemporary—all the way down to the lack of punctuation. Finally, John Ashbery's

sonnet—if we agree it is one—can be identified only by its fourteen-line length and its midpoem break. However, the sestet in this sonnet precedes the octave, and he doesn't use predictable line length or rhyme patterns. This collection of sonnet-like poems may lead you into a fruitful discussion concerning the degree to which a form can be altered and still retain its force and identity.

Sonnet
ROBERT PINSKY

Afternoon sun on her back,
calm irregular slap
of water against a dock.

Thin pines clamber
over the hill's top—
nothing to remember,

only the same lake
that keeps making the same
sounds under her cheek

and flashing the same color.
No one to say her name,
no need, no one to praise her,

only the lake's voice—over
and over, to keep it before her.

House Party Sonnet: '66
ELIZABETH ALEXANDER

Small, still. Fit through the bannister slit.
Where did our love go? Where did our love go?
Scattered high heels and the carpet rolled back.
Where did our love go? Where did our love go?
My brother and I, tipping down from upstairs
Under the cover of "Where Did Our Love Go?"
Cat-eyed Supremes wearing siren-green gowns.
Pink curls of laughter and hips when they shake
Shake a tambourine *where did our love go?*
Where did our love go? Where did our love go?
Stale chips next morning, shoes under the couch,
Smoke-smelling draperies, water-paled Scotch.
Matches, stray earrings to find and to keep—
Hum of invisible dancers asleep.

Romantic Sonnet
CHARLES SIMIC

Evenings of sovereign clarity—
Wine and bread on the table,
Mother praying,
Father naked in bed.

Was I that skinny boy stretched out
In the field behind the house,
His heart cut out with a toy knife?
Was I the crow hovering over him?

Happiness, you are the bright red lining
Of the dark winter coat
Grief wears inside out.

This is about myself when I'm remembering,
And your long insomniac's nails,
O Time, I keep chewing and chewing.

The Heart's Location ❖
PETER MEINKE

all my plans for suicide are ridiculous
I can never remember the heart's location
too cheap to smash the car
too queasy to slash a wrist
once jumped off a bridge
almost scared myself to death
then spent two foggy weeks
waiting for new glasses

of course I really want to live
continuing my lifelong search
for the world's greatest unknown cheap restaurant
and a poem full of ordinary words
about simple things
in the inconsolable rhythms of the heart

At North Farm
JOHN ASHBERY

Somewhere someone is traveling furiously toward you,
At incredible speed, traveling day and night,
Through blizzards and desert heat, across torrents, through narrow passes.
But will he know where to find you,
Recognize you when he sees you,
Give you the thing he has for you?

Hardly anything grows here,
Yet the granaries are bursting with meal,
The sacks of meal piled to the rafters.
The streams run with sweetness, fattening fish;
Birds darken the sky. Is it enough
That the dish of milk is set out at night,
That we think of him sometimes,
Sometimes and always, with mixed feelings?

━ INVENTION EXERCISES ━

1. For those who are mathematically or schematically inclined, sketch out the possible stanza variations you can think of for this four-teen-line form. For instance, you can write a sonnet in seven couplets with space between each couplet. Try recasting one of your sonnet drafts into a different stanza form and also try drafting a sonnet into the most unusual—to you—of these possible patterns.

2. Think of other borrowings you could import into the sonnet form. Elizabeth Alexander imports a refrain. Joy Oliff below turns the sonnet into a lullaby. You might write a sonnet with head rhyme or you might write a sonnet in the form of a letter. In a group, make a list of technique and genre changes you might bring to the form and try one or two.

*Lullaby**

    Joy Oliff

Let me rock you in my arms,
tiny baby, soft and mine,
sing you songs of far off farms,
cows and chickens in unfenced time.
Of far off places not so far,
and some still closer still,
'Twinkle, twinkle little star,
hush little baby, no more tears.'
Swinging slowly, lulling creak
of wood on wood we rock
dark solid oak and antique teak
gold chiming of the clock.
All these and more forever keep
in unseen places, heart's hold deep.

This chapter ends with advice from other novice sonnet writers that may help you as you compose and then revise your sonnets. Like any advice, take and use these suggestions only if they seem appropriate to your needs.

ADVICE FOR WRITING SONNETS (AND SONNET-LIKE) POEMS

- Read different authors' styles from Shakespeare to Kooser to develop a style of your own.
- Become familiar with different rhyme schemes (envelope, English, Italian, etc.).
- Worry more about the content than the form; worry about images, not rhymes.
- Write down ideas for a poem before trying to rhyme.
- Try to carry an image all the way through (the technical term is *poetic conceit* such as two lovers as twin points of a compass, a medical doctor like a queen bee visiting chambers of a hive, etc.)
- Keep the rhyming subtle: use half rhymes if you can (*moon/June* becomes *moon/alone*).
- Don't be afraid to use a metaphor with a double meaning, like *sun/son*.
- Steal another poet's line and work from there.
- Steal another poet's end rhymes and make your own list of possible half rhyme substitutions before you draft.

- Start with little formal structure. Free-write a paragraph and turn it into a ten-syllable by fourteen-line poem.
- Choose a set form or create your own, but follow a pre-ordained challenge, at least for the initial drafts.
- Modernize a sonnet. Use a famous poet's content/message and update to a half-rhyme or 10 × 14 syllabic poem.
- Make a list of terms/rhymes within your topic and have them ready to draw on as you draft. For example, a beach poem uses beach words/concepts/ rhymes (*sand/land/crab/drab* or *sand/beyond* and *crab/fan*, etc.).
- Use lots of colors.
- Adopt a modern tone to offset one hundred years of typical sonnets, avoiding archaic or conceptual diction such as "my princess lost" or "I'll love you through eternity."
- Use strong images.
- End with a strong statement.
- Play with restrictions instead of letting them frustrate you.

ADVICE FOR REVISING SONNETS (AND SONNET-LIKE) POEMS

- Try the same subject in a different rhyme scheme or as unrhymed 10 × 14 syllabic verse.
- Once you've nurtured your content, play with substitutions that take you back toward a form—i.e., revise toward a specific form.
- Cut out unneeded words.
- Expand the line so the syntax is comfortable/normal and then cut back.
- Try to substitute unique, specific, accurate, necessary words for clichés.
- Have several friends read the poem aloud and then tell you what they think it's about. Does your vision match their understanding?
- Try flip-flopping sentences and let the formal rhyme structure become an internal structure.
- Let sentences overflow lines (enjamb) in different ways.
- Look for and eliminate unnecessary prose/connective words: "as soon as," "an," "the," etc.
- Break up descriptive chains ("the red, rough, fall, leaves") to avoid bunched-up accents.
- Avoid an "airy" feel—ground the poem in real life.
- Read aloud for rhythm. Work for regularity and then interesting syllable variations to break overly predictable regularity.
- Identify *poetic* and *sonnet* sounding words and substitute contemporary, everyday language: "You create a longing in my heart" becomes "I miss you," etc.
- Work from a freewrite and then revise to fit a form.
- Expect to revise a lot and don't worry about rhyme in a revision.

POCKET DEFINITIONS

Couplets—Two-line stanzas (or a complete poem in one two-line couplet). These lines are often of the same length. Historically, couplets were metered in a similar manner, often achieving closure through full rhyme or parallel syntax.

Iambic Pentameter—The most common line pattern in English verse. Five (pentameter) iambic (dă-DÁ) feet = one line of iambic pentameter = dă-DÁ dă-DÁ dă-DÁ dă-DÁ dă-DÁ

Quatrain—A stanza consisting of four lines of verse, rhymed or unrhymed. The **envelope quatrain** rhyme runs *abba;* the **couplet quatrain** runs *aabb;* the **alternating quatrain** runs *abab;* and the **monorhyme quatrain** runs *aaaa.*

Sonnet—A historical fixed form. The English sonnet consists of fourteen lines of iambic pentameter verse: three quatrains and a closing couplet, with the rhyme scheme of *abab, cdcd, efef, gg.* The Italian sonnet consists of an octave rhyming *abbaabba* and a sestet rhyming *cdcdcd.* Poets have always adapted this structure, observing most consistently only its fourteen-line length.

Tercet—Three-line stanzas. When all three lines rhyme, tercets become *triplets.* When the rhyme patterns interlock like this—*aba, bcb, cdc*—linking stanzas, the tercet turns into *terza rima.*

13

TERCETS, TERZA RIMA, TRIPLETS, AND VILLANELLES

Thinking in Threes

Rain
RAYMOND CARVER

Woke up this morning with
a terrific urge to lie in bed all day
and read. Fought against it for a minute.

Then looked out the window at the rain.
And gave over. Put myself entirely
in the keep of this rainy morning.

Would I live my life over again?
Make the same unforgivable mistakes?
Yes, given half a chance. Yes.

Separation
W. S. MERWIN

Your absence has gone through me
Like thread through a needle
Everything I do is stitched with its color.

While some of us prefer the thin ladder of couplets and others the four square blocks of quatrains, the braided **tercet** has been the form of choice for poets as varied as Dante, Wallace Stevens, and William Carlos Williams. Tercets have a pleasing balance when unrhymed and feel perfectly off-balanced when two of the three lines rhyme. When all three lines rhyme, tercets are called *triplets*. When the rhyme patterns link up—*aba, bcb, cdc*—weaving a bracelet of sound across the stanzas, we're reading *terza rima*. In this chapter we'll look at tercets, rhymed and unrhymed, and end with **villanelles**, a very particular form of three-lined stanza where lines repeat and the whole poem ends with a quatrain.

While tercets form effective waterfalls of narration over many stanzas, they can also run shorter and produce a more compact, image-filled instant as in Raymond Carver's three stanzas of three lines each, titled "Rain." In his poem, each observation ends for a moment at a stanza break and then continues on, amplified slightly in the next stanza; and we finish with a clear, single-word affirmation that signals closure by its firm typographical placement as well as by its meaning. An even more compact poem, a three-lined poem by W. S. Merwin, extends the haiku's brevity into the lyric's intensity.

Sylvia Plath uses tercets to tell a story, in this case to sing a birth song. Notice how her line lengths alternate as do her sentence lengths, creating intricate patterns of short end-stopped sentences and those that run on across line and stanza boundaries.

Morning Song
SYLVIA PLATH

Love set you going like a fat gold watch.
The midwife slapped your footsoles, and your bald cry
Took its place among the elements.

Our voices echo, magnifying your arrival. New statue.
In a drafty museum, your nakedness
Shadows our safety. We stand round blankly as walls.

I'm no more your mother
Than the cloud that distills a mirror to reflect its own slow
Effacement at the wind's hand.

All night your moth-breath
Flickers among the flat pink roses. I wake to listen:
A far sea moves in my ear.

One cry, and I stumble from bed, cow-heavy and floral
In my Victorian nightgown.
Your mouth opens clean as a cat's. The window square

Whitens and swallows its dull stars. And now you try
Your handful of notes;
The clear vowels rise like balloons.

Louise Erdrich uses three-line stanzas of highly variable lengths, and her poem also tells a story. I've found the tercet form to be quite useful for narration because it moves connectedly but fairly rapidly down the page. Erdrich breaks most of her lines at the ends of grammatical phrases and closes her poem with a quatrain, which is a common technique to signal the finish of a three-line run.

Bidwell Ghost
LOUISE ERDRICH

Each night she waits by the road
in a thin white dress
embroidered with fire.

It has been twenty years
since her house surged and burst in the dark trees.
Still nobody goes there.

The heat charred the branches
of the apple trees,
but nothing can kill that wood.

She will climb into your car
but not say where she is going
and you shouldn't ask.

Nor should you try to comb the blackened nest of hair
or press the agates of tears
back into her eyes.

First the orchard bowed low and complained
of the unpicked fruit,
then the branches cracked apart and fell.

The windfalls sweetened to wine
beneath the ruined arms and snow.
Each spring now, in the grass, buds form on the tattered wood.

The child, the child, why is she so persistent
in her need? Is it so terrible
to be alone when the cold white blossoms
come to life and burn?

Mary Swander's stanzas in "Frog Gig" are both more dense and more regular than those of the previous two poets, leading me to double-check and make sure this isn't terza rima. (It isn't: the stanzas are unrhymed.) While Louise Erdrich did not enjamb across stanza boundaries, Mary Swander does, running stanzas 3, 4, and 5 together as well as stanzas 6, 7, and 8, which no doubt adds to the forward motion and intensity of this frog tale.

Frog Gig
MARY SWANDER

It took a whole plateful to make a meal—
food #7 I could eat without blacking out—
those little white pairs of pantaloons.

Oh, I'd pithed Kermits—needle from the tray,
lab partner, scholarshipped wrestler, locking
thumb and index finger around the squirmer's neck.

No, it was the pileup of those limbs, steamed and soggy
like wet laundry, that made me pick the tendons
from my teeth with special care, and know

those doctors lied who said it'd taste like chicken.
These were no white feathers beside a red wheelbarrow
glazed with rain, no Sunday dinners, the whole family

gathered in the kitchen, home from ten o'clock Mass,
still singing hymns, pressure cooker on the stove
so my grandmother could gum her portion.

Once, due to expense, I went out with friends
to Corker's Pond, the water quiet, clear.
Tiny piece of bandanna dangling from the end

of a fishing line, we groped through the dark,
sun going down, and followed their croaks and plops,
our hooks tangling in the cattails. We lay on the bank

for hours and held our rods just above their heads,
but not one hopped at the cloth, not one crooned
so much depends upon, nor shot out its forked tongue.

⚊ INVENTION EXERCISES ⚊

1. Think of things in threes. For instance, three's a crowd, triangles, triplets (of the human kind), three brothers, three-legged races, pyramids, three-cornered hats, a triple branched candle holder, etc. Choose some of these threes and freewrite. Take the most promising and write a 3×3, a three-stanza tercet poem on your version of threes.

2. Tell a hometown story in the manner of Louise Erdrich. Every town has a haunted house or other infamous spot. Take liberties with the story and be sure to ground the supernatural at all times with realistic images. For Erdrich, the burned girl's dress is "thin white" and "embroidered with fire," and she has a "blackened nest of hair."

3. Like Raymond Carver, use the form to consider a question, and answer it for yourself. You might set up the question in stanza 1, explore it in the following stanzas, and answer it in the final stanza. The question can be as prosaic as "Should I get up this morning?" or as cosmic as "If given a chance would I live this same life over again?" and the answer can be yes, no, maybe, or anything else you choose.

4. Look back at William Carlos Williams' poem "The Red Wheelbarrow" in chapter 3 and then reread Mary Swander's "Frog Gig." How is she using her reference to that poem? Pick any poem—the one you recognize as being the most well-known or the most often anthologized might be best—and weave some quotation from it into your tercet poem.

5. Or like Mary Swander tell an "experience" story without worrying this time about the literary reference. Jason Burns wrote tercets about putting up Christmas lights on a foggy night in un-Christmassy warm Florida. Like most family stories, this has a touch of the absurd, which Jason captures in his mother's uselessly cautionary voice.

*Christmas in Florida**
    Jason Burns

One of the blues twinkles
for a moment, then flashes out,
taking some reds and yellows with it.

Blinded by darkness, I check
my creative footing on my
father's makeshift ladder.

The current vibrates my arm,
making the hairs dance
in the damp night air.

I loosen my sweaty grip,
allowing the string to dangle slightly
out into the soup that surrounds me.

I recognize a faint pulse,
but is it mine? Or electricity itself,
buzzing through my body?

Remembering Dad's lectures of
"Eckerd-brand quality" and the "American
dream," I jiggle the bad connection:

a flicker, then a pop.
Silence.   Darkness.   The steaming
mist envelopes me.

Mom nagging about how
she told me that would happen,
and now just look what I've done.

In the next selection of tercets, the poets push the form this way or that. In "Writing Poems," Mary Oliver centers her tercets on the page in a way that calls attention to the physical shape of her poem and then unravels the form as the poem closes. In "The Buckeye" Rita Dove varies line length a great deal to the point of focusing our attention on a single-word line midway down the poem. She also ends with a single line. Larry Levis' poem about writing poetry closes with an unexpectedly abrupt two-line final stanza. And Maggie Anderson's loose-lined stanzas are interrupted unexpectedly between stanzas 2 and 3 of a six-tercet poem by a single line, "They say these things," which pauses the poem and then pushes the reader on.

Writing Poems ❖
MARY OLIVER

This morning I watched
the pale green cones of the rhododendrons
opening their small pink and red blouses—

the bodies of the flowers
were instantly beautiful to the bees, they hurried
out of that dark place in the thick tree

one after another, an invisible line
upon which their iridescence caught fire
as the sun caught them, sliding down.
•
Is there anything more important
than hunger and happiness? Each bee entered
the frills of a flower to find

the sticky fountain, and if some dust
spilled on the walkways of the petals
and caught onto their bodies, I don't know

if the bees know that otherwise death
is everywhere, even in the red swamp
of a flower. But they did this

with no small amount of desperation—you might say: love.
•
And the flowers, as daft as mud, poured out their honey.

The Buckeye
RITA DOVE

We learned about the state tree
in school—its fruit
so useless, so ugly

no one bothered to
commend the smudged trunk
nor the slim leaves shifting

over our heads. Yet
they were a good thing to kick
along gutters

on the way home,
though they stank like
a drunk's piss in the roads

where cars had smashed
them. And in autumn
when the spiny helmets split

open,
there was the bald
seed with its wheat-

colored eye.
We loved
the modest countenance beneath

that leathery cap.
We, too, did not want to leave
our mothers.

We piled them up
for ammunition.
We lay down

with them
among the bruised leaves
so that we could

rise, shining.

The Poem You Asked For ❖
LARRY LEVIS

My poem would eat nothing.
I tried giving it water
but it said no,

worrying me.
Day after day,
I held it up to the light,

turning it over,
but it only pressed its lips
more tightly together.

It grew sullen, like a toad
through with being teased.
I offered it all my money,

my clothes, my car with a full tank.
But the poem stared at the floor.
Finally I cupped it in

my hands, and carried it gently
out into the soft air, into the
evening traffic, wondering how

to end things between us.
For now it had begun breathing,
putting on more and

more hard rings of flesh.
And the poem demanded the food,
it drank up all the water,

beat me and took my money,
tore the faded clothes
off my back,

said Shit,
and walked slowly away,
slicking its hair down,

Said it was going
over to your place.

Country Wisdoms
MAGGIE ANDERSON

Rescue the drowning and tie your shoe-strings.
—Thoreau, *Walden*

Out here where the crows turn around
where the ground muds over and the snow fences bend
we've been bearing up. Although

a green winter means a green graveyard
and we've buried someone every month since autumn
warm weather pulls us into summer by the thumbnails.

They say these things.

When the April rains hurl ice chunks onto the banks
the river later rises to retrieve them.
They tell how the fierce wind from the South

blows branches down, power lines and houses
but always brings the trees to bud.
Fog in January, frost in May

threads of cloud, they say, rain needles.
My mother would urge, be careful what you want,
you will surely get it.

More ways than one to skin that cat.
Then they say, Bootstraps.
Pull yourself up.

⬤ INVENTION EXERCISES ⬤

1. Mary Oliver's poems show you how to incorporate space and air
   into the tercet form. Try centering lines or try letting each line float
   farther to the right, with the indentations creating a sense of ebbing
   and flowing. Of course in your poem, you could reverse the movement, starting with the first line indented twice, the second line
   indented once, and the third line aligned to the left-hand margin. Or
   you could play with half rhymes and indentation together:

   _____*a*

   _____*b*

   _____*a*

   etc.

As you play with indentation, you might ask what would happen to other tercet poems presented here if they were indented. (Try refiguring several of these poems in that way.) What makes indentation seem useful or necessary? And what provides closure to a three-line stanza poem—the content, the loosening of stanzas at the end, or both?

2. Take a free verse poem and experiment with recasting it into tercets. You might intentionally try to capture some of the feel of Rita Dove's "The Buckeye" where the line breaks sometimes work against the sentence and phrase boundaries: "its fruit/so useless, so ugly//no one bothered to/commend" is not broken into lines quite where one would expect it to be. You might want to play with word or syllable breaks: one word, two words, three words per line in each stanza (or two, four, six syllables) and so on. However you accomplish this, experiment with a mixture of very short and somewhat longer lines.

3. Like Larry Levis, write a tercet poem about poetry, and you might try personifying your poem as he does, making your poem have animal or human qualities. You could give it a setting appropriate to that persona, let it loose, and see what it says or does.

4. In honor of Maggie Anderson's "Country Wisdoms," write your own "Wisdoms" or "Sayings" or "They Say" poem. In Florida, for instance, they say: "It's not the heat, it's the humidity." You might want to collect regional sayings by sharing them in a group or even by doing some library research or by calling family members. Cast this, of course, in tercets.

5. End your poem with one, three, or four lines to place closure on a run of tercets. Rhain Capley does that in this poem. Like Rhain, you might want to talk about a semi-taboo subject—in this case, being stoned while swimming in the Gulf of Mexico—a subject we don't usually expect in a poem but certainly a very human occurrence. You might list things that you think are taboo as poetic subjects and then push to talk about one, either literally or metaphorically, or both. Like Maggie Anderson, you might want to play with interrupting lines—regularly or irregularly. You could alternate three-line stanzas with one-, two-, or four-line stanzas, and so on.

There Is No Such Thing as an Everlasting Moment *
  Rhain Capley

Remember the time we were stoned in the Gulf
Past midnight, the water cold and black
Black as the heaven above, its silvery stars scattered like lost paint

The moment felt real and unreal, my head as light as the night air
We swam far into the black, the fluorescent green of phosphorus
clung to our sea-salted flesh as we emerged to the surface

That night we were gods, our bodies magnificently bright as the stars
So far out, we just floated over the in-coming waves
You were Poseidon, and I one of your mermen

And when I started to come down, a moment of panic struck
Because I could not maintain the facade of the universe which I had created
I could not keep us gods, soon we would be mortals on land

I clenched my eyes shut, and sank beneath the rolling waves
Attempting to stay stoned just a little longer
And for a brief moment I pondered not returning

Becoming one with the ocean and sky
And then I felt your slick, wet hand upon my shoulder
A moment later we were back on land

Our bodies heavy with gravity and mortality.

TOWARD TERZA RIMA AND TRIPLETS

The most famous terza rima poem is Dante's *Divine Comedy* (*La Divina Commedia*), and he is considered the originator of the form, which Chaucer took from Italian to English, and it continued in wide use, particularly in the hands of nineteenth century Romantic poets. The terza rima rhyme pattern runs:

a

b

a

b

c

b

c

d

c

etc.

and the triplet pattern runs:

a

a

a

b

b

b

c

c

c

etc.

Contemporary terza rima is rare, but it does appear with variations. Glover Davis' poem, "The Fish Tank," only approaches and hints at the full terza rima interlock but does so in full rhyme. Try marking the rhymes and see what you come up with. Plath's poem is classic terza rima but in half rhyme (and as a sample of unexpectedly dexterous half rhyme, it's worth paying great attention to). My own terza rima rhymes fall somewhere between full and half—I believe my original drafting intention was to aim for full rhyme, but I sometimes couldn't make sense within such constraints and so reverted to half rhyme. That change probably improved the poem. Davis' and Plath's poems end with a full tercet while mine ends with a single line—my attempt to increase the sense of closure and underline the sense of the line: "the sound of the statue hitting the floor."

The Fish Tank
GLOVER DAVIS

I sit watching TV and a parade
of pills, bottles, soaps and blades punishes
but gives me dreams. Sometimes the dreams invade

my waking hours and I live on the edge of things
where the curtains puff with meaning, the chairs
hold themselves with dignity and the wings

of the ebony table are resilient
with a power which they won't use. The things
I see are tense, disciplined and sapient.

I scoop up pebbles from the goldfish tank.
I touch them for their hardness. One is clouded
and glazed like a dead eyeball that's gone blank

with nothing to see. I see the fish caught there
in the water, their veins shot with stone, the
barbed mouths turned up pulsing at the air.

Medallion
SYLVIA PLATH

By the gate with star and moon
Worked into the peeled orange wood
The bronze snake lay in the sun

Inert as a shoelace; dead
But pliable still, his jaw
Unhinged and his grin crooked,

Tongue a rose-colored arrow.
Over my hand I hung him.
His little vermilion eye

Ignited with a glassed flame
As I turned him in the light;
When I split a rock one time

The garnet bits burned like that.
Dust dulled his back to ochre
The way sun ruins a trout.

Yet his belly kept its fire
Going under the chainmail,
The old jewels smoldering there

In each opaque belly-scale:
Sunset looked at through milk glass.
And I saw white maggots coil

Thin as pins in the dark bruise
Where his innards bulged as if
He were digesting a mouse.

Knifelike, he was chaste enough,
Pure death's-metal. The yardman's
Flung brick perfected his laugh.

The Housekeeper
WENDY BISHOP

While mopping she muses over work undone,
Her daily chores. The blue floor tiles
Reflect where she cleans and her thoughts run

As her hands move smoothly in a mild
Arranging of someone else's life,
The papers and books and clothes in piles.

She removes the signs of domestic strife
By diligently sorting. The long afternoon
Advances like an iron across the clean striped

Shirts that she steams and presses. Soon
She will put away bucket and rags to stand
For awhile by louvered windows in a room

The slow hours fill almost visibly. Scanning
the furniture she considers how, when empty
Of clutter, the house feels abandoned.

Lifting an object, she doesn't see
What she idly fingers: a small bronze man
Blowing on a shell. Sunlight falls in waves so free

She drowns in a clear wash of it, fanned
By breezes and randomly blessed by light before
Weariness slips from her curled hands

With the sound of the statue hitting the floor.

As soon as you read "Pink Dog" by Elizabeth Bishop, you'll be able to see why few poets write in triplets. Certainly it's a challenge—and one Bishop meets beautifully—and can lead to fairly intense humorous verse, but it's also easy to imagine this form turning silly. Still, any challenge is worth undertaking as Rachel Hadas proves in her poem "Three Silences." Look at the way Hadas plays the numbers—three sections, two of three stanzas and the third of six stanzas. She also works with some slant rhyme and enjambment to vary the triplet regularity, yet her choice of threes seems quite appropriate to the speaker's subject—her small son.

Pink Dog
ELIZABETH BISHOP

The sun is blazing and the sky is blue.
Umbrellas clothe the beach in every hue.
Naked, you trot across the avenue.

Oh, never have I seen a dog so bare!
Naked and pink, without a single hair . . .
Startled, the passersby draw back and stare.

Of course they're mortally afraid of rabies.
You are not mad; you have a case of scabies
but look intelligent. Where are your babies?

(A nursing mother, by those hanging teats.)
In what slum have you hidden them, poor bitch,
while you go begging, living by your wits?

Didn't you know? It's been in all the papers,
to solve this problem, how they deal with beggars?
They take and throw them in the tidal rivers.

Yes, idiots, paralytics, parasites
go bobbing in the ebbing sewage, night
out in the suburbs, where there are no lights.

If they do this to anyone who begs,
drugged, drunk, or sober, with or without legs,
what would they do to sick, four-legged dogs?

In the cafés and on the sidewalk corners
the joke is going round that all the beggars
who can afford them now wear life preservers.

In your condition you would not be able
even to float, much less to dog-paddle.
Now look, the practical, the sensible

solution is to wear a *fantasia*.*
Tonight you simply can't afford to be a-
n eyesore. But no one will ever see a

dog in *mascara* this time of year.
Ash Wednesday'll come but Carnival is here.
What sambas can you dance? What will you wear?

They say that Carnival's degenerating
—radios, Americans, or something,
have ruined it completely. They're just talking.

Carnival is always wonderful!
A depilated dog would not look well.
Dress up! Dress up and dance at Carnival!

Three Silences
RACHEL HADAS

I

Of all the times when not to speak is best,
mother's and infant's is the easiest,
the milky mouth still warm against her breast.

Before a single year has passed, he's well
along the way: language has cast its spell.
Each thing he sees now has a tale to tell.

A wide expanse of water: ocean. Look!
Next time, it seems that water is a brook.
The world's loose leaves, bound up into a book.

II

The habit holds for love. He wants to seize
lungsful of ardent new sublimities.
Years gradually pry him loose from these.

---

*carnival costume.

He comes to prize a glance's eloquence,
learning to construct a whole romance
from hint and gesture, meaning carved from chance.

And finally silence. Nothing in a phrase
so speaks of love as an averted gaze,
sonnets succumbing to remembrances.

III

At the Kiwanis traveling carnival
I ride beside you on the carousel.
You hold on solemnly, a little pale.

I don't stretch out my hand. You ride alone.
Each mother's glance reduplicates my own;
the baffled arc, the vulnerable bone.

Myself revolving in the mirror's eye
as we go round beneath a cloudy sky,
eyeing my little boy attentively,

I swallow what I was about to say
(no loving admonition is the way
to bridge this gap) and hear the music play

and later, wordless, reach and lift you down
over the rigid horse's shiny brown
mane, and press your body close against my own.

Stillness after motion,
the creaky music cranking, cranking down,
the carnival preparing to leave town.

If you choose to investigate the triplet form, a rhyming dictionary may be a useful tool to help you find a rhyme word with plenty of variations and lots of full and half-rhyme possibilities. Versions of rhyming dictionaries can be found quickly on the Internet, although I enjoy keeping a book of rhymes next to my computer.

➤ INVENTION EXERCISES ➤

1. Glover Davis' poem invites you to observe the ordinary. Look for your own equivalents to a fish tank. It may be the TV set, the window of your room, the terrarium you keep, and so on. Write a

first-person poem where you observe this object/scene in great detail, and through your observations tell us something about who you are (without stating it directly).

2. There is a body of snake poems that I can call to mind: one by Emily Dickinson, one by D. H. Lawrence. Write your own snake (or reptile) poem or simply observe a creature in nature with your poet's eye. You might consider the squirrel, the jay, the egret, the trout, the bear, the armadillo, the backyard cat. Try in this tercet poem to use half or full terza rima rhyme patterning. To do this, write your first stanza to obtain your *aba* pattern, and then for each succeeding stanza pattern, remind yourself of upcoming rhymes by sketching out some possible rhyme variants in the margin or your journal or on your computer.

3. There is a pleasing regularity to the interlock of the terza rima poem. You might try observing a worker at his or her ordinary work as I did. Consider the bedrock repetition of that worker's day. What motions are repeated and with what effects? Write a terza rima poem where you let us see into that worker's life (without being judgmental).

4. Go back to the invention exercise on threes above and try one of the suggestions, but this time, humorously rhyme the poem in triplet form. Compose you poem in three parts, like Rachel Hadas. Take chances with line breaks like Elizabeth Bishop; she hyphenates the single-syllable word *an* in stanza 10 of "Pink Dog" as a-/n in order to make her triplet.

VILLANELLES

Like the sestina and the sonnet, the villanelle is a poet's Mount Everest: to be attempted because it is there. The villanelle was a more fluid stanza form when it achieved prominence in seventeenth century France, and nineteenth century English poets froze it into a fixed form when they took it up. The villanelle's nineteen lines can be of any syllable length. The poem is divided into six stanzas: five tercets and one quatrain, turning on two rhymes, and built on two **refrains**. This is easier seen than said:

A^1—refrain
b
A^2—refrain

a
b
A^1—refrain

a

b

A^2—refrain

a

b

A^1—refrain

a

b

A^2—refrain

a

b

A^1

A^2

and illustrated, with villanelles by Elizabeth Bishop and Dylan Thomas.

One Art
ELIZABETH BISHOP

The art of losing isn't hard to master;
so many things seem filled with the intent
to be lost that their loss is no disaster.

Lose something every day. Accept the fluster
of lost door keys, the hour badly spent.
The art of losing isn't hard to master.

Then practice losing farther, losing faster:
places, and names, and where it was you meant
to travel. None of these will bring disaster.

I lost my mother's watch. And look! my last, or
next-to-last, of three loved houses went.
The art of losing isn't hard to master.

I lost two cities, lovely ones. And, vaster,
some realms I owned, two rivers, a continent.
I miss them, but it wasn't a disaster.

—Even losing you (the joking voice, a gesture
I love) I shan't have lied. It's evident
the art of losing's not too hard to master
though it may look like (*Write* it!) like disaster.

Do Not Go Gentle into That Good Night
DYLAN THOMAS

Do not go gentle into that good night,
Old age should burn and rave at close of day;
Rage, rage against the dying of the light.

Though wise men at their end know dark is right,
Because their words had forked no lightning they
Do not go gentle into that good night.

Good men, the last wave by, crying how bright
Their frail deeds might have danced in a green bay,
Rage, rage against the dying of the light.

Wild men who caught and sang the sun in flight,
And learn, too late, they grieved it on its way,
Do not go gentle into that good night.

Grave men, near death, who see with blinding sight
Blind eyes could blaze like meteors and be gay,
Rage, rage against the dying of the light.

And you, my father, there on the sad height,
Curse, bless, me now with your fierce tears, I pray.
Do not go gentle into that good night.
Rage, rage against the dying of the light.

> One of its [the villanelle's] major challenges is to make the refrain lines
> fit gracefully and naturally into the form, and to change their meaning
> by varying their contexts. —Jack Meyers and Michael Simms, 335

In the next three villanelles, Frederick Morgan, Mary Swander, and Hayden
Carruth all use full rhyme (although you might want to experiment with half
rhyme), and the villanelle by Hayden Carruth is also about the tricky process of
writing a villanelle. His poem emphasizes the "because it's there" aspect of this
form. Poets can't seem to stay away from the challenge of this poem, perhaps

because it utilizes both line repeats and rhyme patterns. That is, the more we juggle, the more we want to juggle.

The Christmas Tree
FREDERICK MORGAN

In the quiet house, on a morning of snow,
the child stares at the Christmas Tree.
He wonders what there is to know

behind the tinsel and the glow—
behind what he's been taught to see
in the quiet house, on mornings of snow,

when he's snug indoors with nowhere to go
and mother and father have let him be:
he wonders if there's more to know

about their bright, triumphant show
than he's been told. Is the brave Tree,
so proud in the house on this morning of snow,

all that it seems? He gathers no
assurance from its silent glee
and fears there must be more to know

than one poor child can learn. If so,
what stake may he claim in the mystery?
He stares from the house at the falling snow
and wonders how he'll ever know.

Shunning
MARY SWANDER

The doors are always closed to those we know
too well. The well brings up our deepest sin.
To those who stray so far, we must say no.

Amish store: suspenders, hook and eye.
We cannot sell our wares to half our kin,
for the doors are always closed to those we know.

We cannot wave or stop and say hello
to ones who go beyond the daily norm.
To those who stray so far, we must say no.

To some we may seem hard, or mean, or more,
to lock our families out in such a storm,
but we hang on to ours in rain or snow.

Without rules, where would we be now?
Lost souls, by the masses taken in,
like men who hold the sword and not the plow.

A knock. Oh, no, we mustn't even go.
The pain of holding out, is holding in.
The doors are always closed to those we know,
and we leave nothing, no one in the cold.

Saturday at the Border ❖
HAYDEN CARRUTH

"Form follows function follows form . . . , etc."
—Dr. J. Anthony Wadlington

Here I am writing my first villanelle
At seventy-two, and feeling old and tired—
"Hey, Pops, why dontcha give us the old death knell?"—

And writing it what's more on the rim of hell
In blazing Arizona when all I desired
Was north and solitude and not a villanelle,

Working from memory and not remembering well
How many stanzas and in what order, wired
On Mexican coffee, seeing the death knell

Of sun's salvos upon these hills that yell
Bloody murder silently to the much admired
Dead-blue sky. One wonders if a villanelle

Can do the job. Granted, old men now must tell
Our young world how these bigots and these retired
Bankers of Arizona are ringing the death knell

For everyone, how ideologies compel
Children to violence. Artifice acquired
For its own sake is war. Frail villanelle,

Have you this power? And must I go and sell
Myself? "Wow," they say, and "cool"—this hired
Old poetry guy with his spaced-out death knell.

Ah, far from home and God knows not much fired
By thoughts of when he thought he was inspired,
He writes by writing what he must. Death knell
Is what he's found in his first villanelle.

➤ INVENTION EXERCISES ➤

1. Because the full rhyme of the villanelle can sound fairly doom-filled
   and heavy-handed to the modern ear, one class and I decided to
   write slant-rhyme villanelles. One person suggested three words that
   had no true rhymes in English (as far as we could tell): *elephant,
   orange,* and *radio.* We decided we should all write three lines using
   these words as end words and then auction off the lines. Using one
   borrowed line and one of our own (with two of the three
   unrhymable words to ensure our poems would come out without
   true, hard-hitting rhyme), we constructed our villanelles. Here's my
   draft followed by a draft by Jeff Scherzer.

*Waitress, Amarillo**
WENDY BISHOP

Awake at night, I hear the song on the radio.   (*my line*)
(Last time you were here, you called me "Sugar."   (*borrowed line*)
You were so nice when it was time to go.)

I think of you, whistling and blowing
sass in my ear, ordering coffee like a regular.
Talking late that night to the song on the radio,

you tipped me, tipped your hat. We took it slow.
You called me "Sweetheart," winked in the mirror.
You were so nice when it was time to go

to my place. Danced me close, lifted my shirt, folded
it by the bed. You slept in my arms. You didn't stir.
Awake that night, we sang to the radio.

Flash flood, dust storm, or near tornado,
your traveling stories got more spectacular.
You were always nice when it was time to go

back on the road. I'd wave from the window
see snakeskin boots, truck door close, pull out, a blur.
Awake at night, I sang songs with the radio.

This year a drought and business is slow.
(You called me "Sugar" and didn't look in the mirror.)
Late that night, I heard our song on the radio.
(You were always nice. It was time to go.)

*Morning, Mom, and Me**
    Jeff Scherzer

Tropical storm, no school today. I'm glad I listened to the radio.
An insulin shot, wince at the syringe;
divert my attention towards the fruit bowl.

"How'd you get that? Where's the cat? Yoo-hoo Calico!"
I dig into the scab as if peeling an orange;
tropical storm, no school today, I'm glad I listened to the radio.

"There—under the sofa," hiding from the showering cold.
The wind whips newspapers, flyers, foliage;
divert my attention towards the fruit bowl.

An avalanche of whole grain oats, I spot a runaway Cheerio.
Mom smells like Zest and cherry lozenge;
tropical storm, no school today, I'm glad I listened to the radio.

Seventy-five-mile-per-hour winds will continue to blow. . . .
Lighting cracks! then I cringe;
divert my attention towards the fruit bowl.

A mouthful of oatmeal, "I'll make a list of chores before I go."
No matinee for me, "Is that porridge?"
Tropical storm, no school today, I shouldn't have listened to the radio;
divert my attention towards the fruit bowl.

In a group see if you can come up with any other words without full rhyme and/or come up with a set of first lines. Borrow one repeat line, use one of your own, and get started on your first villanelle.

2. Like Elizabeth Bishop or Tara Reynolds, write a lost love villanelle.

Villanelle*
Tara Reynolds

I thought I understood what your promises stood for
But the scent on your shirt contradicts what you've said.
It'd be so much easier if I could walk out the door

And pick up the pieces that you tore
When you cheated and ripped our dreams to shreds.
I thought I understood what your promises stood for

But they lie to me like your letters where you swore
That your feelings for everyone else were dead.
It'd be so much easier if I could walk out the door

And leave behind your stories and poor
Excuses, and all the sorry lines I've been fed.
I thought I understood what your promises stood for

When you'd take my negligee out of my drawer
Or whisper those lines as we'd lie in our bed.
It'd be so much easier if I could walk out the door

And go to someone who could give me much more
Than unfulfilled promises of what lies ahead.
I thought I understood what your promises stood for.
It'd be so much easier if I could walk out the door.

3. Hurricane Andrew crashed into Florida one term when I was teaching, and Chandra Langford poured the overwhelming dislocation it caused into the tight confines of the villanelle form (which also led her, I expect, to draft in these relatively long lines). Write a villanelle in which your content strains against the confines of the form: mix opposites, list objects like Chanda does, put dissimilar things together.

*Too Late Called Me Home**
   Chanda Langford

Turbulences along the Atlantic had, too late, called me home.
Too late to mend crumpled girders or refit jagged gaps,
And the injured wings of seagulls flapped frantic into doom.

Baby crib and notebooks from the downstairs storage room
Were spun inside out, hoisted and blown away unaware.
Turbulences along the Atlantic had, too late, called me home.

Perfume bottle, fragrance of seabreeze, plastic red pocket comb,
A winter sock, long hand of the hall clock all gathered at seaside
While injured wings of seagulls flapped frantic into doom.

Fishing dock so sturdy floated, kindling, in the foam,
Where depraved whirlwinds had split and spit it out.
Turbulences along the Atlantic had, too late, called me home.

Scraps of pool hall jukebox thrashed up and down the dunes,
And cue balls lost the stripes and solids sunken in the sand,
While injured wings of seagulls flapped frantic into doom.

Picked through pieces of humankind were treasure enough for some,
But mementos that might have cemented ties crumbled in my hands,
For turbulences along the Atlantic had, too late, called me home,
And injured wings of seagulls flapped frantic into doom.

4. The villanelle is certainly a challenge. But there is also a variant
   called the **terzanelle** that comes from mixing terza rima into a
   repeat-line form like the villanelle. Inveterate form-finder that I am, I
   had to try it when I read about it. The pattern goes like this:

1. A^1—refrain
2. B—repeton
3. A^2—refrain

4. b
5. C—repeton
6. B—repeton

7. c
8. D—repeton
9. C—repeton

10. d

11. E—repeton

12. D—repeton

13. e

14. F—repeton

15. E—repeton

16. f

17. A^1—refrain or F—repeton

18. F—repeton or A^1—refrain

19. A^2 A^2—refrain

A *repeton* is a single line or phrase repeated *once* after its initial appearance in a poem. A *repetend* is a single line or phrase that reappears more than once after its initial appearance, but at random. A *refrain* is a single phrase or line that reappears at formal intervals throughout a poem, usually at the end of each stanza.
—Lewis Turco, 44

Terzanelle on Drought *
WENDY BISHOP

Drought is the state we are in here.
Blue bowl of sky. No clouds. No rain.
Days steal moisture, parch our tears.

We would speak, if speech could explain.
Slow dust devils; summer fruit unswelled.
Blue bowl of sky. No clouds. No rain.

Or speak to break silence and meld
Together, dance down rains, shape prayer
Against dust devils. Summer fruit won't swell.

Sun hangs high in thin cloudless air.
We share cool sheets, cotton on skin,
Braid limbs to a dance the shape of prayer,

Praise what insists on going missing.
Our bodies mysterious as oceans,
We share cool sheets of cotton on skin

Until summer falters and ends.
Drought is the state we are in here.
These bodies mysterious as oceans.
Day steals moisture, returns it as tears.

Now, if the villanelle isn't challenge enough, or even if it is (sometimes one form just doesn't fit and it's worth trying another), you can try your own terzanelle. To write mine, I borrowed a line from an earlier poem I wrote: "Drought is the state we are in here" and went from there, and that strategy took my poem in a very different direction from the free verse poem I had composed some ten years before, proving that lines never wear out and can often be recycled.

> I think that since I have written almost continuously all these years, I've been able to throw a lot of stuff away because I had a lot of stuff. I think if you write a poem every two months, it's awfully tough to throw it away. If you are writing constantly and trying, and the work is coming you have some faith that the lines you wrote yesterday will not be the last—that since you write yesterday and you wrote Tuesday and Friday, it's likely that you'll get some more. You're going to be able to be tougher and harder on what you did. —Phillip Levine (Duke and Jacobsen 53)

> In high school poetry was a game for me. I don't mean I didn't take it seriously because I think when you're young, games are a serious part of your life—they were challenges—using language in certain rhythms, you'd get a rhyming dictionary, a thesaurus, it was really fun. . . . so I think game-playing is a very good way of starting poetry. . . . But I periodically go into doing it again. I found a wonderful book of forms this summer. —Diane Wakowski (Packard 213)

Try, try again. Reuse. Recycle. Revise. Thirteen times thirteen. That's the message of this book: you can always find new ways to mix and match your forms, to invent new patterns and pathways to follow as a poet. Write enough to throw away what doesn't work. Play long and hard. And you'll find that thirteen ways can become 169 ways into poetry before you're done.

POCKET DEFINITIONS

Refrain—A regular, nearly exact repeat of a phrase or line, often at the end of a stanza.

Tercet—Three-line stanzas. When all three lines rhyme, tercets become *triplets*. When the rhyme patterns interlock like this—*aba, bcb, cdc*—linking stanzas, the tercet turns into *terza rima*.

Terzanelle—A nineteen-line poem divided into six stanzas: five interlocking triplets and a quatrain. Of French and Italian origin, it adapts terza rima to the villanelle form by the use of a repeton: A^1BA^2, bCB, cDC, dED, eFE, fA^1 (or F) F (or A^1) A^2. (A^1 and A^2 are refrains; BCDEF are repetons.)

Villanelle—A nineteen-line poem divided into six stanzas: five tercets and one quatrain turning on two rhymes and built on two refrains: A^1bA^2, abA^1, abA^2, abA^1, abA^2, and abA^1A^2. (A^1 and A^2 are refrains.)

APPENDIX

Three Case Studies in Form and Revision

Any editor will tell you that it's only a moderate thrill to publish a poem by a well-known and established poet. Certainly it takes no great courage to publish a poet who's already been well-received and acknowledged. The real delight is in discovering the work of a new or relatively unknown writer, and in being able to bring this work to the attention of a larger audience. —David St. John (3)

The following case studies by Devan Cook, Bill Snyder, and Rex West take you through the process of composing and revising a poem in form. Each writer was asked to keep a journal of his/her writing and drafting process through a term and at the end of the term write an essay that would teach others about drafting. Each approached drafting and the case study assignment differently, but each felt keeping such records and reviewing them—even if only once in a poetic life— taught them a lot. I encourage you to read these for insights into the process of writing poetry and for ideas of how you might keep your own writing journal to help record and improve your craft as you work to become a poet first published by a sympathetic journal editor like David St. John.

DEVAN COOK—REVISION CASE STUDY

The poem "Whales Off Neakani Mountain" began as a fifteen-sentence portrait exercise.[1] Several years ago, I wrote a poem about the last trip I made to the Oregon coast with my sister. That day has remained evocative and compelling for both of us: it seems to hold or to epitomize a large part of our relationship. I liked

---

[1]Here are brief directions for this exercise:
- Picture a person you have strong feelings for, living or dead, but someone you are/were personally acquainted with.
- For a title, choose an emotion or color that represents that person to you. You will not mention the individual's name in the writing.
- Start by choosing one of the following: a) you stand there, b) no one is here, c) in this [memory, photograph, dream, etc.], you are, d) I think sometimes, e) we had been . . . (complete this sentence).

(continued)

my earlier poem, but I wanted to see if I could expand it in any way, or if I could write about that day differently, since I am a different person now. In short, I wanted to examine my changed perspective in poetry; the way I write has changed, as well as the way I relate to my sister. And maybe (probably) one thing would influence the other. I am one of those people who doesn't know what they think until they see what they say. When I wrote the original poem, it was clear that there was a lot of shared pain in the relationship. Gradually my writing has begun to open and become more explicit, and I wanted to see how that would affect writing about our trip to the beach. The first poem has a powerful emotional impact: Would this one? Would more description make the scene easier to envision, or more difficult? Would telling more of the story help a reader to relate, or would it diffuse and divert the reader's attention? Although at first all I wanted to do was play around and see what happened, since I was missing Oregon and my sister so much, at the back of my mind the whole question of [what are the] ways of writing narrative poetry was simmering.

Here's the original poem, written sometime during the winter of 1989–1990:

At the Beach with My Sister

> We faced the sun's
> edges, and the sea's;
> waves erased our names.
> The wind scraped
> sounds from our mouths;
> pierced, our eyes bled
> tears that wound
> down our faces.

---

[1](*continued*)
- Following your first sentence, build a portrait of the individual, writing the sentences according to these fifteen prompts.
  Sentence 2: has a color in it
  Sentence 3: has a body part in it
  Sentence 4: has a simile
  Sentence 5: is over twenty-five words
  Sentence 6: is under eight words
  Sentence 7: has a piece of clothing in it
  Sentence 8: has a wish in it
  Sentence 9: has an animal in it.
  Sentence 10: has three or more words that alliterate
  Sentence 11: has two commas
  Sentence 12: has a smell and a color in it
  Sentence 13: has a simile or metaphor
  Sentence 14: could carry an exclamation point (but do not use the exclamation point)
  Sentence 15: uses the word or words you chose for a title to help close this portrait
- Use this material as a starting point for a portrait poem.

The day was bright, cold, and windy: we faced west and looked for whales, as we had done countless times with our father. The first fall storms made huge towering scoops of the breakers, and the undertow was so strong it ate the beach: we stood far back and looked out. Foam flew into the sun; all we could see were waves and the sun on them. Only when we left the beach, climbing the coast range toward the Willamette Valley and home, were we sure that no whales swam near the horizon. That was the first time we had been to the beach without our father, who parented heavily on vacations: changes in our family were summed up by our being together now without him.

Too, I wondered what else might be there; my memories of the day are intense and large, and I wanted to write more of them and see what shape they might take. A great deal of the sensuous content of the first versions of the poem, as well as its fragmentary collage nature, comes from the invention exercise I used to start it. The fifteen-sentence portrait, since it calls for similes and for colors and emotions, tends to be like a picture. Since I have photographs of our beach trip—there's one over my desk at school—I thought the "snapshot" approach might work well as a starting point for re-seeing the day. Writing from the portrait would provide exactly the sort of new perspective I was seeking: it was a good place to begin exploring. And of course I miss my sister, and it was fun to write about her.

When I began to shape the exercise into a poem, my only thought was to find places to break it into lines and see what else occurred to me. My writing is full of gaps, ghosts, and shadows, and how successful a particular piece of writing is depends in large part on how intelligently I use them. Often I tend to blunder ahead and pretend they aren't there, and unless the gods of poetry smile on me and arrange the ghosts in a way that works with the surface of the poem, the unspoken hidden truths wreck it. "What do I really mean?" is probably my major question. The next one is "What does this poem want to mean?", and after that comes "How can the two work together?" So here, in the first version of the new poem, is a big unknown: my sister looks like my father, who isn't there. She's there, but she also represents an absence, and the poem doesn't say so: it doesn't even address the issue.

So things left unsaid have been a major issue in the revisions of this poem from the beginning. The kind of writing I have been accustomed to do, both in poetry and in prose, is to find what the writing says and then say it, eliminating anything that does not work toward that goal. Perhaps it is impossible for any piece of writing to be monologic, but what I had preferred was writing directly from Point A to Point B; such a poem tends to have a large emotional impact, which I like, and to be focused and cohesive. If connotations and denotations of the words in the poem work together to make a structure that either supports or comments ironically on what the words of the poem say on the surface, that's good, too. It's also extraordinarily difficult, and as a result many of my poems have been quite short. So I set out here to write a long poem—to explore, to write dialogically if possible, and to let the writing find its own way and its own form as I revised and re-saw the day at the beach again and again.

Most of my writing practice has been in accentual verse: my teacher at Georgia Southern is metrically aware and so skilled that many of his poems, read aloud, sound like music. They're not like songs exactly—more like a new kind of wind instrument, something with the range of the human voice played with breath and a reed—and I have tried to emulate the beautiful sounds his poems make, or that make his poems. Because he mostly writes in blank verse, so have I. Because he writes unrhymed sonnets, so have I. Because he is moving toward narrative poetry while maintaining his moderately formal stance, I've done so also. But I'm not at Georgia Southern anymore; it's time for me to do something new, to look again at forms: are they really so useful in keeping poetic language clean and effective? I wrote the first version of the poem about my sister and I looking for whales without counting beats; it was amazingly difficult. I sat at the computer and bit my lip. I bit my tongue.

Whale Road*

Your face turns toward the Pacific, away
from the camera, away from me. That day
we saw whales, or thought so, near Depot Bay
where we stayed each childhood year, smelled kelp
and sand, squatted by rocky pools where purple
starfish pulsed, gathered, glided, and burst from side
to side and green anemones, poked in the center,
gathered tentacles to close themselves. When someone
down the beach yelled "Whales!", we jumped
to glimpse the curves of glistening backs, spouting
rainbows toward the sun.

         That day we ran away
from home, from canning applesauce and raking
leaves. While with my camera I watched Tommy watch
you—your red-toned skin, high cheekbones, muscular
body—you looked for whales, saw the sun above
October's deep breakers. Of us two sisters, you
are the beautiful one, the one everyone watches.
I would have liked to have been you.
         By Armistice Day
you bought a soft green dress; you looked inexplicably
inextricably like our grandmother, ready for work.
You got a job. We moved; I had another baby, a boy.

When we leave, the coast road is fogged in. Wet
Douglas fir boughs slap the car, cling to the windshield
as we drive out. Winding home toward the Gorge,
climbing haunted Neakani, all we see is mist.

Even I could tell there was way too much going on here: more people, places, and situations than there are in the fifteen-sentence portrait. Somehow our grandmother, whom my sister resembles, showed up, as did Depot Bay, our Oregon farm, and Tommy, my brother-in-law. What I liked were the description of the beach—the sea anemones and starfish—and the phrase "haunted Neakani" because our trip to the beach was haunted by our childhood. The title, "Whale Road," is a kenning used in *Beowulf:* it means the ocean, but implies a sense of loss. Those who go along the whale road in Old English poetry often never return. So I began to see, in this version, that the poem combined the sad, gentle beauty of the Oregon coast in fall with the keener sadnesses my sister and I felt: our father wasn't with us, and she herself was soon to go away to school in New Mexico.

By using the image comparing our past to Neakani, the poem implies something more than nostalgic melancholy: for the Indians, Neakani was a place of evil spirits. It sits right on the coast, but they would go miles out of their way to avoid crossing it. To Western eyes, it looks like any other piece of the Oregon coast range: Douglas firs, deer moss, streams, berries, alders, hemlock, wild roses, mists, and rocks—a *National Geographic* photo. To Indians, Neakani is a place where the dead don't stay dead but come back to torment the living. In this place, my sister and I are tormented by our memories, palpable as we stand on the beach together or drive along the coast road looking for whales. But it's not reasonable to expect that a general reader would know what a bad place Neakani mountain is. That leaves me as a writer with two choices: drop the image, which is perhaps my favorite, or explain it. Rex's [peer reader] comment on this version was that "haunted Neakani" might be a separate poem.

The second version of the poem was the one I shared in a class workshop. In the meantime, I wrote a long poem in long couplets, which had both visual material and emotional impact. The effect was that I was more confident in writing longer lines and saying more in them: I felt looser and better without counting beats. Finally, I found a form that was more appropriate to the loose, undisciplined nature of memory or collage. All I wanted was to try to describe the poem I saw when I looked through my new lens, altered by the experience of having written the long couplet poem.

Whales Off Neakani Mountain

You face the Pacific, turned from the camera and me,
searching beyond October's deep breakers for whales
migrating to Baja. You've got a job; bought a soft
green dress like Grandmother's: you're going
to San Francisco. On our childhood beach
foam hisses toward rock pools where once we watched
purple starfish pulse and glide and anemones clench
their tentacles into fists when we stirred the water.
I run toward you now, shouting "Come on!" but sea sound
surrounds you like the whales below the surface,
swimming south. I touch your shoulder, drag
you further up the beach to walk on spits
of crunchy sand where wide kelp leaves trail.
At the Needle we turn around; head for Moe's
and clam chowder. It's traditional, the way
we've always left the beach; there's no need
to talk. Going home, I stop at the foot
of Neakani to pick a few last salmonberries
beside a shallow stream; we wash the salt
off our feet and faces. It's not safe
to sleep here: Tlingit spirits haunt this mountain
I don't even like to cross, but back in the car,
we're climbing with the road. Fir boughs cling
to the windshield; then free, we wind above the water,
where white and rose would rise from spouting whales,
if they were there, toward setting sun.

When we workshopped the poem, people wondered who the "you" was, but what they didn't realize was how many other people were no longer in the poem: the speaker and one other person are the only ones left. Workshop commentary showed me that it is no longer obvious that the people in the poem are sisters, and that it is important for readers to know who they are. Such knowledge cannot be the exclusive property of the poet if the poem is to work. The other thing that's missing from this version is the whales themselves: we really did not see any whales that day. And their absence (and possibility) is emblematic of other absences that my sister and I felt.

The camera's eye remains in this version, though without Tommy and a description of my sister's beauty, it makes less sense. The starfish and anemones—as much my poetic pets as "haunted Neakani"—are still here and still pretty, and I've described the beach more, too, though I'm not sure why. Lots of physical description made my other "long couplet" poem work, so I thought I'd try it here, and it does seem to draw readers in. But the kelp and sand do little in the poem other than attract readers, although the description of the beach gives the poem's characters a place to turn around. And if they don't turn around and drive off from the beach, they won't be able to get to Neakani, my other "pet." The trip to Moe's for clam chowder sounds cheery, not sad or foreboding, so it doesn't work well to set up what follows.

In this version, too, although I was trying to clean things up and simplify, find some approach to this day at the beach that would make it work as a poem, far too much is going on. For the first time, I began to wonder if the original 1989–90 poem might be the best version of the incident. After three tries that were radically different, I was still left with far too much material that didn't work together. Wendy said she wanted stanzas; Bill [peer reader] suggested several different poems. After class, he asked me if I ever wrote fiction. I told him I'd written a couple of short stories for a class. "This is a book," he said.

I had been warned but refused to believe. If I wrote a series of short poems, perhaps the collage effect would be retained in the snapshots the short poems provided, and if the shorter poems were arranged properly, they could tell a story. Again, I may have been trying to get the form to do too much. Because the sonnet was first used for love poetry and my poem is about love (although not romantic love), sonnets seemed an appropriate choice for the series. Sonnet sequences are hot right now, too: Andrew Hudgins has one in *Saints and Strangers* and so does Seamus Heaney in *The Haw Lantern*. And I had never been able to write sonnets, so I could try to write some.

But the sonnets I wrote weren't especially traditional: they had fourteen lines, but they didn't rhyme—they were alliterative or off-rhymed instead, turning lightly on the couplet. And what I tried to do with them was tell about what haunted my sister and me that day at the beach: why we were having a good time and not a good time at the same time, why, in the first poem about this day, we were crying. The beach was always our father's trip, and in this revision the emphasis shifted away from the collage portrait and the beach description. In the first two versions of the poem, readers had found time problems as the speaker shifts from childhood memories to a remembered trip that is also in the past. Dealing with childhood at the beginning ought to eliminate chronological difficulties, I thought, as well as explain what is going on at the beach between the two adults. The first two sonnets essentially provided background for the poem from the class workshop. I had thought that one sonnet would be enough, but try as I might, I couldn't cram enough material into one to make that work.

The two sonnets are fiction in a way that none of the other versions are, although all the versions written for this class have been more "made up" than the first poem, probably because they contain more facts. They are collages of different trips rather than a poem or poems about one trip, and the combinations lead of necessity to confusion and perhaps generalizations. And some things are simply untrue: we slept once on a motel couch in Wichita, not Coeur d'Alene—something about a sleeper sofa that wouldn't open after we arrived at the motel so late that nothing could be done about it until morning. I never saw the Paloose in Western Oregon until I was an adult, and the description of the Appaloosas in the first sonnet, though it's another of my pets, is too alliterative for it to be a likely childhood observation, even one remembered in adulthood. The most obvious untruth is that our mother and brother aren't in the poem at all; they haven't been in any of the revisions, but the trip to the beach my sister and I made in 1970 was the first we had made without them as well.

In the back of my mind, the idea of writing a story was fighting with the idea of writing poems. What, exactly, is the difference, apart from accentual language and the use of figurative language of some kind? I learned those differences at Georgia Southern and I've read enough narrative poetry—the *Aeneid,* the *Canterbury Tales*—to know that poems can indeed tell stories. But some difference remains in my mind, in my poems. I am struggling with ways that I can tell stories, which I love to do, and still write things that feel like my poems— sensuous, intuitive, and emotional. An old friend and I were talking recently about my school work, and he commented that he was glad I was planning to continue writing poetry rather than fiction. I told him I felt myself grappling with fiction, and he said, "Good. You're resisting."

Since the revised sonnets differ from the originals only in the ways I've described, only the second version is included here. In workshop, I was pleased with the response to the poems in general, and I tried to listen to either matters that bothered a lot of readers or things that I also felt were a problem. The next revision was intended to be personal in one way and democratic in another. Rex felt the semicolons in the second sonnet were excessive; I was irritated because even though he doesn't believe semicolons belong in poems, he was right about them, and I took one of them out. In the first poem, someone suggested changing "rounded hills"—the second use of the word *round* in as many lines—to "mounded," which keeps the sound and sense but avoids the repetition. When I rewrote the first sonnet, I changed the first "we'd," for "we had" to "we," but kept the second, meaning "we would." Maybe it's because I've studied Latin that very specific tenses seem natural to me; maybe it's because I've read comparatively little modern poetry that past tenses also sound better, and present tense grates in my mind's ear. In the interests of naming as well as internal accuracy, the second "crackers" in the first sonnet became "cracker-jacks and Snickers" in the revision, for how could we eat the crackers we'd already smashed in the car? In the second sonnet, the major problem for most readers was the "you," who had been mysterious in the first workshop version and remained so in this one. Someone suggested changing the "you" to "we," which sounded like a good solution to me because it avoided a bald statement about who the other person in the poem is—a reader could tell that "you" is a sibling.

Whales Off Neakani Mountain*

I. Appaloosas

Dad always saw whales first; he drove
two days from Idaho each fall
at first frost and the thought of snow,
glare ice, ground blizzards, wall-
high drifts lining the street. Tangled
in back, we watched him follow the Snake
down, kicked each other and smashed crackers
while he showed us round gray horses grazing
on gray-green mounded hills. Rumpled
and yawning—we slept in our clothes
on a motel couch in Coeur d'Alene—we'd rub
our eyes and stare, wanting breakfast more.
We ate cracker-jacks and Snickers, dozed, groaned,
and colored Prince Charming's horse light gray.

II. Whales

He sharpened his eyes all day; by late
afternoon, we climbed Neakani high
and clear above the ocean. "Whales!"
he'd say, then stop and pull us headfirst
to the front. We'd sight along his arm,
squinting; the low sun hung where he pointed
and we said we saw them. We argued;
he lectured. "Whale families are pods."
His shirt smelled like cigarettes,
sweat, stale whiskey; his hand shook
a little, but his voice was steady.
"Right there—down a little—look"
I'd pretend the curled waves and broken
foam were whales diving, blowing, breathing.

Response to this version was fascinating: most readers liked it less than the other version, though the "you" wasn't there anymore. Other than that, and the addition of subtitles, which I thought would clarify the narrative but which seemed now to be in the way, the poems are substantially the same. Yet reader after reader said they liked the earlier, "rougher" version better. I don't, but I wonder if other problems with the poem are becoming evident since they have been seen so often. As Wendy said, the whole story isn't there, so it's hard to decide how the poems work as part of a larger unit. But I had wanted them to be able to stand on their own, and I think they do.

Then there was the question of the beach trip in the more recent past. Since I had written so much about that already, I thought rewriting and restructuring the lines as a sonnet would be relatively easy and fun, but I was wrong. It has proved almost impossible. The third sonnet is like this:

Now I balance on our childhood beach; you face
the Pacific, searching beyond October's deep
breakers for whales migrating toward familiar
warmth in Baja. Foam hisses toward sleeping
anemones whose startled tentacles clench
into fists when purple starfish pulse and glide
past. Slipping on mossy rocks, I call
"Come on!" and run toward you; sea sounds hide
me till I touch your shoulder, drag you to walk
on spits of crunchy sand where wide kelp
leaves trail. We can't hear each other. Waves
crash spray between us and the whales. Foam covers
our beach as the tide rises, and we turn around
where we used to—head for town, Moe's, clam chowder.

Here's my sister, looking beyond the breaking waves for whales, me standing on rocks and looking at small things, both of us, despite the differences and space between us, doing the traditional things on our traditional trip to the beach. To me, this sounds like the end of the story. Rex was right: "haunted Neakani" is a different poem—right now, it's in tercets:

*Haunted Neakani**

We stop to wash salt from feet and faces
in a snowmelt stream at Neakani's foot.
A few last salmonberries cling to canes

arching over water where we stand,
shoes off, tongues crumbling dry fruit
as we look toward the ocean, where no whale

pods swim. We linger, not ready to leave
our day behind us, and the beach fogs
in fast, graying light that glowed on berries

as we stand barefoot on rocks and moss,
shivering and staring. Waves boom
and crash; foam from the first fall

storms flies and sprays above them.
Douglas firs loom, and deer moss drops
soundlessly from trees and fallen

limbs. Our shirts cling wet now,
our cold feet are heavy as stone:
skin clear and pale as water,

they start to take root under rocks,
to grow downstream toward the sea.
I'd like to stay all night, to sleep

while I dive, descending with my dreams.
But sighing, you step forward and pull me
from water to rocks with one tug.

On the bank, my shoes are warm and dry.
You drive; fir boughs scrape and slap
the windshield as we climb and clear

the fog to twist above the sea where streams
of spray would rise, from spouting whales,
if they were there. In the car, our clothes steam.

From all these revisions, I learned that the same episodes can be re-seen and rewritten over and over; a writer, like everyone else, constantly changes, and her perspectives change as well. Returning to evocative events is a useful writing strategy, and trying different forms helps to find a different point of view. For me, revising means seeing from different angles. Thus, it also means getting a better idea of what it is I see and want to write about. I may not know what I want to say until I've written or said it, but changing form leads me to want to say different things, to choose different words for the sake of sound, like "steam" to rhyme with "streams" in the last tercet of the poem above. I had no idea how I wanted to end the poem until those sounds presented themselves. English itself gives us presents.

WILLIAM SNYDER—REVISION CASE STUDY

Original clustering freewrite in response to listening twice to the Sharon Olds poem "I Go Back to May 1937" [found in chapter 7: Listings and Repetition].

1, 2

"Pleistocene" developed from the family prompt [to write about our parents as Olds wrote about hers] we did early in the semester. I clustered around the words "my mother in Tennessee." What is neat for me is that most of the images that I have in the final poem can be found here in the freewriting: what my mother might have worn in 1945 when she met my father while she was a student at Peabody College (now Vanderbilt U) in Nashville, Nashville being about sixty miles west of Gordonsville where my mother grew up; the boulders and the horseback ride that are in the final copy. And the glacier is in the freewrite too, though no mention of the Pleistocene yet.

I wanted to have Mother take Father home with her, in the poem anyway— I'm not sure if it ever happened really. I'm not sure now why I wrote the poem about both Mother and Father. I guess I liked the story possibilities of a romance.

On the second freewriting page, in the middle, I wrestle with the metaphor: fire or ice—I eventually picked the cold/ice metaphor and the glaciers moving south. What I wanted to present was the idea that two people can be happy early on, but, inexorably like the glaciers, for my parents anyway, problems happen. I'm not sure that comes through in the final copy except in the title per- haps, which may be sort of a conundrum—which is okay.

(1)

What di young women wear I 1944
with the war still on and military men
coming through the towns

I want to say gabardine
I think it was gabardine my mother wore

I dont know if it was gabardine
She could have worn cotton skirts
or searsucker even, or linen.
But the rocks were hard
they wree boulders and they
are still strewn

for school and hell and my mother, wearing, what
why is it important what she was wearing. So I
can see her. So I can visualize her with my
father because I know what he looked like, I
remember pictures. Why do I remember pics of hm

and not of her. He wore a dark brown or dark
khaki, I know that from the movies maybe. A
univorm. Pull back your shoulders he told me.
His wer. Straight. His jaw straight and teeth. A
handsome man, cliched handsome maybe.

The military men, the younjg men
who came through Nashvill,
my father among them, wore
dark brown or dark khaki unierms
and military hats with brown bills with
wings. I know that much. I kow the
pictures.

He was handsome. He sust have been.

But my mother. Mary Caroline. From Gordonsville,
near Carthage, 60 miles east of Nashville. There
she was in Nashville. Far from her pony, her
poney she told me just the other day was almost
as big as a horse, what ever that means. How big
is a horse? I imagin my father didnt know either
then, when he met her. Where. At a dance at
Peabody, where she was in school. College. Which
she never finished because of. Because of me?

Mary Croline came froom Gordonsville though
Not frm Nashville, how much of the
Nashville life she had learned by the
time my father came through
Gordonsville a fraction, a figment on
somebody's map of Tennessee

She took him home with her once to visit. More than once. To the farm.

gaberdeen

It was late fall when she took him there, a cold
spell and the horse's breath, the pony's breath
speared out from the animal's nostrils, and my
father's and my mother's, not my father or
mother then. Only tow people who met at Peabody.
A young woman who happened to be from a small
town near enough to take a train

to or a bus,

(2)

I think it was late fall when,
yes it was, late fall when
she took him home to Gordonsville
to the farm

And the next day, she on her black and white pony
still kept for her to ride
ad he on her granddaddy's mare
they saddled early the next morning
the animal's breath, and theirs,
darting out like spears
the animals from work, or boredom
tehirs from

the man wearing the dark brown uniform with wings

breath from the pny and the black and white
horse side by side in late november, two people
riding among the grey, glacier spread boulders
and rock I the hills. NO I wouldn't call my
father a glacier. Just the opposite, nor my
mother. Yet ice seems more fitting that fire.
Or am I confuming me with them, then in ten.

a kiss on the animals or later, naked in the
spring, but I don't know if he was there that
long. Should I try to get the facts right.

I dojnt know their beginnings. ######

Let me see her. I want to say gaberdine.
I want to say gaberdine is what she wore

Its what she wore that winter, that late
fall when he came.

howinnocent was she then, at Peabody, in a
rororority in Nashville, TN, away from home, away
from the town the size of

He was not. I knv this. He has told me and his
borther hs told me. Male bragging, perhaps
wanting me to live up to their prowess.

I cant imagin sadness then, except when he must
rreturn to the barracks or the bas or wherever
he stayeed in Nashvill. Why was he there?

I can only see love.

It was gabrdine, the jacket she wore

The reason I portray them in a romantic setting, doing romantic things is because that was gone. It is gone.

3, 4

I should date my drafts. This one is about a month or so into the semester. I have the form worked out—the short, enjambed lines, though I don't have any regular stanza lengths, which I won't until toward the end of the process, probably as a result of the looming specter of Form poems that we would be doing and also because I realized that for me, regular stanza lengths looked best on the page and I think make the poem easier to read—a point I made during discussion. (I was forced to take my own medicine.)

I'm still speculating here: about what my mother and father were wearing, what they did together that first night at her home. This speculation—about the clothes, about what they did, though I see I am easing away from this toward the last stanzas—this speculation was a central issue to resolve. Somehow I liked the speculative narrator; the narrator being, in a way, self-reflexive, draws attention to the fact that this *is* speculation, *is* possibly made up, *is* a story. But also, it may just have been trying to work through the story and setting by asking questions.

I do another freewrite on page 2 of this early draft: I was intrigued by my mother's sophistication/innocence when she met my father, coming as she had from a very small town, in fact, living about seven or eight miles from the small town on a farm. I'm interested too, at this point, in the idea of photos—I think someone read a Sharon Olds poem about her mother, mentioning photographs. I think I was influenced by that poem.

(3)

Gabardien? Wool? Ruffled taffeta blous?
What would she wear in 1944,
the war still on
military men haunting through the towns?

A military man, my father, I know
the photographs,
            a h
wore dark bronw, ~~and~~ at with brown
leather bill and wings when he
haunted trhough Nashville.

Mary Davis from Gordonsville *at Peabody*
Gordonsville a dot on ~~the~~ road *feast*
            a

~~though~~
Not from Nashville, how much of the / Nashville life
she had learned by the time my father came through
Gordonsville a fraction, a figment on
somebody's map of Tennessee

was it Late fall, a cold snap0, ~~they said~~ *picked apart*
the degrees
the gents in Maggerts store whe   *and her virginity*
when she walked in with ~~him~~ in 1944   *Bill*
and they all discussed the Bulge
or his wings and they all, the gents
around the stove, wondered at this yankee   *haunting*
through
she'*d* ~~had~~ found ~~in the city~~ *Nashville*

late fall when she took him home
to Gordonsville to the farm

            sleep
Did he ~~would have~~ slept downstaris
int he parlor next tot he porch   *chairs for*
Did she sneak down?
Did the porch swing squeek?
The thin grey boards on the floor?
Did she know him well *?* ~~enough?~~

The next day, she on her black and white pony
still kept for her to ride
and he on her granddady's mare
they saddled early the next morning
the animal's breath, and tehirs,
darting out like spears
the animals from work, or boredon
theirs from

It's what she wore that winter, that late
fall when he came.
I don't know materials, structures
did they know the structures of their hearts,
then
heart strutures
        like gabardine, tough, resilient

(4)

8/3/92

not tough enough, nor resilient as the boulders,
glkacier strewn on the green sheep hills on the
farm

I want to see her, to know and not imagin

I know him, I am him

Dso people marry for the rock-strewn boulder
promises
of pouders, permanence/
But glaciers move south and are unforcasted
in the pleisticien or one of those

ages of cold, like today.
There is noone there to forecast romance
and the loss of it, to forecast encourage
longevity

Glaciers disrupt though,
drive away
pulverize all promise of

for school and hell and my mother, wearing, what
why is it important what she was wearing. So I
can see her. So I can visualize her with my
father because I know what he looked like, I
remember pictures. Why do I remember pics of him
and not of her. He wore a dark brown or dark
khaki, I know that from the movies maybe. A
uniform. Pull back your shoulders he told me.
His were. Straight. His jaw straight and teeth.
A handsome man, cliched handsome maybe.

But my mother. Mary Caroline. From Gordonsville,
near Carthage, 60 miles east of Nashville. There
she was in Nashville. Far from her pony, her
poney she told me just the other day was almost
as big as a horse, what ever that means. How big
is a horse? I imagin my father didnt know either
then, when he met her. Where. At a dance at
Peabody, where she was in school. College. Which
she never finished because of. Because of me?

what I want to get at is the probably
differencebetween their innocences when my
fatherc came through. was she ionnocent? did it
matter?/?? did it matter to this

Did her innocence have anything to do with her
attraction to him Did she see his rigidity?
She took him home with her once to visit. More
than once. To the farm.
gaberdeen.

It was late fall when she took him there, a cold
spell and the horse's breath, the pony's breath
speared out from the animal's nostrils, and my
father's and my mother's, not my father or
mother then. Only tow people who met at Peabody.

A young woman who happened to be from a small
town near enough to take a train
o, or a bus

5

Draft 5. By this draft I have it down to less than a page. I'm still stuck on the
speculation though, and I see that I foregrounded my father in the first couple
of verses. This foregrounding drops out later. The story, though, is here as it is
in the final copy, plus horse breath simile. The whole thing is too loose still. At
the bottom is the theme rather openly stated: "Do people marry for the rock-
strewn boulder promises/of boulders, permanence?/ But glaciers move south in
unforcasted times/. . .". Kind of blatant. I think the poem is better for having
gotten rid of it. The style is more prose-like, informal perhaps. As the poem pro-
gressed though, I began to search for more and more economy—perhaps
because of the stanza form I eventually adopted, partly, I guess for aesthetics,
partly though, because at this point in the semester I felt, I think, that I wanted

to move as close to "poetry" as I could, to break any prosiness, at least for a
while. To see if I could?

(5)

Gabardine? Wool? A taffeta blouse?
What would she wear in 1944, my mother,
with the war still on and those
military boys haunting ~~down~~ the states?
                    through

My father, I know the photography
wore dark brown, a brown hat with
leather bill and wings when he

haunted ~~through~~ Nashville.
          in

Was it late Fall when she took him home
to the farm? ~~Like fall.~~ A cold snap.
Sure enough. The gents in Maggerts picking apart
degrees and Mary Caroline
when she walked in with Bill.
He discussed the Bulge ad wings and the gents
around the stove wondered at this Yankee
Mary Caroline'd found and dragged on home
I declare.

Did he sleep down stairs
in the parlor off the porch?
Did she sneak down?
Did the porch swing squeak?
~~Did she know him well?~~

                         & rode out early
The next day they saddled ~~early, she~~
her black and white pony her still kept   *her mother*
for her to ride, he for granddaddy's mare
The horse's breath, and theirs,
darting out like spears
the animals from burden,
their breath from

ambled   across
They ~~shuffled around the~~ ————— , ~~through~~ the
bouldered hills, boulders left by
glaciers, ~~in the pleistecene, worn smooth~~   *They stopped and*

      the
~~They~~ stood on, ~~one~~ and lay perhaps in a crevice
or a smooth sculpted pocket *smooth*
worn ~~away~~ in the Pleisticine, big enough for
two

Do people marry for the rock-strewn boulder promises
of boulders, permanence?
But glaciers move south in unforcasted times

in the pleisticine or in any age of cold and change the landscape and melt

6

I don't know the number of this draft, but I think it's number ten. Here I, for
some reason branched out with an addition into a whole 'nother area (this
isn't included here) where I try to add to the poem stuff about actually calling my mother and asking her what really happened. Maybe I was getting
tired of speculation at this point. The call to my mother section lasted for a
number of drafts until I got back to the basic story, until, I guess, I decided to
just tell the story as a third-person narrator. But the spirit of the phone call
poem made its way into the heroic sonnet about my mother's health which
some of you [classmates] read.

                I could call her. Ask
(6)   *what was dad like? What were you*
              like in 1944, but it's easier to imagine,
She brought the soldier home to Gordonsville, *we always speak of*
the present
stopping first in Maggert's store   *anyway and somehow it*
for the food her mother called in from the farm. *Makes me uncomfortable.*
The gents in Maggerts picked their teeth,   *I know the future.*
discussed the Tennessee cold snap weather, *Why should I bother with it?*
the Bulge and Rommel's Corp with Bill   *That's probably why what I*
         have already seems stiff—stiff
In the   *about the first time she brought*
Dinner with Ben and Louise, Mary's parents *him home to Gordonsville from*
and Granddaddy Hogan, Mother Fanny, cooked   *Nashville*
by Ella Mae.

Morning they rode ~~together~~,
horse's breath flashing plumes
over hills past stranded gray rock
boulders clustered on the hills, hills and rocks
worn smooth, cut with scoops and spines,
ridges waves in the pliesticine   *called*
pulled up from the earth, thrust ~~down~~ to the hills
by glaciers   *into*
They stood high on a rock   *Bill and Mary warm*
watched the horses crop, the lace of mist above the Caney
Fork. They
lay on a crevice,
a sculpted pocket from the pleisticine.   *Does the remembering by me*
        salvage it? As she lays in bed and watches
Ice moved south in the Pleisticine,   *Oprah, was that choice she made in*
unforecast, in pleisticines to come   *Nashville, bringing him home, the pivotal*
in ages of cold when landscapes change   *mistake in her life?*
Ice melts. Glaciers move south changing land ~~and~~ recede *winter freezes*
changing land, leaving rocks sucked up from the core
~~depending on the weather~~   *deposit rocks*

~~Moved north again, uncovering rocks, moving hills, unforecast~~

With the war still on, military boys
haunted through the States.
        Are there really mistakes anyway?
        In '88 I was living with her and
        watched Golden Girls and Arsenio
        but we never talked about Nashville in '44.
        She always wanted to talk about me only me
        and I couldn't stand it—can't now.

7

In this finished draft there are no questions. My mother is foregrounded more
at the beginning, and my father has been reduced to one line, really, the
"Handsome. Khaki. Wings," line, and the other references to him are as "they."
But, still, he is woven in and out of the story until both are resolved into the
"they" in stanza 5. "They" are together now in stanza 4. Stanza 5 is the idyllic
one to accentuate their togetherness. Stanza 6 is somewhat more of the same,
though it's all setting. Then what's left of my original theme comes in the last
stanza, that is, I see it there. Most readers would probably read this as a continuation of the love story I guess, unless they were to ponder the violence of the
words in the last two lines and the word *pleistocene,* the epoch when glaciers
came. Strange, one might think, that the writer would chose this place and these

words to signal togetherness. That's what I would hope a close reader would think. It doesn't matter though, because I think it works fine on a story level.

I like the use of the single-word lines, the words set off by periods as pauses, a "gimmick" I picked up in the first poem I did, the word-challenge poem where I had to use all the words and the only way I could use some was in strings. But it works, I think, again here, though in the third stanza line 1 is more than one word.

One issue raised with this poem is whether the writer should make every line power-packed, like say, the lines in stanza 2 are—each line is important. But line 2 of stanza 1 seems weaker—though it serves to set the stage.

I included the four pages of freewrites because they seem to be interesting: to recognize how a poem began and then to compare it with the "finished" product, with a few stops in between. This poem wasn't revisioned in a grand way. There were two or three tangents or problems I had to work through: the speculation, the blatant "theme" at the end, and the addition I tried about halfway through of an actual call to my mother, but the end product is very similar, in theme, in tone, in imagery to the first draft.

I like this finished draft. If I do more work on it I might reduce the amount of food in stanza 4—maybe the long list is a bit self-indulgent on my part because I remember those dinners from my childhood visit. Mentioning Lola Mae is problematic—as if I am romanticizing her along with the romanticizing of my parents. I like my resolution to stanza 3, which in a workshop draft was just single words—and was fragmented.

Another "feature," one that I was unaware of as the poem came together, was the spondee triplets: "from the farm," "show him off," "cold snap weath(er)," "fought the Bulge," "Gabardine," "Real live wire," "ate beans snap(ped)," "salt cured ham," "hay-ride quilts," "cold snap plumes," "corn stalks un(der)," "farm house plot," "reins drag free," "grey rock scooped"— "pleis-to-cene." I think these triplets give a sort of finality in terms of tone, and they also serve as a formal structure. Of the 183 words, forty-five make up these triplets. Fascinating, eh?

(7)

Pleistocene*

She brought him home for the first time
in the Fall of 1944.
They stopped at Maggert's store for salt
her mother ordered up from the farm.

And to show him off. I know the pictures.
Handsome. Khaki. Wings.
Gents in Maggert's picked teeth, talked
the cold snap weather, fought the Bulge.

Farm girl. Gabardine. Apple bob.
Gents'd say pretty. Peach.
Real live wire. College down in Nashville.
"May I have this dance?" he asked, on leave.

He met Louise, Ben, Mother Fanny,
Granddaddy Hogan; ate beans snapped,
potatoes mashed and buttered, salt cured ham,
tomatoes, biscuits cooked by Lola Mae.

Night they swung on the porch swing
wrapped in hay-ride quilts.
Morning they rode the steep, bouldered hills,
breath of horses flashing cold snap plumes.

A thin lace of mist twirled above
the Caney Fork. Sheep grazed the slope
beyond the barn. Mules geed corn stalks under
in the farm house plot.

They let the horses crop, the reins drag free,
and lay in a stone pocked big enough
for two, the grey rock scooped, chiseled,
hammered, pumiced smooth in the pleistocene.

REX WEST—REVISION CASE STUDY

I don't believe in muses. I guess I'm an empiricist when it comes to writing: I only believe what I perceive. (Was it Berkeley who said *Esse est percipi?*). When it comes to writing a poem, I can believe in revision drafts; I can see them, touch them, measure them. But I've yet to be visited by a muse. Sometimes I've wondered if a precipitate insight might be my muse finally arriving. But in the end I have to conclude those sudden insights are payoffs for consistent hard work on a draft. In my mind, a poem doesn't just come to you: you earn it. I'll admit this sounds like an investment commercial. Maybe it's just the old Calvinist work ethic that was drilled into me during my middle-class upbringing. Or maybe I'm bitter because my muse has avoided me my whole life. Regardless, this is the approach I espouse.

When I first started writing poems, I was a believer in Robert Creeley's dictum that the poet should not revise much—if at all—because he or she might interfere with the unconscious structure of the writing. (This is a version of the "wait for the muse" argument.) But about the time I started teaching, I read Eliot's essay "Tradition and the Individual Talent"; one line in particular from that essay challenges Creeley's notion: "There is a great deal, in the writing of poetry," Eliot said, "which must be conscious and deliberate. In fact, the bad poet is usually unconscious where he [or she] ought to be conscious" (71). In short, rather than muses and "mysticism," Eliot wants to talk about "practical conclusions as can be applied by the responsible person interested in poetry." That's what I want to do here: talk about the practical conclusions we can draw from what I did in working through several drafts of a poem. If you cling to the muse idea, then at least you can see what follows as a productive waste of my time while I wait for ghostly inspiration to manifest itself.

Let me preface the rest of this case study by saying I draw on the methods of other poets quite a bit. I've learned a lot from Hugo's *Triggering Town* and Stafford's *Writing the Australian Crawl*. Ray Bradbury has a new book called *Zen in the Art of Writing* that's also influencing me a lot. My point is that I don't think you can write in a vacuum or an ivory tower and do much good writing—which is why we have workshops. You've got to bounce ideas off other people—and steal some things too. This is the primary point of Eliot's essay. He says, "No poet, no artist of any art, has his [or her] complete meaning alone" (67). Contrary to the Romantic notion of the poet standing alone atop a jutting crag, shaking a fist at the lightning in a stormy sky, I think Eliot is saying, "Come down off the mountain, talk to folks." Books by other poets are a form of that talk. This case study is a form of that talk.

The following poem is a response to a group challenge from the beginning of the term. We agreed to write a poem using these words:

apricot	leaves	creaking sharp
fly	**butter**	**lips**
open	**fence**	**blossom**

And we agreed on the following rules:

1. You can throw out a word.
2. You can use parts of words.
3. The first line must be end-stopped.
4. The last word must be a verb.
5. [Up to the poet]

I sat down at my word processor and came up with the following first attempt.

> The funeral is today, a bright chilly day.
> I refuse to ride to the cemetery
> and am walking the half-mile instead.
> A long row of apricot trees   **apricot**
> stretches through elderberry bushes and sumac
> along this gravel road which hasn't been gravel
> in years. I swat leaves with a willow branch.   **leaves**

Looking at the first line of my poem above, I begin with a funeral. We usually think of funerals as gloomy occasions. And a lot of writers would use the scene to emphasize the mood: storm clouds, black suits and dresses, maybe rain. But I've picked the opposite: a bright, sunny day. I'm hoping the reader thinks, "That's odd." In the second and third lines, I also tried to pick something unexpected. Most people ride to funerals in black limousines, or in long grieving convoys that cops have to stop traffic for. So I made my character want to walk instead. All these choices go back to one of the practical things Eliot mentions in his essay. He says a good poem has a kind of tension in it; it wants to pull itself apart. So the problem for the poet—according to Eliot—is to "unite what resists unification" (Wimsatt 666). But this doesn't have to sound so theoretical (though Eliot usually does). I've boiled the idea down to a simple—practical—strategy that helps me get a poem written. Simply put: connect things that don't usually go together, things that resist unification. This is what I've tried to do in the first three lines above.

Beginning in the fourth line I write, "A long row of apricot trees/stretches through elderberry bushes and sumac / along this gravel road which hasn't been gravel / in years. I swat leaves with a willow branch." I'm hoping these lines are the opposite of what someone going to a funeral would focus on. I think most people think about times shared with the deceased, or the way the dead body will look in the casket, so the voice in this poem is focusing on the external landscape instead of internal thoughts. In fact, I'm hoping that swatting leaves with a willow switch seems an awfully nonchalant thing to be doing on the way to a funeral. Tension. Of course I'm also being guided here by the challenge words my group gave me, but I'm trying not to let these constraints force me into expected, banal, predictable language.

One note: I wasn't having a good start with this poem at the first sitting, so I left it after spending over an hour on only seven lines. My sittings seem to be several short bursts a day rather than long sessions. In saying earlier that poems are the result of sweat, I didn't mean you have to force a poem out. When things aren't happening like they should, I go have a cup of coffee, or start a different poem. But I always come back to the poem.

Here's what I came up with at the second sitting. Things begin to come together better here. The muse still hadn't shown up when I wrote this draft, so I'm guessing I had a better sense of the poem's mood and direction, and therefore could generate a lot more writing. Notice that the Creeley method (not going back to revise) would have left me with the fragment of the first sitting, which doesn't do much for me—regardless of its "unconscious structure." Here's the second attempt:

The funeral is today.
I refuse to ride to the cemetery,
am walking the half-mile instead.
Electric fence strung along apricot trees   **apricot, fence**
stretches through elderberry blossoms   **blossom**

and sumac along this gravel road
which hasn't been gravel
in years. I swat leaves with a willow branch,   **leaves**
licking the insides of my cheeks
to taste butter from breakfast.   **butter**
I like walking backwards
watching supple lumbering storm clouds,
watching horses group by Garret's pond
pulling serviceberries from the trees with their lips: **lips**
the weedy pond steams in the humid afternoon.
In the ripening tobacco fields
insects creak-beat their rusty wings—   **creaking**
unable to fly in the damp, ripening summer.   **fly**
The casket will be open: the reason for walking.   **open**

After this draft I got bored with the poem, so I abandoned it. I don't see this as failure; it's a creative change of direction. I decided to use the same challenge words in a new poem. I'd recently received a postcard from a friend in Wyoming that had a picture of Annie Oakley on it; on the back was written: "Annie Oakley Once Shot a Cigarette from the mouth of Kaiser Wilhelm of Germany." Below, I run with the idea and am interested in re-creating the scene in a new poem, while using the same challenge words from my group.

Annie Oakley Once Shot a Cigarette[2]

from the mouth of Kaiser Wilhelm of Germany.
No doubt his lips dittered, shuttered, twittered   **lips**
like a leaf the old man shook! said Buffalo Bill,   **leaves**
slapping his rawhide hands against burlap chaps.
The fat monarch came to see the austere desert,
the fuss of the South Dakota gold rush,
and Little Miss Sure Shot astound with rifle and pistol.
But he didn't expect volunteering.
"Folks" sit on a creaky fence. (You are a "folk.")   **creak, fence**
Smell butter beans and chappati at the concession stand.   **butter**
Your program reads: Act I: Indians
                          Act II: Guns and Cowpokes
                          Act III: Buffalo Bill and Annie
The Sioux open the show rain dancing: **open**
a sarabande of porcupine quill embroidery,
shaking apricot headdresses and black tambourines.   **apricot**
They ride out on nervous horses
whooping, their spirits flying like pigeons.   **fly**

---

[2]Annie Oakley (nicknamed "Little Miss Sure Shot") traveled with Buffalo Bill's Wild West Show. She lived from 1860–1926.

I was sickened by what I came up with here, though I've since made it into another poem. But the process of coming to this dead end was important because of the Indian idea in the last few lines. I liked the image of these Native Americans dancing, so I started another new poem with that image, again abandoning the draft.

The Chickasaw Rain Dance

> A sarabande of porcupine quill embroidery,
> shaking apricot headdresses and black tambourines.   **apricot**
> They ride out on nervous horses
> whooping, their spirits flying like pigeons.   **fly**

Chickasaw was a word our small group considered using for the initial challenge words but decided against, so I picked it up here. This draft seemed interesting initially, but after several hours I was still frustrated—it seemed too staged, predictable—so I abandoned it also. Again, I think there's value in knowing when to quit. And the payoff came in the next draft. My interest in the version from the first sitting was renewed, and after some diddling and fiddling, I spliced the Indian section onto the end of the funeral poem. The move goes back to Eliot's notion of opposites: I figured nothing's more unexpected in a funeral poem than Indians dancing. Tension. After three more sittings and various drafts I came up with the following poem that I submitted to a small group workshop. Notice I've made the first line a read-in title.

The Funeral*

> is today. I refuse to ride to the cemetery
> and am walking the half-mile instead.
> Electric fence strung along apricot trees
> stretches through elderberry and sumac.
> I swat leaves with a willow branch
> and lick the insides of my cheeks
> to taste butter from breakfast muffins.
> The casket will be open:
> the reason for walking backwards
> watching lumbering storm clouds,
> watching horses group by Garret's pond
> pulling serviceberries with their lips.
> The weedy pond steams.
> Last night walking with Kristen
> through ripening tobacco fields,
> insects beat their rusty wings
> unable to fly in damp summer:
> we tried to imagine the end of this fleshy world.

Kristen leaned her head on her hand
and told me about watching Indians dance,
their spirits flying like doves,
shaking white headdresses and red tambourines,
whooping.

Those in the class workshop suggested I try to say whose funeral this poem is about, as well as work more with the relationship between the speaker and "Kristen." I've tried to do that below, in a subsequent revision. My goal for this revision was to tighten the poem as much as possible, see how stark and imagistic I could make it. I'm also playing with line lengths and breaks, as a result of reading "On the function of a line" by Denise Levertov.

It's early. Kristen and I walk through a ripening tobacco field
swatting rusty leaves with willow branches.
By Garret's pond horses pull serviceberries with their lips.
The weedy pond steams.
Along the gravel road electric fence strung along apricot trees
stretches through elderberry and sumac.
I lick the insides of my cheeks to taste butter from breakfast muffins.
I say, "Grandma's funeral is tomorrow:
The casket will be open."
We try to imagine the end of this world.
Kristen tells me about watching Indians dance,
their spirits flying like doves,
shaking white headdresses and red tambourines,
whooping.

In the end I was disappointed with this version. Too much was cut out, I think. The poem moves too fast; the reader can't keep up. And in reading this aloud, I don't find it as musical as the previous version. But I did get something out of writing this draft. I think I understand line breaks better. In her article, Levertov says a line break is a form of punctuation additional to the punctuation that forms part of the logic of completed thoughts. Line breaks—together with intelligent use of indentation and other devices of scoring—represent a peculiarly poetic, alogical, parallel (not competitive) punctuation (Hall 266).

Later she says a line break is a sort of "half-comma" (267). This was an empowering idea for me. Whether or not the line breaks above are better than the breaks of the previous draft is certainly a matter for discussion. And you might object, "What exactly is a 'better' line break?" Granted it may be too subjective a thing to resolve. But regardless of the stance you might take on Levertov's notion, the article got me looking closer at my line breaks, and thus re-seeing the whole poem. Working on it some more, I came up with this draft.

Kristen and I walk through ripe tobacco fields
and swat rusty leaves with willow switches.
Quail burst, then a moth.
I tell her about the hospital,
the food tray, the oxygen tank,
about Dad coughing up gray mucus.
We see horses by Garret's pond
pulling serviceberries with their lips—
the weedy pond steams.
Along the gravel road
electric fence strung between apricot trees
stretches through elderberry and sumac.
I tell her Dad's head shook
and the veins in his hands darkened
where he held the hospital bed bars.
I lick the insides of my cheeks
to taste butter from breakfast muffins-
I say, "The casket will be open."
We try to imagine the end:
Kristen tells me about watching Indians dance:
their spirits fly like doves,
they shake white headdresses
and red tambourines,
whooping.

I've added and subtracted lines here. The use of dialogue is new. "Dad" has become the subject. I've tried to evoke the tension we all feel when thinking about hospitals. I generally don't add a title to a poem until I feel it's nearly finished. This draft doesn't have a title yet; looking back, that tells me I wasn't very happy with it. Overall, I think the input from my group was helpful: the poem needs to say more about the relationship between the speaker and "Kristen." So in trying to focus more on that relationship I came up with the following version.

*Kristen**

Last night something in a story by Chekhov made me think of you.
Remember the day of Dad's funeral?
I refused to ride to the cemetery, and walked the half-mile instead.
An open casket: the reason for walking.
You went with me and we walked backwards the whole half-mile.
Do you remember electric fence
strung along maple trees stretching through elderberry and sumac?

Swatting leaves with a willow switch?
Horses by Garret's weedy pond pulling serviceberries with their lips?
The taste of butter from breakfast muffins?
Cutting through a tobacco field, insects beating their rusty wings?
We tried to imagine the end.
You told me about watching Indians dance, shaking red headdresses
and black tambourines, spirits flying,
        whooping.

This draft probably says more about how I write poems than anything I've said so far. It's a statement of how I use form. As I see it, what Hollander calls formal "schemes and designs" (that is, pantoums, villanelles, sestinas, or any formal pattern) are molds you can pour poems into for revision purposes. Let me explain this. When I write a poem, I always begin in free verse. Always. I think this insures that you say what you want or need to say first; it precludes you from coming up with bad lines just for the sake of rhyme or meter (although it doesn't preclude you from coming up with bad lines). Then, after creating an initial free verse poem, I begin playing with the words the way a musician improvises on a tune: I try putting the poem into different forms (however formal or informal). All the drafts you've seen so far are variations on the original. Even the versions I abandoned had elements of the original poem in them. You might say all the versions have some of the notes of the original tune. Finally I abandon the form (unless it results in a poem that's better than the original, which it usually doesn't) but keep the improvements to the poem that I made while working within the form.

   For example, in the draft above, I picked a long-short, long-short form to put the original funeral poem into. In the end I don't like this version much at all. And most of the people I asked to respond to this said they didn't like it much either. But I did accomplish some things. First, I had to look hard at what I would cut in order to fit the poem into the long-short format. Every line was scrutinized. I had to ask myself, "Is the line 'Quail burst, then a moth' necessary? Does it work?" My answer was "no," so I cut it from the previous version above. I've since put the poem back into a looser free verse, but the long-short form helped me pay attention to the moth/quail line and ultimately decide to take it out. I could just as easily make a ballade out of my funeral poem, or a haiku sequence, or a rondeau—all with the same result. My goal is not to write a ballade, haiku sequence, or rondeau but instead to view my poem through the eyes of this form for revision purposes. It's like looking at your poem through a telescope, then a pair opera glasses, then a magnifying glass: all three are ways of seeing more closely, but all are distinctly different in their approach.

   In *Working Words*, Wendy Bishop says good writers use "strategies" to improve their work, "adding and deleting material, for example, but also reordering a text and thinking about its structure and meaning" (31). That's what I see Eliot's and Levertov's ideas as: strategies. Of course not all poems should be attempts to "unite what resists unification." And we could argue ad infinitum about what a good line break is. But the resolution of these discussions seems immaterial to me. Instead I focus on how the ideas can become revision tools—at least until your muse shows up. (I think my muse is Godot.)

I think a self-study like this serves two purposes: it gives you an opportunity to see how I write, and it reminds me of what I do when I write. One thing, in particular, stands out for me now. Looking at these drafts, it seems obvious that I often quit writing when I should keep going. This is something I need to work on. I need to lower my expectations for a draft and just write. I also see some good habits I've learned from other poets. First, I'm willing to completely start over, to go another direction, see what happens. Second, I read poems aloud a lot while working through drafts. Richard Hugo says that if you read your poem aloud and don't enjoy it, there's something wrong with it (39). This is another useful revision "tool."

WORKS CITED

Bishop, Wendy. *Working Words.* Mountain View, CA: Mayfield Publishing, 1992.

Bradbury, Ray. *Zen in the Art of Writing.* New York: Bantam, 1992.

Eliot, T. S. "Tradition and the Individual Talent." *Selected Essays.* Harcourt Brace, 1960. Rpt. in *Prose Keys to Modern Poetry,* Ed. Karl Shapiro. New York: Harper and Row, 1962.

Hollander, John. *Rhyme's Reason.* New Haven, CT; Yale University Press, 1989.

Hugo, Richard. *The Triggering Town.* New York: W. W. Norton & Co., 1979.

Levertov, Denise. "On the Function of a Line." *Light Up the Cave.* New Directions, 1979. Rpt. in *Claims for Poetry,* Ed. Donald Hall. Ann Arbor: University of Michigan Press, 1982.

Stafford, William. *Writing the Australian Crawl.* Ann Arbor: University of Michigan Press, 1978.

Wimsatt, William K. and Cleanth Brooks. *Literary Criticism: A Short History.* Chicago: University of Chicago Press, 1957.

POCKET DEFINITIONS REPRISED

There is never an end to learning about the possibilities of verse forms. These working definitions only start you on your journey into a more extensive poetic vocabulary. You'll certainly want to buy one or more of the prosody handbooks listed at the end of the preface and start keeping your own list of terms, definitions, and illustrative poems. The definitions included here are process-oriented, allowing you, I hope, to better use this book. You can go on to investigate other useful and related terms—*ballad, dramatic monologue, irony, symbol, voice,* and others—that I did not have room to include, to extend your understanding of poetry at work.

Abecedarian Poem—Each line (or stanza) begins with a letter of the alphabet.

Accentual-Alliterative Verse—Poetry that relies on lines of four accented syllables, two on each side of a caesura—a mid-line pause. The lines don't rhyme, but the first three and often the fourth accented syllables alliterate.

Alliteration—Repeated initial consonant sounds, particularly when these are stressed syllables and are close to each other in a line of poetry. For example, in Mary Oliver's poem "Question," (chapter 2), in the line "my horse, my hound," *horse* and *hound* alliterate (have initial stressed syllables), and *my* and *my* repeat and could be said to alliterate (although they are unstressed syllables in this line of poetry) because alliteration is partly a visual device.

Allusions—When a poet intentionally refers to something else—a person, place, time, pop cultural event—she is said to be alluding to something outside, behind, or beyond the work at hand in the hope of enriching your reading of the work (if you understand, or work to understand, that connection or reference).

Anaphora—Initial repetition. This can be a repeated word or phrase ("blessed are they," "a time to"), sentence, or entire line. Used often in biblical verse and many modern list and repetition poems. After a poem is composed in this manner, it is sometimes more effective to drop the originating repetition. Anaphora offers structure and parallelism to a poem and can also help the poet to memorize the verse. Walt Whitman, of course, uses the device in remarkable and memorable ways as do—in variation—authors of hymns, ballads, and poems that use refrains.

Apostrophe—A direct address, often to someone or something that is not there; originally a dramatic term that meant a turning away from the general audience to address a particular audience, present or absent.

Ars Poetica—From the Latin, the art of poetry; in practice, a poem on the art of poetry. The Roman poet Horace (65–8 B.C.) wrote a historically famous one, but Archibald MacLeish's, shared here, is perhaps the best known example from the twentieth century.

Assonance—Repeated vowel sounds, as in "without my mount."

Aubade—A poem, also called an alba, that is literally a dawn song where the lover regrets the coming of daylight and inevitable separation of the lovers. The aubade doesn't have a fixed form but can be in the form of a dialogue, or a speaker may address the loved one.

Blank Verse—Unrhymed iambic pentameter verse. Lines are counted off in five iambic feet (ten syllables, five accents—dă-DÁ), but end rhymes do not occur in predictable patterns.

Caesura—"Caesura" is often used freely to mean a pause within a line of poetry—usually at a syntactical clause or phrase boundary. More technically, the term indicates the place a metrical break occurs as happens in the intentional separation of strong accents within a line of Old English verse.

Chant—A verbal presentation that is a mixture of speech and song and is aided by repetition, accompaniment, recurring rhyme, and/or syntactic patterns. A chant is performed by a single or several performers.

Cinquain—A single stanza poem with the syllabic pattern of 2, 4, 6, 8, 2 syllables per line.

Cliché—Clichéd language is language that offers the easy, the overly familiar, and the predictable and represents, for the poet, a missed opportunity to relate her particular vision of the world through words. Clichés are certainly generational. What is clichéd (old, expected, predictable, like "have a nice day") to one reader, is not necessarily clichéd to a younger person who might hear that phrase for the first time and be enchanted by it. *Trite, stereotyped, platitudinous, predictable, too easy, imprecise* are words you might substitute for *cliché*. Clichés are useful placeholders when you're drafting, but you need to reread and replace the easy with the exact, the first choice with the best choice.

Closure—Readers of poems develop an expectation of how the work will end, what might provide a satisfying resolution or sense of ending and textual stability. This sense of closure can be thematic and/or technical. For instance, an initial line or image may be repeated, or the regularity of a stanza form can be varied to signal that the end of a poem has arrived. Some poets prefer to work against such an expectation of regularity or finish, favoring instead an intentionally open-ended effect that rejects closure.

Couplets—Two-line stanzas (or a complete poem in one two-line couplet). These lines are often of the same length. Historically, couplets were metered in a similar manner, often achieving closure through full rhyme or parallel syntax.

Elegy—A meditative commemorative poem on the loss of a loved one or to mark the passing of a person of fame or importance. Modern elegies can also mourn the death of love or possibilities, the loss of family members, landscapes, and, often more humorously, animals or personal attributes.

End-Stopped—Occurs when phrase, clause, and/or sentence punctuation coincide with the end of a line of poetry.

Enjambment—Occurs when sentence syntax carries on from one line to the next (including movement from one stanza to the next).

Envoi—Final lines of a poem—notably, the final three-line stanza of a sestina. The word literally means a farewell or conclusion.

Found Poem—Originally a poem that represents only a slight change or sub-stitution from words encountered in the environment—from signs, adver-tisements, notices, magazine or newspaper articles, professional jargon, bulletin board notices, printed directions—that already have some notable poetic effects. This language is then shaped into poetic form(s) by the poet (by dividing into lines of regular length, and so on). In a slightly broader sense, a found poem is any poem assembled from borrowed words that are then shaped into lines.

Free Verse—It is often claimed, with Walt Whitman's poetry as an example, that free verse poets discarded poetic conventions like set rhyme and reg-ular meter. However, free verse is not simply free and easy writing. Instead, it is lined verse that works against the ghosts and memory of fixed forms, that plays with jazz, song, and other popular forms, that works into and out of stanzas and with and against a variety of conven-tional expectations. Free verse did not arrive, as one might assume, newly on the scene with Whitman and then, immediately, all other types of verse lost their currency.

Full Rhyme—Full-rhyming words have different initial consonants, similar vowel sounds, and similar consonant sounds. This is a complicated way of describing how *moon* and *June* rhyme—*m* and *J* are different initial consonants, *oo* and *u* are similar vowel sounds, and *n* and *ne* are similar consonant sounds. In *slant rhyme* (also called half rhyme) the vowel sound is not exact: *cloth/growth*, *out/mouth*. Rhymes can come in one, two, or three or more syllables: *hit/sit*, *plastic/drastic*, *librarian/agrarian*. Three-syllable rhymes seem to move toward the humorous. See Adams,

Poetic Designs, Appendix 1, "The Terminology of Rhyming" 198–202 for an extensive list of briefly illustrated definitions of rhyme, including perfect, imperfect, eye, identical, rich, assonant, consonant, macaronic, light, wrenched, one-syllable, etc.

Ghazal—Generally ten to twenty-four lines in length and originally a Persian form, these long-lined couplets develop mystical and/or romantic themes. They may be monorhymed (*aa, ba, ca, da*) and/or include the poet's name in the last line.

Haiku—Growing out of Zen Buddhist philosophy (a version of Buddhism that began in India and then spread widely, in which believers seek enlightenment through introspection and intuition rather than through interpretation of a text or scripture). A three-line poem of 5, 7, 5 syllables; haiku writers seek to capture a moment of perception. Haikus turn on strong natural images—using a word, called the kigo, that indicates the season—and relay intense emotions, often leading to spiritual insights. Contemporary haiku writers may drop the three-line requirement (often writing the poem as a single line) and/or the syllable count and/or the kigo.

Heroic Couplet—A closed couplet of rhymed iambic pentameter, most familiar as the final couplet of a Shakespearian sonnet.

Homonyms—Words having the same pronunciation but different meanings and spellings, like *son/sun*.

Hyperbole—Bold, often ironic exaggeration. We don't expect our claims to be taken literally, but we do expect our exaggeration to draw attention to our point rather ostentatiously, when we claim, for instance, that our love is the truest, deepest, and best.

Iambic Pentameter—The most common line pattern in English verse. Five (pentameter) iambic (dă-DÁ) feet equal one line of iambic pentameter, equal: dă-DÁ, dă-DÁ, dă-DÁ, dă-DÁ, dă-DÁ.

Image—When you use descriptions that rely on the five senses—taste, sight, touch, sound, smell—you are creating a word picture, a mental construction of a felt experience, an image, or a representation of the natural world as you, the poet, experienced it. Contemporary poets rely on creating strong images as much as historical poets relied on rhyme and stanza structures. Visual images are most common, and images using our other senses often need to be intentionally developed.

Imagery—Images may be incorporated into a poem through metaphor or simile or a symbol, as well as through concrete and specific description which evokes a corresponding mental image in the reader's mind. Poems may be composed of a number of images—moon-rise, rain on gardenias, a red wheelbarrow—which provoke vivid sense impressions for readers and can be considered together or alone. The imagistic word or phrase (or entire poem) leads us to imagine or reimagine a similar, visually striking moment, feeling, or effect.

Letter Poem—A form as ancient as biblical epistles and Horace's epistles, contemporary letter poems are often in free verse but perform the same act of allowing readers to peer into private thoughts made public as the speaker addresses a listener, setting up a dramatic monologue situation. Epistolary literature tells a narrative (prose or poetry) in the form of letters exchanged between characters.

Metaphor—A figure of speech, a comparison of one thing to another. If the words *like* or *as* are used to complete the comparison, the writer has produced a different figure of speech, the **simile**. A *conceit* is a metaphor that goes beyond the equation of $X = Y$. Special terms used with metaphor are *tenor* and *vehicle* and *ground*. These come from the work of critic I. A. Richards. The tenor is considered the literal thing being referred to, the vehicle is the metaphorical (comparative term), and the ground is the relationship/similarities between the two.

Metaphysical Conceit—John Donne, George Herbert, Andrew Marvell, and their seventeenth century contemporaries have been termed metaphysical poets because their metaphors are often highly intellectual, complicated and detailed, requiring meditation by the reader to unpack the metaphoric possibilities as in the John Donne poem "The Sun Rising" where the lover is in mock-battle with the power of the sun and claiming, because of the strength of his love, that he has, or should have, dominion over the sun.

Meter—Metered verse in English relies on accent and syllable counts. All words in English receive particular syllabic stress, like par-TIC-u-lar. Poets can arrange stresses in patterns (poetic feet) and feet can be counted off, with so many feet per line. The most common pattern in English verse has been iambic pentameter (dă-DÁ, dă-DÁ, dă-DÁ, dă-DÁ, dă-DÁ) of five iambic (dă-DÁ) feet. Readers interested in meter will want to consult the reference books listed in the preface.

Odes—These poems celebrate, commemorate, and meditate on people or events and were originally structured and written for choruses in Greek plays to sing or chant. In *Pindaric odes* the chorus on stage speaks, then moves left, speaks again and moves right, and finishes with a third response. The left (strophe) and right (antistrophe) movements take the same stanza form, while the final response (epode) differs. The Pindaric ode evolved into the more meditative *Horatian ode* that is composed in regular stanzas (having the same length, number of lines per stanza, and rhyme scheme, if any rhyme is used). The *Cowleyan ode* is composed in free verse although it retains the lyrical, serious qualities of the ode in general.

Onomatopoeia—When poems imitate what they are saying. Often this is an auditory imitation, for instance when the sound of the sea is represented by swishing waves, but it can also be visual, for instance when a long line echoes a discussion of the horizon or when lines are shaped to imitate the ebb and flow of a tide or completely echo the subject of a poem, as in George Herbert's poem "Easter Wings," which appears on the page in the shape of wings. Contemporary poets also embrace concrete poetry, where the typography is part of the content and reader's apprehension of the poem. It is onomatopoeic when the dog in your poem barks "woof" as well as when you shape your poem into a dog-bone typographically or let the line talking about the dog's leash trail far out toward the right-hand margin of the page. Onomatopoeia can quickly become overly cute or trite, but the onomatopoeic impulse can also underlie effective changes of pacing or wording in a poem.

Oxymoronic—An oxymoron is a figure of speech that joins or yokes together two seemingly contradictory or opposite things, often ironically: "non-working mother," for instance, or "cafeteria cuisine."

Pantoum—Sixteen or more lines long, pantoums developed in Malayan litera-ture as rhyming quatrains (*abab*) but developed in English as unrhymed quatrains with repeating lines: the second and fourth lines of each stanza repeat as the first and third lines of the next stanza.

Persona—The persona offers one way of discussing the speaker of the poem (as distinct from the living poet/author of the poem). While most poets prefer readers to assume that the speaker of any poem is always an authorial construction, some poets are clearly choosing a highly autobio-graphical voice. When the poet signals the construction of a poetic per-sona, this speaker may provide a mask or alternate identity for the poet. Personas can be a fictional or historical character or a regular person, but one who clearly leads a life different from that of the poet. This everyday persona allows the poet to explore and investigate different perspectives and lifestyles. A persona can be and often is a fictional character (such as Robert Browning's speaker in the often anthologized "My Last Duchess") or even a character who embodies (readers suspect or poets admit) a side of that poet—a part of his or her personality, now ampli-fied and given voice (as in John Berryman's dream song sequence).

Personification—A rhetorical technique where animals, concepts, or inanimate objects are given human attributes, such as when we claim a tree sways in the wind like a dancer or the sun is a hard taskmaster.

Poetry—A genre (as opposed to novels, drama, technical reports, and so on); like prose it can be unmetered. Historically, poetry has relied on meter since even free verse is based on creating artful exceptions to our expectations of regularity based in metered lines. Poetry relies on attention to line over paragraph and utilizes condensed and shaped language, including recognizable figures of speech (images, metaphors, and similes), sound patterns (assonance, alliteration, rhyme, and repetition), and countable or analyzable rhythm (meter).

Praise Song—In many African societies, tribal bards recite traditional epics of praise and celebration at festivals and coronations and perform these epics in rhythmic prose and verse, often accompanied by percussionists.

Prose Poem—A block-shaped, usually paragraphed text that relies on the poetic techniques of imagery and condensed, rhythmic, repetitive, often rhymed language and often makes its point via metaphor, analogy, or association, yet still may partake of fictional techniques like character building, plot, dialogue, and so on.

Prosody—The study of verse forms, sounds, and patterns in poetry.

Psalm—A song sung to the accompaniment of a plucked instrument; a Near Eastern form best illustrated by the Book of Psalms in the Bible.

Quatrain—A stanza of four lines, the most common form in English poetry. Quatrains consist of four lines of verse, rhymed or unrhymed: the *envelope quatrain* rhyme runs *abba;* the *couplet quatrain* runs *aabb;* the *alternating quatrain* runs *abab;* and the *monorhyme quatrain* runs *aaaa.*

Refrain—A regular, nearly exact repeat of a phrase or line, often at the end of a stanza.

Repetend—An irregular repeat of a word, phrase, or line in a poem.

Rhyme Scheme—The pattern of repeating sound that occurs in a poem, most often in the words that end lines in a stanza; represented by letters of the alphabet, assigned as each new rhyme appears. The rhyme pattern of "Western Wind" is "blow" (*a*), "rain" (*b*), "arms" (*c*), "again" (*b*) ("rain" and "again" rhyme and are therefore given the same letter designation).

Sensory Details—These are usually developed by carefully evoking the five senses of sight, hearing, touch, taste, and smell. Writers tend to rely more on sight and sound, but attention to touch, taste, and smell can turn ordinary observations into vivid expressions of the poet's world.

Sestina—This poetic form requires that six end words be repeated in a set pattern across six stanzas and that all six words be used—again, in pattern—in a three-line final stanza, called an envoi.

Slant Rhyme—See *Full Rhyme.*

Sonnet—A historical fixed form. The eight-line octave followed by the six-line sestet held numerical significance: it could be reduced to 4 and 3 and the total, 7. All three numbers were important in music composition as well as in religious thinking, four signifying the world and three the trinity, and so on. The Italian sonnet consists of an octave rhyming *abbaabba* and a sestet rhyming *cdcdcd.* The English sonnet, which developed out of the Italian, consists of fourteen lines of iambic pentameter verse: three quatrains and a closing couplet, with the rhyme scheme of *abab, cdcd, efef, gg.* Poets have always adapted this structure, observing most consistently only its fourteen-line length.

Speaker—See *Persona.*

Surrealism—A movement to free thought from reason through automatic writing, attention to dream states and free-associational play. In poetry, well-known practitioners include Andre Breton, Charles Baudelaire, Arthur Rimbaud, Steven Malarme, and Federico Garcia Lorca, and in the twentieth century, Robert Bly, John Ashbery, and James Tate. Artists Salvador Dali, Joan Miro, and René Magritte are representative of the breadth of surrealist painting.

Syllabic Verse—Line length in syllabic poems is fixed by syllable count—say, ten per line—or in a shaped pattern like the 5, 7, 5 syllable pattern that signals a Western haiku.

Synecdoche—One part standing for the whole: sunbeams, for example, standing for the heat and force of the sun, or an individual standing for a group.

Tanka (also called *waka* or *uta*)—A traditional Japanese poem that is rendered in English in five lines of 5, 7, 5, 7, 7 syllables. Historically, tankas were combined with prose, linked together, and/or published to include exchanges of verse between poets. Subjects vary but often center on travel, love, and the seasons. As with haiku, in Japan today there are regular tanka competitions and a continuing appreciation of this form.

Tercet—Three-line stanzas. When all three lines rhyme, tercets become *triplets.* When the rhyme patterns interlock like this—*aba, bcb, cdc*—linking stanzas, the tercet turns into *terza rima.*

Terzanelle—A nineteen-line poem divided into six stanzas: five interlocking triplets and a quatrain. Of French and Italian origin, it adapts terza rima to the villanelle form by the use of a repeton: A^1BA^2, bCB, cDC, dED, eFE, fA^1 (or F) F (or A^1) A^2. (A^1 and A^2 are refrains; BCDEF are repetons.)

Villanelle—A nineteen-line poem divided into six stanzas: five tercets and one quatrain turning on two rhymes and built on two refrains: A^1bA^2, abA^1, abA^2, abA^1, abA^2, and abA^1A^2. (A^1 and A^2 are refrains.)

CREDITS

Agard, John, "Listen Mr Oxford Don." From *Mangoes & Bullets: Selected And New Poems 1972–1984*. Reprinted by permission of Serpent's Tail, London.

Alexander, Elizabeth, "House Party Sonnet: '66." From *The Venus Hottentot.* (Charlottesville: Virginia, 1990). Reprinted by permission of the University Press of Virginia.

Alexander, Elizabeth, "Nineteen." From *The Venus Hottentot.* (Charlottesville: Virginia, 1990). Reprinted by permission of the University Press of Virginia.

Ali, Agha Shahid, "Ghazal." From *The Country without a Post Office*. Copyright © 1997 by Agha Shahid Ali. Reprinted by permission of W. W. Norton & Company, Inc.

Alvarez, Julia, "Bilingual Sestina." Reprinted by permission of Story Line Press, Inc.

Ashbery, John, "At North Farm." From *A Wave.* (New York: Viking, 1984). Copyright © 1981, 1982, 1983, 1984 by John Ashbery. Originally appeared in *The New Yorker.* Reprinted by permission of Georges Borchardt, Inc., for the author.

Ashbery, John, "37 Haiku." From *A Wave.* (New York: Viking, 1987). Copyright © 1981, 1982, 1984 by John Ashbery. Originally appeared in *The New Yorker.* Reprinted by permission of Georges Borchardt, Inc.

Balk, Christianne, "Elegy." From *Bindweed.* Copyright © 1986 by Christianne Balk. Reprinted by permission of the author.

Balliett, Whitney, "Back." Copyright © 1995. Originally published in *The New Yorker.* Reprinted by permission of The Conde Nast. All rights reserved.

Barreca, Regina, "Nighttime Fires." From *The Minnesota Review* (Fall 1985). Reprinted by permission of the author.

Becker, Robin, "The Accident." From *Giacometti's Dog.* Copyright © 1990 by Robin Becker. Reprinted by permission of the author.

Behn, Robin, "After Love." From *Paper Bird.* Reprinted by permission of Texas Tech University Press.

Bishop, Elizabeth, "One Art." From *The Complete Poems 1927–1979.* Copyright © 1979, 1983 by Alice Helen Methfessel. Reprinted by permission of Farrar, Straus and Giroux, LLC.

Bishop, Elizabeth, "Pink Dog." From *The Complete Poems 1927–1979.* Copyright © 1979, 1983 by Alice Helen Methfessel. Originally published in *The New Yorker.* Reprinted by permission of Farrar, Straus and Giroux, LLC.

Bishop, Elizabeth, "Sestina." From *The Complete Poems 1927–1979.* Copyright © 1979, 1983 by Alice Helen Methfessel. Reprinted by permission of Farrar, Straus and Giroux, LLC.

Bly, Robert, "Ghazal of the Terrifying Presence." Reprinted from *Lorca and Jimenez: Selected Poems.* Chosen and translated by Robert Bly, Beacon Press, Boston, 1973, 1997. Copyright © 1997 Robert Bly. Reprinted with his permission.

Bly, Robert, "Ode to the Watermelon." Reprinted from *Nerud and Vallejo: Selected Poems.* Edited by Robert Bly, Beacon Press, Boston, 1971, 1993. Copyright © 1993 Robert Bly. Reprinted with his permission.

Bowman, Catherine, "Twins of a Gazelle Which Feed among the Lilies." Reprinted by permission of the author.

Brautigan, Richard, "Haiku Ambulance." From *The Pill Versus the Springhill Mine Disaster.* Copyright © 1965. Reprinted by permission of Houghton Mifflin Company. All rights reserved.

Brock, Van K., "Driving at Dawn." From *The Hard Essential Landscape Poems.* Copyright © 1979 by Van K. Brock. Reprinted with the permission of the University Press of Florida.

Brooks, Gwendolyn, "We Real Cool." From *Blacks.* Copyright © 1991. Published by Third World Press, Chicago. Reprinted by permission of the author.

Carruth, Hayden, "Saturday at the Border." First published in *The Atlantic Monthly.* Reprinted by permission of the author.

President and Fellows of Harvard College. Reprinted by permission of the publishers and the Trustees of Amherst College.

Gallagher, Tess, "Under Stars." Copyright © 1987. Reprinted from *Amplitude; New and Selected Poems.* With the permission of Graywolf Press, Saint Paul, Minnesota.

Gonzalez, Ray, "Praise the Tortilla, Praise the Menudo, Praise the Chorizo." Copyright © 1992. Reprinted by permission of the author.

Gunn, Thom, "The Bed." From *Collected Poems.* Copyright © 1994 by Thom Gunn. Reprinted by permission of Farrar, Straus and Giroux, LLC.

Gunn, Thom, "A Map of the City." From *Collected Poems.* Copyright © 1994 by Thom Gunn. Reprinted by permission of Farrar, Straus and Giroux, LLC.

Hacker, Marilyn, "Almost Aubade." From *Assumptions.* Copyright © 1985 by Marilyn Hacker. Reprinted by permission of Frances Collin, Literary Agent.

Hacker, Marilyn, "Fourteen." From *Assumptions.* Copyright © 1985 by Marilyn Hacker. Reprinted by permission of Frances Collin, Literary Agent.

Hacker, Marilyn, "July 19, 1979." From *Taking Notice.* Copyright © 1976, 1978, 1979, 1980 by Marilyn Hacker. Reprinted by permission of Frances Collin, Literary Agent.

Hadas, Rachel, "Three Silences." From *Pass It On.* Copyright © 1989 by Princeton University Press. Reprinted by permission of Princeton University Press.

Hall, Donald, "O Cheese." From *Old and New Poems.* Copyright © 1990 by Donald Hall. Reprinted by permission of Houghton Mifflin Company. All rights reserved.

Hall, Donald, "Old Home Week." From *Old and New Poems.* Copyright © 1990 by Donald Hall. Reprinted by permission of Houghton Mifflin Company. All rights reserved.

Hall, Donald, "Valley of the Morning." From *Old and New Poems.* Copyright © 1990 by Donald Hall. Reprinted by permission of Houghton Mifflin Company. All rights reserved.

Harrison, Jim, "Drinking Song." From *Selected and New Poems 1961–1981.* Copyright © 1982 by Jim Harrison. Used by permission of Delacorte Press/Seymour Lawrence, a division of Random House.

Hass, Robert, "This road-" "Harvest moon-" "Fleas, lice," "Misty rain," "Don't imitate me:" by Basho, "Coolness-" "That snail-" "Escaped the nets," "The end of spring-?" by Buson, "The man pulling radishes" "These sea slugs" "Writing shit about new snow," "From now on," "A bath when you're born," "The old dog-" by Issa. From *The Essential Haiku.* Edited by Robert Hass. Selected and translation copyright © 1994 by Robert Hass. Reprinted by permission of Ecco Press.

Heaney, Seamus, "Mid-Term Break." From *Opened Ground: Selected Poems 1966–1996.* Copyright © 1998 by Seamus Heaney. Reprinted by permission of Farrar, Straus and Giroux, LLC.

Heaney, Seamus, "Punishment." From *North* by Seamus Heaney (1975). Reprinted by permission of Faber & Faber Ltd.

Henry, Gerrit, "The Confessions of Gerrit." Reprinted by permission of the author.

Hoffman, Daniel G., "The Seals in Penobscot Bay." From *Hang-Gliding from Helicon* (1988) by Daniel G. Hoffman. Reprinted by permission of Louisiana State University Press.

Hudgins, Andrew, "Elegy for My Father, Who Is Not Dead." From *The Never-Ending.* Copyright © 1991 by Andrew Hudgins. Reprinted by permission of Houghton Mifflin Company. All Rights reserved.

Hughes, Langston, "Song for a Dark Girl." From *Collected Poems.* Copyright © 1994 by the Estate of Langston Hughes. Reprinted by permission of Alfred A. Knopf, Inc.

Hughes, Langston, "Theme for English B." From *Collected Poems.* Copyright © 1994 by the Estate of Langston Hughes. Reprinted by permission of Alfred A. Knopf, Inc., a Division of Random House, Inc.

Hughes, Langston, "The Weary Blues." From *Collected Poems.* Copyright © 1994 by the Estate of Langston Hughes. Reprinted by permission of Alfred A. Knopf, Inc.

Hughes, Ted, "The Thought Fox." From *Selected Poems 1957–1967* by Ted Hughes. Copyright © 1957 by Ted Hughes. Originally appeared in *The New Yorker.* Reprinted by permission of HarperCollins, Publisher, Inc., and Faber and Faber Ltd.

Inadad, Lawon Fusao, "To Get to Fresno." From *Legends from Camp.* Reprinted by permission of Coffee House Press.

Jarjo, Joy, "She Had Some Horses." From *She Had Some Horses*. Copyright © 1983 by Thunder's Mouth Press. Appears by permission of the publisher, Thunder's Mouth Press.

Johnson, Denis, "Sway." From *The Incognito Lounge*. Copyright © 1982 by Denis Johnson. Reprinted by permission of Random House, Inc.

Justice, Donald, "An Elegy Is Preparing Itself." From *Selected Poems from Loser Weepers*. Reprinted by permission of the author.

Justice, Donald, "In the Attic." From *New and Selected Poems*. Copyright © 1995 by Donald Justice. Reprinted by permission of Alfred A. Knopf, Inc.

Justice, Donald, "For My Daughter." Reprinted from *The Collected Poems Of Weldon Kees*. Edited by Donald Justice by permission of the University of Nebraska Press. Copyright © 1975 by the University of Nebraska Press.

Justice, Donald, "Little Elegy." From *New and Selected Poems*. Copyright © 1995 by Donald Justice. Reprinted by permission of Alfred A. Knopf, Inc.

Justice, Donald, "Order in the Streets." From *Loser Weepers*. Reprinted by permission of the author.

Kenyon, Jane, "My Mother." Copyright © 1996 by the Estate of Jane Kenyon. Reprinted from *Otherwise: New & Selected Poems* with the permission of Graywolf Press, Saint Paul, Minnesota.

Kenyon, Jane, "Otherwise." Copyright © 1996 by the Estate of Jane Kenyon. Reprinted from *Otherwise: New & Selected Poems* with the permission of Graywolf Press, Saint Paul, Minnesota.

Knight, Etheridge, "Haiku." Permission granted by Broadside Press.

Knight, Etheridge, "The Idea of Ancestry." From *Poems from Prison*. Copyright © 1968 by Etheridge Knight. Reprinted by permission of Broadside Press.

Knight, Etheridge, "Rehabilitation & Treatment in the Prison of America." From *Poems from Prison*. Copyright © 1968 by Etheridge Knight. Reprinted by permission of Broadside press.

Kumin, Maxine, "Appetite." From *Selected Poems 1960–1990* by Maxine Kumin.

Copyright © 1986. Reprinted by permission of W. W. Norton & Company, Inc.

Kumin, Maxine, "Morning Swim." From *Selected Poems 1960-1990* by Maxine Kumin. Copyright © 1965. Reprinted by permission of W. W. Norton & Company, Inc.

Lathem, Edward Connery, "Design." From *The Poetry Of Robert Frost*. Edited by Edward Connery Lathem. Copyright © 1936 by Robert Frost. Copyright 1964 © by Lesley Frost Ballantine. Copyright © 1969 by Henry Holt and Company, LLC. Reprinted by permission of Henry Holt and Company, LLC.

Lathem, Edward Connery, "In Hardwood Groves." From *The Poetry of Robert Frost*. Edited by Edward Connery Lathem. Copyright © 1944, 1962 by Robert Frost. Copyright © 1916, 1934, 1969 by Henry Holt and Company, LLC. Reprinted by permission of Henry Holt and Company, LLC.

Lathem, Edward Connery, "The Oven Bird." From *The Poetry of Robert Frost*. Edited by Edward Connery Lathem. Copyright © 1944, © 1962 by Robert Frost. Copyright © 1916, 1934, 1969 by Henry Holt and Company, LLC. Reprinted by permission of Henry Holt and Company, LLC.

Lee, David, "Loading a Boar." From *The Porcine Canticles*. Copyright © 1984. Reprinted by permission of Copper Canyon Press.

Lee, Li-Young, "Eating Together." Copyright © 1986. Reprinted from *Rose* by Li-Young Lee with the permission of BOA Editions, Ltd.

Levis, Larry, "The Poem You Asked For." From *Wrecking Crew*. Copyright ©1972. Reprinted by permission of the University of Pittsburgh Press.

Lowitz, Leza, Selected haiku by Kiyoko Uda, Nobuko Katsura, and Kimiko Itami from *A Long Rainy Season*. Edited and translated by Leza Lowitz, Miyuki Aoyama, and Akemi Tomioka. Copyright © 1994 by Leza Lowitz. Reprinted by permission of Stone Bridge Press, Berkeley, CA.

Lux, Thomas, "He Has Lived in Many Houses." First published in *The Atlantic Monthly*. Reprinted by permission.

MacLeish, Archibald, "Ars Poetica." From *Collected Poems 1917–1982*. Copyright © 1985 by the Estate of Archibald MacLeish.

Stafford, William, "Ghazal XVI." From *Ghazales of Ghabil*. Translated by William Stafford. Reprinted by permission from *The Hudson Review*, Vol. XXII, No. 4 (Winter 1969–70). Copyright © 1970 by the Hudson Review, Inc.

Stafford, William, "Traveling through the Dark." Copyright © 1962, 1988 by the Estate of William Stafford. Reprinted from *The Way It Is: New & Selected Poems* with the permission of Graywolf Press, Saint Paul, Minnesota.

Steele, Timothy, "An Aubade." From *Sapphics against Anger and Other Poems*. Reprinted by permission of University of Arkansas Press.

Stevens, Wallace, "Thirteen Ways of Looking at a Blackbird." From *Collected Poems*. Copyright 1923 and renewed 1951 by Wallace Stevens. Reprinted by permission of Alfred A. Knopf, Inc.

Stewart, Pamela, "Punk Pantoum." First appeared in *Crazyhorse* (Spring 1979). Reprinted by permission of the author.

Swander, Mary, "Frog Gig." From *Heaven-and-Earth House*. Copyright © 1994 by Mary Swander. Reprinted by permission of Alfred A. Knopf, Inc.

Swander, Mary, "Ode to Okra." From *Heaven-and-Earth House*. Copyright © 1994 by Mary Swander. Reprinted by permission of Alfred A. Knopf, Inc.

Swander, Mary, "Shunning." From *Heaven-and-Earth House*. Copyright © 1994 by Mary Swander. Reprinted by permission of Alfred A. Knopf, Inc.

Swander, Mary, "Two Skulls." From *Heaven-and-Earth House*. Copyright © 1994 by Mary Swander. Reprinted by permission of Alfred A. Knopf, Inc.

Swenson, May, "His Secret." From *The Complete Poems to Solve* by May Swenson. Copyright ©1993 Literary Estate of May Swenson. Reprinted with the permission of Simon & Schuster Books for Young Readers, an imprint of Simon & Schuster Children's Publishing Division.

Swenson, May, "Question." From *The Complete Poems to Solve* by May Swenson. Copyright © 1954 May Swenson; copyright renewed © 1982 May Swenson. Reprinted with the permission of Simon & Schuster Books for Young Readers, an imprint of Simon & Schuster Children's Publishing Division.

Tate, James, "A Guide to the Stone Age." From *Selected Poems*. Copyright © 1991 by James Tate, Wesleyan University Press, by permission of University Press of New England.

Tate, James, "Man with Wooden Leg Escapes Prison." From *Selected Poems*. Copyright © 1991 by James Tate, Wesleyan University Press, by permission of University Press of New England.

Tate, James, "Miss Cho Composes in the Cafeteria." From *The Lost Pilot*. (Yale University Press, 1967). Reprinted by permission of the author.

Tate, James, "Prose Poem." From *Selected Poems*. Copyright © 1991, Wesleyan University Press, by permission of University Press of New England.

Taylor, Henry, "One Morning, Shoeing Horses." From *The Flying Change* (1985) by Henry Taylor. Reprinted by permission of the Louisiana State University Press.

Thomas, Dylan, "Do Not Go Gentle into That Good Night." From *The Poems of Dylan Thomas*. Copyright © 1945 by The Trustees for the Copyrights of Dylan Thomas. Reprinted by permission of New Directions Publishing Co., and David Higham Associates Limited.

Thomas, Dylan, "Fern Hill." From *The Poems of Dylan Thomas*. Copyright © 1945 by The Trustees for the Copyrights of Dylan Thomas. Reprinted by permission of New Directions Publishing Co. and David Higham Associates Limited.

Thomas, Sean, "After the Last Great Anti-War Demonstration." Reprinted by permission of Slapering Hol Press.

Villanueva, Alma Luz, "Crazy Courage." Appeared in *Prairie Schooner*. Reprinted by permission of the author.

Wallace, Ronald, "The Bad Sonnet." From *The Uses of Adversity*. Copyright © 1998. Reprinted by permission of the University of Pittsburgh Press.

Wallace, Ronald, "Sestina for the House." From *Tunes for Bears to Dance To*. Copyright © 1983. Reprinted by permission of the University of Pittsburgh Press.

Index of Authors and Titles

Index of Forms and Themes

Index of Terms